MEANING & VOID

Inner Experience and the Incentives in People's Lives

MEANING
& VOID

INNER EXPERIENCE
AND THE INCENTIVES
IN PEOPLE'S LIVES

Eric Klinger

UNIVERSITY OF MINNESOTA
PRESS □ MINNEAPOLIS

104521

Library of Congress Catalog Card Number 77-81425

ISBN 0-8166-0811-3

Preface

Meaning and Void sets out to show how human inner lives — people's thoughts and feelings — depend on and in turn influence people's commitments to goals. The book casts a wide net. It considers the way in which people's thoughts flow, the meaning of emotion and the nature of value, the causes and course of depression and alienation, satisfaction with work and marriage, the changes in people's inner lives as they get older, people's use of the mass media and of mood-changing chemicals, and the ultimate mood change, suicide. When people talk about the most basic dimensions of their lives, they often couch their thoughts in the language of "meaning" — to what extent their lives feel meaningful or empty. Meaningfulness seems to be a kind of common denominator for people, one that summarizes the way in which they are currently related to their individual world. Because the sense that one's life is meaningful is keyed to so many features of human life, it is a recurring theme in this book.

Clearly, the book deals with humanistic issues, but it deals with them from the perspective of scientific psychology. It presents a picture of the way humans think and feel, a theory of human inner experience as it is bound up with the goals people strive for. The materials for this picture are the many pieces of evidence that psychological investigators have uncovered using scientifically respectable methods. I have drawn on work in both the clinical and the experimental traditions of psychology, on evidence from studies of humans and, where appropriate, from studies of animals. The synthesis that has resulted bears on many parts of psychology and, indeed, on some of the enduring great issues of the human sciences, such as the innate bases of value, the existence of universal symbols, emotion and hedonism, alienation and self-destruction. It also appears to provide a psychological underpinning for the theory of social roles and social organization, and it offers a general unifying theme for the social sciences.

It would be a mistake to conclude, however, that this book is limited to relatively abstract concerns. On the contrary, I have found the ideas I present here extraordinarily helpful to me in thinking about my own life and the lives of others, whether they were friends, family members, or clients in psychotherapy. Many of the students who have read the book in manuscript have told me spontaneously that it has helped them to think about themselves as well. The indications at this point are, then, that people can quite readily apply these ideas in their everyday lives. For instance, the sections concerning depression, alienation, drug use, and suicide should be of interest to professional helpers who encounter these problems as well as to the people who have them. The material on the effects of setting goals and on the ways in which motivation fosters or interferes with productive thinking should interest managers and also people in general who are striving for goals. Clergy may be interested not only in these topics but also in the material on the nature of human values and in the implications of the whole viewpoint for individual freedom and religious commitment. I would hope that people whose lives feel empty to them might increase their understanding of themselves. And I would hope that intellectually curious readers will find the whole range of ideas on meaningfulness, inner experience, and the nature of human nature worth the mulling.

Partly for these reasons I have tried to write the book so that it could be read by readers who are not psychologists or even serious students of psychology. I had in mind the undergraduate student who comes to this book with only a beginning course in psychology or perhaps no course but some general intellectual sophistication, as well as professionals outside psychology such as clergy, managers, and educators. For their sakes I have kept technical jargon to a minimum and have explained all technical terms either in the text or in the notes. I also had in mind pastoral or educational counselors, social workers, and psychiatrists. Finally, psychology has itself become so complex and diverse that psychologists are experiencing increasing difficulty in reading the technical literature in areas of psychology outside their own. I am well aware of my own gratitude toward fellow psychologists in areas other than mine who write clearly enough to make the reading pleasant and efficient.

Readers will have to judge for themselves how well I have succeeded in making the book comprehensible to them. However, there is one piece of evidence: The members of one of my classes thought, on the average, that this book is at about the same level of difficulty as a reasonably challenging introductory psychology textbook. Therefore, readers who already have the equivalent of a beginning psychology course should have no difficulty with it, and many readers who have had no previous background in psychology should find it simply challenging reading.

Because the book is addressed to people with a wide range of backgrounds, the notes take on a special mission. They serve here primarily as communications to readers with special needs or interests. In a few cases, for instance, they clarify elementary concepts with which most readers will already be familiar; but most often they draw out implications, extend arguments, or consider technical matters that will be of interest primarily to psychologists. Most of the footnotes therefore assume in the reader a stronger psychological background than the text does. The notes are not necessary to maintain the flow of the argument, but occasionally they contain important qualifications or even additional theoretical contributions that the psychologist reader will probably wish to consider.

Psychologists will note that the theory presented here rests on a new set of motivational concepts, of which the concept of current concern is the most central. I have developed this construct at greater length here than in previous writings. In its various manifestations it plays a role in the treatment of thinking, emotion, value, depression, alienation, and suicide. In this book I have also formulated findings on emotion into a pattern that can serve as a foundation for a theory of value and that can then be articulated with the motivational theory woven around the concept of current concern. I have somewhat extended here my earlier theory of thinking and present some of the findings of our research on thinking and motivation. Inevitably and gratefully, the work presented here also incorporates many existing theoretical concepts recognizably intact. However, it does try to originate a coherent theoretical framework for dealing with motivation, emotion, and value, and their relationships to thought, adaptation, and social behavior.

My intellectual debts are plainly too numerous to acknowledge fully. The work presented here cannot be identified with any single "school" of thought or theoretical orientation. My thinking reflects a great range of formative influences, most of whom are acknowledged in the body of the book. Viktor Frankl is, of course, the figure in psychology who single-handedly made the case that a sense of meaning is centrally important in a person's life, not as a philosophical abstraction but as a potential life-and-death factor in human functioning.

The theorizing behind this book has gone on in the context of a continuing research program in which abstractions such as current concerns must stand up to the test of usefulness in guiding research. There is no way to disentangle the development of my thought from the countless conversations, seminars, data analyses, reactions to manuscripts, and conceptual crises with my co-workers in this research, especially Steven G. Barta and Thomas W. Mahoney, but also prominently at various times Roxanne M. Anderson, John F. Andrews, Jane Delage, Joseph D. Fridgen, Paul Heyl, Madeline Maxeiner, Mary K. Martin, George A. Peterson, Rachel Froiland Quenemoen, and Deborah A. Smith. My colleague Ernest D. Kemble has provided repeated stimulation and comment during the preparation of this book.

I also wish to thank the following additional people who have commented on parts or all of earlier drafts of this book or on central predecessor manuscripts: John W. Atkinson, Lynn E. Bush II, Charles G. Costello, O. Truman Driggs, John Ervin, Jr., Donald W. Fiske, George B. Flamer, Peter French, Mariam D. Frenier, Clifton W. Gray, Heinz Heckhausen, Ronald O. Hietala, Merle N. Hirsh, Richard J. Illka, Karla M. Klinger, Donald Leavitt, Jooinn Lee, Charles Liberty, Gloria Rixen, Richard T. Santee, Theodore E. Uehling, Jr., Warner Wilson, and Michael Winter.

Our research program has been supported during the preparation of this book by grants from the University of Minnesota Graduate School and by Grant 1-R01-MH24804 from the National Institute of Mental Health. I am deeply grateful for this continuing support.

I was enabled to spend the fall semester of 1975–76 at the Psychological Institute of Ruhr University of Bochum, Federal Republic of Germany, by the generous hospitality of Heinz Heckhausen and his Institute co-workers at Ruhr University and through the generous financial support of a Fulbright research grant and a University of Minnesota sabbatical leave. The semester was an extraordinarily stimulating one whose effects are reflected in several places in this book. In addition to illuminating dialogues with Heinz Heckhausen, I am particularly indebted to the members of a seminar on "Future Perspective and Current Concerns: Neglected Topics in Motivation" for their vigorous interchanges regarding the concept of current concern and related topics.

The manuscript has gone through so many capable hands that I must thank many of the typists without name. However, I wish especially to thank Linda Powers for her extraordinary contribution in preparing the final draft, Marilyn Strand for preparing the figures, Gloria J. Rixen for most of the indexing, Sandra R. Johnson and Gail A. Rixen for reading proofs, and Bonnie Storck and Charlotte Syverson for innumerable services during the years the book was in preparation. I wish also to thank editor Beverly Kaemmer and the other accommodating and skillful staff members of the University of Minnesota Press.

Finally, I wish to express my gratitude to my University of Minnesota, Morris, colleagues, to Social Sciences Division Chairman O. Truman Driggs, Academic Dean Gordon R. Bopp, and Provost John Q. Imholte for their unwavering encouragement and support.

Table of Contents

MEANING & VOID

Inner Experience and the Incentives in People's Lives

Chapter 1

Meaning, Goals, and Action

This is a book about people's sense that their lives are meaningful. It is about the conditions under which people feel that way and about the conditions that erode that feeling; and it traces the consequences in emotion, thought, and action.

These consequences are by no means trivial or superficial. They penetrate the core of a person's being. They wind themselves around all the fibers of body and soul. When the margin of survival has worn thin, they include life and death.

For two and a half years, the people of Leningrad lived under Nazi siege, and many died. Salisbury (1969) wrote of their ordeal: "Living in the cold, hungry, dark city, people held themselves together by the consciousness of being needed. They began to die when they had nothing to do. Nothing-to-do was more terrible than a bombing raid" (P. 463).

Viktor Frankl considers humankind's "will to meaning" the motive central to human existence. His years as an inmate in a Nazi concentration camp convinced him of this. He recounted an especially dramatic instance of another inmate, once a "fairly well-known composer and librettist" (Frankl, 1963, P. 118), who told him about a dream prophecy that the camp would be liberated on March 30, 1945. Frankl wrote (1963):

When F——— told me about his dream, he was still full of hope and convinced that the voice of his dream would be right. But as the promised day drew nearer, the war news which reached our camp made it appear very unlikely that we would be free on the promised date. On March twenty-ninth, F——— suddenly became ill and ran a high temperature. On March thirtieth, the day his prophecy had told him that the war and suffering would be over for him, he became delirious and lost consciousness. On March thirty-first, he was dead. To all outward appearances, he had died of typhus. (Pp. 119–120)

3

. . . Woe to him who saw no more sense in his life, no aim, no purpose, and therefore no point in carrying on. He was soon lost. (P. 121)

People whose life circumstances are more comfortable than these are less likely to die of meaninglessness than to sicken in spirit. People need to be absorbed. They need to be preoccupied nearly all the time with something that can make them feel awe, curiosity, pleasure, love, hate, relief, amusement, pride, lust, devotion, communion. An enormous part of the human drama is taken up with finding content for the form. Young people search for purpose in their lives; older people seek to revive it. People bless their religions, their children, their charities, new lovers, new wars, new careers, social causes, elaborate hobbies, and sometimes even personal catastrophes for having given their lives a new sense of meaning.

This is a certain kind of book about meaning. It is written in the tradition of scientific psychology. It is therefore in the form of a theory based on experimental results and other systematic observations. Theories are constructions, pictures of a reality that transcends individual facts. In some ways scientific evidence is like the numbered dots on a page that can be connected with a pencil to produce a drawing; but in science the dots are not numbered. When there are few dots, a person could conceivably connect the dots in many different ways and still create equally plausible drawings. When there are many dots, the pattern is more obvious, and people are apt to connect them in fewer different ways. The ideas presented in this book vary in the firmness of evidence on which they draw. In each case, however, the book makes clear what the evidence is, so that readers can judge for themselves.

The argument, very briefly, is as follows. People are organized around pursuing and enjoying objects, events, and experiences that are emotionally compelling for them, which I shall call *incentives*. They are organized around incentives in two senses. First, people plan their actions to obtain their incentives; but, second, pursuing and enjoying incentives also determines the nature and quality of their inner experience — the thoughts and feelings that, along with their sensations, make up the sum total of human consciousness. The very tenor and tempo of people's thoughts and feelings depend on how successfully they are achieving and enjoying goals they value. Whether they feel good and their lives feel meaningful, whether they esteem themselves and feel up to accepting challenges, whether they feel invigorated, angry, disappointed, depressed, alienated, or apathetic — all these depend on their relationships to their incentives. The influences are sometimes subtle, and the factors that determine people's relationships to incentives are often more heavily a matter of inner processes than of objective circumstances. When people are deprived of important incentives, either objectively or for reasons within themselves, their lives seem less meaningful and they are then more likely to try altering their inner experience — chemically through alcohol and other drugs, by changing major aspects of their life situations such as their marriages, careers, or life styles, or by committing suicide. Understanding how all this comes about, how it is that even economically affluent people can become psychologically impoverished, and what might be done about it, obviously has much to tell us both about our individual lives and about the soundness of the social policies that to a great extent govern them.

The Meaning of Meaningfulness

When we ask people whether their lives are meaningful, most of them act as if they understand intuitively what the question means. Viewed philosophically, "meaning" in the sense that I am using the term means something akin to "purpose." It is possible to think of "purpose" in two ways, as aim or as function (Baier, 1957). That is, people's purposes can be either the things they intend to do or the things they are put on earth for — wishing to earn a fortune (an aim), for instance, or having been created to glorify God (a function). The second of these meanings of meaning — what humans have been created *for* — poses a theological question, rather than a psychological or a social-scientific one, that we shall not consider further. We shall be concerned with the other sense of meaning: having aims.

This, also, is the sense in which most people seem to interpret the word when asked about the meaningfulness of their individual lives. In order to find out something about how people view their own sense of meaningfulness, we asked college students from large classes on three campuses to fill out questionnaires. One question on both questionnaires asked them how meaningful they regarded their present lives to be. Of the 320 students who filled out the questionnaires, 68 checked "full of meaning" and 146 checked "very meaningful," accounting between them for two-thirds, or 67%, of the respondents. Another 78 (24%) regarded their lives as "somewhat meaningful," 13 (4%) checked "slightly meaningful," and two checked "meaningless." Only 13 failed to answer the question. Most of this group, then, regard their lives to be at least very meaningful, a judgment that might be rather hard to make if the respondent is unsure what it means. To help clarify just what the respondents had in mind, we asked 138 of them to describe in their own words what it was that made their lives meaningful. The main classes of answers are listed in Table 1-1. The overwhelming majority of answers listed either human relationships of some kind or goals that lay in the future, or the feelings and activities associated with them (Table 1-1, column 1).

Most of these students (89%) mentioned one or another kind of personal relationship as something that contributed meaning to their lives. For many, it was the only thing they mentioned. The other things they mentioned are of two principal kinds: immediate pleasures or future goals.

What all these answers have in common is that they are all, in the sense that I shall use the term, *incentives*. An incentive is any object or event that tends to attract a person (or, in the case of negative incentives, to repel him or her). An incentive may be something the person expects to attain in the future, such as an interesting job after graduation, or it may be something the person is enjoying right now, such as the rest of a sandwich. A particular personal relationship is an incentive for someone who values it and wishes to preserve it. People need not choose to pursue and enjoy everything that is for them an incentive, but anything they pursue or enjoy is one, by definition. Incentives provide purposes. People sacrifice *so that* they may finish their educations or *so that* they may better the lives of loved ones. They eat sandwiches *so that* they may enjoy them and be nourished. We can reasonably conclude that when people describe what makes their lives meaningful, they list the important incentives in their lives, which they strive to maintain and obtain when they are not simply enjoying them, and which provide purposes for acting.

The 138 students who wrote answers to our first questionnaire were doing so "off the top of their heads." They had probably never been asked such questions before, and they may have forgotten to list some of the things that contribute to their sense of meaningfulness. To find out what would happen if we jogged our respondents' memories, we presented other students with a list of categories (see Table 1-1) based on the answers of the first group and asked them to estimate how important each kind of thing was in "giving your life meaning."[1] Many more of these respondents acknowledged that the kinds of things listed contribute to their sense that their lives are meaningful (Table 1-1, columns 2 and 3). Nearly all acknowledged friendships to be more than slightly important, and more than three-

Table 1-1. Things That Contribute to the Meaningfulness
of Respondents' Lives

Kind of Contributor to Meaningfulness	Percentage of Respondents Who		
	Listed at Least One Thing of Each Kind[a]	Checked Each Kind[b]	Checked "Fairly Great" or "Extreme" Importance
Friends, communicating, understanding	71%	96%	90%
Parents and siblings	50	85	71
Religious faith, relationship to God	27	52	30
Process of education, finishing college	25	75	57
Spouse, fiance, boyfriend, girlfriend own children	25	79	68
Leisure-time activities	21	92	64
Nature, environment, small pleasures[c]	18	83	61
Happiness, security, things in general[d]	16	79	68
Job, sense of responsibility, success	15	67	43
Helping and sharing, loving others, feeling useful	14	83	67
Inner searching, exploring, growth	11	72	51
Feeling loved and wanted	8	91	76
Having goals to strive for (general)[e]	8	71	48
Plans for vocational future[f]	6	69	54

[a] First questionnaire, open-ended. Other categories were used by less than 5% of the respondents. There were 138 respondents, 55 men and 83 women.
[b] Second questionnaire, response-limited. There were 182 respondents, 103 men and 78 women. Since 14 knew of the theories being tested, the figures are based on 168 cases. The percentage given is for those who regarded each kind as of more than "only slight importance in giving your life meaning."
[c] The category on the second questionnaire was phrased, "Enjoying nature and things around me."
[d] The category on the second questionnaire was phrased, "Being alive and things in general."
[e] On the second questionnaire, goals other than major life goals.
[f] On the second questionnaire, vocational or other major life goals.

quarters considered them to be of fairly great or extreme importance. Only one other category (not shown in Table 1-1) was that important for a majority of these young students: "Being on my own." "Money and possessions" were of great importance to only 19% of this group and drugs to only 7%.

Some theorists have suggested that for one's life to feel meaningful one had to become dedicated to a single, consuming, relatively lofty purpose, preferably spiritual. However, the pattern of our results suggests otherwise. Only 23% of our students claimed a single extremely important source of meaning, and only half reported having any *extremely* important source at all. Furthermore, two of the traditionally loftiest sources of meaning — religion and vocation — were among the weakest. Religion, in particular, was of great importance to only 30% of these students.

This is by no means an isolated finding, true only for our predominantly small-town Minnesotans. A majority of 56 Californians found their greatest source of meaningfulness in their family relationships (Young, 1974), whereas a "particular purpose or belief" was for most members of the group only the third or fourth most important source of meaning (out of eight categories). Elisabeth Lukas (1971, 1972) stopped 1000 Viennese on the street and asked them whether there was something so valuable for them that it gave their lives meaning, and, if so, to describe it. About half found their source of meaning in family, children, or home, and another 9% in love or social relationships. For 17% the major source of meaning lay in their success, work, or education, and for 10% it was general self-development. These categories of personal relationships, vocational development, and personal growth thus account for more than half of the answers. Religion claimed less than 3%, possessions 6%, and general comfort 8%. Thus, most of these respondents found their sense of meaning in pursuing and enjoying conventional, everyday kinds of incentives. Interestingly, those who appeared to have the most clearly ascertainable sense of meaningfulness tended to give the most concrete sources of their meaning: categories such as family, children, vocation, possessions, and hobbies, in contrast to the more abstract replies such as "self-development," "agreeable life," and "social tasks" given by those less certain of their sense of meaning. Few people found their greatest meaning in suffering or in their attitudes toward their lives, such as maintaining a sense of nobility in the face of personal adversity.

Thus, it appears that people derive their sense of meaningfulness from enjoying and pursuing many kinds of incentives, some lofty and remote, but most everyday and homely. Furthermore, there is evidence that the more kinds of incentives people can respond to, the greater their sense of meaning. Thus, among our college students who acknowledged finding meaning in more than 20 of our categories, 81% reported their lives to be "very meaningful" or "full of meaning." That was true for only 35% of the students who found meaning in less than 12 of the categories. (The difference is statistically significant beyond the .001 level.[2]) Other investigators have found that college students who score high in a test of meaningfulness (the Purpose in Life Test[3]) belong to more organizations (Doerries, 1970) and are more certain of their future college majors, vocations, and spouses (Tryon & Radzin, 1972) than those who score low.

The Social Significance of Meaning

Whether or not people have a sense that their lives are meaningful has some very practical consequences. In our second student group, those who feel their lives are less meaningful than average also are more depressed. The correlation is .46 ($p<.001$).[4] Others have found that psychiatrically disturbed individuals report a lower sense that their lives are meaningful (Crumbaugh & Maholick, 1964; Lukas, 1972).

The problem of extreme meaninglessness — "existential vacuum" (Frankl, 1969) or *void* — seems to afflict a significant part of the population. Among our second group of students, 20% claimed to find no meaning in any kind of pursuit. Interestingly, Lukas (1972) also estimated that 20% of her Viennese population suffered from a lack of meaning, and Frankl (1969) estimated that about 20% of patients who come for psychiatric help have problems related to meaninglessness.

The sense that one's life is meaningful is clearly an important part of being human, something with significant practical and social consequences. As we proceed through the remaining chapters of the book, we shall find reason to link people's sense of meaningfulness to a number of additional social consequences: alienation from work and family, immersion in the mass media, alcohol and drug use, and suicide.

How Can We Study Meaning?

Science can proceed only if it casts its subject matter into a form that is manageable by scientific methods. The sense that one's life is meaningful is an ambiguous, slippery subject for investigation unless we can specify just what we mean by it. Fortunately, the kinds of findings described above give us some handholds. We have seen that, when it comes right down to specifying what makes their lives meaningful, people turn to the incentives in their lives — the personal relationships, job goals, recreational activities, inner experiences, and simple daily pleasures that people spend most of their time pursuing and enjoying. The more of these that occupy them, the more meaningful their lives feel and the happier their mood. Meaningfulness seems to arise out of people's relationships to their incentives; these, therefore, would seem to be the place to look for its sources and effects.

Meaningfulness and Inner Experience

The meaningfulness of someone's life cannot be inferred just from knowing his or her objective circumstances. Meaningfulness is something very subjective, a pervasive quality of a person's whole inner life. It is experienced both as ideas and as emotions. It is clear, then, that when we ask about the meaningfulness of someone's life we are asking about qualities of his or her inner experience.

When we speak of inner experience, it is important to realize that we are not referring to a compartment of a person, an appendage of a person's being among other appendages. Experientially, inner experience is all there is. Everything of which a person can become aware is part of his or her inner experience. When we speak of something affecting a person's inner experience, we speak of something that alters the only personal arena in which he or she can perceive, feel, and come to grips with anything.

This is not to say that inner experience encompasses everything that is important psychologically. Experiential totality is less than psychological totality. In the history of psychology some theorists have believed that only conscious events make a difference in human functioning or, conversely, that consciousness itself makes no difference whatever. Today, however, it is becoming clearer that although many of the important processes and influences on a person's functioning remain unconscious, conscious events are of crucial importance and, indeed, the fact that something is conscious alters its impact on the person. For instance, in one experiment children were offered a choice of two rewards, one of which they preferred to the other (Mischel, Ebbesen, & Zeiss, 1972). To get the preferred reward, they would have to wait until the experimenter returned to the room after an absence. However, they could ring a bell at any time to bring back the experimenter and get the less attractive reward. Some of the children were instructed to keep thinking about the rewards during the experimenter's absence. Others were instructed to keep their minds on "fun things" other than the rewards. The children in this "think fun things" group were able to wait much longer than the "think rewards" group before summoning the experimenter. Remaining conscious of the rewards to be had made children less able to put off getting the reward, even though waiting would have gotten them something they liked better.[5]

Consciousness, then, is not just an "epiphenomenon," not simply a reflection of a process that, like a shadow, has no effect on the object casting it. Consciousness is an "emergent property of cerebral activity" (Sperry, 1969, P. 533) whose contents, in turn, influence the course of brain activity. By "emergent property" Sperry meant that consciousness arises out of such complex interactions among the neural units of the brain that it could not be understood from knowing only the single brain events that join together to produce it. Yet, this "emergent" outcome feeds back into the flow of brain activity and modifies the functioning of the parts. To borrow Sperry's example, knowing only the activities of individual molecules in a wheel would provide little basis for predicting that the wheel can roll. Yet, wheels do roll, and rolling is in this sense an emergent property. Furthermore, rolling affects the individual molecules, at least to the extent of changing their locations and velocity. Likewise, inner experience, the content of consciousness, has an impact of its own, and events that change it change the organism as a whole.

Many things may go on at the same time in inner experience. There are typically sense impressions — what one sees, hears, smells, and so on — and also the consciousness of directing one's actions. These both involve a person's ongoing transactions with the outside world. There are also other major components of inner experience that are less firmly tied to immediate circumstances. For the sake of convenience we can classify these into two kinds, *ideational* and *affective*.

"Ideational" here refers to the figurative, imaginal aspects of inner experience that take on qualities comparable to sense impressions — pictures, sounds, touches, muscular movements, and so on — even though nothing is activating the sense organs at the time to produce them. For instance, if people are asked to count in their heads the number of windows in their houses, they are likely to visualize the outside walls or the insides of their rooms, as though taking an actual tour around the house, and count the windows they "see" there. They have created visual images that have some of the properties (though by no means all) of an actual visual experience. When people are thinking through difficult problems or are in stressful situations, they may silently speak to themselves. They may "hear" their own voices, even though their voices are still. There are large differences among people in how vividly they experience such images, but it is likely that everyone has imagery in some form.

"Affective" refers to the feeling tone of experience, to those aspects of emotion that convey the quality of the emotion and perhaps its intensity.

All these components of inner experience — sensory, motor, ideational, and affective — participate in the sense that one's life is meaningful. This book will be concerned with how. Since meaningfulness is bound up with the incentives in a person's life, we shall focus first on the ways in which a person's relationship to his or her incentives influences the components of inner experience. The rest of this chapter considers the powerful effects of incentives on action. Chapters 2 and 3 examine the effects of incentives on thought and affect. Chapter 4 considers the ways in which things become incentives and the ways in which they may gain or lose their value. Subsequent chapters then describe what happens when people lose their incentives or are unable to find new ones: the story of emptiness, of void.

Incentives and Action

Goals Govern Life and Behavior

No person, lower animal, or plant can live very long without keeping up a supply of essential materials. Every organism needs certain substances such as oxygen, nitrogen, minerals, salts, or various organic molecules to fuel the activity of its cells and to replace components which are continuously dissipated into its environment. Plants and simple animals are equipped to draw essential nutrients out of their most immediate environment without much motion and often without leaving the spot on which they are rooted, much as a single human cell is nourished by its immediate surroundings in the body without doing anything beyond its chemical processes of osmosis, metabolism, and the like. All animal species beyond the simplest, however, must do more than this. They have participated in an evolutionary trade-off in which they have freed themselves from the tyranny of their immediate surroundings but have thereby given up the comfort of being nourished in place. Now they are obliged to move around to locate and consume the things they need. No such organism could survive without having built into it the capacity to acquire essential materials and living conditions, and if it must do more than simply absorb the materials into its cells it must have some way of recognizing them. That is, the organism must be equipped to pursue the things it needs and be equipped to recognize — and hence be changed by — the things it needs when it catches up with them. For a *species* of organism, as distinct from just an individual organism, to survive, the members of the species must also be equipped to pursue and recognize whatever things they need in order to procreate.

What does it mean to be "equipped" to seek and recognize things? It means that the organism has an internal communication system for coordinating its actions and that the system specifically directs those actions toward finding and consuming essential materials and conditions. In a real sense, obtaining essentials can be thought of as a set of goals. It may be stretching the term to say that soaking up water is one of a plant's goals, because we normally think of goals as something an organism has to act to achieve; but for any organism that moves around in some sort of directed fashion, the things that it is after can legitimately be called "goals."

When we think about it in this way we can see that organisms — whether they be geraniums, clams, or people — do not really exist separate from their goals. They are part of a larger system that includes them *and* their goals. Not only are they utterly dependent on achieving their goals in order to survive, but they are themselves designed and organized around their goals. Just as a muscle is shaped to fit a certain niche on the skeleton or one gear is cast to mesh with another, organisms fit their goals. They and their goal objects are part and parcel of the same interlocking system of events and processes. To this basic fact of nature, people are not exceptions.

It is this relatedness of people to their goals that this book is about. Goals at the human level include things not often thought of as goals, such as intimacy, understanding, identity, and rapture. Words such as "incentive" and "goal" feel too dry, sterile, and coldly abstract to refer to such warmly and powerfully human experiences. Yet, they are necessary precisely because they refer to such a wide array of events, none of them indifferent to people, ranging from the banal to the divine. These are the things and events to which people are drawn, for which people are designed, to which people are bound by thought, feeling, and act, and in which people find or fail to find a sense of meaning.

Goals and Incentives: Straightening Out the Terminology

I have used two terms, "incentive" and "goal," in ways that are rather similar, but they are not, in fact, synonymous. The reason for having two similar terms is that we need a way of distinguishing between objects or events that an organism values, which I shall call *incentives*, and those that the organism is committed to striving for, which I shall call *goals*. With animals, we can infer that something is an incentive (that it has *incentive value*) when we observe that an individual makes efforts to obtain it when it is available; or we might assume that something probably has incentive value for an animal when we know that most members of the same species strive after the object when they have an opportunity. With people, we can infer that something probably has incentive value when a person expresses something other than indifference to it. However, neither animals nor people actually make efforts to obtain an incentive every time it is possible to do so. They may prefer to strive after a more valuable incentive instead, or they may judge that going after the incentive is too costly or too painful to make it worthwhile. For instance, most people would probably like to own a yacht, but most of those who would are making no efforts to obtain one and have no intention of doing so. For them, owning a yacht is an incentive but not a goal. Dinner, on the other hand, is for most people both an incentive and a goal. An incentive, then, is at least potentially a goal, but it may or may not be one in actuality. Therefore, in many contexts "incentive" and "goal object" may be used interchangeably, but in other contexts they may not.

The terms "incentive" and "goal" tend to conjure up images of people energetically striving to achieve some new outcome. However, they are used here to include some other possibilities. Thus, the objective may sometimes be to attain something, such as a house in the country or a promotion, but at other times the objective may be to keep something (for instance, one's friends' love), to do something (for instance, to go sailing), or, under certain conditions, to injure someone (as in taking revenge).

Although we like to think of incentives in positive terms, there are also negative incentives — objects and events that organisms normally wish to avoid, escape, prevent, or get rid of, such as onrushing cars, electric shocks, and illness. Negative incentives have negative incentive value, in the sense that they are worse than indifferent.

There are various ways to conceive of incentive value, each of which implies different ways to measure it. One way, for instance, would be to establish that something is capable of stirring someone's interest, which renders it an incentive, but then to measure its objective qualities: the size of a pay increase, the duration of a sailing expedition, or the intensity of an electric shock. Another way is not to conceive of the incentive in terms of its objective qualities at all, but rather to assess it purely according to its capacity to attract or repel. These two ways of conceiving value may yield quite different assessments. After all, the twenty-sixth week of sailing may add a degree of value quite unlike the first. Furthermore, the sailor may become seasick, which would change the incentive value of sailing under any conditions.

Another set of alternatives in conceiving of incentive value is whether one is concerned with the value of incentive at a particular point in time — for instance, on the next occasion for encountering it — or whether one wishes to assign to the incentive a single value that can characterize it over time — some kind of average value for the incentive on repeated encounters with it. As we shall see in Chapter 4, the subjective value of an incentive can fluctuate widely for an individual over time in accordance with a variety of conditions.

Which way one chooses to conceive and measure incentive value must depend on the particular purposes for doing it. For purposes of this book, which focuses on the consequences of incentive relationships for inner experience, incentive value is taken as the attractiveness or repulsiveness of something for a particular individual at a given moment in time. That is, the value of an incentive is taken as something that goes on inside the valuing individual. It undoubtedly bears a lawful relationship to the objective qualities of the incentive, but the relationship may be quite complex and variable. Just what it is that goes on inside the valuing individual, and the factors that cause it to vary, are considered in Chapters 3 and 4.

Evidence That Incentives Control Behavior

The fact that actions are generally controlled by incentives is so well known as to require little defense. It is a fact deeply rooted in all major cultures, however it may be expressed. The commonplace of people asking "What's in it for me?" can at best be countered by advising them to equate their self-interest with that of a larger group, such as family, community, or country. The carrot and the stick work well with donkeys and with humans. Major debates in popular culture take place not regarding whether incentives work but regarding which ones are most worthwhile. People who prefer the mystic life are not turning their backs on incentives but are replacing limited material incentives with supposedly more powerful experiential ones. Fundamentalist Christians forgo this world's forbidden pleasures to ensure that they will be able to enjoy the pleasures of the next.

Popular convictions do not, of course, make a very convincing proof. However, all major theoretical positions in psychology incorporate the same basic idea, are reducible to it, or have been found inadequate when they have strayed from it.

Surprisingly, that has not always been so. In fact, some theorists, such as John B. Watson (1930) and E. R. Guthrie (1935), maintained that people's behavior can be explained purely in terms of conditioned reflexes of "habit" without recourse to any concepts such as "goal," "purpose," or "will."[6] Many of their contemporaries and predecessors, who subscribed to the "British empiricist" notion that people build up their inner experience through "association of ideas," recognized that people exercised "will" at times but did not conceive of will or incentive as special influences on virtually all human activity.

However, during the first third of this century — in fact, while Watson's behaviorism was gaining momentum — several major figures transformed psychological thinking. William McDougall (1921) popularized the point that all human (and animal) activity is part of the process of pursuing instinctively prescribed goals. For instance, parents driving their preschool children to nursery school are acting out a parental instinct that, in a real sense, pushes them to protect and care for their young. Sending a letter to the editor is impelled by one's pugnacious instinct. And so on. In Freud's psychoanalytic theories, people direct their behavior toward "objects" of their "instincts" (Freud, 1915/1953). Kurt Lewin's influential system begins with the idea that human actions are guided by psychological "forces," somewhat analogously to the way physical objects (iron filings near a magnet or a space ship near a planet) are guided by magnetic or gravitational forces (Lewin, 1935, 1938). These hypothetical forces are generated by the person's incentives. Thus, in Lewin's view people live in a "force field" of attractions to the incentives of which they are aware. This rather abstract conception reduces in practice to the fundamental premise that people steer toward attaining incentives. The major theories of Tolman (1932) and Hull (1952) both incorporated the principle that organisms act only in relation to goals, and it forms the centerpin for the latest generation of motivational theories (e.g., Atkinson & Birch, 1970; Bindra, 1974).[7]

Some of the most interesting evidence that incentives control behavior has been developed by investigators of two other processes, reinforcement and drive. Both these two lines of investigation began with a rather mechanistic conception of behavior. They agreed that organisms seem to pursue incentives but believed that this appearance of pursuing incentives is a by-product of a different, simpler process. As the research evidence accumulated, however, these original ideas had to be progressively modified and, in the end, either abandoned or redefined so as to be compatible with an incentive theory.

The Law of Effect. Often in science an idea becomes most popular and influential at the same time it is being discredited within the science that produced it. The 1960s saw the concept of reinforcement, as the keystone of behavior modification, become a part of the everyday language of teachers, counselors, clinical psychologists and psychiatrists, corrections officials, and a great many other professionals concerned with changing people's behavior. The concept of reinforcement is part of what must surely be one of the most durable "laws" of psychology, the Law of Effect. First promulgated by Thorndike (1898), the Law of Effect states simply that organisms are more likely to repeat actions for which they have in the past been rewarded than actions for which they have not. A child who discovers that making a fuss gets it some much desired attention is likely to continue making fusses. A bear cub who discovers that overturning garbage cans delivers a feast of squeezed oranges, soggy lettuce, and bacon grease will become steadily more proficient at overturning garbage cans.

The Law of Effect would seem to be a simple way of restating that organisms strive for incentives, and, as an *empirical* law that simply describes a regularity in behavior, it is. However, Thorndike and some of his prominent successors, such as Clark Hull and Kenneth Spence, were not content to leave it at that. They wished to describe in more detailed fashion how the empirical Law of Effect operates. Thorndike supposed that rewarding an animal (that is, awarding it an incentive) for performing an act in a certain situation "stamps in" a connection in the brain between the rewarded act and what the animal sensed in the situation, so that on later occasions being in a similar situation would automatically trigger the same act again. The stamping-in process came to be known as "reinforcing" the connection between what the animal senses in the situation (that is, between the *stimuli* it encounters there) and its response to it. Under the old *theoretical* Law of Effect, then, organisms may seem to pursue incentives, but their movements are in fact controlled in a fairly mechanical way by present stimuli and by the effects of past reinforcements, rather than being an ultimate consequence of their awareness that incentives are available.

The large amount of research stimulated by the various reinforcement theories, however, has shown that the theoretical Law of Effect has serious limitations. Work with animals, for instance, has demonstrated that reinforcement is powerless to teach certain kinds of behavior, especially behaviors that conflict with instinctive patterns, even though the animal is physically capable of performing them (Bolles, 1972). For instance, raccoons that have no trouble learning to deposit single coins in a piggy bank are unable to deposit two: They dip them in and out and rub them together, just as they instinctively "wash" their food in nature. Work with humans shows clearly that people learn actions and associations without specific rewards to stamp in connections, and rewards do not necessarily improve learning (Levine, 1971). Rewards and punishments do have their effects, of course. They inform people whether their actions and thoughts are effective, they attract attention to things in the environment relevant to attaining them, and they determine what things people choose to hold in memory and how they choose to allocate their time and energy (Atkinson & Wickens, 1971).[8] That is, rewards and punishments act as incentives do. Their effects on learning are only indirect. Learning can take place without them, and it takes the form not of "connecting" stimuli and responses but of developing expectations concerning what leads to what (Bindra, 1974; Bolles, 1972; Estes, 1971; Logan, 1971; Nuttin & Greenwald, 1968). As a result, many theorists have argued that the concept of reinforcement is unnecessary, while others have chosen to keep the word but to redefine it. Albert Bandura, one of the leaders of the behavior modification movement in clinical psychology, sums up this trend when he writes (1974) that "reinforcement, as it has become better understood, has changed from a mechanical strengthener of conduct to an informative and motivating influence" (P. 860).

Thus the enormous body of research evidence that has grown up in the tradition of reinforcement theory, the tradition of Thorndike, Hull, Skinner, and their descendants, has ended up supporting and detailing the basic principle that animals and people act in accordance with the incentives they believe to be available to them.

Drives as motivators. For much of this century, most Western psychologists believed that to start a course of action an animal or person had to be in a state of drive. One had to be hungry, thirsty, sexually aroused, angry, frightened, or the like to be motivated to perform any action. Hull (1952) and other early reinforcement theorists believed that increases in the level of drive (for instance, increases in hunger or thirst) motivate organisms and that decreases in drive reinforce the actions performed just before the decrease. Thus, drive was the most important factor in motivation.

As experimenters tested the drive theories, they came upon many kinds of evidence that contradicted the original formulations. It became plain, for instance, that animals worked harder for large rewards than for small ones.[9] Furthermore, very hungry animals often made no apparent efforts to obtain food if food seemed unavailable to them. Therefore, Hull and Spence modified their theories to include incentive as an important factor in motivation.

Meanwhile, important developments in physiological psychology opened up powerful new experimental tools for investigating motivation. Experimenters discovered that animals were willing to work hard for the reward of having certain areas of their brains stimulated electrically, and human patients reported that stimulation to comparable areas of their brains felt extremely pleasant. Since the pleasure derived from this stimulation did not seem to depend on the animal or person being in a state of "drive" as usually defined, psychologists now had a way of administering powerful rewards in animals that were not hungry, thirsty, or otherwise deprived, and they could deliver these rewards much more precisely than before. Furthermore, stimulating these brain areas not only was rewarding in its own right but also made animals act hungry in the presence of food.

These methods therefore led to interesting new experiments. For instance, Mendelson (1966) could now ask whether, in order to motivate an organism to perform an act, it is necessary for the animal to be in a state of drive at the outset of the act, or whether it is enough for the animal to expect a reward at the end. He found that completely satiated rats were willing to travel through a maze for the reward of some food — provided that he stimulated their brain hunger systems when they arrived there. Therefore, it was not necessary for these animals to be in a state of drive — to be hungry — to start working for food. It was enough for them to have learned to expect pleasure at the end. As the animal evidence has accumulated, it has become increasingly plain that drives such as hunger or fear are neither necessary nor sufficient to get behavior started toward a goal; but expecting that the action will yield a reward is both necessary and sufficient (Bindra, 1968).

This is not to say that drives have no bearing on motivation. Some incentives cannot be enjoyed except in an appropriate drive state. For instance, food can be obnoxious on a full stomach, and relief is meaningless to someone who feels safe and comfortable. Thus, the values of some incentives depend almost completely on the organism's state of drive when it receives its reward. Furthermore, severe drive states can make organisms restless and impulsive, and the discomfort that often accompanies drive states reminds organisms to attend to their vital needs. Nevertheless, the crucial factor in motivation is not drive but incentive.

The clearest evidence on this question has so far been obtained with animals rather than with people. The reasons are fairly obvious. In organized society, people can almost always reasonably expect that their needs will be provided for. The hungry expect that they will eventually eat, and they usually know which actions of theirs will bring that about. Faced with a person in dire need, an experimenter cannot ethically withhold help. Therefore, there are for practical purposes no neat ways of separating out the effects of drives and incentives on our fellow humans. However, common observation makes it plain that people work for many kinds of rewards without having to be driven by states of need. Incentives are used by people to control one another's behavior throughout our society. Further, investigators have found considerable systematic evidence that expecting incentives of some kind controls the behavior of humans.

Expecting incentives and human motivation. There are actually relatively few investigations that have set out simply to demonstrate that people are prepared to work harder or take greater risks for what is more valuable to them. The reason is probably that the outcome of such an investigation would be a foregone conclusion. Scientists are not inclined to demonstrate the obvious, at least unless they believe that such a demonstration will lead them somewhere more interesting. Therefore, demonstrations that people work harder if they regard their work as more worthwhile are mainly limited to cases where the demonstration is secondary to some larger investigation. For instance, I once used a test in which students were asked to unscramble some scrambled words — for example, to figure out that "korw" could be unscrambled to spell "work" — as a measure of whether watching someone who was eager to do well would motivate students to work faster. First, however, I needed to make sure that just the challenge of unscrambling words was not already driving students to go as fast as they could. Therefore, I offered some students ten cents for each word over 25 that they unscrambled in five minutes, and — Lo and behold! — they worked faster than the others (Klinger, 1967).

Sometimes, one can infer effects of incentives. For instance, one investigation determined that high school boys who value their parents' and teachers' approval cheat less (Piliavin, Hardyck, & Vadum, 1968). Presumably, cheating less represents a sacrifice to the incentive of remaining in parents' and teachers' good graces.

Beyond these kinds of evidence, psychologists in industry have investigated how incentives affect workers' performance and workers' satisfaction with their jobs. Their research, furthermore, has probed some of the many complications in the way people regard their incentives, especially workers' expectations of whether working hard will in fact get them the things they value.

As early as 1660 the philosopher-mathematician Pascal (1941) had proposed a way of calculating what has since been called the "expected utility" of an action: It is the probability that performing the action will earn a reward, in relation to the size of the reward. An action that is certain to yield a big reward has a high "expected utility." Both an action that has a modest chance to win a big reward and an action that is certain to win a modest reward have medium utilities. Actions that are certain to win nothing have no utility. If one wishes to decide which of several alternative actions to undertake, one can compare the various possibilities and choose the one with the highest expected utility.

This approach to decision-making has some very practical implications for gambling. Poker players who use it are more likely to win than those who do not, apart from other gambling devices such as psychological pressure and rigged equipment. For Pascal (1660/1941, 233 Pensèes), it was also a way of settling a major religious question: Should a reasonable person be a believing Christian or not? He calculated that the prospective value of choosing God if God exists is infinitely great: infinite happiness for eternity in the afterlife. The prospective cost of not choosing God if He exists is also infinite: an eternity in Hell. On the other hand, the gain of not believing if God does not exist and the cost of believing if He does are both finite, and they are insignificantly trivial by comparison. Even if it is extremely improbable that God exists, this small chance (provided it is not infinitesimal) is outweighed by the infinitely greater net rewards of believing. Thus, reasonable gamblers should turn to God.

Pascal was describing the way in which reasonable people *ought* to make decisions. However, others have argued that that is, in effect, the way people *actually* make decisions, and they have elaborated and formalized Pascal's basic idea into what are now generally called "instrumentality" or "Expectancy X (times) Value" theories (for instance, see Edwards, 1954; Festinger, 1942). The principle underlying these theories is simple. Imagine that you wish to choose among a number of alternative actions: for instance, to choose among four job opportunities or between working hard and loafing on the job. What will you do? The theorist predicts that in effect (though, of course, usually not consciously) you will do the following. First, for any one alternative you will consider all the possible consequences of choosing it. Second, you will anticipate how valuable each of these consequences would be for you. Third, you will determine how likely you regard each consequence to be (your "expectancy") if you should choose that alternative. Fourth, you will multiply the anticipated value of each consequence by the probability that it will come to pass and then add up these "Expectancy X Value" products for all of the consequences of a single alternative action. This gives you a "sum of products" for that alternative action. Fifth, you will calculate such a sum of products for each other alternative action. Last, you will compare the sums of products that you have obtained for the various alternative actions — for instance, for every job opportunity available to you — and decide on that action which produced the highest sum of products. With this theory, it is easy to explain why more people do not throw up their modest jobs to make their fortunes in Las Vegas (the probability of a big win is too small) and why not everyone finds it worthwhile to struggle for commercial or professional eminence (the necessary dedication means giving up too many alternative satisfactions that people value highly).

The Expectancy X Value theories have been applied in numerous investigations[10] (Mitchell, 1974). By and large, they have been quite successful in predicting workers' job preferences and attitudes toward good performance. They have had moderate success in predicting workers' satisfaction with their jobs. However, they have been only very modestly successful in predicting work effort and performance.

The fact that it has been harder for the Expectancy X Value theories to predict effort and performance can be explained partly by realities of the workplace which have not been adequately controlled by the investigators: workers vary in ability to perform, there are consequences of working hard or loafing not taken into account by the investigators, and workers' performance depends partly on factors beyond their control, such as equipment and cooperation. Predictions of performance have been most accurate under working conditions in which workers were best able to translate their intentions into performance.

However, there are also other reasons that performance is predicted less well by Expectancy X Value theories. There is growing evidence that the laws that govern the way people choose goals are different from the decisions people make after having become committed to them. First, although people prefer to choose goals that they value highly over goals they value less, they are likely to put in only about as much effort as is necessary to ensure reaching the goal. *Harder* goals lead to higher levels of performance (Locke, 1968). Unless people foresee reasons to take special precautions, however, no purpose is served in working harder for the more *valuable* goal. Second, when people encounter unexpected difficulties in attaining their goals, they are likely to try harder, not less hard, even though the setback probably reduces their expectancy of achieving the goal (Schneider, 1975; Schneider & Eckelt, 1975). We shall see in Chapter 5 that this invigoration of activity in the face of obstacles forms part of a regular sequence of events set in motion when people and animals encounter difficulties en route to goals, a sequence not readily predictable from Expectancy X Value theories. What these findings suggest is that incentives indeed play a vital role in people's actions but that there is not a simple, one-to-one effect. Rather, people's relationships to their incentives are mediated by thoughts and feelings, which this book will attempt to trace.

One kind of goal poses special problems for the Expectancy X Value theorist. This is the set of achievement goals, in which the objective is to demonstrate one's ability to compete against some standard of excellence. Achievement goals pose special problems because the goals that are easiest to attain are, by definition, the least suitable for demonstrating one's ability. To deal with this problem, a number of investigators have modified the Expectancy X Value theories in various ways. John Atkinson (for instance, Atkinson, 1964; Atkinson & Birch, 1970; Atkinson & Raynor, 1974) has led the way in a number of these developments. Instead of simply asking people what consequences they valued, he applied indirect measures of motivation worked out previously (McClelland, Atkinson, Clark, & Lowell, 1953) and *inferred* the value of an incentive for a subject by multiplying the strength of the subject's motive to achieve (or avoid) the incentive times the objective size of the incentive. Thus, the Expectancy X Value theory became in his hands an Expectancy X Motive X Incentive theory. In a large number of investigations, this theory and variations of it have succeeded in predicting how long people persist at tasks, how well they perform, what risks they are willing to take, and what careers they prefer[11] (Atkinson & Raynor, 1974; Heckhausen, 1968).

One thing that the Expectancy X Value theories make clear is that people are motivated not simply by the quality of the incentives around them but by how they interpret them. The Expectancy X Value theories build in an appropriate regard for the person's view of how likely it is that an action will succeed in attaining an incentive. Expectancy is itself a complicated matter, however, and a number of investigators have begun to probe expectancies in much more detail (for instance, Heckhausen & Weiner, 1972). This work is succeeding in linking action not only to incentives but to cognitions about incentives, and hence also to inner experience.

Incentives Work. What Else Do We Need to Know?

Incentives work, at least much of the time. More precisely, people's expectancies of incentives they value usually exercise a controlling influence on their actions. The idea is very old and very useful. Managers of industrial and sales organizations routinely use incentive plans to control the behavior of their employees. Parents regularly use promises and threats to keep their children in line. Demagogues and democrats have long made use of the fact, now demonstrated experimentally (Mitchell & Biglan, 1971), that people's attitudes toward minority groups and public policies depend on the extent to which these seem likely to advance their own interests. That people act to maximize their gains has long been assumed by common sense, systematic philosophy, and classical economics. It is almost as useful as the Law of Gravity.

Perhaps just because it is useful and intuitively correct, the idea that incentives control behavior — what we might call the "Law of Incentive" — manages to hide as much as it reveals. First of all, like the Law of Gravity, it merely states *that* something is so: that actions are controlled by incentives, that bodies of some mass attract each other. Neither law explains *why*. Neither law, by itself, reduces what it describes to simpler terms. It is also easy to overlook that the Law of Incentive, like the Law of Gravity, is in some respects circular. Since there is ultimately no way of measuring the strength of this attracting power (the "gravitational mass") of a physical object without measuring its attraction to another object, stating that masses attract each other is stating that objects that attract each other attract each other. In the same way, there is no objective way to determine what is an incentive except by discovering whether it is attractive to a person or species. To say that incentives control actions is therefore to say that objects that control actions control actions. This circularity can obviously not be all there is to the matter, however, because if it were, neither law would be useful to anyone, and both laws are. The reason for their usefulness is that we do not have to measure the mass or the incentive value of every new object we encounter. It is possible to classify most objects by other means into categories we already know something about, thereby permitting a large measure of prediction. Thus, we can usually tell by the look of a rock that it will fall if dropped, and we can usually tell by the look of money that it will be worked for if offered. Then, too, both mass and incentive value have more than one effect. By holding an object in the hand, it is often possible to estimate what will happen if it is dropped. By asking people what they think about an incentive, it is often possible to predict what they will do about it.

Despite these redeeming features, the Laws of Gravity and Incentive are scientifically useful primarily insofar as they describe events precisely. To build on the Law of Gravity, physics needed to know at just what rate two masses are accelerated toward each other. To build on the Law of Incentive, psychology needs to know precisely what happens between organisms and their incentives. It needs to know under what conditions people come to treat something as an incentive and under what conditions its value for them becomes greater or smaller (see Chapter 4). It needs to know how people manage to stay oriented toward an incentive and how they stay on track to consummation (see Chapters 2 and 3).

The gain of knowing these things is great both for practical purposes and for understanding. Useful as the primitive Law of Incentive is, it is a rough-and-ready generalization that breaks down so often and leaves out so much that its usefulness is severely limited. Why can't people agree on values? How can people be so highly motivated to attain something that their very eagerness disorganizes them? Why do some people immolate themselves to protest a war and others choose to scrabble out a living on a subsistence farm? Why do people become depressed, take drugs, act alienated, give up lucrative careers, tire of good marriages, suffer mid-adult crises, hate their leisurely retirements, enter monasteries, and commit suicide? If incentives control actions, how do they produce phenomena such as these?

Chapter 2

Incentives and Thoughts

In perhaps more than any other single way, we know ourselves according to the thoughts we have. We feel freer to think our own thoughts than to express them in action, and in our thoughts we feel closer to the sources of our actions than we do from simply knowing our actions themselves.

Yet, just as incentives powerfully control actions, they also control thoughts. Judging from the available evidence, all thoughts are in one way or another related to the thinker's incentives. Many thoughts deal quite directly with working to achieve a current goal. Others may dwell on memories of past events or on images of distant places, but these are most likely related in some way to something the person would like to bring about or to avoid, now or in the future.

The apparent fact that incentives govern thoughts raises some important questions. What is there about the nature of thoughts that makes it possible for our incentives to control their content? In what way and under what conditions do our incentives determine what we think about?

The Nature and Organization of Thought

By "thought" I mean the constant stream of images that cross the field of our consciousness and the unconscious processes that organize them. Thoughts are most characteristically streams of inner language, but sometimes thought is made up of mostly visual images and often it includes imagined smells, tastes, touches, and vestiges of movement. The images of thought can tap the whole range of human sensory and motoric experience.

Thought is basically a sequence of responses. That is, the images that make up the conscious aspect of thought operate in many ways like bodily acts. They seem to obey similar laws of conditioning and organization; but whereas motor responses involve neural links in both the central and the peripheral nervous system and musculature, the imaginal responses of thought usually stop with the central circuits.[1] Thoughts have therefore sometimes been called "implicit" responses or "mediating" responses.

The responses of mental activity go on in an almost unbroken stream during waking life, and, insofar as we can infer what goes on in sleepers and infants, mental activity starts very early in life and goes on in some form around the clock. Although the stream of inner activity may be unbroken, it is certainly not undifferentiated. Like all behavior, it is organized into "chunks" of integrated activity. Adults generally tie a knot or shift the gears of a car in a single deft action that requires no coaching and often little attention. In much the same way, a sentence or an individual thought is generally a separate, integrated behavioral unit. I shall refer to these units as *segments*, meaning stretches of homogeneous content. Of course, content may be "homogeneous" at many levels of generality, and one can speak of subsegments within segments, or subsubsegments within subsegments within segments, and so on. For instance, if I am planning to play a game of tennis all continuous content about playing tennis constitutes a segment of a kind, but while I am involved in that segment I may think about where my tennis racket is and that content, concerning the location of the racket, would constitute a subsegment. The term segment, then, provides a very flexible way of referring to units of thought. It also allows us to recast the main question of this section: In what way and under what conditions do incentives affect the launching and content of thought segments?[2]

Kinds of Thought Segments

If one overlooks certain complications, one can classify thought segments for convenience into three kinds: blank states, operant segments, and respondent segments.

Blank States

A lone figure sits in deep meditation. He has spent years training himself to concentrate without deliberately concentrating, to focus sharply on nothing, to feel detached from earthly pursuits, all in order to experience a closeness and even oneness with all creation. He sits now approaching the most poignant and ecstatic moments of his day, when his mind becomes emptied of things and forms.

Another figure sits in another room, stoned on acid. At some point — later he is not sure when — his mind goes blank. After minutes, perhaps hours, he becomes aware that he can recollect nothing since that indeterminate point.

A writer pushes herself to keep working at the typewriter late at night. She has finished a sentence and is fishing for the next. A little later she realizes that for some moments her mind has seemed blank.

Blank states are without content that can be described. Perhaps they lack imagery altogether — introspectively it is impossible to be sure — but at least they lack detectable visual and auditory imagery. It may seem that blank states do not even qualify as mental activity, but at least certain kinds of blanks states, those attained in meditative trance, have a distinctive quality of consciousness, one that meditators strive to create and that in some cases approaches ecstasy.

Very little is known scientifically about blank states. They are, however, accompanied by characteristic EEG brain wave patterns, ranging from frequent alpha waves (8 to 12 cps) down to rare theta waves (4 to 7 cps) in the deepest trances of meditative masters. Aside from meditation, blank states sometimes occur involuntarily, but they constitute only a tiny percentage of thought. Probably they occur most frequently during extreme fatigue and under the influence of marijuana and certain psychedelic drugs.

Just why blank states occur then is unknown, but we may venture a guess. The many techniques of meditation all seem to involve the meditator focusing attention on some simple kind of imagery, either sensory (a vase, a chant, a rhythmic dance, breathing movements, and so on) or nonsensory, such as a repeated thought (a "mantra"). The important condition is that he or she focus on it as though perceiving it, thereby keeping it in the forefront of awareness, and that it be either fairly continuous or repetitive. Now perceptual activity seems to have the effect of blocking other classes of thought, especially the wandering, undirected thoughts described below as "respondent," thus clearing them out of consciousness. However, when a person is exposed to constant or repetitive stimulation, the image of the stimulus tends to fade out. Thus, as the act of focusing perceptually blocks other thought and as the imagery fades out, the person is left with a blank state.

This explanation may account for the way meditators achieve

blankness and it may also explain natural, involuntary blank states. Users of marijuana, for instance, frequently report catching themselves staring at objects — and sometimes at small details of objects — for much longer periods of time than they would when "straight." Although they are more distractible to new stimulation, their attention is arrested by old cues.[3] They too, therefore, are focusing perceptually on constant stimulation and may therefore be simulating spontaneously the conditions that meditators create deliberately. My own experience suggests that during certain periods of fatigue or underarousal I stare more and experience more natural blank moments than at other times. That, however, will require some research to establish.

If this view of blank states is correct, then we can arrive at several conclusions about the way they are related to incentives. First, a blank state is basically an involuntary event. As teachers of meditation stress, one cannot will oneself into a blank state. What one can do is deliberately arrange the conditions that will produce one, and the fact that millions of people spend considerable time and effort to do so leads to a second conclusion: Blank states can constitute powerful positive incentives. Third, however, incentives can have no effect on the thematic content of blank states because blank states have no thematic content, by definition. Fourth, except when a person sets out to produce a blank state the timing of blank states depends on factors that have little to do with incentives.

Operant Segments

Thought is most clearly affected by incentives when one thinks intentionally in order to gain some objective or to solve a problem. Borrowing B. F. Skinner's language (Skinner, 1935, 1953), I shall call this kind of thought *operant* thought. Others have also called it instrumental thought, directed thought, R-thinking, realistic thinking, secondary-process thought, and problem solving. Besides working at problems, operant thought includes searching one's sensory environment for something needed and searching one's memory.

There are at least four ways (four operant elements) in which operant thought segments differ from other kinds of thought. First, a person embarking on an operant thought segment has a subjective sense of trying. That is, the segment is intentional. Second, he or she evaluates the effectiveness of the segment or of its subsegments in advancing him or her toward an objective. Third, the person modifies and corrects his or her thinking if it seems to be in error. Fourth, the person controls his or her attention, bringing his or her thoughts back to the problem if his or her mind wanders away.

Operant segments are often examples of skilled learned responses, just as much as playing tennis or playing Chopin. Instead of moving their limbs or fingers according to well-practiced routines, people who are thinking move their mental images — saying to themselves the right words or creating the right mental pictures in order to think about how best to navigate around a traffic jam, about whom to invite to dinner, or about how to analyze a batch of data statistically. The words and the pictures go through a series of transformations in which one set of words leads to another set, or one picture leads to another. For instance, picturing B and G coming to dinner leads to picturing a conversation in which G is mortally offended by B's opinions, and this in turn leads to a conclusion: B and G must not be invited together. In this way, patterns of mental images are transformed into further patterns until finally the mind yields up an image that can be translated into a useful act. These skilled feats of transforming mental images, which probably involve a great deal of unconscious mental activity besides the images, constitute what are often called mental *operations.*

Although there is no doubt about the influence of goals on the content of operant segments, the simple fact that operant segments are by definition about goals does nothing to explain what it is that determines *when* a particular operant segment will take place. Nor does it explain why irrelevant thoughts keep intruding on a person's attention, making it necessary for him or her to make a deliberate effort to prevent his or her mind from wandering. There are clearly some additional factors at work that relate incentives to thought, and these, paradoxically, become plainest when we consider nonoperant thought.

Respondent Segments

I shall call all mental activity other than blank states and operant segments *respondent segments.* Respondent segments therefore include mind-wandering, most daydreaming, reveries, much play, all dreams, various incidental thoughts and flashes of imagery — all the unintentional ideation that goes on probably a large majority of the time. The waking forms of respondent activity are often lumped together by psychologists and called "fantasy." They have also been called daydreaming, associative thinking, undirected thinking, and autistic thinking. What all respondent segments have in common is

that they are involuntary, unintentional. That is, respondent segments are those that the person did not set out to have. They pop into
one's mind and pass through with no premeditation or conscious
purpose. Having experienced them, it most likely never occurs to one
to evaluate their effectiveness in accomplishing any objective, since
none governed their creation. In most cases it would also never occur
to anyone to steer them, since there is no place they are supposed to
go, and one would not try to keep one's mind on a segment when
one's mind began to wander unless the segment happened to
produce unusually pleasant feelings that one wished to prolong.

A person involved in an operant segment is trying to produce some
consequence. We may therefore say that operant segments are proac-
tive, controlled by the apparent requirements of attaining a certain
future end result. In contrast, respondent segments are reactive, controlled in large part by the events that set them off. In order to make
the difference plainer, it may help to consider some examples.

Providing bona fide examples of thought poses serious problems,
since thought is an internal affair that is impossible to convey exactly
as it occurred. As in all scientific measurement and description (and
perhaps more than in most), we shall have to compromise between
exactness and practicality. Accepting these limitations, there are at
least two ways to find out the content of someone else's thought. In
thinking out loud, experimental subjects speak their thoughts as they
occur to them — preferably as a continuous flow of expression, similar
to talking to oneself.[4] Few investigators have used the method, although one (DeGroot, 1965) undertook an extensive thinking-out-
loud analysis of the thought processes of chessplayers and others
(Bloom & Broder, 1950) used it to analyze students' styles of solving
test problems. In our own laboratory we have asked subjects to think
out loud while performing a variety of tasks. The first example is an
excerpt taken from a male subject while he was working on a "wire
puzzle," the point of which is to separate two twisted metal links:

> Let's see. How can you go about doing this? Ah. Got to get it to turn out.
> Got to turn it, there slide out and that's the way it's done before. Now this
> here one. Ah, let's see. If I turn it around and work it this way. Now let's see,
> I got to turn it so it goes in and around. That ain't going to work. If I turn it so
> that it goes through there. There I got it into that, now I got to get it out from
> here. Ah, same way. Let's see if I turn it, that ain't going to work. Ah, how
> can I do that? If I turn it around, ah, that ain't going to work either. Unless, I
> got to get it worked out. Now I'll try the other one, I can't get that one.

The second example is an excerpt taken from a male subject who
was asked to recline for ten minutes with his eyes shut in a quiet,

dimly lit cubicle, after which he began to think out loud with his eyes still shut (we loosely called this a "hypnagogic" condition):

Got a cramp in my leg. I guess it's starting to go to sleep, I guess. Let's see, tomorrow, think I'll go bow — no — yeah. I'll go see if Pete wants — I'll have to go — to go out hunting — or maybe just target shooting with the bows. I'll have to borrow some of his arrows. Course he said I could buy some but I don't know if I want to buy some. I want to get some of my own I think. Gonna get some aluminum shafts like — like my brother. No he wants fiber glass is what he wants. That's what my brother wanted. Buy a new bow string too. Yeah. I did a nice job on that bow, too. Oh, darn it. Hope Pete is feeling good tomorrow. Oh, he's not feeling too bad today — been kinda sick. I was kinda sick at the beginning of the week myself. Anyway — (Pause) Maybe we'll go out — sometime. Course I gotta study tomorrow too. But I probably won't. I'll play cards more than I'll study.

A second way of finding out the content of people's thoughts (*thought sampling*) is to stop them unexpectedly now and then (for instance, with a tone) and have them describe the thoughts that occurred just before the interruption. The following thought sample was provided by a college woman who was interrupted while listening to someone reading from a short story:

I was remembering when I was in sixth grade and our class we went to the cities and I was thinking about when we went into the conservatory at Como Park. I was walking around in there and remembering how pretty it was. Before that I was thinking about this maid that works in this really nice house. I was helping her rake leaves one day and I was thinking how I felt kind of sorry for her because she wasn't, I couldn't see how she could enjoy just being a maid; she was really nice.

The methods that produced these examples of "thought" are far from ideal. Thinking out loud has the disadvantages of forcing subjects to choose which aspects of their complicated thoughts they will express, of requiring subjects to spell out their thoughts much more communicatively than they probably would in normal silent thought, of making subjects more than normally self-conscious, and, possibly, of causing the spelled-out thoughts to influence the content of later thoughts more than they would have otherwise. Thought sampling suffers from forgetting of detail, from subjects' tendency to summarize rather than to express, and from less accurate information about how long subjects spent on each thought. Both methods suffer from the limitations of trying to put into words experiences that are often ineffable. Despite these weaknesses, both methods seem capable of generating much useful information about the content and structure of mental activity, and since most of their defects are complementary rather than shared they can be used jointly to converge on the nature of inner experience.

From evidence produced by these methods we can already make some general statements about thought. First, we are impressed by the large amount of respondent activity that goes on, even when people are ostensibly involved in performing tasks.[5] Respondent segments seem to intrude on all kinds of thinking. The fewest intrusions seem to occur when people are working on problems that require them to use words or images in the solution (for instance, the mental twister that asks how a farmer can get a duck, a fox, and a bag of grain across a river without any of them eating the others, with the restriction that his boat can only hold one of them at a time). During listening to tapes, performing routine activities, or just sitting with nothing to do, respondent segments form the overwhelming majority of mental activity.

Second, the thinking-out-loud protocols provide evidence concerning two of the "operant elements." People involved in solving logic problems or working wire puzzles evaluate the effectiveness of their behavior and try to focus their attention significantly more often than when they are sitting and resting (Figure 2-1).

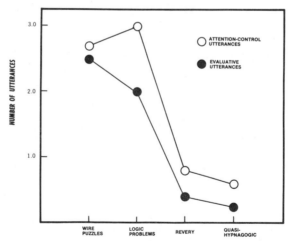

Figure 2-1. Mean number of evaluative and attention-control utterances per five-minute periods of thinking out loud under each of four experimental conditions: working on a wire puzzle, solving a logic problem, revery (sitting up, eyes open), and quasihypnagogic rest (reclining, eyes closed). Means are based on 21 subjects in the wire puzzle condition and 24 subjects in each of the other conditions. Standard deviations ranged from 0.61 to 3.15 for evaluative utterances and from 0.93 to 4.44 for attention-control utterances. (From Experiment 1 in Klinger, 1974.)

Third, even the respondent segments are clearly devoted to the incentives in people's lives, at least in most cases. Some of the incentives are positive, such as tomorrow's fishing expedition. Some are negative or conflicted, such as having to help clean grandmother's house. Some respondent segments deal with memories of events that may be either recent or in the distant past. When we look carefully, it usually becomes apparent that these memories are closely related to people's present concerns with incentives.

This finding is very important. Respondent segments are so pervasive in inner experience that they set the tone of a person's inner life. But since they are shaped by the nature of one's involvements with incentives, those incentives and one's relationships to them determine the quality of one's inner experience.

How do incentives come to have such an encompassing influence on human life? To probe this question further it is necessary to look first at an important aspect of human motivation, the fact of *commitment* to incentives and its effects on human functioning.

Commitment and Concern

Elite groups that wish to select only the most dedicated candidates for membership deliberately require candidates to go through some kind of "hurdle" experience that weeds out all but the supremely motivated. For instance, many graduate programs require graduate students to pass especially arduous courses during their first year of graduate school in order to test their determination to succeed. Fraternities and sororities often ask their pledges to endure drudgery, danger, and indignities before initiating them. Many corporations seem to use the liberal arts college degree itself as a hurdle requirement for admission to the ranks of management. In each case, candidates who lack the proper dedication are either eliminated by the various gatekeepers or themselves decide that passing the hurdle is not worth the rewards. The widely used hurdle technique points up a truth about motivation, that one can best test whether people (or other organisms) are truly motivated to attain certain goals by placing obstacles in their paths and observing whether they try to overcome them.

Organisms are organized around goals. The word "motivation" recognizes that fact and poses a basic question: What mechanisms must exist inside organisms to keep them directed at their goals, even in the face of obstacles? Many species of organisms are attracted to goal objects only when the objects impinge on them directly. For instance, a female mosquito is attracted to warm bodies when it can sense them, but if someone were to place an opaque screen between her and her victim she would not launch a search for that particular body. She would merely go her way until the next warm body attracted her. On the other hand, a dog who loses sight of a stick that someone has thrown for it to retrieve is very likely to search for the stick a while before giving up; and human beings who have decided to pursue an important goal — to win a trophy, obtain a contract, or marry a certain other person — may work hard for months or even years, overcoming repeated obstacles and improvising a long succession of tactics. Dogs and people must, therefore, have something inside them that keeps them striving for goals even when the goal objects are absent and perhaps even without any external reminders of the goal.

In other words, people and higher animals pursuing goals are not just reacting to immediate events going on around them. Deciding to pursue a goal must mean setting off an internal process at the same time, a process that is specific to the goal and that continues to operate until the goal is achieved or abandoned. Without such an inner process, people would stop striving for a goal as soon as they were out of sensory touch with it and with things associated with it. They would be almost as easily sidetracked as a mosquito. The inner goal-related process keeps them alerted to new possibilities for achieving their goal. It enables small children to look forward to birthdays months in advance. It is a process in which the brain stores the information that a certain end result is a goal and then organizes activity around it.

People's activities are organized by this goal-related inner process, even when responding to fairly concrete events. Something outside a person happens — a friend calls, a traffic light changes, it begins to rain — and the person reacts. The important thing here is that none of the things that take place outside the person has a fixed meaning. Few such events dictate a single unvarying reaction. How the person reacts — what the person chooses to do about it — depends on how the thing relates to the person's goals. When it starts to rain, a person might run into the house to get dry or might put on a bathing suit and run outdoors to wash the car. A person watching a traffic light turn from red to green may feel pleasure at being able to go on to where he or she would like to be or may feel dread at being brought closer to doing something frightening. The meaning of anything depends on the goals of the person it happens to; and this is possible only if everyone carries in his or her brain a clearcut representation of what those goals are and a disposition to react in ways that advance the person closer to them.[6]

The "inner process" that can perform all of these functions is obviously very important. We shall be occupied with it and with its implications throughout the remainder of this book. We therefore need some terms with which to refer to it. The onset of the process — that is, the event whereby a person becomes set to pursue a goal — I shall call *commitment*.[7] Thus, we may speak of people becoming committed to goals. People presumably remain committed to their goals until they attain them or until they abandon them as inaccessible or as too costly. The process of giving up a goal I shall call *disengagement*. Finally, I shall use the term *current concern* to refer to the state of the organism between commitment to a goal and either attainment of the goal or disengagement from it.

It is important to understand just what is and what is not meant by this term "current concern." It refers simply to an organism's *state* of being still committed to a particular incentive. It does not refer to the organism's thoughts or actions during this state. "Current concern" is the hypothetical state that underlies those thoughts and actions. Although there must be brain processes that correspond to current concerns, they are at present not known, and the term "current concern" does not refer specifically to them. It refers simply to the fact of having become committed to a particular incentive that has not yet been fully attained or abandoned.[8]

By this definition, people are normally in the grip of several or even numerous current concerns at a time. For instance, a student may be committed to pursuing a degree, completing certain courses, maintaining or improving a relationship with a close friend, finding a part-time job, eating dinner, skiing at year's end, and so on. Each of the ends to which he or she is committed constitutes an incentive (because he or she is attracted to it) and a goal (because he or she is committed to striving for it), and about each he or she has a different current concern (the construct that represents his or her state of being committed to that goal).

People may develop concerns about positive incentives such as reaching a certain income level, buying a certain kind of house, marrying a certain person, seeing a certain play, or having dinner tonight. In each case, the person becomes committed to the incentive when he or she encounters or foresees an appropriate opportunity to pursue or enjoy the incentive. The concern then ends (or becomes transformed into a different concern) when the incentive has been consummated — the income level achieved, the house possessed, the spouse wedded, and so forth — or when the person has given up on it. People may also develop concerns about negative incentives such as ill health, bankruptcy, or the death of someone close to them. Here, the person is likely to become committed to avoiding, escaping, preventing, or getting rid of the negative incentive when it threatens to occur or persist. Such a concern ends (or is transformed) when the threat has been eliminated — the illness prevented or overcome, the bankruptcy averted, the loved one saved, and so forth — or when the person has surrendered to it.

Just how the object of the concern is defined depends on the psychological realities for the individual involved. In some cases, the object may include any of a class of things, as when someone in a strange town goes looking for "some action." In other cases, as in courtship, the object of the concern is likely to be highly specific. The concern may be about finding opportunities for a rewarding commit-ment, as when an adolescent or young adult tries out different roles or jobs in order to assess their rewardingness. Thus, concerns are limited neither to highly specific nor to broadly defined objectives, and neither to immediate nor to very long-term goals. The *concept* can cover the whole range, but particular *instances* of concerns take what-ever more or less precise forms are created by the commitments of the individuals in question.

In our own research, we try to establish people's concerns by means of interviews and questionnaires, and we follow up each per-son for a number of months to see how long evidence of each concern persists. About two-thirds of the concerns we find last less than a month, often appearing just once. For instance, someone may be concerned briefly about protecting his or her privacy from a room-mate's intrusions, about getting a course finished, or about going scuba diving. However, a third of our subjects' concerns last more than a month, and may last as long as we keep interviewing, as in the case of one student's commitment to a career in art which kept pop-ping up for the entire nine months of our acquaintance, or another's unwavering desire to drink beer with his tavern companions.

Concerns and the Content of Thought

Up to the past few years, psychologists studied the content of thought — especially fantasy — mostly by giving subjects one or another variant of the Thematic Apperception Test (TAT). An examiner gives the subject a series of pictures with instructions to tell a dramatic story about the events in each picture, a story with a past (the events that led up to those pictured), a present (what the people pictured are thinking and feeling), and a future (how it will all come out). The subject then narrates or, more commonly, writes down a story. By having subjects write TAT stories under varying conditions, investigators from the 1930s to the 1960s accumulated a mass of information about the influences of picture cues, situations, and subjects' motives on the content of their TAT stories. Investigators commonly assumed that telling TAT stories has much in common with natural silent fantasy, and they therefore accepted the results as at least a rough approximation to what happens in ordinary thought.

Most likely, TAT stories have both some resemblances to and some sharp differences from spontaneous respondent thought. Subjects writing TAT stories are constrained by the features of the pictures they must write about, by their notions of what constitutes an acceptable story, by the need to organize and communicate the story, and by an operant set to do a job — to buckle down mentally instead of letting their minds go where they will. On the other hand, they still must dip into their own mental content to flesh out the story, and it seems likely that the content they dip into is controlled by some of the same influences that control ordinary respondent thought. One must therefore by very cautious about generalizing from TAT stories to everyday thought content, but there is no need to dismiss the TAT evidence from consideration.

All of the TAT evidence available points consistently to a single conclusion: that *one of the major determinants of thought content is the person's current concerns.* Some other determinants of TAT stories, such as picture cues, are specific to TAT stories and have no bearing on normal thought content. All thought, of course, is also shaped by cultural factors such as language, beliefs about the things that people and objects can be expected to do, propriety, and so forth. Apart from these kinds of influences, it seems likely that current concerns are the most important influence on the content of thought.

Although the evidence for this assertion was once largely based on experiments that used TAT stories, the range of TAT evidence is broad. For instance, some experimenters asked their subjects to perform a series of tasks, telling some subjects ("achievement-aroused" subjects) that the tasks reflected their intelligence or ability and telling others ("controls") something else. When subjects were asked to write their TAT stories as if the stories were part of the task series, achievement-aroused subjects told more stories with achieving characters in them than did the control subjects; but if the TAT story writing seemed to come after the end of the tasks that reflected on subjects' abilities — that is, after the incentive of doing well had been reached or failed — there were no differences between achievement-aroused and control subjects in their use of achieving characters.

Other experimenters recruited fraternity, sorority, and dormitory groups, and had some subjects rate one another's likeability while other subjects did something else, after which everyone wrote TAT stories. Subjects who had just been judged for likeability told more stories in which someone was concerned about his or her human relationships. This was especially true if the subjects took the TAT after having been told (without regard to the truth of the matter) that they had been judged unlikeable; but, importantly, if subjects were first reassured that they had been judged to be likeable their stories contained about the same number of affiliative (concern-about-human-relationships) themes as the stories of control groups (Rosenfeld & Franklin, 1966). For all but the last group, we may presume that being rated was a threat to their standing with their friends and therefore set in motion a concern about maintaining their relationships, whereas the assurances given the last group eliminated any special concerns about their friendships. Other evidence for the general proposition that concerns influence thought content comes from TAT studies of hunger, thirst, sexual arousal, aggression, fear, sleep deprivation, and forced inactivity. The evidence is uniformly consistent with the proposition that people think about the incentives to which they are committed and about matters related to them — that current concerns determine the content of a person's thoughts (Klinger, 1971).

Current concerns have also been shown to influence what people dream about (Klinger, 1971). Clinical and various unsystematic studies have provided some evidence that the concerns people carry with them show up in their dreams, but, additionally, people who are instructed to dream about particular content tend to do so (Walker & Johnson, 1974), and concerns created less directly by experimenters also tend to affect people's dreams. For instance, people who are put to bed in sleep laboratories often incorporate elements of the laboratory or the experimental procedures in their dreams.

To say simply that current concerns determine what a person thinks about still leaves a lot unsaid. For instance, a person can think about only one thing at a time, but is in the grip of many concerns. What determines which content one will be thinking about at any single moment? Furthermore, one will think more about some concern-related matters than about others. What determines the relative proportion of time a concern manifests itself in consciousness? It is clear, then, that when we say that concerns determine content we are using "determine" in a rather probabilistic way: We really mean that content related to a particular concern is much more likely to occur in thought than content that is related to no concern. Saying it that way does not specify when a particular content is likely to occur, for how long, and how often; and it does not explain how concerns can control content. The next sections present a probable explanation that permits us to fill in the gaps.

Concerns and Thoughts: The Control of Attention

At any one moment a person receives an enormous number of sensory signals. One's retina is an entire field of visual impressions, one's cochlea is resonating to complex sounds, one's nose and mouth are involved in a wide-range chemical analysis of all the substances that touch them, one's skin is sending up information on touch, temperature, pressure, and pain, and every square centimeter of one's body beyond the skull is reporting on distention, pain, and movement. At the very same time the central nervous system is processing images and instructions to one's muscles. Other things are happening as well, but all of the events listed are capable of becoming conscious. Yet, at one moment in time the person is aware of only a tiny fraction of all these signals.

Most of us go about with a sense of being in touch with a world that surrounds us in space and brackets us in time. We think of our visual world as extending far up and down, left and right, but that is an illusion. Even in our vision we capture only tiny spots of our world at a time. Because our eyes wander in a staccato pattern we can record many bits of the seeable world in a short span of time, and the collection of bits provides the illusion of an encompassing vision. Because our attention can dance from one sense modality to another, from the page before me to the birdsong outside the window to the feel of the typewriter under my hand, I can build up an illusion of a large world that is seeable, hearable, feelable, and smellable. In fact, however, just what I sense and how I sense it depend on which small strips of sensory reality I sample.

At that, a person is likely to become fully aware only of those samples that disconfirm an expectation or that one has been searching for or that pose a special problem one cannot solve routinely. Much of what passes for perception is not really full sensory awareness but a process of routine monitoring to assure that all's well and that all is as expected. If it is, the signals are likely to make little conscious impression and dissipate from memory within a few seconds.

The problem of what bits of reality a person "chooses" to respond to is the problem of attention. It is clear that attention is among those crucial processes that codetermine both behavior and the quality of inner experience. What is the nature of attention, and how can it help explain the control that current concerns exercise over the content of thought?

The problem of attention. When psychologists use the word "attention" they may mean any of at least three different things (Posner & Boies, 1971). They may be referring to a person's level of *alertness* — the extent to which one is primed to detect events going on around one and to respond to them quickly, or they may have in mind one's tendency to *select* only certain kinds of events to attend and respond to — only red triangles, only birds, or only an instructor's voice; or, finally, they may be pointing to one's inability to perform more than one mental operation at a time, such as not being able to answer questions while counting the silverware, which demonstrates the human's *limited processing capacity*. All three of these variables — alertness, selectivity, and processing limitations — affect every mental act. For our immediate purposes, however, it is the second of these, *selective attention*, with which we shall be especially concerned.

That is, we shall examine the notion that current concerns influence mental content by determining which events a person selects to attend to. The process by which concerns determine this is unconscious, of course. It is not at all a matter of the person saying to himself, "I shall overlook the trees and cars as I walk along, and the sensations from the soles of my feet, and instead I shall attend to the face of that person approaching who is my friend." Rather, one's attention is *drawn to* the friend's face and the rest slips by without any conscious decision having to be made.

The process of selecting what to pay attention to is less straightforward than it might seem. There are many ways of selecting, some of which are much more complex than others. Consider, for instance, the case in which an experimenter asks a subject to look at a display of letters and decide whether the display contains the letter "G" (The example and the terms are Treisman's [1969]). In order to answer he must look at the display (select *input*). Second, "he must attend to the shapes of the letters and not their colors, sizes, or orientations, that is, he must select the *analyzers* for shape and reject those for color, etc. Next he must identify the *target* letter 'G' if it is present, and if possible ignore differences between the other letters. . . . Finally, he must select the appropriate *output* of the shape analyzers to control the response, 'G' giving a positive response and all other outputs a negative one" [Treisman, 1969, P. 284].

The person wandering through life sensitized to attend to concern-related events can obviously not be sensitized primarily to certain input variables in Treisman's sense (such as visual cues, upper left events, or things that vibrate) or indiscriminately to certain analyzers (just for shape, for color, for pitch, or the like) because the objects or events that are related to a human concern are usually too complicated to reduce to classes of input or analyzers. A person in love with Betty is presumably responsive to the many complex patterns of inputs and analyzers that go to make up his or her knowledge of Betty: the sound of her voice, expressions she uses, the constellation of her facial features, her favorite overcoat, her gait, her name, her neighborhood, her car, organizations she belongs to, and so on, any of which may produce a flip inside her lover when he encounters them. Thus, if current concerns do in fact control selective attention they must do so at the level of selecting *targets* rather than inputs or analyzers.

This is important because not all of the kinds of selection place equally exclusive claims on attention. Treisman (1969) concludes that whereas a person can efficiently attend to several attributes or dimensions of a certain object at the same time (for instance, notice both the size and the color of something), "division of attention between two or more inputs and between two or more targets is difficult or impossible" [P. 296] unless there is enough time to shift attention from one to the other, one at a time. Thus, a person is limited to attending to one target at a time. In that case, whatever selects the target attended to is wielding virtually dictatorial power over the content of consciousness.

Gatekeeping: the preattentive processes. If a person can attend to only one target at a time, there must be some process outside of attention that directs attention. If such a process did not exist, a person would focus on something and keep focusing on it until he or it vanished, because there would be no way to break the spell. People need a gatekeeper who can work mostly unconsciously, out of the field of focal attention, and who can decide which events to admit into awareness and which to keep out. Ulric Neisser (1967) has called this gatekeeper the *preattentive processes,* and he has described some of their characteristics. Although they work unobtrusively, they are an active, essential, and complicated set of processes. They direct a person's sense receptors toward interesting stimulation. They interpret the world rather crudely, taking in gross outlines of it holistically rather than taking account of details, or being drawn to impressive parts of things without taking into account their full context. They are relatively inaccurate, often overlooking relevant things and occasionally making the mistake of being deceived by something irrelevant. The preattentive processes are basically a quick, rough screening process and they leave to focal attention the job of making the finer judgments and settling the details.

Recall, for instance, what happens to a person walking into a crowded cocktail lounge to meet a couple of friends. Having just left the light outdoors, he has trouble seeing in the dimly lit room. His eye sweeps across dozens of dark shapes. It comes to rest on a young woman with long, dark hair, like the woman of the pair he is meeting, but as he focuses more closely he realizes it is a different face. His eyes dart to a table at which sits a balding young man — the other of his friends is balding — but closer inspection reveals that this is not his friend either. Eventually he sees his friends, perhaps in a spot his eye had already swept once or twice and had overlooked just as it had failed to light on numerous other people, most of whom he did not know but some of whom are also friends who will wonder why he ignored them.

Plainly, in steering attention the preattentive processes are governed by two factors. One of these — the most important — is the person's current concerns: what one is trying to do at that moment or, especially if one is not at that moment trying to do anything in particular, one's commitments to the various goals in one's life. The other factor, of course, is the set of cues available in one's environment or in one's own thoughts that are in some way related to one's concerns.

This conclusion should not surprise us. The way in which the preattentive processes seem to work is simply the most efficient way to set up a search, and for complex organisms life is, after all, a search. It is a search for incentive objects — for basic nutrients and reproductive opportunities in the case of lower animals, for a wide range of additional satisfiers in the case of humans, and for safety in the case of all. Organisms are likely to survive insofar as they can carry out their searches efficiently. This is the role of the preattentive processes, which are immutably cast in the service of search.

Of course, once the preattentive processes have led to the trail of a goal object, selective attention must take over. Most animal organisms cannot efficiently do more than one thing at a time. A dog digging up a gopher needs all of its body to dig well: its front paws scooping, its hind legs bracing, its head pointed at the hole in order to keep best track of what is going on. Its brain can be thought of as a response funnel, focusing all the dog's efforts on one activity while turning back or storing for later processing all of the extraneous stimuli and events going on at the same time. It cannot afford to divide its efforts among all of those stimuli and events because it would become disorganized and ineffective. Whatever mechanisms are responsible for this funneling, focusing process are what we have called selective or focal attention. Focal attention is, of course, interruptable if the preattentive processes should turn up cues related to an overridingly important goal, such as safety.

One more point that should be apparent from the preceding illustrations is that preattentive processes are not processes that act just sporadically between major acts. Rather, they go on to some extent all of the time, a continuous monitor constantly on the lookout for opportunities and trouble, ready to break in on consciousness if it detects something pressing enough.

Looked at from this perspective, the preattentive processes direct not only attention but also behavior in general. Atkinson and Birch (1970) have suggested that when we ask questions about motivation those questions boil down to asking what accounts for the changes in the direction of someone's behavior. Viewing motivation that way, we can see that the preattentive processes stand astride both motivation and cognition, forming the link between motives and the content of inner experience.[9]

Concerns and the Control of Attention: Some Evidence

It appears that when one commits oneself to a goal one's preattentive processes become extrasensitive to cues that one knows are related to attaining the goal.[10] Thereafter, until one attains the goal or gives up on it, one will be more likely to notice things relevant to it. One's preattentive processes act as a constant monitor that scans one's environment and one's own thoughts for relevant events; or so it seems reasonable to think, given the ideas described above. However, nobody has actually every seen such a monitor at work. In everyday life and in common observation, what we actually observe are people tending to their business, expressing thoughts related to their current concerns, and inclined to notice things related to their concerns. Although it seems reasonable to *infer* from this that there must be a silent monitor at work, is there any direct *evidence* that that is really so? There are, in fact, at least three kinds of evidence. The first kind reveals that a screening process is operating even though the person's outward behavior provides no clues that it is going on. The other two kinds of evidence show that people respond to concern-relevant cues even while they are supposedly engrossed in something else or are asleep.

The first line of evidence was reported by two Soviet psychologists, Luria and Vinogradova (1959). Experimenters working in the tradition of Soviet Pavlovian research on attention had long since discovered that when one is presented with an unexpected stimulus one is likely to make an *orienting reaction*, which consists of turning one's head toward the source of the stimulus and undergoing several physiological changes. During the orienting reaction the skin of a person's palms briefly conducts electricity more easily (the *Galvanic Skin Response*, or GSR) and the small blood vessels in the fingers contract, which reduces the volume of blood there. There are also other physiological components of the orienting reaction, but the GSR and finger blood volume are the two most commonly used indicators that an orienting reaction is taking place. Luria and Vinogradova used finger blood volume and also blood volume in the scalp to detect orienting responses. The basic procedure of the experiment was to ask subjects to listen for a certain word (for instance, *doktor*) in a list of words the experimenter read to the subject. When the subjects heard the key word in the list they produced orienting reactions. What is of greater interest is that normal, rested subjects also have orienting reactions to words that mean the same thing as the key word (for instance, *vrach* or *lekar*, also meaning "doctor") even though those words sound nothing like the key word and the subject was not asked to react to them or look for them. Furthermore, these subjects did not give orienting reactions to words that sound like the key word but that mean something different (for instance, *diktor*, which means "announcer").

In these experiments, the orienting reactions tell a story that one could not have gathered from the subjects' outward behavior. Although the subjects did not react outwardly to *vrach* or *lekar*, they did react in a preliminary, covert way. When the target word was *doktor*, for instance, the preattentive processes (as revealed by orienting reactions) were set to admit cues related to doctors. When these cues were not the word *doktor* itself they were admitted to at least a low level of attention just as if they were the target word *doktor*, only to be rejected at a second, more detailed screening (the subject's decision not to respond). The word *diktor*, on the other hand, was screened out at the first stage without so much as an orienting reaction. Clearly, these subjects were benefiting from a monitoring process that was set to react to goal-related cues. Furthermore, the monitor performed in some ways crudely, casting a wider net than the subjects' observable behavior would have suggested; but in other respects the monitor performed a feat of remarkable refinement, reacting to cues related to the target word in meaning but not in sound. It seems safe to conclude that a monitor like the preattentional processes we have discussed must exist. It also seems reasonable to conclude that this monitor is quite automatic and involuntary, since some of its mistaken decisions would surely have been avoided by an intelligent subject acting in the full awareness that normally accompanies the start of voluntary behavior.

In this way, people are constantly alerted to those things going on around them or inside of them that are potentially important to their goals, much as a radar screen alerts the operator to the possibility of an airplane approaching, even though the radar blip will often turn out to have been a false alarm.

In the experiment just described, the subjects were deliberately listening for a particular word, and they turned out to be sensitized also to related words. The kind of monitor we have been talking about should, however, also be able to break in on the person's awareness even when he is attending to something else, at least on those occasions when the monitor spots an indication of something important. Two kinds of experiments suggest that the preattentive processes do work in that way.

In one kind of experiment, the subject wears a pair of earphones that transmit two different messages, one to the left ear and another at the same time to the right ear. He or she is asked to "shadow" the message to one ear — that is, to repeat each word of the message as soon as he or she hears it — and to ignore the message from the other ear. In this experiment, subjects have no trouble shadowing the first message and they remember very little if anything about the other message (Cherry, 1953; Moray, 1959). Subjects, however, do not inevitably block out the messages they are supposedly ignoring. Moray (1959) embedded in the to-be-ignored message occasional instructions for subjects to switch the ear to which they were attending. Subjects rarely noticed these instructions *unless* the instructions began with the subject's name: "John Smith, change to your other ear." Then they noticed the instructions about half the time, and if they had first been warned that such instructions would occur they noticed them most of the time. Evidently, people are especially sensitive to their own names, noticing them even under circumstances when they would not notice many other kinds of stimuli. It seems a safe bet that hearing one's own name becomes an automatic signal to a person that something related to his or her concerns is going on.

Corteen and Wood (1972) in effect created concerns for their subjects. First they asked their subjects to listen to lists of nouns, and they shocked them electrically whenever the names of three particular cities occurred in the list. After this procedure, they placed their subjects in the same kind of "dichotic listening" situation as in Moray's experiment, where they were to hear two simultaneous tape recordings, shadowing one of them. The other channel of the tape recorder played lists of words, including the city names that had previously been accompanied by electric shock, other nouns from the same list that had not been accompanied by shocks, and some new city names and other new nouns. Corteen and Wood subtly led the subjects to believe that they might still receive electric shocks during this second procedure, and they recorded subjects' GSR's, which might indicate orienting responses or arousal of fear. These subjects responded to all city names on the channel they were supposedly not listening to with significantly more GSR's than they produced when other kinds of words occurred on that channel, even though they could not recall hearing any words on that channel and even though they continued to shadow the other channel as smoothly as ever. Thus, these people seemed to be screening out potentially harmful events and responding to them, apparently unconsciously, in just the way we would expect preattentive processes to operate.

There is another small cluster of experiments that have explored subjects' sensitivity to personal material while they are asleep. It has, of course, long been known that the mother of an infant may be sound asleep and yet may awaken to the relatively mild cries of her child. Although some people have trouble not sleeping through their alarm clocks' alarms, others can seemingly awaken themselves at preset times with remarkable precision (Tart, 1970). Clearly, people asleep are still capable of responding, but their responses are highly selective. In the experimental studies subjects are typically put to sleep in a laboratory where the investigator can monitor their brain waves with an electroencephalograph (EEG) in order to be sure that they are, indeed, asleep and in order to determine how deeply they are sleeping. Then the experimenter reads or plays tape-recorded words, some of which are personally relevant to the subject's current life, and looks for indications that the subject is responding selectively to these words. For instance, Oswald, Taylor, and Treisman (1960) played 56 names in a random order, repeating the whole list ten times. One of the names belonged to the subject, who was instructed to wake up and clench his left fist whenever he heard either his own name or one other name arbitrarily selected for purposes of comparison. Subjects did, in fact, clench their fists to about a quarter of the playings of their own names and to about an eighth of the playings of the comparison name, far more often than they did to the other 54 names on the list. In another experiment (Dekoninck & Koulack, 1975), people were shown a frightening film before they went to bed and again the next morning. When the soundtrack of the film was played during the night, it was often incorporated in some way into the sleepers' dreams, especially in the case of those who later experienced the most anxiety when they saw the film a second time.

Again, the evidence confirms the basic idea that people remain sensitive to concern-related cues even while asleep. To this we can add some intriguing results obtained in a casual pilot study by two of my students, Mary K. Nordstrom and Nancy R. Reinhardt. They asked the question, What kinds of words being read aloud would sleeping subjects incorporate into their dreams? It seemed likely that words describing something about a subject's concern would end up influencing his or her dreams and that other words would not. This possibility could be checked by reading words to sleeping subjects, asking subjects about their dreams a few seconds later, and asking a judge to see if he could figure out which dreams came after which word stimuli.

Nordstrom and Reinhardt took turns playing the role of experimenter and subject for each other. This provided the advantage that, since they were very well acquainted with each other, each knew very well the other's principal current concerns. Of course, it also provided the normally grave defect that the subjects knew the experimental hypotheses and had an interest in confirming them. In this particular experiment, however, it can be argued that if the subjects were capable of suiting their dreams to the experimental stimuli according to the predicted relationship, that would in itself be evidence in favor of the hypothesis. In any case, each of the two made up a list of single words that they knew to be related to some of the other's principal concerns and a list of words they thought to be devoid of personal significance. At spaced intervals beginning at 6:00 A.M., when sleep is predominantly REM sleep (that is, *rapid eye movement* sleep, which contains the most vivid dream experiences), one of the pair read to her sleeping partner one of the stimulus words three times and then awakened her about ten seconds later to obtain a description of her dream activity. After they had gathered all of their dream samples, they asked a third person who knew nothing about the purpose of the experiment to match the dream descriptions against the stimulus words.

The results are quite dramatic. For the 11 words related to a subject's concerns, the judge was able to match up correctly the words and the dream samples that followed them 10 out of 11 times. However, he was able to match up none of the 6 neutral words against the dream samples that followed them. The difference is, of course, statistically highly significant ($p = .001$). Equally dramatic were the clearcut changes produced in the dreams by the concern-related stimulus words, changes of a kind never produced by any one of the neutral words. For instance, one of the subjects was excited about shortly obtaining a car, and hence one of the concern-related stimuli read to her was "car." When awakened, she reported:

I was dreaming I had to go to the store for my mother, I'm not sure for what. I started out walking to the corner store and suddenly I found myself in the car inside of the garage. I have no idea how I got there. I was attempting or trying to get the car out in order to go to the store for my mother.

Another stimulus was a subject's boyfriend's address. (Both subject/experimenters were then enrolled in a very demanding laboratory course and at the time of this dream sample had arrived at a unit in that course entitled Motivation-Conditioning-Learning [MCL].) The subject reported:

I dreamt I was sitting at the table in my apartment. I was doing homework — I think I was working on my MCL lab report results 'cause I remember trying to draw graphs. It must have been late at night because the curtains were open so I could see outside and it was completely dark out. Then suddenly I was waiting for a letter from ——— [her boyfriend]. I was ignoring the papers and stuff that was cluttering the table. I remember listening for the mailman because you can always hear when he comes. I walked to the door once and looked out when I thought I heard him but he wasn't there. I came back in and sat down. Then I woke up.

This dream clearly starts out dramatizing one pressing concern and shifts to another theme almost certainly induced by the experimental stimulus.

The judge who had done the matching of words against dream samples in the Nordstrom-Reinhardt experiment performed his matching on the basis of thematic similarities. He found these similarities only in the case of stimuli that were related to the subjects' concerns. Thematic similarities are not, however, the only kind of similarities one could look for. Berger (1963), in particular, instructed his judges to look also for very minute, formal similarities such as assonances. For instance, if the stimulus was "John," Berger accepted such words in the dream report as "Pond," "Marchmont," "Jim," or "just going on" as apparent assonant connections that suggest that the stimulus had been incorporated into the dream. Berger found that his judges were able to match up the stimulus names and the dreams that followed them at a statistically significant level, that most of the matches were performed on the basis of assonance, and that neutral names had been incorporated about as often as names of friends. Does this finding contradict the notion that people are especially sensitive to concern-related stimuli? It may well be that people are influenced in their choices or words or images by those they have recently encountered. (This is the phenomenon of *priming*, which I have discussed elsewhere [1971].) I often self-consciously find myself using words that someone else has just used, words I probably would not have used otherwise, but being influenced in my choice of words is a quite different matter from being influenced in my formulation of ideas or themes. Perhaps people appropriate bits and pieces of others' behavior regardless of the concern-relatedness of that behavior, but become alerted enough to change the major themes of their thoughts only when confronted with stimuli that are related to their concerns.

All of the evidence we have reviewed is consistent with the basic notion that a person's attention is under the control of preattentive processes which shift attention from whatever it was focused on to new events in the environment or in one's own thoughts that are in some way connected to one's current concerns. These observations therefore lead us to an important principle of human inner experience, the *induction principle*.

The Induction Principle:
Concerns, Cues, and the Content of Thought

Induction in Respondent Thinking

An experimental subject sits in a small sound-insulated room listening to a narrator on the intercom read a passage from some stream-of-consciousness fiction by Beckett. She is a college freshman whose name was selected from a directory and she agreed to participate in the experiment for an hourly wage. Earlier, she had been trained to report her thoughts to the experimenters according to a standard reporting format. Now, however, she is listening to the narrator's soft voice reading:

The distant sea is hammered lead, the so-called golden vale so often snug, the double valleys, the glacial loughs, the city in its haze, it was all on every tongue. Who are these people anyway? *What do they need, what can be given?* Did they follow me up here, go before me, come with me? Do they see me, what can they see of me? *Perhaps there is a want, perhaps I can share with them for them, these people: Will I reach them?* I listen and it's the same thoughts I hear, I mean the same as ever, strange. To think in the valley the sun is blazing all down the ravelled sky. BEEEEEP!

The pure tone interrupts the reading and rouses the subject to report, as she has learned to do, first the very last thought segment just before the tone, then the one before that, and so on back as far as she can remember clearly. She says:

A valley reminds me again of my experiences in Stanton Lake State Hospital caring for these people who are put away down into their own valley, but they're happy there. Hank's coming to see me in a week, skiing would be fantastic right now on the hills on Lenton, going down the main hills if it's snowing like it is outside right now, I really like the snow.

Then she answers a questionnaire about those thoughts, including her belief that she had not been listening to the taped reading very attentively.

Unbeknownst to her, not all of the reading was pure Beckett. Here and there, experimental passages (those, for instance, italicized in the sample above) had been embedded in the Beckett story, passages composed to touch on one of the subject's current concerns or composed deliberately *not* to touch on one. In the example above, the embedded passages were intended to touch on her concern about being helpful to people and, perhaps, one day entering one of the helping professions, such as psychotherapy.

In response to these passages, the subject could recall two segments of thought, the latest clearly combining her concern about being helpful with the words of the passage. The segment that went just before dealt with another of her concerns, her plan to go skiing with Hank, and it may well have been cued off by the allusions to valleys and glacial loughs.

This example supports the notion that people are sensitized to those cues in their environment that relate to their current concerns, for this subject's thoughts seemed clearly to reflect the narrated passages even though she had been paying little conscious attention to them. Furthermore, those passages were capable of triggering many other kinds of thoughts, but the subject responded with only those thoughts that bridged both some selected passages from the tape recording *and* her current concerns.

Experiments using techniques like these are beginning to pull together a picture of how cues that are relevant to people's concerns influence their mental activities (Klinger, Barta, Mahoney, et al., 1976). In these experiments, subjects listen "dichotically" to two narrations at a time, each piped to a different ear. While the tapes are playing, subjects continuously indicate with a toggle switch whether they are listening to their right ear, left ear, both, or neither. Each time the subjects report their thoughts, they also try to recall the last taped material they can recall. In this way, the experimenter can obtain measures of the subjects' thought content, memory for cues, and, at least crudely, attention.

The results are presented in Figure 2-2. They show that people attend more often to cues related to their concerns, although they also attend at least briefly to other material, perhaps to assess its possible relevance. More strikingly, they are much more likely to recall and have thoughts related to concern-related than to unrelated cues.[11] ("Related" and "unrelated" here refer, of course, only to what the experimenters thought about the cues when they wrote them. Their judgment is quite fallible, both because they have an imperfect knowledge of subjects' concerns and because words sometimes have unpredictable associations for subjects.)

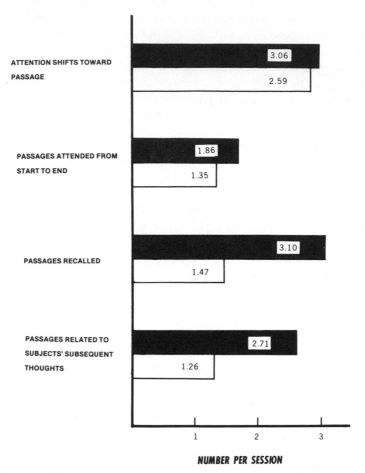

Figure 2-2. Mean number of times experimental subjects attended to, recalled, or had thoughts related to tape-recorded passages, 12 pairs of which were presented in each session. Black bars represent activities with respect to the passages in each pair written to be related to the subject's current concerns. White bars represent actions with respect to passages intended to be unrelated to subjects' current concerns. (After Klinger, Barta, Mahoney, et al., 1976.)

We can form a picture, then, of the way in which much human inner experience is determined. One travels through one's world of stimulation ignoring most of it, processing primarily those features of it that fit into one or more current concerns. As one does so, one's respondent thoughts are continually shaped by the coincidences of cues and concerns. We can say, in other words, that concerns and cues *jointly induce* relevant thoughts that best bridge them, and that the process goes on continuously. This, then, is the *induction principle.*

Stated in this simple way, the induction principle raises many questions, most of which cannot be answered very precisely without much research that has yet to be performed. There are three main questions. First, what is the relative importance of cues and concerns in determining the content of a person's thoughts? Second, granted that thoughts are induced by concern-related cues, and that the thought will have something to do with the concern to which the cue is relevant, of the many possible concern-related thoughts, what determines exactly which one the person will have? Third, what determines how influential a particular concern will be in influencing thought?

In answer to the first question, clearly concerns are the most important influence, since they determine which cues people will select to incorporate into their thinking. Moreover, we have found it extremely difficult to write neutral passages for subjects — that is, passages unrelated to any of their concerns. In the absence of cues that are strongly related to their concerns, subjects react to cues that are weakly related, and it seems as if almost any cue has at least some distant connection with one of the subject's concerns. For instance, such an apparently ambiguous and innocuous cue as a reference to a "gray mass" plunged one subject into the thought that her friend was inordinately fond of gray circus elephants. Friendships, of course, create concerns, and those concerns carry with them an interest in one's friends' interests. Therefore, a neutral cue must be unrelated not only to subjects' own personal concerns but also unrelated to what subjects know to be outstanding concerns of their friends and relations. Thus, people's concerns dominate their thoughts, picking up with whatever cues there are, however distant their relevance, to launch new segments of thought.

Of course, the experimental situations in which we are studying thought are rather artificial. Our subjects have been instructed to listen to the taped stories with moderate attention and they cannot escape the narrations without ending the experimental session. No doubt in a more natural setting subjects exercise some choice of cues to which to expose themselves and are more likely to ignore cues that are very weakly related to their concerns, perhaps more completely choosing their own thoughts in preference. People's own thoughts are undoubtedly an important souce of cues to which they respond much as they might to cues from outside of themselves. Thus, there are probably practical limits in any given kind of situation to how irrelevant a cue may be before it ceases to have any discernible effect on the course of a person's thoughts.

The second main question raised by the induction principle is what determines the exact form of the concern-related thoughts induced by the concern-related cues. For this question there are no answers based on research. We do know that respondent segments may take the form of a brief image of something related to the concern — of a friend, for instance — or a more extended recollection of the person doing something in a past situation. It may consist of imagining events in the future, of remembering something the person intends to do, of self-pity, of hoping for something to happen, of inquiring about what kind of a person the thinker is, of wondering about the effect something he or she did may have, or of many other things. It seems reasonable to speculate that when one takes into account the many facets of a cue and the many facets of a person's various concerns, the thought that they jointly induce will be that response which best encompasses all of those facets. For instance, in the example described earlier, the cues regarding terrain and helping may have locked into the subject's concerns about helping and about her related worry of how to set limits on what will be demanded of her, thereby reviving a memory of a summer spent working in a rural state hospital in which the demands on her sometimes constituted a problem. Perhaps a slightly different constellation of cues would have joined with different aspects of the same concern to produce a different thought. For instance, cues that touched on feeling useless and incompetent to help people may have led her to think about her plans for academic preparation in the helping professions.

The third major question is what determines how influential a particular concern will be in affecting thought. There is evidence (Klinger, Barta, Mahoney, et al., 1976) that at least three kinds of factors determine this: the importance of the incentive to the individual, the amount of time left before the incentive will be consummated, and the probability that a consummation will in fact take place.

In some sense, of course, the distinction between something that is the focus of a concern and something that is not already implies a great deal about the relative importance of the two things. There are, however, a number of ways in which something can be important. It can be capable of arousing strong emotionally felt desire, for instance, or it can be something which one dispassionately recognizes as important to one's future welfare. We asked a number of people to tell us what things they had been thinking about most during the previous 36 hours and what important things they had not thought about much, and to rate each of these "things" according to how important (on several dimensions), near in time, and likely to occur it was. There was a slight but significant tendency for the things most thought about to have been more important than the others, especially in the sense of being more strongly desired.

Distance in time has long been recognized as something that affects the psychological "pull" that goals exert. Even rats work harder as they approach their goals (Miller, 1944). Subjectively, people feel more emotionally involved in events, such as economic depressions or natural disasters, in the near as compared with the distant future (Lundberg, von Wright, Frankenhaeuser, & Olson, 1975), and students waiting to receive electric shocks during an experimental session (Lundberg, Ekman, & Frankenhaeuser, 1971) or to take an important examination (Lundberg & Ekman, 1970) become more anxious as the time for it comes nearer. In our own research, the things people reported thinking most about were also nearer to them in time.

Respondent thought and special states of consciousness. When we considered blank states at the beginning of this chapter, it seemed that the purpose of specialized techniques used by meditators was to block out respondent thoughts. Dancing, looking, chanting, and so forth, when they are repetitive, continuous, or routinized, can all block out the flow of respondent thought if the meditator concentrates on them. In addition to these kinds of methods, however, the sects and religions that practice meditation also prescribe guides for living that make it possible or at least easier to achieve the spiritual plane at which they aim. Nearly all of them — from Christian mystics to Buddhist monks — prescribe as one guide renunciation of material goals: poverty and chastity.

From what we have learned about respondent thought, it is apparent why this should be so. If respondent thoughts are triggered by concern-related cues, and if they are triggered most vigorously by cues related to the most important and imminent incentives, then the best way to keep from thinking about those cues when one is trying to meditate is to disengage oneself from worldly incentives.

Although respondent thought may make it hard to meditate, people may turn out to be especially receptive to subtle information during respondent periods, including to extrasensory information. Investigators have reported a number of circumstances in which, for instance, experimental subjects can guess the content of a card someone else is holding (e.g., Honorton, 1975), or an "agent" concentrating on a picture in one room can cause the free associations of a waking subject (Honorton, 1974) or the dreams of a sleeping subject in another room to reflect elements of the picture (Ullman & Krippner, 1973). Although large numbers of psychologists still doubt the reality of extrasensory communication, a number of psychologically trained investigators in parapsychology have not only established its reality according to conventional scientific criteria of evidence, but have begun to explore the conditions that support or impede it. These conditions seem to have a single common element: They are the kinds of conditions associated with respondent thought. Thus, some of the most convincing and replicable evidence comes from studies of dreams and free association. Among the experiments that use more traditional ESP procedures, the best results are obtained when subjects are relaxed, show an increase in brain alpha waves (which are associated with relaxed, respondent thought), are not trying to produce particular kinds of results, spend more time in "random, disconnected thoughts," and are generally inclined to be spontaneous (Stanford, 1974a, b). We have seen that respondent thoughts are responsive to concern-related cues. Now it appears that some of these cues may be extrasensory!

Induction in Operant Thinking

The main differences between operant and respondent thought are that in operant thinking thinkers try to keep their attention on a problem, evaluate how well they are doing in moving toward a solution, modify their thoughts and actions to improve their chances of succeeding, and have a subjective sense of trying. All of these "operant elements" go on continuously as long as the person remains in an operant segment. By themselves, however, they are far from the whole story of what takes place during thinking. The four operant elements are things that the thinker does about the content of thought, but they do not contain in themselves the actual content of the steps one takes to solve one's problem. One must come up with specific images and transformations of images in order to arrive at a solution one can apply. If one is planning a trip somewhere, one must have some kind of mental representation of where one is, where one is going, what kinds of vehicles there are that link the two, what their schedules and requirements are, and so on. If one cannot do that, one cannot plan one's trip. Where does the content come from? How is one able to conjure it up when one needs it?

Remarkably little is known about this question. The psychology of thinking has focused much more on the strategies and methods that people use to solve problems than on how they get hold of content, and the psychology of memory has focused more on the ability of people to retain bits of information than on their ability to tap their memories in the course of thinking about problems. Although psychologists are at least beginning to consider the problem (for instance, Greeno, 1973), their ideas are still in a very preliminary, abstract stage that permits few concrete predictions about how the process might work.

In the absence of any conclusive evidence, I shall suggest what seems to me a strong possibility: namely, that the process of injecting content into a person's operant thinking is the same as that involved in induction during respondent thinking. In both cases the content of thought consists of responses (perceptions, images, words, mental operations, or outward motor responses) that the person has learned to make in regard to a certain concern when faced with certain cues. In both cases, the person thinks whichever thought provides the best combination of the cues around him or her and the concerns he or she carries inside, taking into account the extent to which various facets of the cue situation are compatible with the various facets of the several concerns. Thus, we would predict that if a person has a very important Concern A (for instance, in the earlier example, a strong need to feel helpful to people) and cues that clearly relate to some aspect of that concern (for instance, talk about people who need help), the person will have a thought about helping people. In order to predict more exactly what the person will think about helping people we would need more information about the person's concern and about the cues in the situation, including those that occurred recently enough to still be in short-term memory and those that the person is producing in his or her own thoughts.

In this view, then, operant and respondent thinking are not two totally different, mutually exclusive modes of thinking but, rather, operant thinking is the result of imposing certain additional processes on what would be occurring during respondent thought. There are two parts to this proposition. The first is that, apart from the things imposed on respondent thought to make it operant, thought obeys the induction principle during operant thought pretty much the way it does during respondent thought. In our dichotic listening research, described above, we have been finding that our subjects notice and think about concern-related cues about as often when they judge their thoughts to have been operant as when they judge them to have been respondent. Of course, the experimental task they are in is quite undemanding — to listen to a tape with only moderate attention — and their responsiveness to the cues might be expected to diminish if they were involved in a task that requires hard concentration. Nevertheless, it is important that the tape-recorded cues launched operant thoughts about as readily as respondent thoughts.

The second part of the proposition is that something is *imposed* on respondent thought to make it operant, rather than that these are two totally different kinds of thought. What could be imposed? First, clearly, what I have called the four "operant elements" are imposed. The idea that these — or at least the attention-control element — are actually *imposed* on a process that would otherwise lead elsewhere is supported by recent findings (Patterson & Mischel, 1976) in which children were instructed to ignore a tempting "Clown Box" (whose tape-recorded voice kept cajoling them to play with him) and instead to keep working on a dull pegboard task. Children were able to resist the Clown Box better if they told themselves not to pay attention to it, but telling themselves to keep their attention on the pegboard made no difference. In this case, then, the effective way to control attention was to inhibit the tendency to stray, rather than to emphasize the task they were straying from. However, another of these elements, "trying," may well have the effect of temporarily strengthening one concern — what we might call *hyperenergizing* it — so as to make it a more powerful factor in the situation. Once the concern is hyperenergized, the person will be in a better position to think thoughts related to that concern rather than to others.[12]

There are also other important differences between situations in which people can think operantly and situations in which they cannot that may affect the results of induction without altering the way in which the induction process operates. When one has a problem, knows what to do, and is in a situation that permits one to do it, one will, most likely, simply go ahead and solve the problem. If one does not know what to do, but knows some steps to take which may help one find out what to do about solving the problem, one is very likely to take those steps. That, however, is to say in other words that the person's concerns have many specific facets — many clearly defined subgoals, for instance — and that the cues in the person's situation fit well into the important facets of the concern. With the facets so well specified, the thought that the concern and cues induce is very likely to be a thought that constitutes a solution to the problem.

If, for instance, the subject of our earlier example who was eager to help people had run not into our taped story but into a lost child, we might predict that her thoughts would be about helping the child and, assuming nothing stops her, that she will act to help.

Viewing operant thinking in this way leads to a number of predictions. For instance, it predicts that a person working on one mental task who is in the grip of a very strong concern about something else will have trouble keeping his or her mind on what he or she is doing — he or she will be fighting a lot of mind wandering. In addition, he or she will be thinking relatively inefficiently even when not mind wandering because, through the induction process described above, the large extraneous concern will keep inducing thoughts that are off the mark for purposes of the task at hand. This kind of interference has been documented by Wine (1971), who showed that anxiety about taking tests leads test-takers to think too many thoughts related to their plight, thereby interfering with thinking about the test questions themselves.

Another prediction is that problem-solving, especially the complex kinds that require "creativity," will proceed best if solving the problem is one of the person's dominant concerns both in *and out of* the problem-solving situations, so that the induction process can provide those rich, creative insights that occur during fantasy or even during dreams. By the same token, this view predicts the importance of having this low-key, "incubation" stage of creative thinking.

Sometimes people who are thinking, writing, playing basketball, swimming, or conversing lose all sense of distinction between operant and respondent activity. They are continuing to produce at their very best level, but they experience a sense of flow, of specifically *not* trying. For many people this kind of state leads to a "peak experience" (to use Abraham Maslow's term) of exultation in their oneness. It is as though the demands of the situation, the necessary cues and props, and the individual's current concerns have come together to produce a single productive thrust, one that has no need of operant elements and that draws on every last shred of the individual's psychological resources. Perhaps these are the cases when respondent and operant activity are equivalent, the organism unified in a total effort.

Yet another prediction is that the person is most subject to distraction when work is nonroutine, requiring one to piece together a solution rather than simply to follow a well-worn trail of rules. It would be interesting to investigate whether working amid conversations or radio programs is indeed more disruptive at the point of formulating a solution than during the period of carrying it out.

This discussion is by no means, of course, a complete theory of operant thought. It leaves out the notion that the thought segments induced by concerns and cues are structured in particular ways, a matter I have considered elsewhere (1971) but which is unimportant for present purposes. It also leaves out what has been the main focus of psychological research on thinking: the strategies, transformations, and structures involved in complex human thought. It does not dwell on the many ramifications of the theories that view thought as continuously regulated by the feedback of its consequences. Nevertheless, it makes one central point, which is that insofar as the theory is correct, not only respondent segments but the content and effectiveness of operant thought itself are determined by the thinker's current concerns — by the person's commitments to pursue incentives.

Summary

The figurative features of our inner experience, what we call our thoughts, are in essence responses. They partake of the properties of all responses and they can be studied, therefore, in the same spirit. It is convenient to classify segments of mental content into three classes: blank states that lack all figurative features, respondent segments made up of unintentional and undirected thoughts, and operant segments that are intentional and are aimed at particular goals. Blank states take up only a tiny proportion of total thought but are sometimes sought out through meditation. They may thus constitute incentives. The content of both respondent and operant segments reflects the incentives to which people have committed themselves — reflects, that is, their current states of *concern* over attaining their goals. The content of inner experience, in short, depends on the world of the person's incentives.

People can generally attend consciously to only one target of attention at a time. However, they are not completely impervious to other things happening around them. While one is attending to one thing (or is asleep), one's *preattentive processes* maintain a constant vigil for cues that are relevant to one's concerns, and if they detect something pressing, one shifts one's attention to it. Because preattentive processes are sensitized to concern-related cues, one's current concerns determine which cues one will attend to. We can therefore say that one's concerns and the concern-related cues around one jointly *induce* thoughts that encompass both the concern and the cues. This is true of respondent segments of thought as in fantasy and dreams, but it probably also applies to operant thought, even though operant thought works under greater constraints. In conclusion, then, the qualities and sequence of the figurative features of inner experience depend in largest part on the person's relationship to his or her incentive world.

Chapter 3

Incentives and Emotions

Many people think of their thoughts as the main characters of their inner life. Yet, thought — the "cognitive," imaginal part of our inner life — is one part only. An inner life without emotion would be eerily detached. Most of the time emotion is less prominent than figured thought, just as the sets, lighting, and music of a theatrical production command less attention than the speeches going on among the actors. Nevertheless, the role of emotion is entirely central to human functioning. "The emotions," writes Carroll Izard (1971), "are viewed not only as the principal motivational system but even more fundamentally as the personality processes which give meaning and significance to human existence" [P. 183].

Wundt, Titchener, and their theoretical allies believed that human consciousness contained *only* two kinds of elements, sensations (including imagery) and feelings. That was the assertion introspectionist psychologists were unable to agree on in the early years of this century. It was also the issue that revealed most clearly the limitations of introspection as a scientific method.[1] It would be foolish now to insist that either their position or that of their antagonists is correct. Either way, no one is likely to dispute that imaginal and emotional processes are at least the two dominant contributors to inner experience.

There are a number of peculiarities about the way in which emotions are experienced. Whereas thoughts seem to occur in the head, people are inclined to localize feelings elsewhere. We speak of chests bursting with pride, hearts breaking with grief, butterflies in stomachs, people getting something off their chests — all, apparently, cases of "gut reactions." Besides localizing feelings in the viscera, people also identify their feelings with facial expressions. Can you imagine feeling joyous without a happy smile? Or deeply depressed with one? Evidence is mounting that facial expressions are an integral part of the emotions they express (Ekman, 1972; Izard, 1971; Tomkins, 1962, 1963).

In this chapter I shall try to show that emotions are an aspect of all behavior, that they are a crucial part of the process by which organisms evaluate incentives, and that it is therefore the emotions that tie people to their goals. That is, objects and events become incentives by virtue of their capacity to arouse emotions. Therefore, emotions form the linchpin of the system that binds organisms to the world around them, and they make possible the effects on thought and behavior that we have attributed to incentives. We shall begin by considering the nature of emotion and then, in view of its nature, how it performs its vital functions.

Keeping the Terms Straight

There are at least four words in common use for naming somewhat similar things: feeling, emotion, affect, and mood. There are at present no reliable conventions for how these are used. Different investigators use different terms to mean the same thing and even a single writer is likely to use the terms in ways that overlap. The definitions used here seem to correspond with the tendencies of the field. First, I shall use *feeling* as the broadest possible term to include all aspects of the phenomenon. In that sense it is virtually synonymous with emotion, but *emotion* has come to be used by some writers to emphasize the peripheral physiological aspects of emotion — the racing heart, loose bowels, and sweaty palms of fear, for instance — without excluding the other aspects. "Emotion" may also emphasize the brain processes involved. *Affect,* on the other hand, emphasizes the experiential aspect of feeling, focusing away from the peripheral physiology of the response, without, of course, denying that the experiential component must also rely on brain mechanisms. *Mood,* finally, also describes feeling, but whereas emotions and affects refer to states that are often very short-lived, perhaps only a few seconds long, moods refer to relatively longer-term feelings. Thus, if we wish to describe people's states of feeling sad, we are likely to talk about their affect; if we wish also to draw attention to their tears or their very slow movement, we are likely to talk about their emotions; if we are describing the feeling frameworks in which they worked yesterday, we are likely to speak of their depressed moods; but all are descriptions of feeling states.

Thus, the four terms differ not so much in denotative meaning as in the different aspects of the same process that they emphasize. Because of the thrust of this book, I shall tend to write most often of affect.

What Are Emotions?

There is no simple, single statement that can cleanly define "emotion." First, any emotion is so much a *system* of responses, with so many components, that a precise definition would have to be an elaborate enumeration that would go on and on and that would, in any case, eventually outrun our knowledge. Second, emotion is not a single entity. There are many kinds of emotion and they do not all operate in the same way even at a fairly abstract level of description. To answer the question of what emotion is will therefore require a somewhat leisurely consideration of the various aspects that are involved.

As Carroll Izard wrote (1971), "Emotion is a complex concept with neurophysiological, neuromuscular, and phenomenological aspects" (P. 185). The phenomenological aspect — emotion as we consciously experience it — is, of course, the most direct route by which people come to know their emotions. However, investigators have begun to associate activity in particular brain circuits and actions of particular chemical substances in the brain with particular emotions. We shall look at some of this evidence in sections and chapters to follow. Furthermore, some emotions are also accompanied by characteristic postures and, especially, facial expressions, such as smiles and frowns. These are very much part of the emotional process, not just signals that people learn to put on when they are communicating.

Three experiments illustrate just how closely facial expressions and emotional inner experience are intertwined. In one (Schwartz, Fair, Salt, Mandel, & Klerman, 1976), people were asked to imagine situations in their lives that had made them clearly happy, sad, or angry, and also to imagine a "typical day." Movements of their facial muscles were recorded electromyographically. The patterns of movement were systematically different for happy, sad, and angry situations. Some of the participants in this research were depressed at the time, and their "typical day" expressions were like those they slipped into when imagining "sad" situations, whereas the "typical day" expressions of the others were more like their "happy" expressions. Even though these people had been asked only to "imagine," not to "make faces," their faces reflected the emotions evoked by their imaginings.

In the second experiment (Laird, 1974), people *were* asked to make faces, but they did not know that the faces were supposed to reflect emotions. They were asked to contract particular facial muscles in what they thought was simply a study of muscles. However, the instructions in fact led them to smile or frown. Those who were led to smile afterward described themselves as feeling happier than those who were led to frown, who described themselves as feeling angrier. Furthermore, people who had been led to smile in this way also thought a group of cartoons was funnier than did a group who had been led to frown. Thus, just as the first experiment had shown that feeling a particular emotion changes the expression of the face, the second experiment shows that adopting a certain expression changes the emotions one feels.[2]

In the third experiment (Lanzetta, Cartwright-Smith, & Kleck, 1976), students were given series of electric shocks. Each shock was preceded by a signal a few seconds earlier. Typically, people become uneasy between such a signal and the shock that follows. In this experiment, the students were sometimes asked to hide their feelings while waiting for the shock, and at other times they were asked to reveal their feelings clearly. When they hid their feelings, they experienced less fear, reacted less strongly on a physiological measure (skin conductance), and judged the shocks to be less painful than when they made no effort to hide their feelings; and when they revealed their feelings fully through facial expressions they were more fearful, more physiologically reactive, and more sensitive to the pain. Thus, by controlling their faces these students were able to either weaken or strengthen their emotional reactions to electric shock.

Emotions, then, are brain-based response systems that reach into glands, muscles, and inner experience, thereby coloring the entire state of the organism. How do they get organized and where do they come from?

Emotions and Instincts

Complex animals come into the world already "programed" to respond to certain cues in preset ways. The nervous system is able to interpret a limited number of perceptions and set in motion orderly, primitive responses to them as early as birth without the animal having to learn the connections or the motor skills. I shall call these acts and the brain processes underlying them *instinctive,* a term much in disfavor by psychologists for several decades but very serviceable nevertheless. It is easy to find examples of instinctive behavior. Male stickleback fish attack other fish that have red bellies, and they also attack wads of red color. Fledgling thrushes gape when a parent approaches the nest, or when approached by a connected pair of cardboard discs. Hungry human newborns move their heads left and right when touched around the mouth by a nipple or by nearly any other object, and they suck when they find it. These instinctive responses depend on the stimuli outside and the organism's chemistry inside in very complicated ways.

Every animal comes into an unfamiliar world equipped with a repertory of instinctive reactions that give it a chance to survive.[3] Its repertory forms a "wired-in" base upon which to build a larger repertory — immensely larger, in the case of humans — through learning. However, the instinctive processes that form this base are merely molded, bent, and extended through learning; they are not abolished by it.

There is reason to believe that at least some emotions start out as aspects of instinctive reactions. This is an old idea, one advanced by William James (1890) and popularized by William McDougall (1921). To McDougall, for instance, the emotion of fear was part of the "instinct of flight," the emotion of anger part of the "instinct of pugnacity," the emotion of wonder part of the "instinct of curiosity," and so on. The trouble with McDougall's theory is that he had only a very weak basis for labeling particular kinds of behavior "instinctive" and an equally weak basis for identifying them with particular emotions. He also wrote as if calling something instinctive explained more than it in fact does. The theory has been roundly damned by psychologists since the 1930s. It has served as a classic "bad example" of theorizing in generations of psychology textbooks. One hesitates to espouse any part of a theory so disreputable. Can it nevertheless be partly valid? I believe that the answer is "yes."

McDougall's major point was that organisms, including humans, are motivated entirely through instinctive processes. In this view, all of the subtle, varied motives of adult humans are refinements and variations of basic instincts. The theory was badly defective in its specifics and oversimple even in its general outlines; but its conceptual thrust is gaining support. For instance, animal psychologists are finding what they call "preparedness for" or "constraints on" learning — members of a species can learn some things with surprising ease and other things very slowly, if at all. They and child psychologists are finding patterns of behavior and preferences for incentives that were almost certainly not learned.

The emerging view of these instinctive influences is vastly more sophisticated and complicated than McDougall's. No one today would deny the overwhelming importance of individual life experiences in shaping behavior; but then McDougall wouldn't have denied it either. Let us, therefore, examine the following arguments that emotions have evolved as aspects of instinctive reaction patterns: First, some important patterns of emotional expression are determined innately. Second, some of the events that set them off are also specified innately. Third, emotions can be controlled by stimulating particular sites in the brain electrically or by removing them surgically, sites that are also involved in innately organized action patterns.

Emotions as innate reaction patterns. Not long ago, most social scientists were so impressed by the great variety of human societies around the world that they believed nearly every kind of human behavior to have been learned, including the facial expressions of emotions. There is no doubt that emotional expressions do depend to a great extent on the particular customs of one's home culture; but there is a common core of human expressions that are unlearned. Children's smiles and cries of distress are recognized in very similar ways the world over. People who live in societies virtually cut off from contact with the West recognize many of the same expressions and assign to them much the same meaning. (We shall come back to this evidence below.) Perhaps some of the most convincing evidence comes from films of children who were born deaf and blind (Goodenough, 1932; Eibl-Eibesfeldt, 1970). These children are almost completely cut off from the chance to mimic those around them. It is hard to teach them anything even with great exertion. Yet they display normal human emotions. They laugh when they find a lost doll or discover a way to dance. They wrinkle their brows, pout, clench their teeth, or stamp their feet when angry. They push away people whom they fail to recognize by smell.

Events that set off emotions. If one looks just at the concrete events that cause people to smile, they seem to have little in common; but on careful consideration some common elements emerge. The basic outlines can be seen in the development of smiling in young infants

(Sroufe & Waters, 1976). Newborns smile only during states of deep relaxation, generally while asleep. When they are about a week old, infants smile a few seconds after being touched lightly, blown on, or very gently jogged, provided that they were relaxed at the time. During the third week, infants may smile at voices, and in the fourth week at the mother's voice or at a vigorous game of patty-cake. As the infant becomes more sophisticated, the events necessary to evoke a smile must keep pace: A stranger must put on a mask, blink lights, or be a clown. At about four months, infants begin to laugh, at first over having their stomachs kissed in a mock threatening way and then over the mother saying "Boom Boom" resoundingly.

What all of these events seem to have in common is a rise in tension followed by a drop in tension. At the earliest ages, the tension is produced by sheer stimulation and the drop occurs after it ends. At the older ages, the tension occurs because someone does something slightly novel or arousing and the tension drops when the infant recognizes the something as benign. If it does not recognize the thing as benign, it is more likely to cry or withdraw than to smile. As infants get older, events that were once arousing or novel become familiar and lose their capacity to challenge. At that point they also cease to cause smiles or laughter. One could add to these carefully controlled observations of infants that children also smile when something they have looked forward to comes true, when someone they want around them returns after an absence, and when they succeed at a task or game.

The observations of infant humor have a parallel among adults. Arthur Koestler (1964) argued that something is funny insofar as it shows that two things that seem unconnected have an unexpected connection. The strategy of good joke-telling is to create tension by challenging the listener to make sense of the story and then swiftly to resolve the tension by drawing on an unexpected angle. The swift resolution is the punch line; but the punch line depends for its "punch" on a prior buildup of tension. Riddles create the tension by a direct challenge to the problem-solving ability of the listener. (For instance, what has 18 legs and flies?) The riddle poser must wait long enough for the listener to confront and wrestle with the problem, so that the surprise answer will be funny. (Answer: a baseball team.) Jokes create tension by involving the listener vicariously in the problems of the protagonist or by implicitly challenging the listener to anticipate the punch line. Jokes are often funnier when one expects a joke to occur, perhaps because they then combine both kinds of challenge. When the punch line comes, it must be neither too obvious nor too far-fetched if it is to be funny, since in the first case the joke would provide no challenge and in the second case no resolution.

Evidently, people smile or laugh when they master a challenge. The challenge may consist of surviving a threat, recognizing a threatening situation as benign, discovering a solution to something, taking delivery of something that was uncertain, or being reunited with a loved one. Simply doing something one values is not enough. People do not typically spend dinner smiling or laughing at their meals, for instance, and spouses do not typically go through their evenings together smiling or laughing over the fact, unless perhaps it is a rare, sought-after occasion. But when people find a happy love, finish writing a long-awaited first book, or visit Greece after wishing to do so for 20 years, they may smile almost incessantly for days on end. The smile, and the inner affective experience that goes with it, is the spontaneous result of mastering a threat or achieving a goal.

One kind of smile that takes place world-wide is the "eyebrow flash" — raising one's eyebrows for perhaps half a second when warmly greeting someone. This is a subtle, ephemeral expression that draws little attention to itself. Yet Eibl-Eibesfeldt (1970) has photographed it among the widely separated native peoples of Bali, New Guinea, and France; and it seems to occur each time in the same kind of context.

Stimuli that evoke fear, concludes Jeffrey Gray (1971), include very intense sensations, such as pain or loud noise, unfamiliar stimuli that cannot be analyzed into benign or familiar qualities, and certain stimulus configurations that are specific fear stimuli for the members of a species. One can easily find examples of the latter among animal species, such as the fear reaction of chaffinches to owls. Humans, too, show rather specific fears. Human infants, for instance, hesitate to climb over the edges of cliffs, and human adults commonly report fears of snakes and heights.

With humans it is hard to be sure that these fears have an instinctive basis, since nearly everyone has watched other people's reactions or read about them. However, with other higher primates, such as chimpanzees, one can rule out such factors. Chimpanzees who have never experienced snakes or mutilation nevertheless become frightened when they are presented with snakes or with a head detached from the body. Interestingly, infant chimps are unmoved by these kinds of stimuli, half-grown chimps begin to show signs of agitation, and adults express their fear full-blown. This progression also occurs in human children, who display increased fear of snakes between infancy and adolescence.

Fear is closely tied up with action to avoid the danger. When there appears to be no way to avoid it, the fear grows and diffuses, and thus gives rise to anxiety (Szpiler & Epstein, 1976).

When people fail to reach a goal or lose incentives they are used to enjoying, they become depressed. When they are confronted with obstacles to something they are striving for, but before they have accepted failure or loss, they give evidence of anger and, often, of aggression. We shall consider the evidence for these conclusions intensively in Chapter 5. For present purposes, it is enough to say that loss regularly precipitates some degree of aggression and depression both in humans and in the animal species for whom depression has been investigated.

At least some kinds of emotion, then, seem to be instinctivelike consequences of specific kinds of events. The events we have examined are not necessarily the only ones instinctively able to evoke emotions, and these emotions are not necessarily their only instinctive consequences. In some cases, the emotion-producing events are defined quite narrowly, as in the case of snakes, whereas in other cases they are defined broadly, as in mastering challenges or losing incentives. Interestingly, McDougall did not regard joy and sorrow as emotions because it is hard to associate them with specific patterns of action, in the way that fear can be associated with flight. McDougall notwithstanding, they may carry action patterns with them nonetheless, such as reaching out arms with joy or withdrawing into the listless slump of sorrow. In any case, they are responses to specifiable events, and the link seems to require no learning.

It is not the case, however, that these instinctivelike emotional reactions occur self-sufficiently. One can appreciate novelty only in comparison with what has become familiar, which is a matter of learning. One can celebrate success or mourn failure only in relation to one's aspirations, the details of which were bound to be learned. Cultures specify the occasions on which emotions are appropriate and the appropriate manner in which they are to be expressed, and people soon learn to follow the culturally prescribed forms. What we have examined in this section is an instinctive core — the organism's original contribution to its own development, and the inexorable givens from which any acculturation process must start.

Emotions and the brain. One striking way to show that emotions are organized innately is to demonstrate clearcut relationships with particular sites in the brain. A number of kinds of animal activity, especially "consummatory" acts such as feeding and gnawing, are heavily influenced by instinctive processes. If these can be turned on and off by stimulating certain locations in the brain, and if stimulation there can be shown to arouse affect, then we have evidence that the action patterns and the affects have evolved together, probably as aspects of the same response system.

In order to investigate these relationships, investigators embed long wire electrodes into the brain, the ends of the electrodes coming to rest in those brain areas under investigation. After the electrodes are mounted permanently into place and the animal or person has recovered from surgery, the investigator can stimulate the target brain areas electrically, while the subject can move about and live normally. In animal studies, there are two basic experimental plans. In one kind of plan the experimenter arranges that if the animal makes a particular response (such as pressing a bar in a Skinner box) it receives electrical stimulation through the electrode. This is called a *self-stimulation* design. In the other plan, the experimenter keeps complete control over the stimulation and observes its effects on behavior.

Olds and Milner (1954) were the first to report cases in which rats seemed eager to stimulate themselves through electrodes to certain parts of their brains which were soon dubbed "pleasure centers." Stimulation to other brain regions seemed clearly unpleasant, and animals learned to perform acts to avoid stimulation there. The work by Olds and Milner led to an enormous volume of research by hundreds of investigators which has greatly enriched our understanding of brain functioning. Despite the great complexity of their observations and the many controversies over how to interpret them, there is now general agreement that animals are willing to work hard for the reward of stimulation to particular brain regions and that intracranial stimulation acts as an incentive like less artificial incentives.

Other investigators found that if rats are, for instance, placed in the presence of food and are stimulated in parts of the lateral hypothalamus, they will proceed to eat even if they have just previously eaten to satiation. (The effect of this stimulation is not necessarily highly specific. The same animals might gnaw or drink instead when stimulated in the presence of things to gnaw or drink.) These satiated animals will even search and work for food when stimulated. Studies of stimulation are by no means limited to eating and drinking. Limbic stimulation often produces aggression in cats. "Cats stimulated in this way will learn to seek objects to attack. . . . [S]timulation in other parts of the brain will stop the attack . . . and some are points which are apparently rewarding, judging by results of other experiments in which so-called self-stimulation was used. In the attack situation . . . the animal no longer seems angry or fearful" [Mark & Ervin, 1970, Pp. 30–31]. It is very likely that the brain locations stimulated in these experiments are involved in the organization of instinctive behavior patterns.

The main point of interest in these studies is that the places in the brain that, when stimulated, seem to reward the animal tend to be the same as those in which stimulation sends the animal into action (Glickman, 1973; Valenstein, Cox, & Kakolewski, 1970). For example, the same brain locations that a rat will work to get stimulated are also those which can be stimulated to start the animal looking for food, to copulate, to attack prey, to explore, to sniff, and so on. If being rewarded is assumed to involve an emotional process, then these studies provide evidence that emotions and actions share some of the same neural machinery.

Inference about animals' emotions is, of course, somewhat chancy. However, work on stimulation of people's brains supports these conclusions. Neurosurgeons have been able to produce a wide variety of emotions and actions by stimulating patients' brains through implanted electrodes. Unlike animals, these patients were able to report their emotional experiences. For instance, following stimulation in an anterior hypothalamic location, one patient reported a euphoric feeling "like two martinis" [Ervin, Mark, & Stevens, 1969, P. 57]. Much of the evidence concerning human subjects has been collected by neurosurgeons treating people who become intractably depressed or uncontrollably violent. In some cases (especially Heath, 1963, 1964) the patient receives a permanently implanted set of electrodes for stimulating his or her own pleasure centers when depressed. In other cases of patients who for neurological reasons become uncontrollably violent (Mark & Ervin, 1970), the purpose of the temporarily implanted electrodes is to locate the brain regions which, when stimulated, render the patient violent. Once they are located, they can later be destroyed. Moyer (1971) has summarized much of this work. Describing observations reported by Heath, Moyer writes: "One patient, for example, was on the verge of tears while discussing the illness of his father. At that point, the electrode implanted in the septal region was activated, and within a 15-second period, the patient grinned and shifted the conversation to a discussion of his plans to seduce a particular girl friend. The patient was not aware that he had received stimulation and could not account for the sudden change in his train of thought. Another patient in a severe depressive state expressing feelings of hopelessness smiled and began to talk about a youthful sexual experience within one minute after septal stimulation" [Moyer, 1971, P. 116].

These data are, of course, fascinating from a variety of viewpoints. They demonstrate the effects of emotional arousal pervading the person's mood, expressive behavior, and conversation. They point up the important effect of emotional activity on the content of thought, and they support the theory that new segments of thought are launched with emotional reactions.

Heath's patients reported changes in feelings and thoughts as a result of stimulation, and they gave outward signs of their changed feelings, such as grins and manner. Mark and Ervin tried to recreate violence in their patients in order eventually to eliminate it surgically. Their graphic accounts leave little doubt that emotions and actions occurred together in their patients. When they stimulated affected brain regions, their patients experienced rising rage and uncontrollable impulses to violence, which they often acted upon. If we can assume that the electrodes stimulated the kinds of preprogramed response systems that we have been calling instincts, then the evidence from these studies supports the proposition that emotions are aspects of instinctive behavior.

Kinds of Emotions

The experiences and events that we lump together as "emotions" are a very mixed bag. A bit of reflection will quickly confirm that dejection feels drastically different from fear, joy from disgust, and shame from anger. Furthermore, any one of these can occur at quite different intensities. The hundreds of words that describe different emotional experiences in any major language attest to their variety and subtlety. Does it, then, make any sense to even try to treat these as having something in common? Is there an infinite variety that defies classification?

All writers on the psychology of emotion have lists either of emotions that they regard as basic or of dimensions of emotion. Dimensional theorists may describe all emotions as different levels on only a single dimension, such as Duffy's arousal, or on a small number of dimensions, such as Wundt's pleasantness-unpleasantness, relaxation-tension, and calm-excitement. Other theorists have listed discrete types of emotion, of which the most recent and best documented is a list of eight "primary" emotions originated by Tomkins (1962, 1963) and investigated by Ekman (1972) and Izard (1971, 1972): enjoyment, interest, surprise, distress, disgust, anger, shame, and fear. The list should be considered tentative — it may well be too long or too short. Izard, for instance, has added a ninth primary emotion, contempt. These workers assume that different primary emotions can be experienced at the same time, thereby giving rise to subtle mixtures of emotion. For instance, "some mixture of happiness and anger . . . could account for the blend emotion of *smugness*" [Ekman, 1972].

The emotions are "primary" in the sense that they are unlearned reactions to certain basic kinds of situations. For instance, anger may be an unlearned reaction to interference with a goal-directed sequence of behavior. However, people learn that a wide variety of new situations are equivalent to the basic situations for which the primary emotional reactions are programed. They then respond emotionally to these new situations as well. People also learn to inhibit or to mask their emotions according to the teachings of their society ("display rules" [Ekman, 1972]), thus greatly complicating the picture.

Given the great variety of human experience, both within the same culture and among different cultures, it may seem foolish to offer up a list of primary emotions that apply universally to the entire human species. In and of itself, such a list would be an unimpressive achievement. Many theorists have in the past suggested other lists. However, Ekman, Izard, and their associates have marshaled an interesting array of evidence to support the belief that at least some members of this list are experienced universally, are recognized by people regardless of cultural heritage, and are usually precipitated by specifiable kinds of situations.

Their work across different cultures assumed that each type of emotion is a complex response pattern that includes characteristic facial expressions. They first prepared photographs of facial expressions to represent each of the primary emotions. Then they variously asked subjects to describe in their own words what the people pictured must be experiencing (Izard), to pick the correct description of each photo from a prepared list of labels (both Ekman and Izard), or to rate their own attitudes toward the emotions (Izard). These subjects agreed in their ability to label emotions a very high percentage of the time. In nearly all of these procedures, enjoyment was the emotion with the greatest recognizability, cross-cultural stability, and desirability.

Particularly impressive is the evidence collected by Ekman and his associates (Ekman, 1972; Ekman, Sorenson, & Friesen, 1969), who found as subjects groups of preliterate New Guinea tribesmen who had had no contacts with Western languages, governments, employers, or mass media. They also were able significantly to match up verbal descriptions of various emotions with photographs of Western faces expressing those emotions. Some of the tribesmen were then, in turn, themselves photographed while posing emotions that they would feel in specified situations. Just as they had recognized the Americans' emotions, American students were able to recognize their happiness, sadness, anger, and disgust. Both groups confused each other's surprise and fear.

Equating Ekman's "happiness" with Izard's "enjoyment" and "sadness" with "distress," these data impart considerable confidence in the belief that joy, sadness, anger, disgust, and fear/surprise (separately or combined) are universally distinguishable, universally experienced human emotions. In view of the enormous differences among human cultures in all modes of expression that are not fixed through physical necessity, it would be very surprising if the human species could maintain such universality of emotional expression unless the emotions rested on an instinctive base, one that provides for distinctively different emotional reactions to specifiably different kinds of situations.

Dimensions of emotion.[4] To say that certain emotions are universal and universally distinguishable is not necessarily to say that they are in any way more basic or more important than others. All major theorists of emotion agree that, if there are "basic" or "primary" emotions, people often (or even usually) experience them not in pure form but in some blend of two or more emotions. This, however, raises some interesting questions: How can one tell which emotions are the basic ones being blended? Is smugness a blend of happiness and anger, as Ekman would have it, or is anger a blend of smugness and, say, distress? Does it even make sense to think in terms of "basic" emotions? One can describe physical spaces by their height, width, and length without insisting that "real" length always points north and that other length measurements are really blends of length and width. Can it be that human emotions are also just variations in an emotional "space" of several dimensions, none of which is any more "basic" than the others?

A dimension is just a variable that can be used to describe or measure something. Things being described are described *in terms of* their dimensions. Just as a box can be described in terms of its dimensions of height, length, and width, it is possible that an emotion can be described according to the proportions of (say) fear, anger, and disgust that go to make it up. A number of psychologists have tried to find out what dimensions people in fact do use to describe emotions. One investigator, Lynn Bush (1973), asked several hundred American college students to read lists of adjectives that describe feelings and to judge how similar each adjective is to each other adjective. He then subjected these judgments to a statistical analysis (multidimensional scaling) able to suggest two kinds of things: first the approximate number of dimensions the students were actually using in judging whether adjectives are similar, and, second, what those dimensions probably were. He found three significant dimensions, which he called "pleasantness-unpleasantness," "activation," and "aggression." He gave them these labels on the basis of which adjectives represented the extreme points of each dimension. However, if one looks at these extreme adjectives carefully, it is apparent that the dimensions could have been labeled less abstractly. On the pleasantness-unpleasantness dimension, for instance, the extreme high adjective is "delighted" and the extreme low adjective is "depressed." The high end of the activation dimension is marked by "startled" and "alarmed," and the low end by "unfrightened" and "sleepy." The high end of the aggression dimension is marked by "outraged" and the low end by "needed" and "sympathetic." Put in these terms, the dimensions take on a somewhat different significance. Their extreme poles now correspond to some of the emotions on Tomkins's, Izard's, and Ekman's lists. The positive and negative poles of the first dimension clearly correspond to "joy" and "sadness," the positive pole of the second dimension corresponds to "fear," and the positive pole of the third dimension corresponds to "anger."

These findings are really not about the dimensions of emotions, but about the ways in which people use their language to talk about emotions. Nevertheless, it is interesting that when one uses this approach as a way of studying the dimensions of affect, one finds dimensions that correspond to the "primary" emotions suggested by other investigators. These findings cannot, of course, be conclusive evidence that these emotions are primary in a biological sense, or even that primary emotions exist. However, it seems likely that emotions have evolved as reactions to certain kinds of situations which are critical for the survival of animal species — situations that require particular kinds of responses such as success, flight, attack, or regurgitation. These would have to be represented in the brain by specialized structures. Even though human emotions may have evolved to be more flexible and less closely tied to such response systems, they can still be expected to reflect their ancestry. On balance, therefore, it seems likely that some dimensions of emotion do correspond to biologically basic or "primary" emotions.

It is also possible, however, that some kinds of affect transcend the primary emotions. For instance, it may be that all pleasant affects, besides their separate distinctive impacts on inner experience and behavior, also give rise to a common component of "pleasantness," and similarly for all unpleasant affects. In other words, just as there are brain mechanisms for particular kinds of pleasant affects, any of these affects may also feed into a central "pleasantness" brain mechanism. Thus, if the separate primary affects constitute a set of value codes, pleasantness may be a kind of supercode for value. This supercode leaves out the nuances of the separate affects and, conceivably, conveys no instructions about how to react, but serves as a basic, primitive answer to the question, "Is it good for me or is it bad?" Certainly, "good-bad" is the most important dimension used by people in all known cultures when they judge the fixtures of their worlds (Osgood, May, & Miron, 1975). Whether it is really different from primary affects such as joy and sadness, or whether it may have evolved as a generalized form of them, we cannot yet tell.

Components of Emotion: Affect and Gross Physiology

Everyone is aware that when they become emotionally very aroused their bodies become aroused too. Some people, including theorists William James and Carl Lange, thought people distinguish among their emotions chiefly on the basis of their bodily reactions. However, this is almost certainly not the case. The gross physiological reactions that accompany emotions are an important part of emotional responses, but there is also another part. It probably operates entirely within the central nervous system and is probably responsible for imparting the distinctive subjective "feel" of the emotion. I shall refer to this component of emotion as *affect*.

A number of investigators have tried to establish whether there is, indeed, something to emotion besides gross physiological activity. There have been basically two ways to go about this. First, the investigator could try to produce the physiological state without producing anything else, in order to see whether the subject experienced a genuine emotion. Second, the investigator could put the subject into an emotion-arousing situation and interfere with the physiological reactions that would normally accompany the emotions, in order to assess the effects of diminished physiological activity on the subject's behavior and inner experience.

Marañon (1924) took the first of these tacks. He injected people with adrenaline, which produces many of the bodily reactions found in strong emotion. However, most of his subjects reported not feelings of emotion but simply bodily symptoms, and most of the rest reported that they felt "as if" they were emotionally aroused but knew they were not. Clearly, then, adrenaline did not produce authentic emotional experiences or behaviors.[5]

The opposite tack, that of inhibiting the physiological component of emotion, is much more difficult. Hohmann (1966) therefore made use of tragic "natural experiments." Himself paraplegic, he interviewed quadraplegics and paraplegics. These patients, of course, have injuries of the spinal column that interfere with brain control over bodily functions. If the lesion is high enough in the spinal column, it virtually eliminates the gross physiological components of emotion as well as many of the sensations they produce. Hohmann asked his patients to compare their inner reactions to emotionally arousing situations before and after their injury. All of these patients continued after the injury to experience some kind of emotion,[6] but it tended to be a changed experience, the more so the higher the lesion. Those with the highest (cervical) lesions described their feelings as "cold," "mental," "thinking," and so on. Yet, they were still capable of experiencing anger, fear, and grief. They were still capable of expressing preferences. What they had lost was the "heat" of emotion, the bodily turbulence that seems so characteristic.

It is apparent, then, that there is much more to emotion than gross physiology. The question now becomes one of establishing what this "something more" is. Schachter (1971), summarizing more than a decade of his research, concluded that what I am calling "affect" is not truly emotional at all. He suggests that people's "cognitive" appraisals of their situations determine the quality of their emotional experiences — for instance, tell them whether they are happy or angry — whereas the degree of their physiological arousal informs them about the intensity of their emotions. That is, one knows that one feels angry not because there is anything distinctive about the feeling — as far as one's emotion is concerned, one might as well be feeling scared or overjoyed — but because the situation warrants anger.

There are a number of reasons for believing that this view of emotion is mistaken. For one thing, key experimental results on which it was based have been misinterpreted. Also, other investigators have been unable to replicate the original results (Marshall, unpublished, in Zimbardo & Ruch, 1975). However, the most dramatic evidence against this view comes from the studies of human brain stimulation described above. Surgeons such as Vernon Mark are able to produce very distinctive emotional experiences, ranging from anger to euphoria, by starting and stopping brain stimulation at times unknown to the patient and without any significant changes in the patient's momentary situation. The evidence suggests that there are indeed two components of emotion, a gross physiological component and a central affective one, that the two are ordinarily closely related but can be separated experimentally or accidentally, and that both are important in the total experience and function of emotion.

Implications of This View

If the argument up to this point is correct, emotions are aspects of instinctive behavior, which is to say aspects of an organism's relationships to instinctively dictated incentives. There are many kinds of emotions because there are many kinds of instinctive behaviors and incentives, and each carries with it a distinctive experiential feeling. Emotions have both physiological and experiential (affective) components which often occur together but are separable, with the result that a person can experience affect without readily detectable changes in his or her bodily activity.

These are all very important properties of emotion for purposes of our theory. Because emotions begin as innate reactions to incentives, they can serve as an organism's channel of information about which objects do and do not have incentive value for it. Because emotional reactions to different incentives are distinguishable from one another, emotions can provide information about which are positive, desirable incentives and which are negative, unpleasant incentives, and something about the ways in which an incentive is positive or negative. Because the affective component of emotion can occur without much physiological dislocation, affect can operate as an efficient, unobtrusive flow of signals that normally makes few heavy demands on the organism's physical resources. All of these capabilities are essential to the function of emotion to be described in sections below.

One more characteristic of emotion is important. Emotional responses can be conditioned. That is, an organism can learn to make emotional responses automatically to ever new events. Their conditionability frees them to occur at times and in places not fixed by instinct or physiological stringency and thus makes possible their occurring in anticipation of future events. Hence, emotions contain the ingredients necessary for foresight (Tomkins, 1962) and hindsight, and therefore they have the basic properties necessary to maintain the concern-related flow of mental events in humans.

The Roles of Emotion in Human Functioning

Emotions as Incipient Behavior

Emotions usually contain some instructions about what to do next. People who feel ashamed speak of feeling so small they would like to crawl into a hole. People feel so happy they could dance or so angry they could slug somebody. Often, perhaps more often than not, they disobey the instructions and instead of dancing they merely glow or instead of slugging the other person they ask him whether he would prefer coffee, tea, or milk. Nevertheless, the more intense the emotion, the greater is the impulse to "act out" and the more likely that the person will break his or her socially learned facade by behaving in accordance with his or her feelings. If emotions are indeed part of a larger complex of behavior with instinctive origins, we can think of emotional arousal as a case in which the other parts of the behavior are potentially there but inhibited. Then the emotions are in a sense their representative and carry with them implied instructions to run, hide, fight, enjoy, or whatever, depending on the emotion that happens to be getting expressed.

In other words, the emotions are directors of behavior. The directions are, to be sure, quite primitive and they become overlaid in mature adults by an enormous repertory of learned actions that substitute for the primitive ones. If one suddenly becomes angry in a conversation, one's first response may be to find a category of condemnable behavior in which to place one's partner and then to appeal to one's partner's understanding of social proprieties in order to extract redress. With some sophistication in these matters, one may alternatively try to identify precisely what one's partner did that angered one and what the partner's provocation may have been for doing it, as a means of finding a friendly basis for reconciliation.

Whichever one does, the conversation will have been changed in some way by one's having become angry, and the basic tendency will have been to attack, even though the attack may have been forestalled by a variety of learned ploys for dealing with hostile confrontations. If this view of emotion is correct, it is inaccurate to say that anger causes a person to attack just as it would be inaccurate to say that a runny nose causes a fever. Both the runny nose and the fever are part of the same cold; both the anger and the attack are part of the same behavioral complex.

The same may be said of emotions aroused in fantasy. Suppose that something in a person's thoughts reminds him or her of something else in his or her life. If this arouses an emotional response, it also arouses some action tendencies, which the person will probably experience as a new segment of fantasy in which he or she imagines taking the kind of action that goes with the emotion aroused. Since these emotional upsurges are related to the person's incentives — that is, they are about things he or she values or wishes to avoid — they represent another way in which current concerns control the content of thought.

Emotions and Incentive Value [7]

No object has incentive value for anyone simply by virtue of being the thing it is. No matter what its potential benefits for a person, they will go unrecognized and untapped unless they can be translated into the language of the organism. That language is the language of affect. Things and events are incentives insofar as they can influence feeling. They are positive incentives insofar as they can make one feel good (or less bad) or negative incentives insofar as they can make one feel bad (or less good).

Silvan Tomkins (1962) has made the case well that affects, not drives or the reduction of drives, are the direct motivators of human beings, that whereas drive states such as hunger or thirst are important signals, they gain the power to motivate behavior only when they are amplified by affects. Hunger pangs are relatively mild, quite tolerable sensations, but self-pity, fear of pain, and anticipation of pleasure drive the dieter to the snack machine against his or her better judgment.

We come to associate pleasure with certain sensations and assume that the sensations themselves are what attract us, but what attracts is really the affects produced by the sensations. When experimenters or physicians stimulate brain "pleasure centers" through implanted electrodes, there are no objects or sensations to value. There is just good feeling, according to human subjects, and their animal counterparts work long and hard to prolong it when it becomes available. When there are sensations to value, their value can fluctuate widely. Consider, for example, how becoming ill and vomiting up a favorite food temporarily destroys one's liking for that food. It is often a long time before the person is able to enjoy eating it again. There are also many other ways whereby something that had been a positive incentive loses its positive value or even becomes a negative incentive. These will be discussed in Chapter 4. Conversely, negative incentives including even pain itself may under some conditions become positive incentives. It is hard to explain these kinds of changes by appealing to drive reduction or stimulus patterns, but they are readily explainable in terms of what we know about affect.

Emotion as Evaluative Feedback

A certain sign reads, "At 40 miles per hour you are driving your car. At 80 miles per hour, you're aiming it." The difference between guiding and aiming something is fundamental for engineering and for organisms. In order to guide something, one must continually compare its present state with whatever is necessary for it to reach its target and then make midcourse corrections as necessary. Aiming is in some ways simpler: You point the object carefully in the best possible direction for hitting the target and send it on its way. Once underway it is beyond control and correction. All organisms are to some extent self-guided. A purely ballistic organism would have small chance of surviving.

The information received by a guidance system to check its whereabouts is called *feedback*. In a guided system, feedback constantly depends on what the object does in relation to its environment (for instance, too little power may produce feedback announcing too low a trajectory) and what the object does constantly depends on the feedback it receives (for instance, speeding up or changing its angle to return to a desirable trajectory). The feedback and the correction together constitute a *feedback loop*. Organisms make constant use of feedback to modify their outward behavior and physiological functions. Moths spiraling toward a light, drivers slowing down to avoid crashing into the car ahead, and breathing rate increasing in response to a buildup of carbon dioxide in the blood stream are all examples of feedback loops at work.

In some relatively simple kinds of feedback loops the feedback produces responses through a fairly automatic mechanical or chemical process. The breathing response to carbon dioxide in the blood is an example of this. Simple organisms probably operate entirely through this kind of feedback loop. However, as animals become more complicated higher up the phylogenetic scale, they must be sensitive to more and more kinds of incoming information. Having to link every important kind of information with an innate response to it would create an enormous burden for the animal's brain. At the human level, people must act on incredibly subtle and varied kinds of feedback, much of it symbolic feedback that may come in thousands of possible languages. There is simply no way that evolution could have fitted out humans to deal with so much information by means of a separate innate response for each kind of important information. There must be some way by which a person can reduce the huge number of possible communications to a manageable number of implications for his or her life. There must be some way of coding the information so that one can decide what to do with it.

Emotions seem to offer the coding system that is needed. The code is quite primitive at birth, consisting of emotional responses to only a very few innately meaningful stimuli. It becomes somewhat more refined with the individual's biological maturation; but what vastly expands the number of stimuli to which the individual responds with emotion is learning. We shall examine this process, whereby formerly neutral objects and events gain value, in Chapter 4. Its result is that adult humans respond with affect to a great range of things in their worlds, and it is the affect that makes them meaningful.

To put this another way, most of the raw perceptual information a person receives is useless without something more happening. If I walk toward a table, I see the table taking up an ever larger part of my visual field. I can recognize the image as that of a table and may be able to state that if I keep going I shall bump into it and perhaps bruise myself. There is nothing in this rich perceptual and cognitive feedback, in and of itself, to make me change course. It is only the wish to avoid pain, embarrassment, and inconvenience that enables me to decide to walk around rather than into the table; and whereas I know of no direct evidence other than intuitive to support the assertion in the case of the table, the factor that makes me decide to change course is my *fear* of pain, embarrassment, and inconvenience. That is, I am proposing that an essential part of the coding by which a person interprets the action implications of sensory feedback is his or her system of emotions.

In still other words, the great world of sensory feedback that is essential for locating oneself in space is insufficient to guide behavior. It must be supplemented by a system of *evaluative* feedback, one which can quickly code events as good in a certain way or bad in a certain way. The system that provides evaluative feedback is emotion. Just as sensory feedback is experienced along an array of dimensions — colors, brightnesses, pitch, temperature, sweetness, and so on — that permit the organism to distinguish differences in physical qualities, so also emotions are experienced along various dimensions — fear, anger, joy, and so on — that permit people to distinguish differences in value.

A number of investigators have shown the power of emotion to guide behavior by interfering with it in various ways. Schachter and Latané (1964), for instance, experimentally administered chemical agents in order to affect emotions. They thereby changed students' dispositions to cheat and they changed other subjects' ability to learn to avoid electric shocks.

In the first experiment, college women were put into a situation in which they could falsify their scores on an examination without being detected. All of the students first took what they thought were vitamin pills, but half of them actually swallowed the tranquilizer chlorpromazine and the other half swallowed ineffective placebos. The students who took the tranquilizers were expected to be less fearful than the others and therefore less afraid to cheat. Of the placebo subjects, 20% actually cheated. Of the tranquilized subjects (excluding some for whom the tranquilizer was physiologically ineffective), twice as many — 40% — cheated. We may infer that the tranquilizers reduced subjects' fears of detection. Without the guidance of their normal evaluative feedback, some subjects who would otherwise have remained honest cheated.

The second experiment is more complicated. Subjects were seated in front of a panel that contained four switches. Their task (invented by Lykken, 1957) was to discover and learn to make a series of 20 correct choices, each being a choice of one among the four switches. The task was intended to be a "mental maze." It simulated the situation of finding one's way through a maze with 20 "choice points" at each of which the subject must choose the one out of four possible turns that leads out of the maze. Making the correct choices at all 20 choice points was the "manifest task." However, there was also a secondary ("incidental") task. At each choice point, one of the incorrect switches was wired to give the subject an electric shock. Subjects were led to believe that the shocks were unrelated to their actions. Nevertheless, normal adult subjects unwittingly learn to avoid the shocked errors faster than they learn to avoid the other errors.

Some people, however, have difficulty learning to avoid the shocked errors faster than the other errors, even though they are just as quick as normal subjects at learning the manifest task. These people, who have been called "psychopathic" or "sociopathic," tend not to learn to inhibit behavior that gets them into trouble. Consequently, they form a significant part of prison populations. One possible explanation for their psychopathy is that for some reason they have a less effective emotional feedback system for guiding them away from dangerous behavior.

Schachter and Latané operated on the premise that there is a problem in the psychopath's fear responding. Since they had already shown (Latané & Schachter, 1962) that adrenaline increased rats' ability to avoid electric shock, they arranged to inject half of a group of psychopathic prisoners (and half of a control group of prisoners) with adrenaline. The other prisoners were injected with a placebo. After adrenaline injections, the psychopaths learned to avoid the shocked errors markedly better. Directly manipulating their emotional feedback dramatically improved their performance.

Another drug that seems to reduce fear is alcohol. A number of studies have shown that when rats are under the influence of alcohol they can learn to escape an electric shock as quickly as sober rats, but they perform the responses necessary more slowly (Pawlowski, Denenberg, & Zarrow, 1961) and less often (Scarborough, 1957). Furthermore, when rats are put into a conflict situation, for instance by placing food where the rat has been shocked, rats under the influence of alcohol become more "reckless": They are more inclined to approach the food and shock (Barry & Miller, 1962; Freed, 1968).[8] Here, again, chemically manipulating the animal's emotional feedback system leads to just the kinds of behavioral changes one would predict if emotions serve as evaluative feedback that guides the organism.

One might object that in most day-to-day behavior there is little indication that emotions are ever involved. For instance, the theory described here would suggest that people are kept from walking into a street in front of an oncoming truck by fear of being run down, but every day millions of people wait patiently at curbs for trucks to pass without feeling much detectable emotion. The answer to this objection is that affect, unaccompanied by much general physiological arousal, can operate at a very subtle level and still be effective in guiding behavior. The classical demonstration of this was performed in a series of experiments by Solomon and his associates (Solomon, Kamin, & Wynne, 1953; Solomon & Wynne, 1953).

Solomon placed dogs into a "shuttlebox," a box with two compartments separated by a barrier the height of a dog's back. The floors were metal grids that could be electrified to give the dogs severe shocks. The boxes were also equipped with gates above the barriers which could be lowered to block access between the two compartments. The dogs soon learned that ten seconds after a buzzer sounded and the gate lifted they would be shocked unless they had jumped over the barrier into the neighboring compartment. During the learning (acquisition) period the dogs acted very emotionally, as one would expect, but after they had mastered the task of jumping to avoid shock and the shock was no longer used (the "extinction period") they became markedly less emotional.

> The types of emotional signs which usually disappeared during the course of ordinary extinction were defecation, urination, yelping and shrieking, trembling, attacking the apparatus, scrambling, jumping on the walls of the apparatus, and pupillary dilation. Whining, barking, and drooling tended to decrease in magnitude but often persisted throughout the 200 trials. . . . Some dogs showed no overt emotional signs during the latter part of ordinary extinction [Solomon, Kamin, & Wynne, 1953, P. 293].

Nevertheless, the affective process almost certainly continued to operate during this apparently placid period. There are two reasons for believing this. First, many trials after the dogs had experienced their last shock, the amount of time it took them to jump (the *latency*) after hearing the buzzer continued to decrease. If there were no continuing affective process and the dogs had merely learned cognitively that jumping helped them to avoid shock, and if the speed with which they were jumping already accomplished that, why should the latency of their jump grow shorter and shorter? The only plausible explanation that suggests itself is that even though they were no longer experiencing shock there was still something unpleasant for them to escape: the unpleasant fear of being on the shocked side of the shuttlebox. The sooner they jumped, the sooner they could end their fear. Thus, an affective process too mild to produce outward indications of emotional arousal seems to have continued to operate and continued to shape the dogs' behavior.

There is a second, less compelling but more dramatic demonstration that the dogs' emotions were merely latent. Hundreds of jumps and several weeks after some of the dogs had received their last electric shock, the experimenters placed a glass partition above the barrier so that after the gate rose and the buzzer sounded, the dogs could not jump into the next compartment. Under these conditions, even though there was no new shock, the dogs' panic immediately returned in full. The dogs had not lost their fear of the shock. They had not forgotten the shock nor gained overriding trust in the experimenters. As soon as they were prevented from making the jump that could save them from shock, they panicked. (Imagine, as an exercise in empathy, your own feelings if you were crossing a busy four-lane street, traffic was beginning to bear down fast a half-block away, and in the middle of a lane you suddenly found yourself rooted to the spot, unable to move — the makings of a nightmare.)

Occasionally, a dog, faced with the glass partition that prevented escape, failed to jump. By this time, the dogs were no longer being shocked. Nevertheless, such a dog would "typically" jump especially quickly after the buzzer on the next trial as if making up for the previous lapse.

We see here, then, animals turning in calm, workmanlike performances after they have mastered a procedure for avoiding pain. Insofar as they are forced to deviate from this pattern, their emotion rises. Is it not likely that the relationship between deviation and emotion is a functional one — that it is precisely this relationship that keeps behavior regular and efficient, guided by the principle of minimizing unpleasant affect and maximizing pleasant affect?

One might ask how we know that emotions contain the judgments on which action is based rather than simply accompanying the actions we observe. Which comes first, the emotional response or the impulse to action? The answer is almost certainly that the emotional process occurs first. We have seen that investigators can change actions such as cheating by using drugs aimed at changing emotions or by inducing people to disregard certain emotions. These investigators did not try to manipulate the subjects' actions directly, nor their decisions directly. Manipulating affect was enough. Observations of infants support this conclusion. When a mother puts on a mask and approaches her infant, "the infant ceases ongoing activity, quiets, and stares intently at the masked face. . . . [T]he face then brightens, the infant smiles or laughs, and *then* reaches. The reach and smile may occur simultaneously, but the reach never precedes the smile. This suggests that the smile is the final point of the appraisal process." (Sroufe & Waters, 1976, P. 184).

Affect as a homing device. The concept of affect that all these varied pieces of evidence lead up to, then, is that of affect as a homing device, something like a radio beam to an aircraft approaching an airport. When one is on course toward a goal, one's affect is mild and perhaps seems neutral, although it may also involve hope or relief (Mowrer, 1960). As one approaches one's objective, one may feel anticipatory joy. But as one's feedback says that one is deviating from a goal-bound course, affect turns unpleasant, toward fear, disappointment, distress, disgust, shame, or anger, depending on the circumstances. The radio beam (or the pilot's visual contact with the airport) is essential to the flight, despite all of the other instruments, because it directly reports on success. Unlike the other instruments, its strength depends on a *comparison* between the plane's position and the course it is supposed to hold. Just so, affect provides a direct answer to the question, "How'm I doing?", and serves as a basis for correcting the course.[9]

Cognitive processes: the role of interpretation. When it comes to human beings, hardly anything is simple. People are guided not by sheer physical events but by the meanings they give them; and people have a vast capacity to alter the meaning of events. When people misinterpret the bodily evidence that they are emotionally aroused, they act in accordance with their misinterpretation. For instance, Dienstbier and Munter (1971) led subjects to misinterpret their natural, actual states of emotional arousal. All of their subjects took placebo pills and were put in a position to cheat seemingly without risk of detection. Half of them were told that the pill would produce side effects identical to those of fear ("— a pounding heart, hand tremor, sweaty palms, a warm or flushed face, and a tight or sinking feeling in the stomach") and the other half were told to expect side effects unrelated to fear. When the first group began to feel afraid, therefore, they could blame the bodily effects on the pill and ignore their message that cheating is dangerous. Sure enough, a much larger proportion of them cheated than of the other group.[10] There are therefore two ways to interfere with a person's evaluative emotional feedback. One is to alter the peripheral-physiological expression of the emotions directly. A second is to alter the meaning the subject supposes the expression to have. Both kinds of interference can affect decisions and performance.

Evidence of this kind has sometimes been taken to indicate that all emotions are always indistinguishably a matter of general arousal and that their differences are due purely to the person's different interpretations of their causes (Schachter, 1971). That is, just as in Schachter and Singer's experiment, whether subjects become angry, euphoric, or indifferent depends not on any biological differences in the emotions but on whether people attribute their arousal to happy or provoking situations, or to a pill.

However, there are a number of reasons for rejecting this conclusion.[11] First, animals as well as people depend on emotional feedback for deciding what to do next; it seems highly unlikely that dogs and rats form cognitive interpretations of situations before deciding whether to run or fight, or that lower species could have survived very long without a more direct set of decision rules. Second, different emotions incorporate distinctive facial expressions that seem universal for human beings, which means that there are indeed biological distinctions among different emotions, not just general arousal. It seems inconceivable that organisms would evolve such distinctions without also evolving ways to use them in the business of surviving. Third, eliminating most of the peripheral physiological reactions that occur during strong emotion still leaves a recognizable residue of affect that is enough to motivate behavior. Consider, for instance, a patient with a very high (cervical) spinal cord lesion, who told Hohmann (1966), "I used to have a hot temper but now it's nothing compared to what it was. Now I get kinda mad one minute, and the next minute it'll be like nothing happened. Seems like I get thinking mad, not shaking mad, and that's a lot different" [P. 151]. Despite the lack of general arousal, this subject still experienced affect that he could recognize as anger, even though it seemed strangely changed without the usual physiological arousal. The changes experienced by Hohmann's subjects seemingly resulted from this elimination of arousal — they felt less disorganized by emotion and it passed more quickly, presumably because there was less need to clear biochemicals slowly out of their bloodstreams after an emotional upset. However, a "cold" affect seemingly remained to act as a guidance mechanism.

Overall, then, the evidence supports the notion that emotion acts as a system of evaluative feedback to steer an organism toward its goals.

Happiness, Mood, and Incentive Relationships

The theory spun in the previous sections states that emotions make up an evaluative feedback system and hence measure progress toward goals. So far it rests on a base of reasoned argument and experimental data. How well does it hold up in the larger world outside the laboratory? What predictions does it make about human happiness?

It might seem as if the theory simply predicts that people will be happy insofar as they are well off — that the rich, healthy, and privileged are happier than the poor, sick, and oppressed. Despite occasional people who romanticize the poor (who are sometimes said to be happier because they lack the cares and satiety of the rich) it probably comes as no great surprise to learn that rich people and white people consider themselves happier on the average than those who are poor and black (Bradburn, 1969; Wilson, 1967). The differences, however, are averages. There are many happy poor people and many miserable rich ones. Money, another platitude says, cannot buy happiness. What, then, does money have to do with happiness, and what else is involved?

The theory permits no broad generalizations as answers to these questions, but it does point to specific factors in individual lives. We can predict, for instance, that people will experience happy moods when they believe they are successfully pursuing incentives they value highly. We can predict that obstacles to this pursuit will produce unhappiness; but just what kind and amount of unhappiness depends on the kind of obstacle and the kind of incentive. Obstacles may be temporary or permanent, expected or not, early or late. They can take the form of directly blocking people's efforts at pursuing goals or they may be threats to well-being with which people must grapple immediately, thereby diverting them from attaining their positive goals. The incentives may be momentary sensual pleasures, primary human relationships, long-term career objectives, and so on. The obstacle may have no redeeming value or it may carry with it substitute satisfactions. All of these factors make an important difference in a person's emotional responses.

Some of the factors that are especially important and subtle, especially the conditions that give rise to depression, despair, and apathy, we shall examine closely in Chapters 5 and 6. There is, however, some evidence from investigations concerning happiness, mood, and incentive relationships that illuminate the theory of emotions already presented and are therefore of interest here.

One investigation (Wessman & Ricks, 1966) focused on students' ratings of their own moods every day for six weeks. The students had also filled out a number of personality tests. A second study (Bradburn, 1969) used survey research methods to ask questions of 2787 people living in eastern and midwestern U.S. cities; some of them were interviewed as often as four times over the course of a year. The primary objective was to probe "the relation that events in a person's life — the kind of social life he leads, the state of his health, how he gets along with his wife, and what he is doing at work — have to his feelings of well-being" [Bradburn, 1969, P. 17]. The extensive interview schedule contained 10 questions that were intended to measure "affect" and that yielded separate scores for positive and negative affect. The questions in the two scales are as follows (P. 267): "During the past few weeks, did you ever feel . . . "

Positive Affect
a. Pleased about having accomplished something
b. Proud because someone complimented you on something you had done
c. Particularly excited or interested in something
d. On top of the world
e. That things were going your way

Negative Affect
f. Bored
g. Upset because someone criticized you
h. So restless that you couldn't sit long in a chair
i. Very lonely or remote from other people
j. Depressed or very unhappy

Despite the enormous differences in the methods of these two studies, they come to similar conclusions: The crucial factor in happiness is not past accomplishment or accumulated wealth so much as, first, people's outlook on their prospects and, second, the extent of their participation in pursuing incentives, especially social incentives. Wessman and Ricks's "happy men valued warmth and friendliness as much as their academic goals" whereas the unhappy men valued only "efficient work and ambition" [P. 111]. The data "suggest a basic association between happiness and ease vs. difficulty in social relationships" [P. 116]. The happy men were more likely to agree with optimistic statements affirming the worthwhileness of their endeavors and the high chances of success, whereas the unhappy agreed more with statements that view life as disillusionment and hopelessness. The happy felt successful, the unhappy felt like failures. Happy men view time as "something that may be employed in the projection and realization of goals and purposes. . . . Their time is *filled*," scheduled and planned (P. 118). The unhappy men "express a feeling of *passive subjection* to time. . . . Their time is *unfilled*: they shy away from long-term responsibilities; they keep the future open and uncommitted; they are ready for anything, prepared for nothing" [P. 119].

Bradburn, too, found his happy subjects to be more involved with people socially and more active in pursuing a variety of interests. Bradburn allowed subjects to register their positive and negative affect separately. That is, a person could be experiencing a great deal of positive affect and also much negative affect; or a person could be experiencing little affect of either kind; or, of course, a person could be experiencing a great amount of one and little of the other. Bradburn found that positive and negative affect were related to quite different kinds of life events. This is perhaps an artifact of his method. After all, his questions about affect were worded to imply success in the positive case and rejection in the negative case. Be that as it may, people seem generally to respond with "positive affect" to the pursuit of varied and interesting goals, especially social ones, and they seem to experience negative affect when they are blocked or when stable elements in their life situations are threatened: "Specifically, variations in negative affect are associated with difficulties in marriage and work adjustment, interpersonal tensions, and feelings of having a 'nervous breakdown,' as well as with some of the more standard indicators of anxiety and worry. . . . On the other hand, positive affect appears to be related to a series of factors concerning the degree to which an individual is involved in the environment around him, social contact, and active interest in the world. The factors include such things as the degree of social participation, which is reflected in organizational membership, number of friends, and frequency of interactions with friends and relatives; the degree of sociability and companionship with one's spouse; and exposures to life situations that introduce a degree of variability into one's life experiences" [P. 12]. Thus, the conditions that govern positive affect consist of involvement with opportunities whereas those that govern negative affect consist of preoccupation with threats.

Our own research findings support these results. Chapter 1 described a study in which 168 college students answered questionnaires concerning the things that made their lives meaningful. They also described their moods. Of those who reported that 12 or more categories of incentives contributed meaning to their lives, 80% described themselves as generally happy (positive ratings on the

Wessman-Ricks Elation-Depression Scale) as compared with only about half (53%) of those who reported fewer than 12 sources of meaning ($p < .003$ for a correlation coefficient[12] of .23). A still unpublished survey, which found very similar results, led its authors to conclude: "People seem to arrive at a sense of global well-being by simply adding up life's pluses and minuses" (Andrews & Withey, 1976, quoted in "Americans' View of Life's Satisfactions," 1976).

Conclusions

The main component of inner experience other than thought is emotion; and like thought, emotion is also determined in large part by the person's relationships to incentives.

Emotions are complex response systems. In fact, they probably originate as parts of larger "wired-in," instinctive response systems, and since these response systems are organized around incentives that organisms need in order to survive, emotions are also inherently responses to people's relationships with incentives. As parts of larger response systems, emotions include physiological, facial, postural, visceral, and phenomenological responses.

There are a number of distinct "primary" emotions that probably include at least joy, sadness or distress, anger, disgust, and fear. Each kind of emotion is programmed into the brain and hormonal system with its own pattern of responses, each reporting that something has gone well or has gone badly in a particular way with respect to some incentive object: It has been enjoyed, attained, lost, blocked, or spoiled, or it constitutes a threat.

Emotions have an affective aspect, physiologically quiet but phenomenologically prominent, that provides information about where the person stands relative to each incentive and about which objects have value. Emotions also have an aspect of gross physiological arousal that amplifies the affective component. The affective and arousal components of emotion normally occur together but can be teased apart experimentally and clinically.

Emotions constitute a continuous stream of signals informing a person where his or her incentives are, how important they are, and what his or her relationship is to them. Because emotions are part of a larger behavioral complex, they are incipient behaviors with respect to incentive objects. They therefore prepare the person for a certain class of response — to seize, fight, run, or desist, for instance. Emotions can be conditioned and generalized to new objects and events other than those laid down innately — to the full range of objects and events that people come to regard as incentives. Also, because emotions can be conditioned and generalized to the signs and symbols of real events, they can anticipate real events or occur long after the events are past. Emotions therefore make possible foresight and hindsight.

Because of these characteristics, emotions serve as a constant stream of evaluative feedback, telling people how they are doing in their many ventures and forming a basis for decisions to change course if necessary or to proceed ahead. Emotions thus form an essential feedback system that codes sensory feedback according to its implications for action. Emotion can therefore be thought of as a kind of homing device that enables organisms to zero in on their goals. Because of its role as the system that evaluates, emotion is the ultimate basis for all judgment of value.

Because emotion is the system that links people to incentives, interfering with people's emotional feedback changes their behavior. At least two kinds of interference have been shown to change behavior: altering emotional reactions physiologically and altering people's interpretations of their emotional reactions. The latter kind of interference shows that humans can transform the effects of emotion (as they can transform the psychological effects of most events) by assigning them a different significance.

Studies of people's emotions outside the laboratory indicate that happiness arises out of pursuing opportunities, especially social ones, and that unhappiness arises out of threats to basic incentives.

Chapter 4

The Ups and Downs of Value

The previous three chapters have tried to show that the qualities of people's inner experience depend on where they stand with respect to their incentives. This chapter and to some extent the next two explore a further question: What does the value of an incentive depend on?

The question is important for two reasons. First, the value that an incentive has for a person can and frequently does change, either up or down, even though there are no changes in the incentive object or event itself. That is, incentives are incentives by virtue of their ability to attract or repel someone, which means (if we can accept the argument of the previous chapter) that they are incentives by virtue of their control over a person's affective reactions. However, if value depends on being able to stir emotion, incentive value is not an "out there" property of an object or event but is rather something that goes on inside the person. Emotional reactions to things change, and the values of incentives change along with them; and whatever it is that changes value also changes people's inner experience — what they think about, notice, and feel — as well as their actions.

There is a second reason why the question of incentive value is important: Knowing which events influence incentive value helps to understand and predict changes in behavior and inner experience that might otherwise seem somewhat mysterious. Consider some examples. A person of twenty becomes inflamed with dedication to a social cause that would have bored her at sixteen and mystified her at twelve. An adult party-goer has trouble restraining himself from gobbling up olives he spurned a few years ago. A sharecropper envies the twelve-thousand-dollar income of the person who runs the nearest grocery, who in turn envies the forty-thousand-dollar income of his grocery chain's lawyer, who is seriously considering chucking it all for a subsistence farm. A couple with a comfortable, good marriage wonder whether to end it because it has ceased to be fully exciting. A manager is promoted to vice president of his firm and becomes seriously depressed. His competitor again failed to be promoted and also becomes seriously depressed. A *nouveau riche* family feels rebuffed socially and spends itself into financial straits to gain acceptance. A successful physician becomes alcoholic. Here are some of the human stories that a theory of inner experience — a theory of the sense that life is meaningful — must be able to shed light on. What are the qualities of inner experience that underlie such stories? What can we say about the interplay between such people's life situations and their inner experiences?

The Growth of Value

Some things are inherently valuable. That is, everyone comes into the world programed to pursue some things and to avoid others. Human infants seem to value the opportunity to suck on a nipple that provides milk and seem to respond to being held. Just what it is about sucking or being held that signals "Value!" to the infant brain is still a matter of dispute. Nevertheless, it seems clear that there are such signals — particular properties of transactions with the environment that somehow feel good or bad from the very beginning. From birth on, human infants prefer curved contours to straight ones (Fantz, Fagan, & Miranda, 1975) and they pay the most attention to things that move and are sharply set off from their background (Lewis & Brooks, 1975). These are, of course, properties of the human face — properties that can be much more easily programed into the brain than something as abstract as "human face." Perhaps they provide the instinctive base whereby babies gaze at their mothers' faces and charm them into putting up with babyhood. Women's pupils dilate with pleasure when they look at pictures of babies. Their dilation is, of course, an involuntary sign of emotion, not something put on to meet social expectations. Furthermore, when they look at cartoons, the more the babyish features have been exaggerated — proportionately larger heads, eyes lower on the face, and so on — the wider women's pupils grow (Hess, 1970). Men are also attracted to pictures of babies (Berman, 1975) and, in fact, so are other babies (Lewis & Brooks, 1975)! Human infants also come wired to avoid certain negative incentives such as pain, sudden loud noises, and stimuli that are too different from what the infant has learned to deal with.

Not all values that are programed into the organism need be operative at the beginning of life. Just as a person is programed biologically to end up walking but does not display this until a year or so after birth, so some values require maturation or special biological conditions to take place before the values can be manifested. Infants cannot become afraid of strangers until they have learned to tell them apart from familiar people, for instance, and they cannot smile at a clown's antics until they have learned enough about what to expect from ordinary people. Judith Bardwick (1971), an investigator on the psychology of women, was taken aback at her own inner experiences when she gave birth to her first child. She felt an overpowering tenderness and protectiveness toward her new infant for which neither decades of living nor specialized professional experience had prepared her.

It would be easy to multiply these examples, for instance by describing inherently negative incentives — such as being cold or suddenly being dropped — or by citing the extensive evidence of programed values in other species — young ducks fleeing the silhouette of a hawk, mice working for the chance to attack another mouse, paradise fish working for the chance to threaten their mirror images, and so on. The important point here is that organisms have built into them a certain set of positive and negative values — a set of specifications about what to go after and what to avoid — that forms an innate basis for action.

Granted that this is true, it is also true that this repertory of values begins to change as soon as it is exercised. Especially in the case of humans, it soon becomes modified and greatly enlarged. Even small children develop attachments to objects and events that could not possibly have been foreseen in their neurology: particular stuffed animals, people, toy trucks, shirts, spoons, games, grandparents, sounds, tastes, rituals, and so on, and on! Clearly, values grow and spread until each item in an enormous inventory of items has a certain value. How does this come about? We shall consider three kinds of ways: various forms of conditioning and learning, changes in the context of the thing valued, and obstacles to attaining it.

Learning to Value

There are different ways to learn and therefore different ways of learning to value. There are times in one's life when simply being around and paying attention to something endows it with value. Probably throughout life, things gain value when they occur in association with other events that are already valued. Finally, of course, realizing that something can help one to attain a valued goal gives the helping instrument value it would not otherwise have. We shall look more closely at each of these ways of gaining value.

Imprinting, attachment, and other biologically "prepared" learning. During the first 30 or so hours of a duckling's life, it is inclined to pay attention to moving objects around it and, if it is not confined, to follow the object, whether the object be a person, toy train, or decoy. In nature, of course, it is likely to be a mother duck. Once the duckling has had this kind of exposure to the object, it forms a strong attachment that may be lifelong. It follows the object around, seeks shelter with it, and, in adulthood, may court it sexually. Once it has formed the attachment and the first 30 hours of life are past, the duckling forms no further such attachments. The object of the attachment will have no serious competitors. This process of forming an attachment is called *imprinting*. Because it happens only or most strongly during a certain time in the organism's life, that time is called a *critical period*.

The behavior of the ducklings after they have been imprinted is an example of "attachment" behavior, which is by no means confined to ducks or to other birds. Imprintinglike phenomena have been observed in a number of mammalian species. For instance, ewes develop an attachment to their lambs, but if the lamb is removed during the first few hours after birth the ewe will reject it. Furthermore, if the lamb is removed from its flock for a few days during a critical period when it is older, it loses its attachment to the flock and becomes a maverick. Whether a dog becomes a "house dog" that is intimately attached to people or a "kennel dog" that keeps its reserve depends on whether it spent a critical period during its "juvenile" stage with people or other dogs. Infant rhesus monkeys that are deprived of their mothers or even deprived only of play with their agemates develop various kinds of social abnormalities that are very hard or impossible to reverse through later experience. A mother-deprived monkey, for instance, even though otherwise well cared for, seems unable to mate and unable to form a normal attachment to its own offspring.

Not only is attachment widespread among mammals, it is actually only one of many forms of biologically "prepared" forms of learning (Seligman & Hager, 1972). For instance, organisms can learn to fear certain kinds of stimuli much more readily than they can learn to fear others. In all likelihood, some of the most common human phobias, such as fear of the dark or of snakes, are examples of fears which humans are "prepared" to learn easily. Another, especially powerful example of prepared learning is learned aversion to foods that were tasted, perhaps coincidentally, just before the taster became nauseated (Garcia, Hankins, & Rusiniak, 1974). For instance, western sheep ranchers have discouraged coyotes from attacking lambs by leaving around pieces of mutton poisoned in such a way as to produce severe nausea.

There is little question that humans are also biologically "prepared" to learn certain behaviors: certainly food aversions, certain fears, and attachment to other humans. Interestingly, human infants and infant monkeys and dogs show very similar kinds of distress when they are separated from parents or placed in strange surroundings — similar enough to suggest that humans, too, have a built-in motivational basis for social behavior (Scott, Stewart, & DeGhett, 1973). This basis, in all likelihood, consists of an innate process such as imprinting by means of which humans learn to value particular people and objects, but only further research can tell us whether, when, and to what.

Conditioning. Granted that people may begin their lives with a natural program of possible satisfiers, and granted even that some of these wired-in satisfiers do not become effective until sometime later in life, it is still obvious that most of the things and happenings that people enjoy and work for are different from these and could not have been wired in. Most psychologists have supposed that the many kinds of incentives that delight people are nevertheless derived from the basic innate ones. The question, then, is how were they derived? One important kind of process that seems to imbue new things with the incentive value of older ones is conditioning.

The basic idea of conditioning was developed by I. P. Pavlov beginning at latest by the 1890s. While studying the factors that cause dogs to salivate, he unexpectedly noticed that dogs often began to salivate before he had put any food in their mouths. Upon investigating further, he saw that the dogs were slobbering not just to the taste or smell of food, but to whatever stimuli regularly preceded it, such as the sight of an experimenter or the sound of a bell; eventually they even responded to stimuli that preceded the stimuli that preceded the taste and smell of food. The taste and smell of food Pavlov called *unconditional* (or unconditioned) stimuli (that is, stimuli whose ability to stimulate salivation was not conditional on a learning process). The formerly neutral stimuli whose occurrence seemed to predict the unconditional stimuli he called *conditional* (or conditioned) stimuli, since their effect on salivation depended on a learning process. This particular kind of learning process has come to be called *conditioning* (*classical*, *Pavlovian*, or *respondent* conditioning). The particular form observed by Pavlov has since then been found to be a far more general process than one that affects salivation, and it has, in fact, been proposed as the basis for all learning. Its main characteristic in these more general forms is that an organism comes to treat a formerly neutral stimulus in some of the ways it had previously treated another stimulus that regularly followed the neutral one.

Of course, an organism does not react to the conditioned stimulus in precisely the way it would to the unconditioned one — the dogs did not (so far as was recorded) try to eat Pavlov or his bell — and there is a considerable body of opinion that conditioning sets up not a true reflex but rather an expectation (Bolles, 1972; Brewer, 1974). In this view, it is not that the conditioned stimulus (say, the ringing of a bell) produces reflexive salivation, but rather that the bell leads the dogs to expect a feeding, for which they salivate in anticipation.

This point is important to our discussion, because if conditioning does nothing more than arouse expectations, how can it explain the passing of value from one thing to the next? Fortunately, there is evidence that conditioning does transmit value, in humans as well as animals.

First of all, people and animals can be conditioned to fear things. If the original fear was powerful enough, the conditioned fear may become virtually permanent. Twenty years after one group of World War II veterans had broken down emotionally in combat, they were still experiencing marked stress (Archibald & Tuddenham, 1965). Among their many psychiatric symptoms, they still found certain stimuli unpleasant that reminded them of combat: sounds of airplanes, firecrackers, other sudden loud noises, and combat scenes in films and on television. The lasting effects of traumatic fear have also been shown in a rather brutal laboratory experiment (Campbell, Sanderson, & Laverty, 1964). These investigators surprised a group of alcoholic patients by injecting a substance (Scoline) that temporarily paralyzes skeletal muscles, including those needed for breathing. Thus, these patients unexpectedly found themselves unable to breath or move for up to two minutes. Understandably, they were extremely frightened. During the period in which they were paralyzed, the experimenters played them a certain tone. Although the patients never again received Scoline, they continued to show ever stronger signs of physiological (GSR) arousal when presented with the tone up to three weeks later, which was as long as the investigators followed them. Clearly, people try to avoid things that remind them of terror, even if the things themselves are quite harmless.

Things also gain value if they are associated with rewards and they lose value if they are associated with lack of reward. There are both animal and human experiments to show this. In the case of rats, for instance, investigators rewarded their animals in one place when they were very hungry and in another place when they were only slightly hungry. Presumably, eating is more pleasant when one is hungrier. When the rats were tested with medium hunger, they chose to feed in the place they had fed in when very hungry (Kurtz & Jarka, 1968). The *place* had apparently gained enough value to attract the rats, even though it was the same as the other place in every other way. Places in which animals experience disappointments, on the other hand, become downright unpleasant. When hungry rats who are used to being fed in a certain place are disappointed by putting them there without food, they are willing to work in order to get out of that place, even if it means learning a new response to escape the scene of their disappointment (Daly, 1969a, b).

People can be shown to change their preferences through conditioning, as well. Jum Nunnally and his associates (Nunnally, Duchnowski, & Parker, 1965; Nunnally & Faw, 1968; Nunnally, Stevens, & Hall, 1965), working with children, measured value in two ways: what the children said about a thing and how much time they spent looking at it. The experiments were set up as games in which the children would associate an object — a particular geometric figure, for instance, or a nonsensical combination of letters (a *nonsense syllable*) — with winning something, another object with losing something, and yet another object with neither winning nor losing. Then the experimenters could discover whether the children later said nicer things about the objects that had been associated with winning and whether they later looked at them longer than at the others when they were all on display. The apparatus they typically used was a carnival type of gambling game, such as a spin wheel with a pointer that could come to rest on one of 18 spaces. Each space was marked, for instance, by one of three nonsense syllables, and the child player would receive two pennies if the pointer stopped on a ZOJ, would receive nothing if it stopped on a MYV, and would have to give back a penny if it stopped on a GYQ. In each of these cases the child was a helpless beneficiary or victim — there was nothing to *do* with the nonsense syllables or geometric forms, but they provided information about whether the child would win or lose. (In the experiment by Nunnally and Faw the child did have to use the nonsense syllables. It had to learn which nonsense syllable on a lid meant reward, which syllable meant loss, and which meant neither, in order to choose the right lid; but the results were consistent with the other experiments.) These experimenters used several kinds of games, stimuli, rewards, ages of children (from five to twelve), opportunities to say things about the stimuli, and measures of how long the children looked at each. The results were quite consistent. Children said the nicest things about stimuli that had been associated with winning and spent the most time looking at them. They said the worst things about the stimuli associated with losing and spent the least time looking at them. In the only test to see how long these effects would last, the children were still giving greater praise for the reward-associated stimulus three weeks after the last conditioning (game) session.

Thus, in these experiments, simple stimuli about which the subjects could have had no systematic preferences took on different values according to the events that immediately followed them. It seems as if value can be conditioned. This is not, of course, to say that these conditioned values were very strong — it is doubtful that any subjects would have laid down their lives for a ZOJ — but these values were there, both in what subjects said and in what they chose to look at, and they persisted over time.[1]

All of these findings, a little stark because of the need for tight experimental controls, confirm more rigorously what we have suspected right along. Popular songs have long had the singer declare the high value of "the street where you live" and "all the old familiar places," and folk knowledge is aware that the way to a man's heart is through his stomach. The folk knowledge, as introductory psychology textbooks are fond of saying, is of course overgeneralized and often contradictory. The experimental results help to specify what is necessary in order for something to be true and what is not. Most crucially, the neutral stimulus must *predict* the already valued one in order to gain value; that is, it must frequently occur before or along with the already valued stimulus and must occur less often without it.

Familiarity. It is sometimes hard to know in a particular case what the factors were that caused something to become valuable. For instance, what is it that causes people to take on such pronounced preference for some foods rather than others? Why are certain grubs, fat and sweet when roasted, a delicacy to Australian aborigines and utterly repulsive to shoppers in Sheboygan? Why do Americans eat shrimp by the ton and retch at the thought of grasshoppers? Is there an imprinting process at work here that sanctifies the familiar and condemns the exotic? Is it a matter of conditioning, in which familiar foods are associated with pleasant times and strange foods are associated with the disdain of parents and friends who have disparaged them? It is too soon to say. However, beyond imprinting and conditioning, there appears to be yet another factor at work, which Zajonc (1968) calls "mere exposure." Simple familiarity changes feelings about things.

Human infants, human adults, and rats change their preferences for nonsense words, photographs, abstract pictures, mobiles, Chinese ideographs, and other things after seeing them repeatedly. The results show that familiarity can foster either liking or disdain, depending on circumstances, through at least three kinds of processes: reducing fear, enabling the person to master the stimulus, and arousal.

Repeatedly showing someone something that at first frightens them reduces fear by demonstrating that the thing is harmless. During the second six months of life, human infants often develop a strong fear of strangers, for instance — until, of course, the person is no longer strange.

At first, people dislike or even fear complex stimuli to which they are unaccustomed. Faced with a new type of picture or musical composition, for instance, they may feel overwhelmed by what they experience as a sea of unorganized and uninterpretable intricacies. People like their world to have a degree of predictability, which complex, "different" stimuli lack. However, when people are shown strange stimuli repeatedly, they have an opportunity to inspect them, find patterns in them, begin to develop a sense of predictability about them, and therefore gradually increase their liking for them.

Observing this, Zajonc (1968) concluded that, as a general law, "mere exposure" to things increases liking for them. However, this is true only if the stimuli were originally not only new but also strange, and mere exposure to strange stimuli increases liking for them only up to a certain point of familiarity. After that point, continued exposure causes people to like them less, presumably out of boredom (Greenberg, Uzgiris, & Hunt, 1970; Harrison & Crandall, 1972; Smith & Dorfman, 1975).

Just where the critical point of familiarity lies at which interest begins to wane is still debatable. Probably, however, it is the point at which the stimulus seems completely explored, at which no surprises remain (see Stang, 1975) and viewing of it has become relatively automated (or *integrated*, to use a concept developed elsewhere [Klinger, 1971]. At that point, stimuli become less able to command conscious attention — they are "taken for granted" — and cease to arouse the viewer.

Arousal seems to play a part in this picture in yet another way. Organisms seem to prefer to maintain a certain moderate level of physiological and experiential arousal, a level somewhere between harassment and boredom. Consequently, their preferences for stimuli depend in part on how aroused they feel at the time. A great variety of experiments has shown that after animals and humans have been aroused by noise, electric shocks, listening to incomprehensible recordings, and the like, they are more inclined to prefer familiar stimuli (familiar pictures, places, objects, and so on), but after having been subjected to a dull or familiar routine they are more likely to prefer novel experiences (Berlyne, 1967).

New challenges. As strange things become more familiar, they pass, as we have seen, through a period when they actually seem pleasing. In Chapter 3, we saw that whether an infant smiles at something depends in part on whether the thing is just different enough to pose a challenge but familiar enough so that the challenge can be mastered. For instance, an infant who has developed a firm concept of what its mother is like might smile if the mother dons a mask, but it might cry if the person approaching it is a stranger. Most of the investigators who have observed smiling in infancy have done so by giving their young subjects various things to look at and noting which ones they smiled at. It might appear that smiling is purely a spectator activity, but, of course, it is not. In fact, speaking of things that make infants laugh, "in the second half-year those items in which the infant *participated* became more potent (pulling the cloth from mother's mouth, reaching for the protruding tongue), and later, infants laughed more at their *own productions* (attempting to stuff the cloth back into mother's mouth)" (Sroufe & Waters, 1976, Pp. 179–180). In later infancy, children smile when they succeed in solving puzzles, especially hard ones (Kagan, 1971). Evidently, the reason that very young infants smile a lot at things they *see* is that making sense of what they see is at that stage the crucial challenge. As they come to know their way around the world of crib and family, and as they gain skills in manipulating that world, the challenge shifts toward doing things with it.

The fact that much of this interesting information comes from studies of smiling and laughing is very significant. It allows us to conclude that smiling and laughing — and the delight they reveal — are innate responses to overcoming challenges. Of course, once something has been thoroughly mastered it ceases to be a challenge and dealing with it is therefore no longer able to delight one so directly. However, mastering one thing usually brings into range other challenges that would have seemed too hard before. They would therefore now gain value, as the person recognizes that they are within his or her range and are therefore able to yield delight. Thus, new games, new academic courses, new jobs, and new tennis partners gain value as one's competence grows.

There is one more very important aspect of this idea. Arthur Koestler (1964) has already noted that humor and creative insight are matters of seeing new or unexpected relationships as ways out of confusion or difficulty. We can now see that the insights of humor and creative thinking in adulthood are part of a larger fact — conquering challenges is pleasing. But that means that there is an innate basis for many of the activities that we think of as distinctively human. Making scientific discoveries, exploring new lands, inventing a new machine, reaching a new understanding of some reality, portraying a landscape or a design with a new perspective, recognizing a new variation on an old theme, and so on — all are gratifying for the same basic reason, wired into our brains. It is an idea that greatly extends the range of innately specified human incentives.[2]

Instrumentality. People can change the value they place on something or someone sharply if they suddenly see that the object can help them get something they want or if they suddenly realize that it cannot. Consider your sudden warm feelings for the total stranger who just happens to be driving in your direction after you have missed the last train. For the would-be sailor, an obliging friend with a yacht may be valued more highly than the same obliging friend without one. The basic idea here is that one values things (and other people) partly according to how *instrumental* they are in helping one achieve valued goals.

This idea that instrumentally useful objects are valued has been woven into a number of theories, often called Expectancy X Value theories, for predicting various kinds of behavior, such as someone's attitude toward other races, a businessperson's preference for a moderately risky undertaking, or an employee's inclination to work hard. Let us take working hard as an example. Various Expectancy X

Value theories suggest that the forecaster find out (a) what things the person values that might be affected by hard work (such as a pay raise, promotion, longer vacation, or greater prestige), (b) how much he or she values each of them, and (c) how likely it is in the person's estimation that working hard might bring about (or block) each of these valued things. Then the forecaster would multiply the value of each thing times the probability it will be affected, and add up all of these products. The sum of the products is an indicator of the person's inclination to work hard.

Using this general approach, investigators have been able successfully to predict a wide range of attitudes and behaviors, such as attitudes toward other races, effort spent working, or engaging in sexual intercourse (Mitchell & Biglan, 1971). Raynor (1974) and his associates have found that students who believe that their grades are important for fulfilling longer-range goals earn higher grades than students who consider grades less instrumental. If people's attitudes and working patterns indicate how they evaluate their incentives, then people must value more highly those things they regard as instrumental in helping them achieve further goals.

There are also other ways in which being instrumental changes the value of something. Many of a person's goals are in effect subgoals that take on value only because they serve as stepping stones toward something else. Ever since the dawn of the Western university, professors have lamented the fact that most of their students value their educations not for the value of education as such but because higher degrees are passports to attractive careers. Sometimes, of course, an activity engaged in as a stepping stone may prove enjoyable in its own right, in which case the person may continue to value the subgoal when it is no longer useful for other purposes. Gordon Allport (1937) spoke of motives becoming "functionally autonomous" of their original bases, such as the retired sea captain who continues to love the sea. Often, however — perhaps more often — regard for the subgoal dissipates when it has outlived its previous usefulness, such as a worn-out car or a worn-out alliance.

When a person comes to value something because it is instrumental for gaining something else, we are assuming that the person starts out with little interest in the thing for its own sake. (Interest in something for its own sake is called *intrinsic* interest, the rewards of which are *intrinsic* rewards. If one performs an activity to get something else, one's interest is called *extrinsic*. One is then working for *extrinsic* rewards.) A two-year-old, who doesn't know yet about the extrinsic value of money, would much rather have two shiny pennies than a wrinkled old dollar bill. When the child finds out what the dollar will buy, its value in the child's eyes rises sharply. However, if we start out with some activity that the person already enjoys for its own sake and make it instrumental for achieving something else, the person is likely to gain less enjoyment from it later — its intrinsic value will fall. That is true at least when the extrinsic rewards for the activity have little in common with the activity itself (Eden, 1975). For instance, if children are given special rewards for drawing, which they already enjoyed for its own sake, they will lose some of their intrinsic interest in it (Lepper & Greene, 1975).

In general, it seems as if being instrumental makes activities more attractive if they were originally things in which the person had little interest but makes them less attractive if the person already enjoyed them (Calder & Staw, 1975; Kruglanski et al., 1975). There seem to be at least two exceptions to this rule, however. First, take the case in which people already find an activity interesting. Rewards will make them like it even more if the rewards are an inherent part of the activity. For instance, children enjoy tossing coins more if they get to keep the coins than if they have to turn them in for points; but they enjoy building with wooden blocks more if it is for points than if it is for money (Kruglanski et al., 1975). Winning money is part of coin-tossing, but it is not part of building with blocks. Second, there is a limit to how much instrumentality can raise the value of a dull activity. If an activity is intrinsically uninteresting, people like the activity less if they feel overpaid than if the rewards seem appropriate (Gerard, Conolley, & Wilhelmy, 1974). How can we explain all these complexities?

There are at least seven ways in which extrinsic rewards can make something less enjoyable. First of all, if someone feels overpaid for doing something, they may conclude that the task must be objectionable for anyone to pay so highly to have it done.[3] They may even feel guilty about it, thus leaving the task encumbered by unpleasant emotions.

Second, getting rewarded for some activities robs them of their intrinsic value quite directly. For instance, if a person volunteers to give blood in order to feel good about helping people, offering the person payment for the blood defeats the purpose of giving. As a result, volunteer blood donors are actually *less* likely to give blood if they are offered $10 payments (Upton, 1973, described by Condry, 1975).

Third, extrinsic rewards may set up an "incentive contrast." That is, the activity was intrinsically rewarding to begin with. Now, with the addition of extrinsic rewards, it is even more rewarding, in total. Later, however, when it is no longer rewarded extrinsically, there is a letdown. People judge things not by absolute standards but by what they are used to. They judge the activity as less rewarding than before, and hence lose some of their interest in it.

Fourth, if people become accustomed to thinking of an activity as something they do in order to get something else, they may overlook it as a possibility when they search for something enjoyable to do. To perform the activity for its own sake might not occur to them, or it might seem strangely out of place (Greene & Lepper, 1975).

Fifth, when one does something for an extrinsic reason, one must also accept outside criteria of how good it must be and how long it must take. Such criteria do not emanate from one's enjoyment of the activity itself (Greene & Lepper, 1975). For instance, if one paints pictures as a hobby, one can decide just how to paint them and when to stop when one tires of painting. Commercial artists, on the other hand, have to keep the client in mind when deciding how to execute a painting and may have a deadline by which it must be done. They may have to stop before a painting feels right or may have to keep working after they are bored with it; and when it is done they may feel that it is not completely "theirs" if it is not the way they would personally have preferred to do it. Thus, they may come to enjoy painting for its own sake less than before.

Sixth, doing something for an extrinsic purpose may distort the activity itself. For instance, students in one study (Condry, 1975) were offered money to solve problems. Some were given all the money at the start of the session and others were given 50 cents for each problem they solved. The second group chose easier problems and were more interested in getting right answers than in learning good methods that would make them more competent.

Seventh, when one is doing something for the sake of getting something else, one's attention may be distracted from the activity to the extrinsic framework of rewards and demands within which one is doing it. Distraction from something enjoyable may reduce one's enjoyment of it (Reiss & Sushinsky, 1976).

In short, it may be that when one starts to do something for extra pay that had been enjoyable before (drawing, writing, or potting, for instance), one does it differently. Perhaps one works more efficiently and pays less attention to the pleasant experience of the activity as such. In the process, it is possible that the activity loses some of the very characteristics that had once made it a pleasure in itself. These factors are not likely to be as prominent if the "extrinsic" reward is an integral part of the activity, since it is then unlikely to change the way the activity is performed and the good feelings evoked by rewards are more likely to become directly associated with activities of which they are a part.

Learning to appreciate. Finally, there is one more kind of learning that raises the value of things in a person's eye, and that is learning to recognize the rewarding features of things with which one is already acquainted. A jacket that a person buys for its looks may turn out to be made of a pleasantly soft fabric, which adds to the pleasure of wearing it. A simple-appearing game that a competitive player tries out disdainfully may turn out to be harder than it looked and may therefore gain the status of an appealing challenge (e.g., Weiner, 1966).

Changes in Value Resulting from Changes in Context

Quite often the value of something changes for a person without any change in the thing itself and without the benefit of any new learning having occurred, but simply because the thing has been placed in a new context. We tend to think of ourselves as seeing the world in absolute terms and as making judgments about the world purely on its absolute merits, but the fact is that in most instances our perceptions and judgments are relative. When we are children earning half a dollar an hour for helping out, two dollars an hour seems a handsome wage. Later, it will seem the minimum tolerable. Still later, it will be an insult. During a Minnesota January, a day when the temperature rises to 40° F seems balmy. In July a night that cold seems insufferable. A twenty-pound backpack feels quite different depending on whether we put it on after having carried nothing or whether we put it on after having carried a forty-pound backpack.

These everyday observations have parallels in the scientific literature of psychology. Harry Helson has tried to answer the question of how people arrive at their standards of size (or weight, brightness, and so on) against which to judge other things as being large or small. For instance, when you speak of having seen a large mushroom, compared to what was it large? How did you decide to call it "large"? Helson concluded from his experiments that people build up inside them a subjective notion of the average size (or amount) of each kind of thing they have encountered recently — in our example, the average size of the mushrooms you have seen recently — and use that as their standard of what is medium. (Technically, the "average" is the geometric mean [Helson, 1964].) This subject standard he called the person's *adaptation level* for the kind of thing being judged. For instance, if a person lifts a series of weights weighing 200 grams, 250 grams, 300 grams, 350 grams, and 400 grams, the theoretical adaptation level is 254 grams, and experimental subjects in fact were observed to regard 249 grams as a "medium" weight.[4]

Not only do things seem different depending on the framework in which they are experienced, they may also then have different incentive values. Even rats, for instance, will work harder for a certain size of reward if it follows a series of smaller rewards than if it follows a series of larger rewards (Adamson, 1971). And so it seems to be with people. The children of the wealthy suburbs mock the housing developments of other suburbs that the ambitious poor of the central cities are striving some day to occupy. The clothing industry is able to sell unneeded new clothes by deliberately shifting the public's adaptation levels for hemlines, lapel widths, trouser flare widths, and color brightnesses, and therefore a suit that once looked "just right" now looks outmoded and a bit bizarre.

A number of theorists have even proposed that pleasure itself depends on having experiences that are slightly different from the person's adaptation level, and that larger discrepancies are the cause of displeasure (Hebb, 1949; McClelland, Atkinson, Clark, & Lowell, 1953). A number of experiments support this idea (reviewed by de Charms, 1968, and Eisenberger, 1972). For instance, substances that are slightly more sour, bitter, or salty than average are generally experienced as pleasant, whereas more strongly flavored substances are experienced as unpleasant. Music that is very different from what we are used to — very discordant, for instance, or involving very different beats and scales — seems unpleasant at first, but after we have listened to enough of it the new music comes to seem pleasant. If one listens to it too often, it becomes monotonous, except, perhaps, if it is complex enough so that a listener can keep fixing his attention on different aspects not closely attended to in the past.

Taken at face value, this discrepancy theory of pleasure obviously does not apply in all cases, and the experimental evidence for it is rather weak (Eisenberger, 1972). However, the general idea embodied in it can be taken a step further and made to apply to a wider variety of cases. What we need to add (the idea is Berlyne's, 1971) is the notion that deriving pleasure from something depends not on the qualities of the objects and events as such, but on the effects those qualities have on the person. Specifically, Berlyne suggests that the pleasantness or unpleasantness of something depends on the extent to which it succeeds in "arousing" the person: whether, for instance, it puts one to sleep (extreme low arousal) or sends one into panic or fury (extreme high arousal). Arousal can occur at any level between these two extremes, and the various degrees of arousal can be defined in terms of brain electrical activity, muscular tensions, visceral and glandular activity, and so on. In Berlyne's view, for which he marshals an impressive array of evidence, being aroused from a low starting level of arousal is pleasant but, after a certain point, increasing arousal is less and less pleasant until one reaches the level at which still further arousal is definitely unpleasant. For instance, a favorable, unexpected turn of events — your best friend telephones — may be a pleasant surprise, but when a good friend pops in unannounced from another part of the world the pleasantness may at first be outweighed by a distinctly unpleasant sense of "shock," which may take a period of readjustment to dissipate.

This idea, that medium arousal is pleasant but high arousal is not, rescues the discrepancy-from-adaptation-level theory because many of the characteristics that make something arousing depend on discrepancies from adaptation level. For instance, very loud sounds (compared with those you have become used to) are more arousing than soft sounds. So, too, is unexpected silence when you have been used to a certain level of commotion. Stimuli (music, works of art, conversations, and so on) are more arousing if they are complex compared with those in a person's recent average experience than stimuli that are about average. Therefore, the "arousal potential" of objects and events often (but not always) coincides with departures from the person's previous adaptation level.

It consequently seems safe to conclude that the value of something depends on how it compares with the person's adaptation level for that kind of thing. It also follows that if the person's adaptation level for something drops, its value may become greater than before. For people in love, other friendships sometimes seem to lose some of their significance. When their passion subsides, the older friendships regain some of their lost value. To someone who has always enjoyed financial security, financial security as a life goal seems banal, but its value quickly rises after a period of extended hardship.

Obstacles

It is one of the well-known perversities of the human character that people value highly what they cannot have. At least, that is so at certain times. Evidence is mounting that the value of something desirable rises when it is encumbered by obstacles or by the threat of constraint.

Give adults a set of choices (for instance, of phonograph records) and then let them know that one of them will be unavailable after all. On the average, the unavailable option will come to seem more attractive than if it had remained available (Brehm, 1972; Worchel, 1974). After the city of Miami banned phosphate detergents, Miami housewives rated phosphate detergents as more effective than did housewives in Tampa, where phosphates remained available (Mazies, 1975). The same general effect can be produced by making one of the options costlier than the others. Even when a person makes his or her own choice between a set of alternatives, there is a sense of regret about having deprived oneself of the other options, and they briefly seem more attractive than before (Brehm, 1972).

Children experience the same kind of effect as adults. When a film that children are watching is interrupted and they are led to believe that it cannot be resumed, they suddenly think of it as being a much better film than children do who see it uninterrupted (Mischel & Masters, 1966). When children are asked to rate the attractiveness of good-tasting foods, they rate food they cannot have for another week as better-tasting and more exciting than the same food if they can have it right away (Nisan, 1973). Knott (1967; Knott, Nunnally, & Duchnowski, 1967), in a series of experiments, had children play a "fishing game" in which they were to fish for pill boxes with a magnet. Landing a box got the subject a coin that had been placed inside it. The magnet, however, was electric, and the experimenter had the switch. Half of the subjects found the box dropping off their magnet every time they were close to landing it. These frustrated subjects later overestimated the sizes of coins. They spent more time looking at pictures of coins and of nonsense syllables (such as KEB) that had been printed on the boxes that got away when these pictures were displayed along with others. When they were faced with three stick figures, each having the "name" of one nonsense syllable, and were asked to choose statements to describe the stick figures, such as "Who has the most friends?", or "Who is mean to animals?", they said nicer things about the stick figure named after the boxes that got away than they said about other stick figures.

One way that the value of something may rise, then, is through the thing becoming unavailable, harder to get, or delayed.[5] It seems as if there is a psychological law of supply and demand that operates parallel to the economic law. When things are in demand and their supply is curtailed, their subjective value rises, whatever may happen to their price.[6] It is possible, of course, that the rise in subjective value occurs because of the person's experience with the fact that at least Western white society tends to place a higher value on things that are hard to do or get. However, it seems likely that blocked incentives rise in value without benefit of special cultural conditioning. Apart from expressions of subjective value, people and animals behave in certain ways quite similarly when their efforts to achieve an incentive are frustrated. This matter will concern us again in the next chapter.

Summary

The values people place on things, we have seen, are far from fixed. We come into the world predisposed to value certain things — certain sensory experiences, actions, and meeting of challenges — and from this baseline our values rise and fall according to a variety of factors. Through conditioning, the values we assign to things innately are gradually extended to a large array of new things. Often things become somewhat more highly valued as we become more familiar with them. We value things according to how well they promise to advance goals beyond themselves, and the value we assign to them may rise or fall as our belief in their instrumentality toward these further goals rises and falls. Value depends on context, too: how something compares in our experience with others of its kind, especially recently. Since contexts may change drastically within a lifetime, so may the value of something. Finally, valued things temporarily gain even more value if obstacles arise between us and them.

Each of these factors that may increase the value we place on something can also, of course, work in reverse to reduce the value, but reductions in value are most likely not simply mirror images of gains in value. They include some additional factors, and they involve psychological complications. These are the subject of the section that follows and of the next chapter.

The Decline of Value

One feels inclined to say that the intention that man should be 'happy' is not included in the plan of 'Creation'. What we call happiness in the strictest sense comes from the (preferably sudden) satisfaction of needs which have been dammed up to a high degree, and it is from its nature only possible as an episodic phenomenon. When any situation that is desired by the pleasure principle is prolonged, it only produces a feeling of mild contentment. We are so made that we can derive intense enjoyment only from a contrast and very little from a state of things. (Freud, 1930, P. 23)

In this world there are only two tragedies. One is not getting what one wants, and the other is getting it. The last is the real tragedy. (Oscar Wilde, quoted by Richard Fernandez, 1973, P. 19)

"Highs" are always transitory. People experience deliriously happy moments that quickly fade, and all attempts to hang on to them are doomed to fail. Robert Frost once wrote wistfully that "Happiness makes up in height for what it lacks in length" [Thompson, 1970, P. 488]. Steak every night, or lobster every night, or Strudel every night — whatever may be your favorite food — soon loses its special attraction. Sexual relations — so often experienced by adolescents as awesomely magnificent — eventually often become just another (albeit pleasant) physical and interpersonal activity. Folk lore challenges newlyweds to place a bean in a jar every time they have sexual intercourse during their first year and then to take one out on each occasion thereafter, with the expectation that the jar will never run out of beans. Romantic love notoriously cools if it ripens into a close, open relationship. Prestige, power, and fame pall with time. People envied because they lead "the sweet life" or because they are celebrities nevertheless become bored. Happiness, it seems, not only cannot be pursued directly, except as a by-product; when caught it cannot be captured. That is Wilde's "real tragedy."

The rest of this chapter probes some important questions about the consequences of "getting it." Must everything that people attain lose value? Are there no dependable joys? How basic is this erosion of satisfaction? What is its cause? What is its function? The next chapter will then consider Wilde's first "tragedy," the one that feels most tragic at the time: losing something one values.

Let me stress at the outset what this view of man does *not* mean: It does not mean that all humans are doomed to lives of continuous misery. A great deal depends on the person's expectations. Someone with very modest expectations of life may very well lead a life of quiet and satisfying contentment, particularly if the person feels adequately loved and provided for, and therefore has nothing to compensate for in future life. In our Western society, however, such a person may well be a rarity, for three kinds of reasons.

First, society holds out to all young people the prospect of over-powering elation, elation both now-and-then and forever-after. Con-tentment is all well and good, but it cannot hold a candle to elation for sheer emotional power. Often, of course, the promise of elation is a systematic commercial lie, as when it lurks just behind a given hair rinse, a certain refrigerator, or a particular car. At other times, the promise may be fulfilled as a now-and-then high, as people experi-ence the thrill of an audience on its feet with applause, or the expan-sive freedom and ease of sudden great wealth, or the social privileges of high status. In cases like these, the promise will turn false only as these joys turn out not to be forever-after guarantees of great happi-ness.

Second, people in many social strata of our society make it plain to their children that they ought not to be satisfied *unless* they achieve the wealth, power, and prestige that is supposed to provide great happiness. The mass media, the schools, the churches, and many families keep pointing to the models their children are to follow, people who model "success" in all of its many conventional forms. Those young people who manage to resist the pressures for social climbing often succumb to the lure of a special magnificent love that will transform their lives forever. Thus, it seems likely (but I know of no sound social-scientific evidence) that most children from working-class, middle-class, and upper-class families labor under one or another of these expectations.

Third, many people whom society may have instructed to expect little (and quite a few of the others) have experienced some of the most fundamental emotional deprivations from which humans are capable of suffering, and they therefore genuinely need to demon-strate to themselves their basic worth. Besides, while they may have been relegated to live lives unenriched by success and romantic love, they can very easily observe the promises made to others — made as though to them. If, therefore, they do not actually strive to fulfill these promises by legitimate means, they may nevertheless live in hopes that they or their children will achieve them, one way or another, or they will live in bitterness at their exclusion.

Therefore, the people of Western society about whom we know most value and strive after elevating emotional experiences — elevated pride, love, lust, and joy. They are accordingly at the mercy of the sapping of value from their attainments, the gradual debasement of their gains, that this section is about. When the emptiness has set in, they may be far better off materially than their contented, unpresuming neighbor, but they may feel far worse for having lost a towering elation. (Remember the principle of the adaptation level.) It may be that only people who aspire after things of great value can fully experience great emptiness.

Satiation, Extinction, and Habituation

Psychologists use a number of terms to refer to a number of somewhat different kinds of experimental observations, all of which have some of the central characteristics of declining value, whether declining from positive value to neutral, from negative value to neutral, or, sometimes, from positive value to neutral to negative. For instance, Karstens (1928) asked people to perform a single kind of simple task for as long as they could stand to — tasks such as writing rows of hashmarks on sheets of paper or reading poems aloud. Despite her subjects' continued desire to cooperate, they eventually found the tasks so cloying that they had to give them up. Karstens called this satiation.[7] Pavlov found that if he repeatedly presented a conditioned stimulus (for instance, the sound of a bell) without the unconditioned stimulus following it (for instance, meat powder), the conditioned stimulus would soon lose the capacity to produce the conditioned response (for instance, salivation). Pavlov called this process extinction of the conditioned response. In general, experimental evidence indicates that all conditioned values extinguish if the valued objects are not at least occasionally paired with objects having unconditioned value (Wike, 1970). Many experimenters have found that if they repeatedly present a mild stimulus to animals or persons, the subjects respond to the stimulus progressively less strongly until eventually they do not respond at all. For instance, a person presented with a regular series of background clicks will make orienting responses (head turning, galvanic skin responses, contraction of peripheral blood vessels in the fingers, and other changes) to the first click and probably to several more, but eventually he or she will stop responding to the click, assuming that the click is truly "background" in the experiment and not a meaningful signal or cue, even though he or she hears it just as loudly as before (Hirschman & Brumbaugh-Buehler, 1975). This phenomenon is called habituation of the orienting response.

It is important to distinguish all these forms of habituation, satiation, and extinction from two other factors, fatigue and monotony. Karstens's subjects, for instance, were physically quite well able to continue after the point at which they quit their tasks. Indeed, some of them unwittingly did perform more of their tasks without even noticing it when the task was presented in another context. For instance, a subject whose task had been to write letters of the alphabet had no trouble whatever signing her name to the papers she had used, even though that involved writing, and even though her name included the letters she had rebelled at writing more of. Subjects in habituation experiments who have stopped making orienting responses to a repeated stimulus suddenly start orienting again if the old stimulus is accompanied by some new element — for instance, the same tone played longer than usual, more briefly, or at a different interval. (This is called *dishabituation*.) Therefore, the habituation or satiation observed in these experiments could not be due simply to fatigue. Karstens also tried varying the tasks assigned to some of her subjects in order to reduce monotony and found that variety did not save her subjects from satiation. Whatever is responsible for habituation and satiation operates in addition to fatigue and boredom.

On the other hand, as in the case of fatigue, a habituated or satiated response recovers with time off. Given some time away from clicks, a person will again make orienting responses to another click. Karstens's subjects were willing after a period of days or weeks to come back and resume their tasks. However, it generally takes fewer stimuli or fewer tasks for a person to habituate or satiate the second time around, and it takes fewer still on each successive occasion.

The kinds of experimental observations described above are by no means isolated cases. Sometimes, indeed, it seems as if everything habituates or satiates. Habituation of some kind has been observed at every level of animal life more complicated than protozoans, and it is possible that even the protozoans can habituate (Goodman & Weinberger, 1973; Wyers, Peeke, & Herz, 1973). There may be some kinds of reflexes that are not habituable — no one has ever found turtles' head-turning responses to habituate to a change in their balance, for instance (Goodman & Weinberger, 1973) — but nearly all reflexes do habituate (Thompson, Patterson, & Teyler, 1972). These reflexes include, of course, the orienting responses by which organisms turn their attention to unexpected events.

Habituation or something like it also affects incentive values. If birds such as ducklings, quail, and chaffinches are exposed repeatedly to models of their enemies, such as hawks and owls, they react with progressively less alarm (Melvin & Cloar, 1969; Petrinovich, 1973). When male Siamese fighting fish are exposed repeatedly to another male, they become less aggressive toward them (Peeke & Peeke, 1970). For fish like this, the opportunity to attack a rival is rewarding. Paradise fish, for instance, will "work" (by swimming through a certain ring, for instance) for the chance to see themselves in a mirror and to threaten their image; but after two hours of this, when they are swimming through the ring at the rate of more than 130 times per hour, the attraction begins to wear off, and their swimming-through-the-ring plateaus at about 48 times per hour (Melvin & Anson, 1970).

There is also evidence that sexual attraction habituates, owing to what has come to be called the "Coolidge Effect." The Coolidge Effect refers to the observation that when sexually "exhausted" males (rat, bull, ram, monkey, guinea pig), who have stopped copulating with a particular female partner, are presented with a different female, they revive sexually, whether by mounting and entering (Fisher, 1962; Fowler & Whalen, 1961; rats) or by increasing ejaculations (Beamer, Bermant, & Clegg, 1969, rams; Hsiao, 1965, rats; Wilson, Kuehn, & Beach, 1963, rats). Their revival is in comparison with their behavior when they are presented repeatedly with the same partner. The commotion and movement of partners is not enough. The partner must be different.[8] In fact, efforts in one sheep study (Beamer et al., 1969) to disguise the appearance of the partner failed to stimulate the rams, but introducing a new ewe five minutes after each ejaculation kept the rams responding at a high level.

These are instances of sexual habituation within a single session. There was no evidence in these experiments to suggest that the animals responded to any female less enthusiastically on later occasions. However, Fisher (1962), whose rats produced the largest Coolidge Effect ever observed, cautioned that although he obtained this effect with young males he was unable to make it work with "sexually experienced older males" [P. 618]. Perhaps they had become jaded by their experience — had become habituated to variety of females. Clearly, that kind of habituation takes much longer to establish than other kinds that have been observed.

Usually when people or animals totally habituate to something they simply stop responding to it. Presumably, then, the thing has taken on a neutral incentive value, since it ceases to have any impact on their behavior. Sometimes, however, if the stimulation keeps up or if the subject is forced to continue responding, the activity or stimulation becomes unpleasant. For instance, when a hungry human infant is touched on the cheek, it turns its head in the direction of the touch. If it is touched on the cheek repeatedly at intervals of from half a second to two seconds, its head-turning habituates and it stops responding. If the repeated touching continues, then after 30 seconds or so of no response it begins to turn its head *away* from the direction of touch (Prechtl, 1958). It is as if the infant were satiated with this game and sought to get away from it.

On a very different time scale and with a very different type of behavior, Karstens's subjects went through a rather similar process. Many of these subjects rather enjoyed the experimental tasks at first. For instance, reading poems was for some of them very pleasant. All of them were eager to cooperate with the experimenter. The first signs that satiation was setting in occurred when the subjects introduced some spontaneous variations into their tasks, such as grouping the hashmarks, writing them down in the shape of stars, or singing the poems. Later they often turned the task into a secondary activity, doing it automatically while turning the focus of their attention to something else. It became ever harder for them to pay attention to the assigned tasks, but they seemed determined to continue and actively fought the satiation that was engulfing them. As their satiation thickened, they began to devalue the task as stupid or became strongly attracted to alternative activities. Now subjects sometimes engaged in angry outbursts, sometimes destroying the products of their efforts, such as crumpling sheets of hashmarks. The anger was directed not at the experimenter but at the task and their reaction to it. Finally, often reluctantly and apologetically, subjects felt compelled to break off their activity. They could stand it no more.

When one considers this sequence of reactions in general terms — spontaneous variations, automatization, forced effort, devaluation, destructive outbursts, and finally quitting — it seems strikingly similar to the progression of events in major life involvements. Many marriages undergo similar progressions. So do many careers. In university life, for instance, one meets faculty members who begin with normal dedication to teaching, begin to feel a strong need to innovate in their methods, tire of innovation and seek major satisfactions and stimulation outside teaching — in politics, research, administration, consulting, fishing, and so on. While continuing to perform their major teaching duties, they find themselves having to exert increasingly explicit self-discipline, begin to question the value of their teaching at all, become hostile toward their students and institution, and change jobs if it is socially and economically feasible. Fortunately, academic life offers enough opportunities for varying one's activities so that many satiated teachers are able to find acceptable alternatives within academia. Then, too, the sabbatical system permits the satiation to dissipate from time to time.

Of course, the satiation process just described is not at all inevitable, for reasons we shall consider below. Nevertheless, the satiation process described by Karstens seems strikingly to fit the course of events in major life involvements. The resemblance raises the question of whether all are parallel consequences of a single process that debases incentive values.

Is It All One Process?

There are theorists (e.g., Thompson & Spencer, 1966) who believe that all of the various forms of habituation, extinction, satiation reflect a single kind of process in the organism. The evidence for believing this is that the behaviors involved follow a similar course and obey similar laws, even though these may take place on a drastically different time scale and even though the parallels may sometimes be obscured by the different kinds of circumstances in which they occur. Other theorists (e.g., Graham, 1973; Ratner, 1970) caution that the superficial differences in these behaviors probably reflect real differences in the underlying mechanisms. No one can at this time be very sure which view is correct. It is possible that both are correct, with appropriate qualifications.

The fact seems to be that habituationlike phenomena occur at all levels of nervous system complexity. Habituation has been observed in the activity of single neurons in the brain. It has been measured at the cut ends of a lingual nerve leading from a cat's tongue, the nerve sending fewer and fewer signals as the experimenter repeatedly washed a quinine solution across the tongue (Wang & Bernard, 1970). It has been studied intensively at the level of the spinal column, as cats whose spinal cords had been severed from their brains jerked their legs progressively less to repeated electric shocks (Thompson, Groves, Teyler, & Roemer, 1973). It has been found, as already described, in intact animals from the protozoa to humans, where, for instance, brain mechanisms cause infants to habituate to touches on the cheek and cause adults to stop orienting to repeated sounds. Finally, at the highest levels of complexity, we find animals and humans habituating or satiating to goals ranging from aggressive attack in fish to reading poems in humans. That is the range involved in experimental studies. If we add satiated marriages and careers to this list, we increase the range still further.

Despite the fact that all of these forms of "habituation" follow somewhat similar rules, it may not be safe to consider all of them the work of a single underlying set of neural mechanisms. That is primarily because the time relationships are drastically different. Habituation, we saw, dissipates to some extent with the passage of time (*spontaneous recovery*), but the rate of that recovery seems to depend on the kind of àctivity that is habituating. The kinds of intervals one finds in experiments that involve satiation with goals — for instance, the intervals between copulations or between attacks — would be more than enough to permit some simple reflexes to recover from habituation. Furthermore, there is some evidence (Davis, 1970) that animals exposed to rapid-fire stimuli become more habituated to them than to more widely spaced stimuli by the end of the same experimental session; but their habituation carries over better to the next day if the stimuli are more widely spaced. That is, the short-term results of the stimulation are different from the longer-term results.

These observations led Graham (1973) to propose that the reason the rapid-fire, short-interval stimuli are more effective in the short run is that in a rapid-fire sequence the next stimulus arrives before the organism has had time to recover from the previous one. (Technically, the next stimulus arrives during the *refractory period* of the previous one.) Therefore, two things happen. First, the organism is less able to respond to successive stimuli, which gives the appearance of habituation. Second, however, because the organism is not responding as fully to the stimulus as it could, it is not accumulating as much lasting habituation as it would if the stimuli were more widely spaced. Therefore, on the next day it will display less carried-over habituation. This assumes that, especially when faced with more widely spaced stimuli, the organism undergoes a kind of "learning" not to respond to the repeated stimulus, a learning that produces long-term, lasting habituation. Thus, Graham is suggesting that some forms of habituation are "refractory" phenomena and others are "learning" phenomena. It is the learning phenomena, of course, that are most relevant to the problem of declining incentive values. This theory suggests that under certain circumstances people "learn" to attach less value to the incentives in their lives.

Of course, even disregarding the refractory forms of habituation still leaves us with an awesome range of behavior to explain by a single mechanism — all the way from a rat's becoming less startled by repeated noises to a person becoming cloyed with reading poems and perhaps on to a person shucking a career or a marriage that has begun to pall. It is quite possible, however, that there is a basic habituation mechanism that can operate on many different levels of complexity. Perhaps such a mechanism can produce different results depending on the complexity of the neural machinery that it links up with. One might imagine, for instance, that if the mechanism were fastened just to the relatively simple machinery underlying the startle reflex, it would dampen startle behavior. But if it were also linked with the machinery of memory and motivation, the same habituation components might be able to dampen the person's affective reaction to all of the remembered characteristics of a complicated other person or professional activity. Furthermore, depending on the memory connections, that habituation (or satiation) might well be long-lasting.

For our present purposes, I shall assume that habituation or satiation does indeed operate at many levels, including the level of major human incentive values, and hence at the level of human values in general. There are many profound implications of this view, some of which we shall pursue through the remainder of this book. One immediate implication concerns a benefit of a person understanding that this process works in his or her own life. When people become satiated with a personal relationship or with an activity, they are inclined to criticize or belittle it, perhaps in order to justify their satiation. Knowing that satiation saps all values under some circumstances takes the onus of self-justification off the person experiencing the satiation, and it may therefore save the other person or the activity from being vilified while being abandoned.

What Habituates? What Does Not?

Although it must seem by now as though every conceivable kind of activity habituates, a little reflection makes it obvious that this is not so. Nobody habituates so completely to food that they stop eating. Although some physically healthy couples do stop engaging in sexual intercourse, most continue, though typically at a declining rate. Albert Schweitzer did not seem to habituate to his vocation in the Congo, and a very large number of less well-known individuals maintain their dedication to their work throughout life. At this date, a majority of American marriages are still terminated by death rather than divorce, and a significant number of these continue to be deeply gratifying to both members. Obviously there must be conditions that limit or prevent the decline of incentive values.

First of all, it is almost certain that some kinds of innate, wired-in incentives remain valuable to at least some extent. The taste of food, warmth on a cold night, orgasm, rest when tired, and undoubtedly some other sensations normally remain valuable. It is true that during a single occasion it is possible to satiate them, and this satiation may carry over to some extent to future occasions, as when one has had cheese for lunch so often that the thought becomes repulsive. However, the extent of carried-over satiation is limited, and it is reversible under certain conditions, such as extreme hunger.

There are probably also negative incentives to which people cannot become completely habituated. For instance, habituation of responses does not occur in the case of very intense stimuli, such as strong electric shocks or painfully loud sounds (Thompson et al., 1973). This is not necessarily because no habituation takes place in these cases, but rather because the effects of habituation are outweighed by a contrary "sensitization" process whereby the person becomes progressively more responsive to the stimulus each time it occurs. For instance, a person might one day notice a certain rattle in his or her car and might become concerned about what it portends. For a time the person may become extremely sensitive to the rattle and may even imagine it to be far more noticeable than it is. Thompson et al. believe that some sensitization goes on in most responses to stimuli and some habituation goes on in all. In most cases, the habituation becomes stronger than the sensitization (because, they believe, the sensitization itself weakens over time), and hence the response to the stimulus becomes weaker. But in some cases of very strong stimulation the sensitization remains stronger than the habituation and then the response to the stimulus continues indefinitely.

The human organism therefore is equipped to consider certain things as incentives under nearly all conditions. To be sure, it is possible to spoil one of the innate positive incentives by conditioning negative affect to it. For instance, cats who are shocked electrically each time they begin to eat may after a few shocks starve themselves rather than resume eating. Freud's discovery of rampant sexual inhibitions in middle-class Victorian Vienna testifies to the ease with which sexual pleasures can be spoiled by anxiety. Furthermore, depression (as we shall see in the next chapter) reduces appetites of all kinds. On the whole, however, there are abiding sensory pleasures that resist total habituation.

Beyond these considerations, there is one more very powerful factor that determines whether the value of something will decline. In order to describe this factor it is first necessary to recognize that actions vary according to how satisfying they are in and of themselves — how great their *intrinsic* value is — as contrasted with the extent to which they are valuable purely because they serve to produce some valuable result (and are *extrinsically* valuable). Chewing good-tasting food, for instance, and copulation are intrinsically valuable. Shifting gears in a car has little intrinsic value but a great deal of extrinsic value since it helps get us where we wish to go. Apart from flavor and orgasm, people learn to value a great many other incentives, as we saw above, by attaching pleasant affect to previously neutral objects and events. While these incentives are capable of stirring good feeling (or bad feeling, in the case of negative incentives), they can be said to be intrinsically valuable.

Now, the evidence strongly suggests that *only intrinsically valuable incentives lose value through habituation.* Extrinsically valuable incentives, which people use instrumentally to get something else, do not seem to lose value except as the ultimate goal may do so. Therefore, successful instrumental responses do not habituate. Of course, if these responses cease to be successful in attaining a further objective — if the extrinsically valuable incentive ceases to have extrinsic value — then the response will continue to be made and the incentive will continue to be valued only insofar as it might offer intrinsic satisfaction, and it is then subject to the same decline in value through habituation or extinction as other intrinsically valuable incentives.

The evidence for this idea comes from several sources. The orienting reaction, for instance, which habituates so readily to background stimuli, remains strong when the stimulus is one the subject is searching for. When incentive values that were produced by conditioning are reconditioned from time to time, the conditioned incentives remain valuable (Wike, 1970). Finally, Karstens (1928) reported some fascinating observations from her experiments with satiation. Not all of her subjects experienced satiation. Most of them were unpaid volunteers, and they usually satiated. One who was a psychologist experienced the usual amount of satiation in her first session with Karstens's tasks, but not when she undertook the second session with the goal of finding out just how long she might be capable of keeping on. For her, there was an objective, and each task she completed took her further toward it. For her, then, the tasks in the second session took on extrinsic value and she did not satiate. From this standpoint, it is particularly significant that there was an entire group of Karstens's subjects who experienced little satiation — a group of unemployed workers who were participating for pay. For them, too, the value of the tasks was largely extrinsic — they were a way of earning money.

Interestingly, Karstens found that subjects were slowest to become satiated with the tasks they were most indifferent toward, and they became satiated fastest with tasks they found either the most pleasant or the most unpleasant. The subjects who experienced satiation often reported their feeling as one of futility, as a sense that it was useless to go on doing these tasks because it made absolutely no difference whether they filled yet another page with hashmarks or read yet another poem. In other words, their satiation became complete when they ceased to take pleasure in the activity and viewed it as useless in accomplishing anything else.

It therefore seems reasonable to conclude that *what habituates during satiation is the affect associated with enjoying an incentive.* For habituation to take place, it is probably necessary that the incentive be attained and consummated, perhaps repeatedly. Until it does habituate, objects and actions that derive their value from being instrumental toward it will keep their value intact. Some incentives are innately satisfying and these will never habituate to the point of having zero value. Other incentives, whose attraction rests on no innate basis, may eventually become completely valueless through repeated enjoyment of them.

We can see these principles operate in one kind of behavior that people wish were not so stable — neurotic behavior. One of the features of neurotic behavior is that it seems insatiable. For instance, people driven by neurotic ambition seem never to have enough of what they seek. People who stay homebound because of their anxieties actually become more frightened to go out as time goes by. One common view among psychologists is that such people are driven or restricted by anxiety — by their diffuse fears of what might happen if they do not succeed or of what might happen if they do. Such people lead a fairly joyless existence; but as long as they do what their anxiety compels, they stave off what they regard (unconsciously, perhaps) as the worst that could befall them. They too are committed to a long-range incentive — a negative one — which they never experience. It, too, avoids becoming habituated — and their anxiety avoids being extinguished — because the negative goal is never met.

Habituation and Satiation of Innately Valued Incentives

Although innately valued incentives probably do not usually become valueless, experience with them does change the way in which they are valuable. The person who has tired of eating high cuisine shows no willingness either to go hungry or to settle for rice and beans. The person whose romantic love for a spouse has waned may nevertheless be unwilling to end the marriage and is likely to experience severe grief should the spouse die. Thus, incentives that can no longer provide the same high level of positive feeling as before can still produce strong negative feelings by disappearing.

One possible explanation for this (Solomon & Corbit, 1974) assumes that whenever anybody feels an emotion, whether positive emotion such as joy or negative emotion such as fear, the first emotion stimulates an "opponent process," an opposite emotional process whose effect is to reduce and eventually to cancel out the first emotion. The idea here is that organisms are designed to maintain a certain biological and psychological balance, which any strong emotional response disturbs. The effect of the opponent process is to bring the organism gradually back to normal neutral. Therefore, the love one person feels for another comes, after a long enough acquaintanceship, to be largely counterbalanced *in the presence* of the other person by loneliness. While the other person is there, the loneliness is not apparent, only the fact that the love is less fervent. When the other person is gone, the pleasure of his or her company (which the opponent process had been neutralizing) also ends, thus revealing the full extent of the opponent emotion: strong loneliness.

There are some other assumptions in this explanation. First, Solomon and Corbit assume that the strength of the opponent process grows with each occasion on which the person experiences the original emotion (pleasure, love, fear, or whatever) because of the incentive involved (food, spouse, falling, and so on). Therefore, the incentive is fully appreciated only on the first occasion and on successive later occasions the appreciation grows less and less. Second, they assume that the opponent process grows weaker with disuse. Therefore, long periods away from the incentive will revive some of the original subjective reaction, because the opponent process will be less able to spoil it by canceling it out. Third, they assume that the opponent process can be conditioned to various stimuli just as the original emotion can be.

What is the evidence for this explanation? First of all, the theory has several points in common with various theories of habituation and satiation. The idea of two processes operating in reaction to stimuli is fairly common, whether they are called sensitization and habituation (e.g., Graham, 1973; Thompson et al., 1973), instigating force and consummatory force (Atkinson & Birch, 1970), excitation and inhibition (e.g., Hull, 1952), or opponent processes. All of these theories can point to evidence that, with continued stimulation, responses to the stimuli change in strength, usually becoming weaker. The opponent-processes notion can rest partly on the same data as the various habituation theories in that the extent of observable habituation grows from one occasion to the next if the interval between them is not too long, and weakens from one occasion to the next if the interval between them is long enough to permit spontaneous recovery. However, opponent-processes theory differs from the habituation theories in two important respects. First, the habituation theories assume that sensitization and habituation are parallel *independent* reactions to the same stimulus, whereas the opponent-processes theory proposes that the second (opponent) process is a reaction to the first (original) emotional response. Second, the habituation theories seem implicitly to regard habituation as simply a lessening (perhaps by inhibition) of the habituating response, whereas the opponent-processes theory proposes that the dominant emotion is not reduced but is *opposed* by a second emotional process that is also capable of being experienced as a definite subjective state.

What is the evidence to support the opponent-processes view in these differences from habituation theory? There is some experimental evidence, the key feature of which is the phenomenon of emotional "overshoot." When a dog is first subjected to electric shocks, it reacts, as one might imagine, with panic, and when the shocks are over it acts subdued and stealthy. After many experiences with being shocked, however, it reacts to shocks with fairly well-controlled unhappiness, rather than with panic, but it greets the end of shock with great joy. During shock, the heart rate of an experienced dog rises sharply. At the end of shock, its heart rate plummets well below its normal baseline rate and then gradually recovers back to baseline. Novice parachutists are often terrified of their first jump and when they land they often act stunned. Experienced parachutists may be tense while anticipating their next jump, but not terrified; and when they land they feel exhilarated and jubilant. Thus, in each of these cases, an experienced subject greets the negative incentive involved with less negative feeling than before, and greets the end of the negative incentive with exaggerated pleasure.

Besides this evidence on fear responses, there is also some experimental evidence on attachment behavior in ducklings. If ducklings are left in the environment they were hatched in, they behave quite placidly, and they placidly accept a mother duck or an artificial "imprinting object" (for instance, a block of foam rubber) introduced by an experimenter. If the experimenter then removes the "imprinting object," the duckling emits distress calls, even though it is in the same environment in which it had seemed contented before the foam rubber block had been introduced. This is, of course, one kind of demonstration that "imprinting" takes place. However, only Solomon's opponent-process theory makes certain other predictions about the timing and course of the ducklings' distress. For instance, only opponent-process theory predicts that if the imprinting object is reintroduced briefly at short intervals, the ducklings will make increasing numbers of distress calls each time the imprinting object is removed; but if the intervals between presentations of the imprinting object are long enough, the number of distress calls after each presentation will stay the same. Furthermore, only opponent-process theory predicts that, if the ducklings have stopped calling and the imprinting object is presented briefly, the ducklings will resume their distress calls; and only opponent-process theory predicts further that the longer the presentation, the more calls they will make. These are quite nonobvious predictions, and they have all been confirmed in experiments with ducklings (Hoffman & Solomon, 1974). The fact that the theory is able to predict such detailed features of behavior is quite impressive.

The theory can make these predictions because it sees the opponent process as a reaction to the original emotional process, and also because the opponent process grows while the original emotion lasts and declines after it is over. Therefore, if a duckling is "grooving" on having its motherlike imprinting object nearby, it is building up an opponent process of distress that becomes evident when the imprinting object is taken away. The longer it enjoys the imprinting object, the greater its distress later, even though it had started to seem indifferent to the imprinting object while it was still there. If the imprinting object is kept away for a while, the distress will subside. However, if the object is reintroduced while the duckling is still very distressed, the duckling once again becomes contented, its hidden distress builds up even further, and its overt distress will be greater yet the next time it loses the imprinting object.

Solomon has applied this analysis to drug abuse (Solomon, 1976;

Solomon & Corbit, 1973). When people use a drug such as nicotine, alcohol, or heroin — all of which have a high potential for addiction — the drug makes them feel good for a while and therefore sets in motion an opponent process of discomfort. If the user waits until this has worn off, the opponent process will decay and no great craving will develop. However, if the user turns to the drug again while the opponent process is still strong — while still feeling the aftereffects of going off the drug — then the opponent process will build up even higher, and the user's distress and craving will be still greater the next time the drug wears off; and so on, into a thoroughgoing addiction.

Solomon's predictions concerning drug use have not yet been specifically tested in ways that clearly distinguish this theory from others. If they can be supported, drug-abuse treatment programs will gain some powerful new tools, and the theory will be on the path to forming a broad new theoretical basis for viewing human motivation and emotion.

Implications for the Meaningfulness of Human Lives

The ideas developed in this chapter have a number of important implications for the ways in which people order their lives. We have considered ways in which things come to take on value for people — ways in which the limited number of incentives that we are born to enjoy expand to the huge number that fully functioning adult humans can appreciate. We have also considered ways in which incentives lose value, after which they cease both to attract and to act as a focus for a person's sense that his or her life is meaningful. Although we cannot be sure that these views will turn out to be correct, they seem to provide the best approximation to truth that scientific information on the subject permits. It is therefore time now to trace out some of the implications of these views.

On Finding Habituation-Resistant Incentives

First, simple pleasures that are innate satisfiers, and perhaps some not-so-simple ones, would seem in the long run to be the most reliable incentives. These may include food, sex, drug-altered states of consciousness, rest, elimination of wastes, warmth and coolness (depending on body conditions), stroking, cuddling, other people's smiles, and perhaps a much longer list of experiences: a yawning chasm at one's feet, fire, changes in stimulation, the configuration of a baby, romantic love, attack when angry, benign surprises, seeing a familiar thing in a new way, exercising skills and capacities, and so on. The science of human ethology is not yet advanced enough to tell us with any assurance which human experiences have an innate basis for pleasing or displeasing us, but in the meantime the things listed seem to be likely candidates.

Beyond the innate pleasures, the most reliable incentives may be those that we believe will be highly satisfying but that are still in the future, safe from habituation and from the disillusionment of finding out they are not all they were cracked up to be. Pegged to these, of course, are all of the intermediate, extrinsic incentives and instrumental actions that derive their value — their ability to please and delight — largely from the more distant incentive, still untested and unhabituated. Perhaps for these reasons, devotion to other-worldly goals such as salvation or Nirvana provides such a stabilizing influence in the lives of the devout. For this reason, too, great ambition toward some future status — to be a billionnaire, a president, or a Nobel laureate — may keep people constantly working toward it, provided they receive enough encouragement to keep the goal subjectively realistic.

For these same reasons, the incentives that should be most subject to habituation are those whose value has been acquired through the influence of social learning, that are not intended to serve any purpose beyond themselves, with which a person can have ample experience. Thus, a career or a marriage that is by itself supposed to ensure living "happily ever after," or likewise membership in a church, being on one's good behavior, winning an election, or becoming executive vice president of a company, are likely to be disappointing if the person believed in the importance of their intrinsic value, rather than in their helpfulness for attaining some further or more elemental objective. That kind of faith is likely to pave the way for disillusionment and discontent.

The distinguishing feature of these habituable incentives is that, once attained, they cannot be long enjoyed, at least not in themselves. The status of having "married a wonderful person" or of having become the executive vice president may elate people when they first attain it, but thereafter they are forced simply to enjoy the *idea* of having made it. Of course, often a change in status brings with it other rewards that may be more lasting, but these are outside the status itself. If the person now discovers that the marriage also entails some inconvenient adjustments to the peculiarities of another real, individual human being, or discovers that executive vice presidents come under brutal pressures of work and politics, and if these outweigh the positive benefits that go with the new status, then disillusionment is bound to set in.

Yet, people do often strive after a goal not for what the goal might bring them in the way of realistic, day-to-day pleasures but because of their strong feelings about the goal, a goal that, once attained, cannot be savored except in the fading satisfaction of an abstract idea. This leads to something of a paradox. In earlier chapters we saw that when people become committed to striving for an incentive, their commitment sets in motion a "current concern," a state of being that organizes the person's thoughts, perceptions, and actions around pursuing or enjoying the incentive in question. In order to become committed, there is no reason that the person's view of the incentive must be realistic. It is enough that the person expects to experience pleasure upon attaining it. Sometimes, therefore, the incentives that will turn out to be most habituable or disillusioning may in prospect seem most attractive. Think of all the children and adolescents who reply firmly and proudly that they will become physicians, lawyers, professors, engineers, and so on, with only the most distorted idea of how people in these occupations spend their days. Therefore, one may become committed to alluring incentives, thereby providing a thorough-going organization of one's thoughts, perceptions, actions, self-regard, attitudes, and so on, and yet find after attaining the incentive that one's life is empty.

According to the viewpoint developed here, there are then two kinds of stable incentives, those that are innately satisfying and those that cannot be fully attained. However, these incentives are responsible for creating a great many other fairly stable incentives that are instrumental in helping to achieve them. The instrumental incentives consist of convenient living arrangements (which may include marriage or various forms of communal living), memberships in clubs, jobs, and many others, prominently including money.

It may seem as though this scheme has left no place for what Viktor Frankl (e.g., 1967) considers the central motivating force in human life, the will to meaning, or the need for basic purpose in one's life. Frankl opposed this to Freud's will to pleasure and Adler's will to power, saying that these were but partial reflections of the broader human need for a sense that life and suffering serve some acceptable purpose. Frankl's most vivid and moving evidence for this belief derives from his experience in Nazi concentration camps during World War II, as he observed and ministered to the medical and spiritual needs of his fellow inmates. He saw that as long as the people in the camp kept a sense of purpose, they were able to survive hideous brutality and debility. When they lost their sense of purpose, they sickened and died. Of course, these supremely unfortunate people were almost totally bereft of pleasure, power, and other conceivable here-and-now incentives. The only possible basis for self-organization and meaningfulness, apart from minimizing their misery, was the sense of ultimate purpose — of accomplishment that transcended the bounds of the camp — that Frankl nurtured in them. If there are other bases around which to organize a satisfying life, they would not have become evident there.

Nevertheless, it is true, as we have seen, that simple sensory pleasures (of the kind usually implied by "pleasure") do not constitute an especially powerful basis for living a full life. People do habituate to them to some extent, and in our society many people are aware that they are capable of feeling greater elation than what a stale sensory pleasure can evoke in them. It should also be noted that "simple sensory pleasures" do not exhaust the category of innately satisfying incentives, which probably include love (that is, the act of loving someone else), attack when angry, and a variety of pleasures that are often thought of as social and intellectual.

Therefore, although the will to meaning probably does not constitute a pure principle of human motivation, the kinds of long-term incentive commitments that Frankl regards as especially effective sources of meaningfulness do seem to incorporate a very large share of the most stabilizing and purpose-giving influences on human lives.

Reviving Sensory Pleasures

Frequently repeated actions become automatized to the point that they require little focused attention and hence they receive little. When a person is in a familiar kitchen and decides to throw something into the wastebasket, he or she pays little attention to the action of throwing away, only just enough to make sure the refuse goes into the basket rather than next to it. Repeated perceptions also become automatized. Experienced drivers somehow can negotiate blocks of traffic and suddenly realize that they cannot remember anything they saw or did. When it comes to automatizing perception, however, there is a serious loss to offset the gain in efficiency. Sensory pleasures require sensory attention. The person who has automatized his or her walk to work may cease to drink in the colors of the leaves against the sky, may not notice the chickadees scurrying through the branches or the quality of the breeze against his or her face. Many things can be automatized that thereby eliminate pleasure. People eat their food mechanically, preoccupied, not focally savoring their food. People make love mechanically, preoccupied, hastening on to orgasm oblivious of what is happening to them en route.

One of my more vivid experiences occurred once when I decided to restrict my food intake so as to lose some weight. In order to make my reduced portions more tolerable, I tried eating very small bites and chewing them longer. I was amazed at the flavor, which I had been routinely ignoring while gulping large amounts of food.

It is possible to increase pleasure simply by once again experiencing it. This is a process of "deautomatization" (Deikman, 1969). There are a number of systematic methods for deautomatization. The various forms of meditation seem to be among these, for they involve fully experiencing something that is either unchanging or repetitive by keeping it at the focus of attention — a vase, a word ("mantra"), a dance movement, one's breathing, or whatever. Probably marijuana and other psychedelic drugs also foster deautomatization of one's sensory experiences. Marijuana users report spending more time staring at details of things or totally absorbed in a musical experience (Tart, 1971), and physiological investigations of marijuana effects report brain-wave changes that suggest deepened attention but impaired performance (Low, Klonoff, & Marcus, 1973). Apart from meditation and marijuana, however, one can increase enjoyment of one's daily sensory experiences (assuming that they are potentially enjoyable) simply by paying deliberate attention to them and savoring them.

Moderation and Restraint

One way of preserving the value of an incentive is not to enjoy it too often or too early. One problem of contemporary American childhood is that the average nine-year-old child is already surfeited with the entire range of childhood pleasures — bicycle, electric train, complete set of Barbie dolls, dozens of educational gadgets and novelties, uninhibited quantities of carbonated and flavored sugar water, ice cream, hamburgers, travel to beaches, amusement parks, zoos, and relatives, televised fantasies of omnipotence and violence, instant social communication with almost anyone by telephone or chauffeured automobile, and so on. What is there to look forward to other than adult pleasures he or she is considered too young for? If the present position is correct, there is something to be said for holding back many of these incentives, making them contingent on constructive contributions to family and society or keeping them in the realm of the future. They are then likely to be better enjoyed, for, as we shall see in the next chapter, obstacles and waiting time enhance the attractiveness of incentives; they will provide a phased antidote to boredom; and they will maintain a sense of stable organization around constructive objectives.

Synergy and Peak Experiences

Perhaps the most satisfying life is one that combines many enduring sources of satisfaction — high goals in science, religion, politics, social service, the arts, or commerce; appreciation for a wide, varied range of simple sensory pleasures; cultivation of ways to experience intellectual and aesthetic pleasure; and a variety of loving relationships with others. When one can combine these so that they interweave without much conflict, all of one's thoughts — respondent as well as operant — will concern one's sources of satisfaction and meaning. Each current concern meshes with the others. In fact, the distinction between one's respondent and one's operant thinking becomes blurred. There is little need to push oneself or to control one's attention because one is attending and doing the right things spontaneously. One's work begets respect and love, one's loving accomplishes human ends. Pleasure, love, and work cease to be separate compartments and become facets of a single, integral life thrust. One can then mobilize tremendous energy for living one's rich life — for solving one's problems creatively and taking one's satisfactions fully. That is the "synergy" Abraham Maslow (1971) wrote about, the synergic living that yields "peak experience" of feeling and that enables an individual to live in a unified flow of personal experience.

Chapter 5

Consequences of Losing

The essence of tragedy is that humans are the playthings of the gods: that people's lives are vehicles for the expression of cosmic forces, that people's fortunes must often submit to forces beyond their control. Human lives are organized around commitments to particular incentives, and many of life's great personal upheavals arise from disappointments in pursuing them.

There are many ways in which a venture can come to grief. First, there is disillusionment. A person may strive hard for something, only to find out later that it was not worth the effort. Second, there is partial defeat, when the end result is less glittering than hoped for, though still substantial. Third, there are escalations of cost, when the goal turns out to require more time, effort, money, or other sacrifices than it is worth. Finally, there may be insurmountable obstacles to reaching the goal.

All such disappointments, ranging from disillusionment to total defeat, exact a cost in the person's psychic economy. Given the ideas we have sketched out in previous chapters, it would be surprising if they did not. We have seen that becoming committed to a goal sets in motion a continuing psychological state, which I have called a "current concern," that is reflected in changed patterns of attention, perception, and thought content. If such a state is set up to be enduring, we should expect that turning it off will require a definite, positive neural act. If the state involves a large part of a person's psychological organization, we might expect that eliminating it will set in motion a massive reorganization, a kind of psychic earthquake that will send shudders and rumbles through the person's life until all of the forces have settled into a new secure balance.

The upheavals that follow defeats spring at least in part from one

137

central issue: The person is committed to incentives that are either no longer available or no longer worth the cost. If one regards the defeat as final, one must *disengage* from the incentive, to release its grip on one's psychological functioning. What had been an incentive, in some cases a very powerful incentive, must now become functionally a nonincentive.

This process of *disengagement* appears to follow a predictable sequence of events, which we shall call an *incentive-disengagement cycle*. Since such a cycle probably occurs in all cases of disengagement, even when the incentive is minor, it will be well to illustrate it with a common occurrence, common at least in the industrially advanced countries of the world.

In order to appreciate intuitively the cycle I have in mind, imagine that you are thirsty, have just a few minutes to refresh yourself, and are putting a quarter into the only soda pop dispenser around. You hear the quarter plop down into the machinery and nothing happens. You begin to push the selector buttons, but there is no response. You push the coin return button, but the coin fails to return. You now take out your only other quarter and repeat the sequence. Your thirst is mounting. You reread the instructions with concentrated care, pushing the appropriate buttons, your motions perhaps becoming stiffer and choppier, the beginning, perhaps, of a flush on your face. The button pushes by now have become punches, and you whack the dispenser on its side once or twice. You may be writing a mental letter to the company, complaining of their negligence and threatening to take a class action on behalf of all consumers. Eventually, perhaps after an additional attack on the machine, you depart, your irritation melting into disheartment, a lump rising in your throat. Your hope for refreshment has turned to disappointment mingled perhaps with some strains of self-pity and lingering irritation. After a while, however, the bad feelings fade as you produce other satisfactions and they are eventually forgotten.

In miniature, the saga of the jammed pop dispenser appears to be a reasonable paradigm for the consequences of losing in general. In it we can discern a sequence of events that can for convenience be described as a sequence of phases: first, behavior becomes more vigorous, then it becomes somewhat aggressive, but eventually the aggression melts into a sinking mood of disappointment or depression, which is in turn eventually followed by a recovery as the disappointment fades into the irrelevant past.

Many students of frustration, aggression, and depression have noted one or more of these consequences of losing, and some have noted the entire sequence. For instance, the Swiss psychiatrist Bleuler (1948) concluded that any loss could lead to depression, and he speculated that whether the loss would lead to aggression or directly to depression depended on circumstances. He picked as his paradigm a small child who has lost its balloon or has suffered some other hurt, and divided the sequence of reactions into three phases: first, the child's loudly crying out against its pain and misfortune; second, the child's moody withdrawal into itself; and finally, recovery of interest in the world around. From the standpoint of an experimental clinical psychologist, Davis (1952) ascribed retarded depression "to an unfavourable environment, the essence of which is the withholding of reinforcement from responses previously reinforced. . . . [T]he first phase in the development of depression is expected to be an increase in the force and extent of responses and a varying degree of agitation, and the second phase to be a weakening and slowing in the same way as comes about in the laboratory during experimental extinction" [P. 112]. Bull and Strongin (1956) took as their starting point frustration, defined (as it customarily is in modern psychological usage) as interference with goal-directed activity. Then, "aggression in the hostile sense is open to interpretation as a primitive method for getting rid of interference . . ." [P. 533]. Continued frustration, however, produces a sense of helplessness. "Right here we have the point of entry for further complication — the downward path into *depression* — where the organism, having lost its goal, becomes fixated on some aspect of its own entanglement and consequent discomfort, while it perseverates in a display of helplessness and protest, designed, like screaming in a baby, to call attention to its plight" [P. 533]. Finally, Bowlby (1960) has summarized the various kinds of psychological responses noted by observers of grief and mourning:

(a) Thought and behavior still directed toward the lost object;
(b) Hostility, to whomsoever directed;
(c) Appeals for help;
(d) Despair, withdrawal, regression, and disorganization;
(e) Reorganization of behavior directed toward a new object. (P. 17)

Bowlby's summary is based almost entirely on the observations of psychoanalysts and other clinical observers. We shall look later at more systematic evidence gathered by both clinical and experimental workers. In the meantime, however, it is already plain that there is considerable agreement among different observers concerning the kinds of behavior produced by frustration — that is, by interferences with goal-directed activity or, to put it still another way, by the loss of incentives. It is also plain that there are many ways of classifying these consequences, many ways of dividing them into "phases." In fact, there is no basis at present for deciding that particular phases exist except as convenient ways of grouping observations. Consequently, I shall be referring to five "phases" that follow frustration — invigoration, aggression, downswing into depression, depression, and recovery — with the understanding that this is just a convenience for purposes of naming things, and that I could as easily talk about three or seven. These phases shade into each other. They may overlap. There are probably circumstances in which one or more of them is absent.

There is one more point to bear in mind. This theory supposes that a person goes into an incentive-disengagement cycle every time he or she sustains a loss, no matter how small. At any one moment in time, however, a person is usually committed to a number of incentives and is in the process of pursuing several goals. For instance, a student may be trying to write a certain term paper, obtain certain grades in his or her courses, find or conciliate a girlfriend or boyfriend, arrange a vacation trip, launder clothes, cook dinner, and so on. Some of these enterprises will at any one moment be going well and others will be in one or another kind of difficulty. Since every loss produces an incentive-disengagement cycle, and since losses are likely to be staggered over time, a person may be in different phases of more than one incentive-disengagement cycle at a time. In the theory presented here, what a person feels at any one moment is a combined effect of all the phases of incentive-disengagement cycles in which he or she is at that time. Thus, if a person suffers one moderate loss among many continuing success stories, he or she is likely to experience not outright depression but rather a diminished sense of elation. If several ventures turn sour at about the same time — a special friend left town abruptly, the soup burned, and one misplaced one's notes for writing a term paper — one is likely a little later to feel somewhat blue.

So far, then, we have sketched the consequences of losing incentives and have found that the sketch amounts to a theory of depression. How can we be sure that the sketch is accurate? And if the evidence for it is persuasive, what can it tell us about inner experience, individual differences, and the sense that life is meaningful?

The Phases of the Cycle: Features and Evidence

Invigoration

Adversity is a well-known energizer. Challenge is said to bring out the best in people. The prospect of failing or losing does things to people's perspective, sometimes concentrating their attention and focusing their energies on something that had for a while diminished in importance to them, and at other times exaggerating the importance of a goal out of proportion to its real value. Under some circumstances and for some people, however, adversity has the opposite effect. They give up, relinquish their goals, retreat. What sense can we make of these commonplace observations? What happens, when, and under which circumstances?

To begin with, it is now clear that, on the average, individuals become more energetic right after having experienced a disappointment. This seems to be true whether the individual is a normal child, a retarded person, a rat, or a pigeon.

One of the most common experiments for studying this matter places a rat at one end (the "start box") of a straight runway. If the rat runs the length of the runway, it is usually fed at the other end (the "goal box"). Following the first runway is a second one, so that after eating in the first goal box the animal is allowed to run to a second goal box, where it is also fed. Ocasionally the food reward in the goal box of the first runway is omitted. When that happens, rats tend to run faster in the second runway than they do after they have been fed as usual in the first. This change in running speed is called the "Frustration Effect" (Amsel, 1958, 1962). It is one of experimental psychology's most stable and robust findings.

Many investigators have tested the Frustration Effect to determine whether it is an artifact of special conditions that might have nothing to do with the frustration of not receiving an expected reward. They have found, for instance, that the Frustration Effect occurs whether or not the type of reward used in the first runway is similar to the type used in the second runway (Berger, 1969). It is not necessary to confine the animal in the first goal box to find the effect (DiLollo, Davidson, Hammond, & Donovan, 1968). Even if the experimenter makes reward in the second runway contingent on the animal's running slowly, rats run faster there after rewards are omitted in the first goal box (Logan, 1968). The Frustration Effect seems to occur very reliably.

The effect is not limited to rats. In some experiments children are given opportunities to obtain rewards through certain actions, for instance turning a handle on a dispenser to crank out marbles or pulling a lever for peanuts. If the machine fails to produce a reward on one occasion, the children are likely to act more forcefully on the next (Gilbert, 1969; Holton, 1961; Ryan & Watson, 1968). After high school students are told they are performing a task much less well than average (or other such tasks), they try harder, do better and have higher pulse rates than if they are told they are doing well (Schneider, 1975; Schneider & Eckelt, 1975).

Some investigators have argued that these experiments really show not that disappointment invigorates behavior but rather that reward makes behavior more lethargic (Staddon, 1970, 1972). Since most of the experiments compare running speeds or response force after rewarded occasions with speed or force after unrewarded occasions, many experiments could support either interpretation. Staddon showed that if one trains pigeons to *refrain from* pecking a key in order to be fed, then after an occasion on which the pigeons are not rewarded they peck it *even less* than before. From one standpoint, this would seem to be the opposite of invigoration, but if one considers invigoration to refer not just to the physical energy expended but to performing a frustrated response more intently, then it is easy to credit the pigeons with redoubling their effort not to peck the key. Even Staddon's evidence, therefore, fails to cast serious doubt on the notion that frustration invigorates.

There are a number of other reasons for accepting the conclusion that frustration invigorates. One experimenter never rewarded his rats in the first goal box of his double runway, but occasionally kept them there momentarily by blocking their path to the second goal box (Uyeno, 1965). On those occasions, they ran faster in the second runway. These results cannot be explained on grounds of reward having slowed any rats down. Children respond especially forcefully if their expectaton of reward had been established by many experiences with reward rather than by few and if they are stopped close to achieving a goal rather than farther from it (Holton, 1961). There is no way that one can account for such results by supposing that reward dampens behavior, but they are easy to recognize as frustration effects.

There is another set of reasons for believing that frustration invigorates, but in order to appreciate these it is necessary to draw an important distinction. In the experiments with children just described, and in Staddon's research with pigeons, the investigators were looking at the effects of frustration on instrumental actions — in fact, at repetitions of the actions that the investigators had failed to reward in order to produce frustration. In the double-runway Frustration Effect experiments, however, the experimenters frustrated one response (running to eat in the first runway) and found that this invigorated a different response (running to eat in the second runway, which was always rewarded). Frustration, it appears, invigorates not only repetitions of actions that have been frustrated but also other actions that immediately follow frustration.

There are many pieces of evidence to support this conclusion. As early as 1936, Neal Miller observed that when he withheld rewards from his rat subjects they became agitated (Miller & Stevenson, 1936). When rats are removed from the goal box of a single runway and placed directly into an activity box, they run around more if they have just found the goal box empty (Gallup & Altomari, 1969; Klinger, Barta, & Kemble, 1974). Retarded persons rock themselves more after frustration than after reward (Forehand & Baumeister, 1971).

Taken together, these various results suggest that frustration — that is, interference with goal-directed behavior — invigorates probably all kinds of immediately following behavior. If the person or other organism has a chance to repeat the frustrated act, it is repeated more intently. If not, the actor is likely to explore the situation, to try completing the act successfully (Mandler, 1964), and to be generally agitated. This conclusion holds most of the time. We shall see later that it probably does not apply to depressed individuals.

Frustration does more than invigorate behavior. As we saw in the previous chapter, people faced with obstacles to a goal place a higher value on it as a result. This is apparently the subjective aspect of behavioral invigoration. People feel greater desire for things they are in danger of losing.

There is seemingly no information concerning what happens to the value of other incentives while the value of the blocked incentive rises. However, there are reasons for believing that their value declines. First, the value of an incentive is lowered if it is overshadowed by a more attractive incentive (Adamson, 1971; Fowler, 1971). For instance, an animal will work less vigorously for a food reward of a certain size if it has been accustomed to larger rewards than if it has been accustomed to smaller rewards. Second, there is the general principle of the adaptation level (Appley, 1971): things are judged in light of the average of recently experienced things in the same class. If the new item is less than this average (than this *adaptation level*), it will be judged smaller or less attractive than it would have been judged had the adaptation level been lower. When the value of one incentive increases, that should raise the adaptation level for incentive values, and hence other incentives will seem less desirable.

Probably, then, frustration both makes the blocked goal seem more desirable than it would seem otherwise and makes other incentives seem less desirable. Very likely, this phenomenon accounts for the loss of "perspective" often noted in people who have become embattled in pursuit of a blocked goal. Rejected lovers, drivers whose paths are blocked by other cars, adolescents forbidden to frequent a certain hangout or to associate with a certain friend, negotiators who face severe compromises — all may come to overvalue their objectives and to become temporarily heedless of losses in the other areas of their lives.

Aggression

Although frustration seems to invigorate behavior, invigoration is not frustration's best-known effect. Modern psychology has come to think of frustration as producing primarily aggression. Individuals become angry when events interfere with their actions and societies become especially violent when times are hard.

As a broad generalization, it is undoubtedly true to say that frustration produces aggression. However, this generalization requires much qualification. If we define our terms carefully, if we make some important distinctions, and if we recognize that under certain conditions the statement is false, then we can accept the notion that under the other conditions frustration not only invigorates but incites to aggression. First of all, we must recognize that to say frustration produces aggression is not to say aggression is produced only by frustration. Second, we must remember that we are using the term "frustration" in a special sense: interference with goal-directed actions. Third, we must realize that "aggression" can mean many different things, not all of which can be explained in the same ways.

"Aggression" or "aggressiveness" is popularly often used in the sense of asserting oneself, of persisting, of initiating many actions aimed at attaining one's goals. Insofar as these are especially vigorous forms of behavior, they may, in fact, become more likely following frustration, but they are not part of what we shall here mean by "aggression." Rather, I shall use "aggression" to refer only to thoughts or behavior aimed at hurting someone or something — aimed at injuring, destroying, defeating, humiliating, or depriving someone or something.

Even limiting the meaning of "aggression" in this way still leaves many different forms of aggression. Moyer (1971) lists seven kinds of aggression, each of which probably has a somewhat different neurological organization in the brain. The seven are (1) predatory aggression (cats killing birds), (2) inter-male aggression (stags fighting it out for attractive does), (3) fear-induced aggression (cornered rats fighting back), (4) irritable aggression (produced by pain, fatigue, hunger, and interference with goal-directed actions), (5) territorial aggression (male stickleback fish chasing intruders out of their nesting ranges), (6) maternal aggression (lion mothers protecting their cubs), and (7) instrumental aggression (destroying a competitor's business in order to take over his or her customers; releasing bombs as a routine act of bureaucratic soldiery).

There is little reason to believe that humans are neurologically specialized to engage in predatory, inter-male, or territorial aggression (see, for instance, Fromm, 1973). Much human aggression, including some of its most widely devastating forms, such as modern war, can be classified as instrumental aggression. Irritable aggression is probably the category accounting for the second largest portion of violent aggression, and it undoubtedly accounts for the largest amount of day-to-day minor aggression. It is to "irritable" aggression that we must restrict the generalization that frustration produces aggression.

Anger. There is one more complication. It is easy to find situations that are plainly frustrating to someone, but in which the person engages in no detectable aggression. For instance, a professor hands back a test with a low grade, an employer requires an employee to give up weekend plans in order to work overtime, or a policeman stops a motorist to write a ticket for speeding. Sometimes such situations evoke great spoken aggression, but more often they do not. The reasons, in incentive terms, are fairly clear. In each case, the victim wishes to stay in the other person's good graces or wishes to avoid still worse treatment. We would suppose, however, that the encounter nevertheless affects the victim emotionally. Most likely, the victim experiences annoyance, irritation, or deep anger.

During the behaviorist period of American psychology, psychologists avoided talking about anger on grounds that it was a subjective event not verifiable by an outside observer, and they therefore preferred to talk about aggression, which anyone can see. However, that decision has probably caused the science a considerable setback in theory and research on aggression. Although aggression is easy to observe, it is not always easy to identify or to tell apart from nonaggressive action, and at the human level it is especially hard to divide into different types. Anger, on the other hand, is subjectively fairly easy to identify. It is in part observable from the outside, in that it carries with it distinctive facial expressions that can be identified by other humans virtually regardless of their cultural background (Ekman, 1972; Izard, 1971).

It seems very likely that irritable and instrumental aggression can be told apart by whether they are committed in anger — a distinction upheld in law between actions committed in the heat of emotion or in "cold blood." In that case, the statement that frustration leads to aggression could be restated more precisely as frustration leads to anger.

Anger, of course, predisposes people to aggress, but whether it does so in a particular instance, and what form the action takes, depends on many other factors. It seems safe to suppose that there is an innate tendency to react to frustration with anger. Apart from facial expressions, extreme emotional arousal, and possibly a tendency to shout and thrash around, there is no innate prescription for what form the angry actions will take, or whether there will be overt actions at all. Therefore, the emotional response of anger may well be the purest consequence of frustration. Although people can learn to dampen and disguise their anger, it seems less subject to modification than aggressive actions. Even when subjects report no anger following failure, their blood pressure rises (Gentry, 1970).

Although it would be best for us to focus now on frustration and anger, very little evidence has been collected regarding anger as such, and a great deal of evidence has accumulated concerning one or another form of aggressive behavior. It is therefore to this evidence that we must briefly turn next.

Frustration and aggression. As early as 1931, Tamara Dembo reported some experiments from Kurt Lewin's Berlin laboratory in which she systematically frustrated her human subjects, probably the first such experiments. She persuaded these people to undertake tasks that seemed reasonable, if difficult, but that were in practice impossible to complete successfully. For instance, one task required subjects to practice until they could toss small rings around bottle necks twelve feet (3.5 meters) away ten times in succession. Dembo's experimenters recorded the gradual rise in subjects' hostile and eventually overt aggressive behaviors, beginning with slight irritability and ending sometimes with undisguisedly contemptuous actions, with vividly described wishes to destroy experimental property and with occasional gestures in that direction. Yet, these subjects were completely uncoerced. All that kept them in the situation was their desire to cooperate, the experimenter's deceptive assurances that the tasks could be performed, and, presumably, the subjects' own wish to complete what they had set out to do. Thus, their anger against the experimenter reflected their frustration at not being able to reach their goals.

A few years later, a group of investigators based at Yale (Dollard, Doob, Miller, Mowrer, & Sears, 1939) formalized what has come to be known as the "frustration-aggression hypothesis." They gathered the evidence then available from a variety of sources, ranging from rat experiments to social movements, and they concluded that frustration produces aggression. Their conclusion was stated too broadly and unqualifiedly, as it turned out (see, for instance, Berkowitz, 1962), but they made a powerful case.

The evidence has continued to mount. Not only do species at virtually all levels from crustaceans to man tend to attack when they are subjected to pain, but species as widely separated as pigeons, rats, monkeys, and humans are inclined to attack when they are deprived of expected rewards (Hutchinson, 1973). With different species, investigators have produced attack behavior by withholding food, morphine, freedom to move around, rewarding brain stimulation, money, and signals that had been associated with reward. Different species directed their attacks at targets as diverse as another animal of the same species, an animal of a different species, a stuffed animal, a piece of rubber hose, and an experimental response panel (Hutchinson, 1973). In the latter case, human subjects worked for money rewards by pulling a knob, and they could turn off periodic annoying tones by either pressing a button or punching a padded cushion. After a while the experimenters stopped issuing money rewards for pulling the knob. During this extinction period, their subjects turned off the annoying tones progressively more by punching than by pressing (Kelly & Hake, 1970).

Investigators who have observed the effects of personal catastrophes have documented a predictable cycle of events. They all seem to describe the first phase of the cycle as one of protest. Whether the catastrophe is sudden blindness (Fitzgerald, 1970), separation of children from their parents (Bowlby, 1973), or the death of a spouse (Marris, 1958), people often express disbelief that things are as bad as they seem — their sight will return after all, their spouse could not really be dead — and they express angry protest, whether the screams of children or the accusations of the newly blind or bereaved. Much the same nonverbal behavior occurs with monkey infants separated from their parents (McKinney, Suomi, & Harlow, 1971). They scream and they attack their monkey peers (Seay & Harlow, 1965).

Probably the most reliable way to make people angry is to insult them. It is most likely that insult can be considered in the same class of events that we have called frustration, for two reasons. First, everyone beyond the cradle has had ample opportunities to learn that an insult is often the first event in a chain that leads to some kind of pain or deprivation — a punch in the arm, a broken toy, or social exclusion. Second, an insult is in any case a challenge to one's social status. Whether the insult is a name — sissy, bum, kike, stupid — or a manner, its effect is to downgrade the status and dignity of its target, and losing status usually also means deprivations ahead.

Even pain can be thought of as a loss of incentives, since it involves the loss of comfort and safety. Consequently, if frustration is interference with goal-directed behavior, unremitting pain — which the person is helpless to relieve — represents just such interference with the person's efforts to maintain comfort, and therefore is an instance of frustration. In fact, the pain itself may be less important than what it portends for the person's control over comfort and safety in the future. For instance, people retaliate much more aggressively when they believe they have been hurt purposely than when they believe their pain was accidental (Nickel, 1974).

Although the evidence that frustration leads to "irritable" aggression is strong, frustrated organisms do not always aggress, and it is possible that they do not always feel angry. In order to aggress, there must be a handy victim. In order to be angry, there may need to be a plausible target. When the frustrated person can attribute the cause of his or her frustration to someone or something (the *instigator* of the aggression), then the instigator is most likely to be the target, and successful retaliation seems to satisfy the aggressor. At least, the aggressor's blood pressure, which rises upon frustration, comes down nicely if he or she has been allowed to retaliate against the instigator, but it takes much longer to come down if the frustrated person is allowed to aggress only against other people or to engage in mere fantasies of aggression (Baker & Schaie, 1969; Hokanson & Burgess, 1962; Hokanson, Burgess, & Cohen, 1963). Following frustration, it feels good to attack the frustrator, and the opportunity to attack then becomes a positive incentive.

It may happen, of course, that retaliating is impractical, in which case aggression may not occur, and it may also happen that the frustrated person can find nothing on which to pin blame. However, even though there is here no hope of successfully retaliating against the instigator, and even though aggression against others does not satisfy the need for retaliation, the person is nevertheless likely to remain for a time diffusely hostile and irritable. A new instigator of a new frustration is very likely at that point to get more than his or her fair share of retaliation. This may account for the commonly observed case of someone — perhaps a business or professional person — who handles important frustrations with apparent equanimity, only to leave work and blow up over a trifle. As we shall see, depressed individuals who are in the process of giving up a blocked goal are also exceptionally irritable.

It is probably a mistake to think of aggression as a discrete phase of an incentive-disengagement cycle. Some irritability persists into the depression phase, and some tendency toward aggression probably begins immediately after a frustration. As a person's efforts continue to be frustrated, aggression is likely to become gradually more evident and behavior gradually more primitive. Children who were arbitrarily forbidden to play with certain attractive toys in a room played with the other toys more destructively than before (Barker, Dembo, & Lewin, 1941). Business school students who became increasingly frustrated as their academic term wore on responded with less original and resourceful answers to tests of originality in midterm than they did at the start of the year (Hinton, 1968). It is only in the sense that behavior following frustration often eventually becomes blatantly hostile that we are justified in considering aggression to be a phase and not just a facet of the incentive-disengagement cycle.

The treatment of aggression that we are attempting here does not pretend to be exhaustive, and hence it need not include all of the many scientific problems of describing and explaining human aggression. However, there are two further problem areas in which the formulation sketched above may be helpful. These two are vengeance and sadism.

Vengeance and sadism. Some instances of vengeance, of course, fit directly into the theory as already described. A person blinded with rage over an atrocity committed against him or her may be able to overtake the tormentor and exact revenge while still in the heat of anger, when attack is itself satisfying. In other cases, however, vengeance occurs long after the original offense. The avenger has awaited an opportunity, nursing a grudge long past the end of hot anger. Sometimes, revenge is compelled by the offended person's society, which would compound the injury already done him or her by demoting him in social status if he did not attempt revenge. In other cases, revenge might serve the purpose of restoring the offended person's sense of being effective, of retaining some control over his or her fortunes. In either case, the avenger is eliminating future threats to his well-being. Here, revenge has become an incentive in its own right, and perhaps its consummation is all the sweeter if the avenger can whip himself up into a state of anger like the original one by dwelling on memories of the offense. Finally, there is a possibility that long-term revenge not compelled by cultural pressures occurs when the disengagement process is incomplete — when the person has for some reason not been able to grieve away his attachment to the lost incentive. Clearly, the psychology of revenge is still very poorly researched, but the conceptual framework of the incentive-disengagement cycle suggests some of the directions it might take.

The psychology of sadism is also still unclear, but it has been given a major boost by Erich Fromm (1973). Fromm distinguishes between "benign aggression," which includes all of the kinds described above, and "malignant aggression," which includes cruelty, destructiveness, and necrophilia. Benign aggressions are natural *re*actions to threat. Malignant aggressions are part of a life pattern by which a contorted *character* seeks satisfactions. People need a certain minimal level of excitement and they need a feeling of being effective, of having an impact. Destructiveness can fulfill both of these needs, because destruction dispels boredom and certifies the destroyer's effectiveness. When people, for one reason or another, cannot create enough excitement and impact through loving, constructive means, they learn to channel their needs for excitement and impact through a pattern of destructive and cruel domination. This is the sadistic character. Since the needs for excitement and effectance are continuous, so are the person's sadistic urges. Unlike the ordinary aggressor, whose aggression is a momentary reaction to frustration, the sadistic character seeks opportunities to be destructive, frustration or no. His continuous sadism constitutes a "transformation of impotence into the experience of omnipotence" (Fromm, 1973, P. 290).

The people Fromm writes about seem not only to be chronically sadistic but also chronically more or less depressed. Although they seem formidable and even frightening from the standpoint of someone eager to avoid being their victim, they are at the same time vulnerable and needy. It seems possible to think of them as people whose limitations, either of opportunity or of personal resources, have consigned them to a life of repeated disappointments which continually revitalize the value they place on aggression; and, as Fromm proposes, they have woven into their routine ways of managing their lives destructive expressions of their hostility, deeply satisfying to themselves.

Depression

At some point during sustained, unrelieved frustration, organisms begin to give up. Rejected suitors go away hurt. Defeated contestants leave the field of contest and lick their wounds, literally or figuratively. The bereaved mourn. Abandoned lovers share their sad/bitter hurt by "singing the blues." So do people who have lost their jobs or fortunes: "Nobody knows you when you're down and out." Indeed, a large part of folk music consists of complaint by losers and compassion for losers — the stories of losers told by themselves and their sympathizers. Irretrievable loss and its emotional consequences are the common lot of humankind.

However suddenly a person may give up deliberately pursuing a lost cause, giving up is emotionally a drawn-out process. It seems to occur in spasms, for amid the apathy and withdrawal of depression the person is likely to experience pangs of yearning, waves of sadness, and fits of irritation, bitterness, and anger. It is as though the person who has lost an incentive periodically loses his or her resignation to the loss and turns again to search and contend for the person or thing he or she had apparently given up.

This account of the giving-up process describes a common pattern of what most people experience. In detail, however, probably every person experiences grief and depression somewhat differently. At the extremes there are wide variations in this experience that depend not only on the nature of the person's loss and on the nature of the person's circumstances, but also on the person's biological makeup and emotional history. Nevertheless, there are some common elements in these experiences. Most people feel some sadness, although some do not and those who do are likely to experience it now and then rather than all the time. Many depressed people doubt their own adequacy and worth, but some do not. There are, however, two kinds of elements so common in grief and other depression that they may be considered characteristic: pessimism and apathy. Depressed people believe that their personal future is gloomy, that things will not work out to their satisfaction, and, probably, that the world's future is itself rather clouded. To use the phrase of most clinical observers, they feel "hopeless and helpless." Furthermore, depressed individuals experience a marked loss of interest in incentives they would ordinarily find attractive. They do not care to socialize with their friends. Sports and games are too much bother. Their work seems uninspiring and even futile. Nothing in their lives seems able to rouse in them lively feelings or, in some cases, identifiable feelings of any kind. Jacobson (1971) writes that "some of the patients who complained about their lack of feelings did not experience 'sadness'; they were even longing for it" [P. 172]. Depression carries with it an often profound sense of meaninglessness (Wessman & Ricks, 1966).

Depression is, in a sense, the collapse of invigoration, the aftermath of determined effort or of keen hope. It follows the exaggerated, often hostile invigoration I have called the aggression phase of the incentive-disengagement cycle. Nevertheless, aggression continues into the depression phase. Depressed people are significantly more hostile, often in a diffuse, irritable kind of way, than they are when not depressed. At one time, under the influence of psychoanalytic theory, clinicians believed that depression occurs when people are unable to express or feel the anger they harbor toward others, that they therefore turn their aggression inward toward themselves, and that this inward-directed aggression is depression. It seems very unlikely that this is so, however. A number of investigators have now found that although depressed individuals are indeed more critical of themselves than when not depressed, they are also more critical of others. They become angry more easily, especially with the people closest to them, such as their children and spouses; but they are not especially hostile toward psychiatric interviewers, which may help to account for the earlier conclusions by psychiatrists that depressed patients have turned their aggression inward (Weissman, Klerman, & Paykel, 1971)! Depressed patients are more resentful than nondepressed individuals, and both their resentments and their verbal expressions of hostility decline as they become less depressed (Friedman, 1970). Outside the realm of clinically depressed patients, other investigators have found that college students' feelings of anger fluctuate in accordance with their feelings of being depressed, and the students who are chronically most depressed also feel chronically most hostile (Wessman & Ricks, 1966). Most widows experience intermittent excessive anger for several months after bereavement, often in the form of "general irritability or bitterness" (Parkes, 1970). One must conclude that depression is in no sense either the inverse of aggression or aggression aimed inward. Rather, both depression and aggression seem to be consequences of prolonged frustration, the aggression usually showing up earlier but both continuing together after the onset of depression and both gradually subsiding together during recovery.

What precipitates depression? All of the above discussion has assumed that depressions are processes of giving up incentives to which the person had become committed, such as a relationship to another person, a career goal, a certain kind of recognition, or reaching some other goal. That is, we have been assuming a frustration-*depression* sequence, one that parallels and sometimes replaces the better-known frustration-aggression sequence. What evidence is there to justify such a conclusion? There have, after all, been many explanations for depression, most of which have been thoroughly discredited (see, for instance, Beck, 1967; Becker, 1974) and will not be considered here. Among theories that treat depression as something precipitated by external events, rather than as purely biological events or as reflecting chronic personality traits, three are still very much in contention: a theory that depression occurs as a result of incentive losses (which actually includes a number of different theoretical contributions and research traditions), Seligman's (1975) theory that depression is a case of learned helplessness, and the behaviorist view, exemplified by Lewinsohn (1974), that depression is brought about by an abnormally low rate of "reinforcement," perhaps caused by the depressed person's lack of social skill.

Modern systematic observations of *incentive losses* probably began with some of the natural tragedies produced by World War II. London parents, fearing for their young children's safety, sent them to nurseries outside the city, where some of them were cared for and observed by Dorothy Burlingham and Anna Freud. Relatively safer from Nazi bombs, but separated from their parents, these children fell prey to the most profound personal unhappiness. Later investigators repeated and refined Burlingham and Freud's observations (Bowlby,

1973). They found a regular sequence of reactions, which Robertson and Bowlby called "protest, despair, and detachment." These children screamed and pleaded for their parents and often turned against the nursery staff and plant. Later they became sullen, withdrawn, and apathetic. Eventually, they resumed relatively normal activities and accepted the nursery's care. But they were often warier about forming intense personal relationships, and they often rejected their mothers after being reunited with them. Their "protest" clearly corresponds to our "aggression" phase, or perhaps also to the transition from aggression to depression. "Despair" corresponds to our "depression" phase, and "detachment" to our "recovery" phase. Without heroic efforts to maintain a sense of cheer, comfort, and optimism, children separated from their parents eventually despaired. Even heroic efforts — taking the children into the professional worker's home after a period of familiarization, bringing to the foster home the child's own bed, toys, and other artifacts, occasional visits with the parents, and assurances that the separation would be temporary — could not erase the distress of these one- and two-year-old children completely.

During the 1960s, workers in Harry Harlow's University of Wisconsin Primate Laboratory were beginning to observe the severe disturbances displayed by young rhesus monkeys when separated from their mothers. These monkey infants displayed much the same sequence of protest, despair, and detachment as the British workers had observed in human infants (McKinney, Suomi, & Harlow, 1971). It began to seem that separating primate infants from mothers, whether monkeys or humans, is a natural means of inducing distress. It can now be seen, however, that while this is certainly true, the truth of the matter is much broader. Later work in the Harlow laboratory has shown that the same sequence of protest, despair, and detachment occurs when monkeys are separated from objects other than their mothers, such as their peers (McKinney, Suomi, & Harlow, 1973). Furthermore, it seems likely that these effects are not restricted either to primates or to interpersonal relationships. When rats, who have been accustomed to finding food at the end of a runway, are repeatedly denied food in the same runway, their activity levels following the early disappointments rise sharply, but following later disappointments they are less active than normal, and after still more disappointments in the runway their activity returns to normal (Klinger, Barta, & Kemble, 1974).

Back at the human level, there are many other indications that what precipitates depression is not just separation from others but incentive losses of every kind. All sorts of personal catastrophes send people into periods of grief or depressed despair after their initial surge of protest: losing personal relationships, social roles, reputations, or important objects (Averill, 1968), becoming blind (Fitzgerald, 1970), and becoming physically disabled (Orbach & Sutherland, 1954; Talbott, 1970). People are more likely to be hospitalized for depression in communities that offer fewer economic opportunities (Linsky, 1969). People who have recently become poorer are more depressed than others, especially if they were poor to begin with (Levitt & Lubin, 1975).

Izard (1972) asked 332 college students to describe a situation in which they had been depressed. Their replies, categorized in Table 5-1, run the gamut of college students' incentive losses: academic failure, breaking off with opposite-sex friends, loneliness, death, difficulties with parents, and so on. Most people experience such losses, of course, and apparently most people tend to become depressed about them. Usually, the depression lifts with time and the person requires no special treatment; but if the person is especially susceptible, and if his or her troubles come in clusters, it is harder to bear up unaided. Psychiatric patients who have been hospitalized for depression have gone through a much higher proportion of upsetting events a short time before their admission than a matched group of ordinary community residents (Paykel, Myers, Dienelt, Klerman, Lindenthal, & Pepper, 1969).[1] One can almost always find upsetting events in the weeks of a depressed patient's life just before the onset of the depression, usually several such events clustered over a relatively short time period (Leff, Roatch, & Bunney, 1970; Grinker, Miller, Sabshin, Nunn, & Nunnally, 1961). The kinds of events involved in these depressions are the nonstudent's equivalent of the depressing events reported by Izard's students. The most common are changes in sexual and marital relationships, moves to new neighborhoods, job changes, losses of loved ones, and illnesses.

All of this evidence taken together strongly supports the generalization that losing one's incentives is depressing, and being depressed is something that follows incentive losses. Considering only reactive depressions (that is, depressions that are in reaction to external events), hardly anyone disputes the truth of this as a generalization. Theorists who disagree question whether the real precipitators of depression are losses *as such*. They propose that other aspects of loss situations are the ones directly responsible.

Table 5-1. Classification of Free-Response Descriptions
of the Depression Situation[a]

Category	Percentage of Total	Examples of Responses
1. Academic failure, pressure of school work and competition for grades, and related problems	22.3	(a) Failed a course. (b) Failed math exam, first one taken in college. (c) Poor performance on tests and quizzes. (d) Did poorly on exam for which I thought I was prepared. (e) Behind in schoolwork, trying to catch up, but it does little good. (f) Too much homework, too little time, seem to be under it all — super bleak.
2. Heterosocial (boy-girl) problems	21.0	(a) Being away at school, separated from boyfriend. (b) The aftermath of breaking up with a girlfriend. (c) Breaking of an engagement. (d) When my boyfriend dumped me. (e) No letter from girlfriend. (f) After a really terrible date, finding out that the boy I liked had a great time on his date with another girl. (g) My boyfriend found out that I had a "summer fling" and had been unfaithful.
3. Loneliness, separation from loved ones, being left out	14.7	(a) Nothing specific — just alone in a single room. (b) First two weeks at school, knowing no one. (c) Completely alone at home, when relationship with father was poor. (d) Dropped from fraternity rush list. (e) Feelings of total failure and worthlessness when unable to find a date.
4. Loss or failure in nonacademic competition — sports, campus elections, honors	5.7	(a) Losing an important athletic contest (baseball) that was ultimately "blown." (b) Lost a football game in which I didn't get to play, though I thought I was better than those who did. (c) Lost an election for an office in a club I really wanted.
5. Death or illness of loved one or friend	4.7	(a) Death of my father. (b) Death of my brother and its impact on my family. (c) Death of a friend in combat. (d) When a teacher of mine became an alcoholic and lost his coaching job.
6. Difficulties with parents	3.3	(a) Separation of my parents. (b) Parents still treating me like a child. (c) Constantly restricted by uncle, who replaced parents and behaved in totally opposite manner from that of parents.

Table 5-1 continued

Category	Percentage of Total	Examples of Responses
7. Categories with less than 3% of total responses: loss of friendship or contacts with people; personal failure; life itself and world situation	18.0	
8. Responses combining two or more categories	10.0	

Source: Reprinted with permission from C. E. Izard, *Patterns of emotions: A new analysis of anxiety and depression*. New York: Academic Press, 1972, Table 10-3, Pp. 246–247.
[a] College sample ($N = 332$).

This is the position taken by the theory of *learned helplessness* (Seligman, 1975). The earliest support for this theory came from experiments with dogs in shuttleboxes. A shuttlebox is a small walled enclosure with two compartments separated by a low barrier. The floor consists of an electrifiable grid. As it is usually used, a dog is placed in one of the compartments, a signal tone or light comes on, and after a constant interval the floor is suddenly electrified, delivering continuous shocks to the dog's feet. In this situation, most dogs become frightened, bound around the compartment, and eventually leap over the barrier into the second compartment, thereby discovering that leaping the barrier ends the shock. After a few such occasions, dogs learn to leap the barrier immediately when they feel shock under them; and if the shuttlebox gives them a warning tone or light, they learn to leap the barrier at the onset of the signal without waiting for the shock. It is a fairly easy lesson for average dogs, and veterans do their leaping with studied nonchalance.

However, the dogs in the learned-helplessness experiments entered the shuttlebox after experiences with Pavlovian hammocks. A Pavlovian hammock is a contraption made up of a sling and straps for keeping dogs stationary in Pavlovian conditioning experiments. Dogs are unable to escape Pavlovian hammocks. Bruce Overmier and Martin Seligman (1967) subjected dogs to inescapable electric shocks in a Pavlovian hammock and then a day later put them into a shuttlebox. Remarkably, these dogs seemed unable to learn how to escape shock. Even when the experimenters dragged them across the barrier in order to make the point, they were slow to catch on. They acted as if having been unable to escape shock in the Pavlovian hammock had taught them that shock could not be escaped ever. This phenomenon Overmier and Seligman called "learned helplessness." Subsequent research has established that helplessness can be learned in a wide variety of situations, by rats and people as well as by dogs (Seligman, 1974).

What most struck Seligman, however, was that these helpless dogs endured their shock in the shuttlebox with a demeanor not unlike that of depressed humans. They became passive and slow to recognize that they could now control the shock if they wished. Like depression, the dogs' learned helplessness dissipated with time. Later studies showed that rats who had been taught helplessness ate less, lost weight, and kept less of the transmitter substance norepinephrine in their brains — all of which are changes that have also been observed in severe depression. These experiments made clear that the important factor is not the shock itself but rather its uncontrollability. Seligman (1974) therefore concluded that reactive depression is caused by inescapable stress and is identical with learned helplessness. That is, depressed persons are passive and withdrawn not because their emotional state has undermined the motivational base for action but rather because they have learned the uselessness of doing anything. Losing important incentives is depressing not because of the loss itself but because it teaches the person that he or she is helpless to prevent the loss; this lesson then generalizes to other areas of the person's life. The central issue in this theory is not loss of incentives but loss of control. In Seligman's view, "noncontingency" — events occurring without being contingent on the person's actions — is unpleasant and depressing.

Attractive as this theory seems, there are a number of reasons for preferring an incentive-loss view of depression. First of all, noncontingent events are not always unpleasant. Pigeons and rats are willing to work for the chance to have time periods in which they get "free" food rewards that do not depend on their actions (Neuringer, 1973), and many humans are devoted to gambling.

Second, teaching humans that they are helpless in an experimental situation does not necessarily produce the effects of "learned helplessness" that Seligman found in animals. To be sure, certain things that are consistent with the learned-helplessness theory have become clear. First of all, people *can* be taught that there is no use trying to solve the problems given them by an experimenter (for instance, Gatchel & Proctor, 1976; Hiroto, 1971; Klein & Seligman, 1976; Miller & Seligman, 1975; Racinskas, 1971; Roth & Kubal, 1975). For example, students might be told that there is a way to turn off periodic loud noises or that there is a way to tell certain cards apart, but in fact the experimenter makes this impossible. Then they are given a new task — for instance, to move a switch in order to avoid electric shocks or to solve a different kind of intellectual problem. People who have been taught that they are helpless in the first task are much slower to learn the new task than people who had been allowed to solve the original problem or who had not suffered the noise. They seem to have little faith that the problem can be solved, so why try? A second finding has also been well established: Failure to stop the noise or to solve the problems is depressing (Miller & Seligman, 1975; Roth & Kubal, 1975). However, the question is whether learning that one is helpless produced the depression — directly and automatically — or whether the real factor was losing incentives. Let us look at the evidence further. Not all experiments have found the learned-helplessness effect. In one study, people had to learn to press buttons quickly after a signal in order to avoid shocks. Those who had earlier received inescapable electric shocks learned to press the buttons as quickly as others who had received no shocks (Thornton & Jacobs, 1971). Yet another study asked people to learn an unlearnable task and then made it appear that some of the equipment had broken down (Roth & Bootzin, 1974). These "helpless" subjects were more likely than the others to try helping the experimenter fix the equipment.

What might account for exceptions like these? One factor might be the importance of the task. If the participants believe that their performance does not reflect on their ability — the experimenter is just trying something out — they do at least as well after experiencing helplessness as if they had experienced success; but if they are led to believe that their performance reflects on their basic ability, helplessness has the usual effect of impairing their performance on the next task (Roth & Kubal, 1975). There is nothing in the theory of learned helplessness to suggest why the importance of a failure should make a difference. On the other hand, it is clear from the incentive-loss viewpoint that it should: The participant's self-esteem is at stake if doing well reflects on one's basic ability, but nothing much is at stake if it has no bearing on oneself. There is one more interesting feature in these results. When the participants in Roth and Kubal's experiment were given just a short lesson in helplessness, rather than the longer one that impaired their performance, they actually did *better* on the next task. This looks very much like an invigoration effect, and it is completely out of keeping with a learned-helplessness interpretation. After all, why should a little helplessness teach someone to try harder but more helplessness teach them to quit, if teaching is all there is to it?

Third, depression afflicts many people who have had a history of success in achieving their goals and who, even at the time of the loss that depressed them, continued to be successful in other pursuits. For instance, a person who loses a spouse may remain successful in his or her career — indeed, the person may deliberately have chosen the career over the spouse — and yet experience some depression. Alternatively, someone who loses a job may become depressed despite being on continued good terms with loved ones. Why should the helplessness learned in one sphere of life generalize to other spheres, rather than success in the others preventing a feeling of helplessness in the first?

Seligman's experiments with dogs have shown that if dogs are first taught to escape shocks and then subjected to inescapable shocks, they do not learn helplessness. He has therefore suggested that early successes "immunize" against learned helplessness. But one of the causes of depression sometimes seems to be success itself. For instance, a doctoral student may become depressed after obtaining his or her PhD, an author may experience depression after finishing a major book, or an executive may become depressed after becoming the company's president. In cases like this, it is easy enough to perceive possible ways whereby what seems like a triumph carries with it, paradoxically, incentive losses. For instance, a person with no major goals beyond the one attained has lost the organizing focus of his or her life. Success may force him or her to abandon comfortable old friendships, working relationships, skills, neighborhoods, and excuses. The emotional punch of success may turn out to be less intense or shorter-lived than expected. In each of these eventualities, we would predict some tendency toward depression. But if the learned-helplessness view of depression is correct, why would the history of successes not have immunized against the success depression?

The upshot of all this evidence seems to be that animals and people can indeed learn that they are helpless, but that learned helplessness is not the same as depression. In circumstances that depress people they may well also learn that they are helpless, and those circumstances surely include pain and failure. However, depressed individuals behave as they do not because they have learned the general futility of action but because the depressed state produced by incentive losses undercuts the motivational base of normal behavior.

We have so far considered two theories of what events precipitate depressions: the incentive-loss theory and the learned-helplessness theory. The third theory that we shall consider briefly is the behavioral theory that depression is really only a rough category of quite diverse behavioral events, that the main thing these events have in common is lower-than-expected activity on the part of the depressed person, and that the main reason for the person's inactivity is that he is *receiving too few "reinforcements"* (for instance, see Ferster, 1974, or Lewinsohn, 1974). In other words, "depression is conceptualized as an extinction phenomen[on]" (Lewinsohn, 1974, P. 175). More generally, the behavioral view of depression is that anything that lowers the rate of behavior is by definition depressing; but most events that have this effect involve reducing the rewards that people can reap through their deliberate actions. For instance, losing a parent, spouse, or job makes it harder for a person to find the satisfactions they provided or made possible. There will be fewer opportunities for the person to do satisfying things, and some of the things may fail to provide the rewards they once brought.

Superficially, this theory is much like the theory that depression follows incentive losses. However, it raises some serious difficulties. First, this theory accepts the notion that behavior is maintained specifically by reinforcement — that a certain schedule of rewards strengthens connections between stimuli and responses. We saw in the first chapter that there are sound reasons for disbelieving the reinforcement principle, except, of course, for the simple idea that behavior is directed at expected rewards.

The second problem is that the theory does not suggest an adequate way whereby the "extinction" of behavior toward the lost incentive would generalize into other areas of the depressed person's life. One of the most common clinical observations is that the depressed person seems to lose interest in almost everything, including activities quite different from those that involved the lost person, job, or whatever.[2] Of course, there are ways in which extinction can spread beyond the lost object. If a complicated chain of actions is required to achieve a goal, then there are likely to be many subgoals whose value depends on the ultimate goal. For instance, if a child has learned to organize much of its behavior around a parent's approval, then losing the parent may make all of the actions learned to please him or her meaningless and unattractive. Costello (1972) has suggested that this domino effect — losing an ultimate incentive saps the value of intermediate incentives — accounts for the spread of "extinction" to so many areas of a depressed or bereaved person's life. However, it seems unlikely that the pervasive loss of interest by depressed patients can be explained that way. Nor does this explanation account for the experimental findings of Gouaux (1971) that people become temporarily less attracted to others after they have seen a depressing film, or the findings of Ludwig (1970) that people like excitement less during depressed moods. Nor does this explanation indicate why people afterward recover their interest in most of the activities to which they had become indifferent during their depression. The theory that depression is an encompassing state that accompanies disengagement from incentives has no difficulty in accounting for these kinds of evidence.

Some reinforcement theorists reason that if depression is caused by a low rate of rewards, it can be cured by arranging a better rate of rewards.[3] For instance, one might teach the depressed person to become more skilled socially so as to win more approval and attention from others.

Peter Lewinsohn (1974) and his colleagues have taken this approach. They have found that in social situations depressed individuals initiate fewer social acts toward others — such as asking them questions, praising or criticizing them, requesting help, and so on — and others direct fewer toward the depressed person. Furthermore, depressed individuals are less adept at timing the social responses they do make, with the result that their actions have a less favorable social impact on others.

Lewinsohn and colleagues believe that their depressed patients' low level of social skill is responsible for the low social returns they reap and therefore for their depression. There is, however, an opposite possibility: that the depression has affected their social behavior. There is, after all, no evidence that these depressed patients had been socially less skillful than others before they became depressed. Furthermore, it is well known that depressed individuals lose interest in a wide range of incentives, including social ones. Widows, for instance, initiate fewer social contacts after the death of their husbands than they were accustomed to initiating before; and as their bereavement gradually lifts, one of the early signs of recovery is that they initiate more social activity again (Glick, Weiss, & Parkes, 1974). When normal subjects are shown a depressing film, they are afterward less attracted to an "anonymous stranger" (Gouaux, 1971). People also find excitement less appealing when they are in depressed moods (Ludwig, 1970). All in all, it seems likely that depressed patients are socially inept because their depression has made them less interested in social interaction and has therefore impaired their social functioning by attenuating its motivational base. In that case, they will be helped little by efforts to improve their social skills, but their skills will recover spontaneously as they recover from their depressions.

To sum up, depression is a process of giving up incentives. It is a state of affairs that must run its course, during which other incentives in the person's life are less appealing than they would be otherwise. The person feels relatively more helpless and experiences relatively less satisfaction, but the helplessness and joylessness are accompaniments of depression, not its causes. Until the recovery phase begins, direct behavioral assaults on the person's unhappiness and inactivity will be of little help.

Are all depressions reactive? If it is true that incentive losses lead to depression, does it also follow that all depressions are produced that way? The answer seems to be that not all are. To consider for a moment very mild depressions, it is possible to put children into depressed enough moods to make them share less and eat more just by asking them to dwell on events in their past life that had made them sad (Moore, Underwood, & Rosenhan, 1973; Rosenhan, Underwood, & Moore, 1974). It is possible to make adults feel and act somewhat depressed by asking them to read gloomy statements (Strickland, Hale, & Anderson, 1975).[4] We have already seen that showing people depressing films can also affect their moods (Gouaux, 1971). Judging from these results, depressing thoughts and images carry with them depressed feelings which, when aroused, produce depressed behavior.

There are, however, reasons to believe that even more profound depressions can occur without the person having lost major incentives. We know, for instance, that women's moods fluctuate with changes in the amount of the hormone estrogen in their blood (Bardwick, 1971), so that many women feel depressed during menstruation (Sommer, 1975), just after childbirth, and at certain other times. Finally, there is a long-standing debate regarding the existence of what is most often called "endogenous" depression.

Originally, "endogenous" meant that the depression began without any outside precipitating cause, that it commenced through some kind of unknown bodily disorder rather than as an emotional reaction to an unhappy situation. Endogenous depression was often contrasted with "reactive" depression, for which the clinician could discern a clearcut situational cause, such as the death of a spouse or the loss of a job. Eventually, clinicians reached some degree of consensus that patients with endogenous depressions displayed certain symptoms that did not characterize people with reactive depressions: a pervasive feeling of hopelessness and dejection that seems unresponsive to whatever happens around the patient, regular differences in the amount of depression experienced in the morning as compared with evening, and a loss of most feelings, such as affection, happiness, and even sometimes grief (e.g., see Beck, 1967; Klein, 1974).

The question of whether it makes sense to distinguish between endogenous and reactive forms of depression has consumed a large research literature. Many of these studies proceeded by the method of factor analysis, with which investigators try to determine what symptoms go with what other symptoms, how many basic dimensions of depression seem to underlie the many possible symptoms experienced by depressed patients, and how best to characterize the underlying dimensions. A number of such studies seemed to agree that "endogenous" depressed patients moved and spoke more slowly, were deeply depressed, were unreactive to changes in their surroundings, showed a loss of interest in life, and experienced visceral symptoms (Mendels & Cochrane, 1968). There was fair agreement that such patients were older, had a history of previous depressed episodes, lost weight, awoke too early in the morning, reproached themselves, and did not display certain neurotic symptoms. It does seem, then, that an endogenous syndrome exists.

The next question, however, concerns what it is that the endogenous syndrome is different from. The reviewers of the studies described just above (Mendels & Cochrane, 1968) concluded that the endogenous factor may be "simply measuring a pure or 'classic' depression picture" [P. 9], that "the so-called endogenous factor might represent the core of depressive symptomatology" [P. 10]. In other words, it may be that what clinicians have been calling "endogenous" might in reality be nothing more than "very severe." Such a conclusion seems strengthened by the rather surprising finding that patients who are considered endogenously depressed had experienced distressing life events almost as often as other depressed patients (Paykel, Prusoff, & Klerman, 1971; Leff, Roatch, & Bunney, 1970). This finding is, of course, ironic, since the endogenous syndrome had been named in the belief that patients with these symptoms become depressed without any external precipitating cause. In another study, intensive inquiries into the lives of 40 depressed patients showed that all of them could be regarded as having been precipitated into depression by a definable set of events, even though these were often extremely subtle and would have been hard to detect with less thorough probing (Leff, Roatch, & Bunney, 1970). For instance, one young woman, the daughter of a prostitute, had spent much of her life trying to demonstrate to herself and others that she, unlike her mother, was virtuous and deserving. She became depressed when her generally rejecting husband, during an argument, called her a whore. The investigators included 13 "endogenously" depressed patients among their 40 and found no differences between them and the other patients in the number or nature of the events that occurred in the months before the patients became depressed.

What sense can we make of these findings? First, it seems safe to continue regarding depression as a complex psychological and biological response to losses of incentives. Second, however, the depressive reaction involves many components of the nervous system. Just as any other bodily mechanism, these nervous system components can be disrupted, in which case they can produce a depressed state even without the usual frustrations. Just as it is possible to change the function of any organ through direct electrical, chemical, or mechanical stimulation, the brain systems responsible for depression are undoubtedly capable of being switched on "downstream" from and independently of the psychological events that usually govern them. Whether depressions begin that way has apparently very little to do with whether the symptoms conform to the "endogenous" syndrome or not, but there is little question that such depressions can occur.

Second, it seems likely that people vary greatly both in their susceptibility to becoming depressed and in the form that their depressions take. All biological characteristics vary among the members of a species, not just length of nose and color of skin but also size and function of the liver, reactiveness of the adrenal glands, and the anatomy and physiology of the brain. These biological differences are due to the interaction of genetic and environmental factors, and they undoubtedly affect the conditions and forms in which people experience depressions. In addition to varying biologically, people are also subject to sharply different cultural influences and personal histories. We shall examine these differences among individuals in a later section. For now, it is important only to recognize that because of them some people become depressed much more easily than others and experience their depressions somewhat differently than others; and this may be admitted without invalidating the theory that depressions are designed into the organism as reactions to losing incentives.

Recovery

Most depressions, even a majority of those severe enough to receive clinical attention, gradually clear up without specific treatment. In fact, except for antidepressant drugs and electroconvulsive shock, there are no reliable treatments. For most depressions, therefore, there is a phase during which the depressed person is gradually returning to normal. This period is what I am calling a "recovery" phase.

When the recovery phase has ended, several changes have taken place. In comparison with the depression phase, of course, people's moods are relatively happier. They have regained interest in various incentives to which they had been indifferent. They have perhaps become interested in new incentives. Perhaps most striking, in comparison with all previous phases of the disengagement cycle, the person no longer acts committed to the incentive he or she had lost.

The existence of the recovery phase therefore raises some interesting questions. What happens to the person's original commitment to the lost incentive? What happens to its incentive value? How long does recovery from depression normally take? What determines how long recovery takes in a particular case?

What happens to the value of the lost incentive? It might seem that if someone gives up striving for an incentive, its affective value for him or her has most likely declined. However, as we saw in Chapter 1, people usually strive after valuable incentives only if they have a reasonable expectation of attaining them. People might abstractly assign high value to cruising the world in their own yacht, becoming President of the United States, or winning the Nobel Prize, but most people regard such achievements as unfeasible, given their life circumstances, and are neither very excited to think that they could pursue such goals nor very much saddened to think that they may never achieve them. In these cases, however, the person has never become committed to pursuing them. How does a person regard an incentive after having become committed and having had to give it up?

One thing that has clearly happened is that the person is no longer committed to the pursuit. In all likelihood, however, the lost incentive has become not neutral in value but ambivalent. Whereas earlier the person wanted very much to achieve the incentive, he is now both attracted and repelled by it; and this ambivalence is so painful that he may avoid the very situations in which he can contemplate the incentive. Bowlby (1973) describes some observations by Heinicke and Westheimer (1966) with children aged 13 to 32 months who had been separated from their parents:

On meeting mother for the first time after the days or weeks away every one of the ten children showed some degree of detachment. Two seemed not to recognize mother. The other eight turned away or even walked away from her. Most of them either cried or came close to tears; a number alternated between a tearful and an expressionless face. (P. 12)

Interestingly, when such reunited children overcome their initial "detachment" from their mothers, it is often followed by clinging. Sometimes, indeed, detachment and clinging alternate. It seems clear that these children are in sharp conflict. They want their mothers close, but are deeply pained by having them there.

Similar reactions have been observed in young monkeys (Kaufman, 1973). Pigtail and bonnet macaques were separated from their mothers. The pigtails became depressed and the bonnets were adopted by other bonnet mothers. Periodically, the original mothers were reintroduced into the infants' cages, but they were put there in small cages within the infants' larger cages so that the infants could not make contact.

Each time, the first [pigtail] infant, after a cursory look, continued what it was doing; but each time, the second infant, after looking at its caged mother, collapsed into a ball and remained withdrawn and immobile until its mother was removed, whereupon it quickly resumed playing. For 23.5 hours of each day, it explored and played and ate and slept like the other infants, but during the half-hour of its mother's caged presence it showed the depressive response. An identical experiment was done with two bonnets . . . [w]hen the caged mothers were returned, each infant ran to its *adopted* mother and remained with her until the cage was removed. (P. 50)

Adult humans also experience this kind of pain. We have seen that having people read depressed statements tends to depress them. People who have been bereaved experience moments of pain even long after their recovery is apparently complete. "At anniversaries, for example, or when an old friend comes to call unexpectedly or when a forgotten photograph is discovered in a drawer all the feelings of acute pining and sadness return and the bereaved person goes through, in miniature, another bereavement" (Parkes, 1970, P. 464).

Evidently, then, the value of the lost incentive remains strong, and even the depressive form of pursuing the incentive, pining, can persist. What must happen, then, is that the person's commitment to the incentive, the impulse to attain it, and the influence of that commitment on moment-to-moment thought and feeling become progressively inhibited. The sphere within which the lost incentive still controls behavior and inner experience is gradually narrowed. As the lost incentive becomes a much smaller part of the person's inner reality, he or she experiences more and longer periods of pleasant feeling. As the lost incentive becomes a less dominating force in the person's life, other incentives seem more valuable again and attract the person's interest, perhaps through a shift in his or her adaptation level for value.

What conditions promote recovery? It is impossible to state a specific length of time during which depression and recovery take place, partly because different indicators of recovery may occur at different times and partly because recovery depends on the person's history, life situation, and constitution. Kaufman (1973) can state that infant pigtail macaques recover their normal levels of playfulness within four weeks after being separated from their mothers, and Parkes (1970) can state that widows' appetites for food recover during about the third month of bereavement, but other functions may return to normal more slowly, and in some respects the individual may never recover fully.

Nevertheless, there are conditions that promote recovery better than others. In general, life situations that offer substitute incentives seem to shorten at least some aspects of depression. To return for a moment to monkey evidence, Kaufman's (1973) pigtail macaques became severely depressed after losing their mothers but the bonnet macaques did not, although they had both become quite agitated. The probable reason for the difference is that pigtail adults are relatively isolated from each other whereas bonnet adults are close, with the consequence that pigtail adults reject and even harass the orphans in their midst, whereas bonnet adults quickly adopt them. Therefore, the pigtail orphans were left completely motherless and became depressed, but bonnet orphans were adopted and escaped at least the worst outward symptoms of depression.

People, too, seem to respond to available incentives. Widowed adults are less likely to become deeply depressed if they have close relationships with children (Clayton, Halikas, & Maurice, 1972), and those widows in Parkes's (1970) group who held jobs "found fresh interests and new friends earlier than the widows who had no job to take them out of the home" [P. 462].

Another factor that may speed recovery is to take the person away from the cues associated with the lost incentive. There is some intriguing anthropological evidence on this point (Rosenblatt, Walsh, & Jackson, 1976). For instance, some societies impose taboos against speaking a deceased person's name, especially in the presence of close relatives of the deceased. Furthermore, widows and widowers remarry more often in societies that have "tie-breaking" customs, such as destroying or burying the deceased's possessions, tearing down the house they shared, and moving away from the old locality. The rate of remarriage seems to be particularly high in societies with the "levirate" (the custom of marrying the husband's brother) or with the "sororate" (marrying the wife's sister). Presumably, siblings-in-law make more accessible "incentives" than more distant acquaintances or total strangers.

It might seem from this evidence that the remedy for depression is obvious: Surround depressed persons with attractive incentives and eliminate cues that remind them of what they have lost. Unfortunately, many depressed individuals would find the most promising of incentives unappealing, because their appetite for all incentives other than the one lost has virtually vanished. Clinical observations suggest that the ability of the person to respond to alternative incentives gradually improves during depression (Jacobson, 1971). In fact, it may be possible to define the "recovery" phase of the incentive-disengagement cycle as that period during which the depressed person increasingly comes to appreciate incentives other than the one lost. At some time during clinical depression, patients become unusually responsive to small successes. For instance, depressed patients working on small laboratory tasks try harder after successfully completing a task than after failing one, which is a pattern opposite to that of nondepressed individuals, who try harder after failure (Loeb, Beck, & Diggory, 1971). Whether this responsiveness to success is something that marks only the later stages of depression — the portion included within our "recovery" phase — or whether it characterizes all of depression, there is too little hard evidence to be sure, but at this point it seems likely that depressed individuals become progressively more responsive. Therefore, neither the generalization that "Nothing helps" nor the generalization that depressed individuals respond to alternative incentives is exclusively correct. However indifferent the depressed person may be at some early stage of his or her depression, he or she may become responsive later on; and it would then be the task of a therapist, caretaker, or friend to discover the point at which the change takes place.

Do the Disengagement Phases Really Constitute a Cycle?

We have seen that the frustration of losing incentives makes a person's behavior become more vigorous and eventually more primitive and aggressive, and that eventually unrelieved frustration becomes depressing. The fact that frustration produces these effects, and the fact that these effects take place at somewhat different times following frustration, does not necessarily mean that the "phases" really make up a coherent, lawful sequence or that the sequence is governed by a single brain system. Could these various reactions to frustration be a group of fairly independent, separate effects that just happen to coincide in time? It is possible but, given the mounting evidence, very unlikely.

One problem in thinking that all of these consequences of frustration obey a single set of laws is that we are talking about such superficially different events. There is a world of difference between being annoyed and disappointed over a broken pop dispenser and grieving for one's lost spouse. There is a vast difference between a rat not finding a food pellet at the end of a runway and a college student being unable to solve an experimental problem. Can we really think of these things in the same scale?

Different as these cases are, they nevertheless do follow certain regularities. They differ chiefly in the duration and intensity with which the person or animal is affected. Bereavement takes much longer to get over and is a vastly more profound experience than frustration over a pop machine. We have only a few clues to what determines how long and deep the experience will be. Probably, people grieve longer and harder over something to which they were strongly attached than over a passing fancy, and their lives are probably more disrupted if the thing they lost involved a large part of their daily acts and thoughts than if it involved only an isolated and restricted part. Thus, losing a spouse or a gratifying job is more depressing than losing a friendly cashier or a favorite pocket comb.

The diversity of these things need not necessarily suggest that they are governed by different laws. Alternatively, it could suggest that the laws and underlying mechanisms are basic for higher animal organisms — that they must have first emerged at a point in evolution so early that the diversity we see today had not yet developed. What evidence is there to suggest that this may be so?

Behavioral Evidence for a Cycle

Whenever investigators have observed people or animals following a loss, they have reported a very similar sequence of events. This is particularly remarkable when one considers the variety of losses and species involved: spouses, eyesight, and physical health among human adults; mothers among human infants; mothers and peers among monkey infants; and food rewards among rats. Despite occasional differences in the language the investigators used, they were clearly referring to similar events: a phase of activity, disbelief, or invigoration, followed by a second phase of protest, blame, or aggression, leading then to grief, apathy, despair, or depression, ending finally by detachment or recovery. The end result is disengagement: the actions of the person or animal no longer seem to be directed toward the lost incentive, even though contacts with the incentive or thoughts about it may continue to be painful or conflicted.

Perhaps the only quantitative record of an incentive-disengagement cycle was obtained in the unlikely study of extinction in rats (Klinger, Barta, & Kemble, 1974). The rats in this study had become accustomed to finding food at the end of a runway. Following some of their runs down the runway, the animals were placed directly into a box in which the amount of their spontaneous running-around activity could be recorded. The floor of this activity box had been divided into small four-inch (10 cm.) squares, and an observer could count the number of squares each rat entered in one minute. Figure 5-1 shows how these activity levels changed as the rats were repeatedly frustrated, with number of squares entered after each runway trial scaled along the ordinate and the successive trials (that is, experiences with reward or disappointment) scaled along the abscissa. It is easy to see that after the first few disappointments, the rats' activity levels rose far above those typical while they were still getting their food rewards, corresponding presumably to the invigoration and aggression phases. After four such trials, however, the activity levels began to drop again, and after the ninth to twelfth disappointments the rats were considerably less active than they had been while they were still being rewarded regularly, presumably corresponding to the depression phase. However, their activity levels had reached their lowest point just following the eleventh trial of disappointment, and activity levels on succeeding trials gradually rose back to normal. The curve that charts these rats' activity levels, then, embodies quantitatively the sequence of events reported by other observers with human and monkey losses ranging from eyesight to mothers and spouses.

Evidence on Brain Mechanisms

The behavioral evidence on the incentive-disengagement cycle strongly suggests that there is, indeed, a lawful sequence of events that unfolds whenever a person loses an incentive and is forced to give up trying for it. One would expect that such a well-regulated sequence of behavior would be served by a single, interconnected system of brain mechanisms. Although the evidence on this point is still extremely sketchy, it does seem to point in the expected direction.

The evidence that exists focuses on two aspects of brain function. The first is biochemical and involves the catecholamine substance, norepinephrine, which is involved in transmitting nerve impulses across the "synapses" between pairs of certain neurons. The second is an anatomical location in the brain called the amygdala, which is an inside part of the brain's temporal lobe (behind the ear) and forms a part of the brain's "limbic system," which has frequently been implicated in emotional activity. Norepinephrine and the amygdala are particularly interesting in connection with an incentive-disengagement cycle because they seem to be involved in both aggression and depression.

Norepinephrine seems to become more plentiful in the brain during aggression (Kety, 1970), and it seems to become depleted during depression (Schildkraut & Kety, 1967). If rats are given a drug (tetrabenazine) that depletes their stores of brain norepinephrine they become passive and helpless like Seligman's animals that had been subjected to inescapable stress; but if they are given a drug (pargyline) that protects their brain norepinephrine from becoming depleted naturally, they are able to sustain inescapable stress without collapsing into helpless passivity (Weiss, Glazer, & Pohorecky, 1974).

Norepinephrine also affects rats' responsiveness to incentives. Rats can have needle electrodes implanted into their brains so that the tips of the electrodes rest in the animals' "pleasure centers." Rats will then learn to press levers in their cages for the reward of brief electric stimulations through the electrodes. When they are given a drug

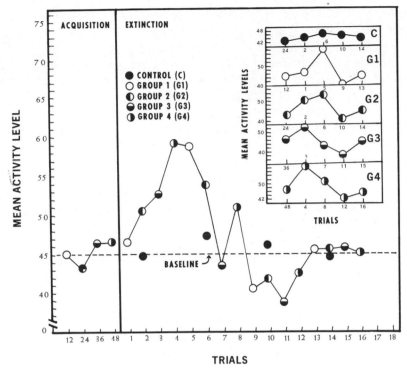

Figure 5-1. Activity levels (number of 10-cm. squares entered per 60 sec.) as a function of preceding runway trials. (The large curve is a composite of data from four experimental groups whose separate curves are presented in the upper right. The unconnected black dots represent the activity levels of Control Group 5, also presented in the extreme upper right. The second point from the left in the large curve represents identical activity means for Group 2 and Group 5 (control). Reprinted with permission from "Cyclic Activity Changes during Extinction in Rats: A Potential Model of Depression," by E. Klinger, E. D. Kemble, and S. G. Barta, *Animal Learning and Behavior*, 1974, 2, 313–316. Copyright 1974 by the Psychonomic Society.

(tetrabenazine) that releases norepinephrine from brain cells and depletes it, the rats press the lever less frequently; but when they are also given a drug (a monoamine oxidase inhibitor) that prevents norepinephrine from being taken up again by the brain cells, they press the lever more often than usual (Schildkraut & Kety, 1967).

In clinical work with humans, the antidepressant drugs in greatest use protect the patient's store of brain norepinephrine either by preventing its breakdown inside brain cells (the monoamine oxidase inhibitors) or by preventing it from being absorbed by those cells (the tricyclics) (Klerman, 1973). It therefore seems that brain norepine-phrine is associated with aggression, vigorous pursuit of incentives, helplessness, indifference to incentives, and depression.[5]

The amygdala also seems to be involved in aggression, depression, and striving for incentives. When an animal's amygdala is stimulated electrically, the result is emotional behavior such as attack or flight (Ursin & Kaada, 1960). Surgically destroying the amygdala "tames" wild animals (Schreiner & Kling, 1953, 1956) and makes animals less responsive to various positive and negative incentives (Kemble & Beckman, 1969, 1970; Kemble & Schwartzbaum, 1969).[6] The psychosurgeons Mark and Ervin (1970) have reported instances in which the seizure-produced rages of their human patients gave way to episodes of depression, and other clinical evidence implicates the amygdala in many such seizures. Finally, surgically destroying the amygdala of rats abolishes the "frustration effect" first noted by Amsel (Henke & Maxwell, 1973), and it also abolishes the other phases of the incentive-disengagement cycle that can be inferred from activity levels — depression and recovery as well as invigoration (Barta, Kemble, & Klinger, 1975).

Undoubtedly, things are not as simple as they may seem from the foregoing description. For instance, if it is true that norepinephrine and the amygdala support aggression, how do we account for the fact that depressed people are unusually hostile? A large part of the norepinephrine effect may have to do with the organism's willingness to put forth physical effort, for animals that seem too helpless to jump a hurdle (after either inescapable stress or the appropriate drug) are quite able to learn a less effortful response, poking their noses through a hole (Weiss, Glazer, & Pohorecky, 1974). Finally, both norepinephrine and the amygdala are parts of very complex systems, biochemical and anatomical, respectively. Therefore, the effects that seem to implicate them may in fact be due to the functioning of larger systems that merely include them or to other parts of those systems — for instance, other substances related to norepinephrine, or other brain structures connected with the amygdala.

Nevertheless, the evidence looks intriguing and promising. In any case, a theory of an incentive-disengagement *cycle* emphasizes the interconnectedness of the processes involved in commitment to and disengagement from incentives, and therefore prompts us to look for unitary or closely interconnected brain and biochemical systems un-derlying them.

Adaptive Functions

If animals and people come designed biologically to go into incentive-disengagement cycles whenever they give up on incentives, they must have acquired the machinery for doing so in the course of their evolutionary development; but, in that case, incentive-disengagement cycles must somehow provide organisms with special advantages in helping them to survive, either as species or as individuals. In fact, a number of adaptive advantages have been suggested.

Adaptive benefits for individuals. One way to think about the benefits of the disengagement cycle for individual organisms is to imagine what they would be like without its various components. For instance, an organism without a capacity for invigoration would go after each incentive with a fixed level of effort and a fixed approach to it. If the approach at that level of effort failed, there would presumably be no mechanism for doing anything further. Since this organism is clearly not using its capacities to their limits, it is bound to lose many incentives that it is otherwise capable of achieving. If we give our organism the capacity to vary its approach but not to increase its effort, then we must also provide it with some means to persist — to "lock on to" the incentive and to keep up its goal-striving until the incentive is achieved. However, although such an organism will succeed more often than the first, it will still not maximize its biological opportunities for achieving incentives that may be crucial to its individual survival. After all, sometimes success requires not new approaches but more vigorous, faster, or more concentrated efforts. Therefore, the invigoration phase clearly confers an advantage.

Sometimes, of course, even moderately invigorated behavior is insufficient when crude, brute strength or a frontal assault on an obstacle can succeed. It would be unfortunate if our organism became unduly forceful at the beginning, since technique is often more helpful than force and is always physically less taxing. Nevertheless, organisms are likely to survive better if they have at their command a last-resort capacity for directing maximum effort at achieving important incentives. Therefore, the aggression phase confers an adaptive benefit.

Unfortunately, there will be occasions when the best efforts fail. If an organism were equipped only with invigoration and aggression phases, it would presumably keep working for the first incentive to which it had become committed that was truly beyond its capacities, and, necessarily, it would work itself to death. If there is to be a commitment process, if there are to be invigoration and aggression phases, there must also be a shut-off mechanism so designed that when the costs of pursuing something become too large compared to the probable gains, the organism stops. Stopping, however, may carry emotional benefits of its own. If we assume that our organism has already been designed to appreciate rest when tired or to feel relief at the end of hard striving — which is itself adaptive and is obviously the way organisms are constructed — then stopping after an aggression phase would in each instance be rewarding. That is, the organism's emotional apparatus would systematically reward failure, thus turning failure into a positive incentive, and hence encouraging organisms to stop prematurely. To counter this reward-of-failure effect, it would be necessary to make stopping after unsuccessful striving emotionally unpleasant. Depression embodies both of these characteristics: depressed organisms stop striving and feel bad. In at least these respects, then, depression is a positively adaptive process, one that helps organisms to survive in the real world. Perpetual depression, of course, would leave the organism incapacitated. Therefore, there must also be a provision for recovering from depression.

When the lost incentive is an infant's mother, and the species is one in which infants depend on mothers to satisfy their vital needs, the incentive-disengagement cycle may play a special role. Infant monkeys and humans react to losing their mothers by crying and searching. Kaufman (1973) points out the great value of such behavior in helping the mother locate her infant. If such behavior goes on too long, however, the infant will wear itself out and will attract the attention of predators. Consequently, the depressed phase also serves an adaptive function after the initial distress calls and wandering have failed.

Adaptive functions for populations. In some important respects, depression is harmful to individuals, especially when it is profound and prolonged. Not only are depressed people often hypochondriacal (Jacobs, Fogelson, & Charles, 1968), they also incur a much higher-than-normal risk of actual illness and accident. Bereaved individuals often experience deteriorating health (Marris, 1958) and they face higher rates of mortality (Rees & Lutkins, 1967; Young, Benjamin, & Wallis, 1963). Life changes that require major social readjustments increase the risk of illnesses, especially of chronic illness (Holmes &

Masuda, 1973). The most pathogenic life changes often involve losing major incentives and often produce depression: "death of spouse," "divorce," "marital separation," "jail term," "death of close family member," and "personal injury or illness."

In the face of these grim statistics, how can depression as it is usually lived — apart from stopping striving and feeling bad — be adaptive? Viewed in terms of the welfare of a population, there are actually a number of advantages in having depressed individuals die. First, since severe depression is usually a reaction to losing important incentives, there is a good chance that the individual has lost a mate, progeny, or territory. Insofar as the individual lost the incentive out of greater-than-average incompetence, there is a eugenic advantage to the species to weed him or her out of the breeding stock. Second, whether incompetent or not, individuals who have been prevented from breeding still lay claim to a share of the food supply. Therefore, their deaths would enlarge the food supply for the breeding population and hence help the species to survive. Viewed from this rather harsh perspective, depression can be seen as a kind of screening or hurdle period. Having lost major incentives, individuals must pass special tests of their fitness to survive. If they fail them, the odds are that the species will be better off without them. If they survive, the species will be strengthened.

The grief that attends separation from loved ones may also have another adaptive function for those species whose members survive better in social groups than alone. If such individuals grieve every time they are separated from their group, grief serves as a reliable signal to them that something has gone wrong (Averill, 1968). That is, grief provides a form of strong evaluative feedback to the individual that overrides most other signals and impels him or her back to the safety of the group.

Price (1972) has suggested two other intriguing arguments for the biological usefulness of depression. First, there are times when losing incentives is more the fault of an inhospitable environment than of the individual's incompetence. In such cases, the population would be served best if individuals conserved their energies and put the least possible pressure on the food and other resources available to them, thereby minimizing the metabolic cost of waiting for better times. Price therefore draws a parallel between "stay-put" depressions and hibernation, which is another low-cost response to inhospitable environments, and he even suggests that they may share some of the same physical processes.

Price's second argument is that depression keeps members of some species from killing or wounding each other. The members of a number of primate species, for instance, compete for dominance not by violent fighting but by ritual symbolic displays. By snarling, bristling, posturing, or screaming, one monkey may convince the other to step down. However, such ritual competition would succeed in preventing violence only if there is some way for it to override the aggression phase of the incentive-disengagement cycle. If the loser

has merely received signals, he is physically fit and might choose to ignore the ritual contest and engage in destructive fighting, or he might claim that the ritual was null and void in some way and insist on repeating it. This sort of behavior would counteract all the gains to be derived from ritualized fighting; in fact, the ritualization of fighting requires that the loser should yield. . . . The simplest and most effective way that he can be induced to yield is by being incapacitated. It does not matter whether he is physically or psychologically incapacitated, except that in the latter case recovery is swifter and more complete. (Price, 1972, P. 135)

Consistent with this notion, vervet monkeys that have lost a competition for social dominance undergo marked physiological and behavioral changes, including depressed-appearing behavior and an increased chance of death (Gartlan & Brain, 1968).

It is apparent, then, that a psychological characteristic disadvantageous to certain individuals may nevertheless benefit the species and may therefore be selected for in the course of evolution. Depression may well have begun as a single process basic to the biological and psychological functioning of higher animal species and have been gradually adapted to the special needs of more advanced social species. Since depression could then serve a number of adaptive functions for individuals and for species, it may have evolved as a compromise mechanism serving several of them.

Individual Differences

The fire that melts the butter hardens the egg. People vary drastically in their reactions to stressful situations. The concept of the incentive-disengagement cycle helps us to think about some of the sources of these differences.

We can safely assume that the biological machinery of depression, like all biological characteristics, differs from person to person because of hereditary differences interacting with differences in the physical environment, such as nutrition, stimulation, and disease.

The result must be that some people are biologically destined to become more severely depressed than others facing similar circumstances, to experience the qualities of their depressions somewhat differently, to become angry with less provocation than others require, and to recover more quickly. If the process of becoming committed to an incentive and of maintaining a current concern about it has a specific biological basis, then we can further assume that some people become more firmly committed to incentives and hang onto their concerns more tenaciously.

The only significant body of evidence that bears on these assumptions suggests strongly, though not conclusively, that one can inherit a disposition to become severely depressed (Rosenthal, 1970). Not only is there probably a genetic basis for depression as a whole, genetics also seems to determine what form the depression will take, whether it will range from nondepressed to depressed ("unipolar") or whether it will include both depressed and manic episodes ("bipolar") (Winokur, 1973).

Apart from their genetic inheritance, people are more likely to become depressed if they have in certain ways been deprived of parental care during childhood. The most obvious way of being deprived is through one or both parents having died or deserted. Depressed patients, especially those severely depressed, are more likely than others to have lost a parent, particularly during their first five years or from ten to 15 years of age (Heinicke, 1973). There are, of course, other ways of suffering parental neglect, including financial neglect and parental illness. In one group of depressed patients, 23 out of 36 either had lost the parent of the same sex or had otherwise been deprived of that parent, whereas only three out of 16 spouses of the patients had been so deprived (Leff, Roatch, & Bunney, 1970).

The human evidence provides few clues to how losing a parent inclines one toward becoming a depressed adult, and, in fact, it even leaves some questions about whether it is really so. We are therefore fortunate to have an experiment performed with animals that points in a somewhat similar direction. In this study, monkeys were separated from their mothers for one or two periods of six days when they were about half a year old. At one year of age and to some extent even two years after the separations, these monkeys were more timid, less active, and less inclined to play with other monkeys than were normal monkeys who had never been separated from their mothers (Spencer-Booth & Hinde, 1971).

Evidently, interfering with a monkey infant's mothering even relatively briefly can have lasting effects. One must always be cautious in generalizing from one species to another, of course, but the monkey results are consistent in this instance with the human results. We do not know whether parental deprivation makes humans more timid, less active, and less sociable, but it does appear to incline them toward depression. Furthermore, being timid, inactive, and unsociable seems likely to handicap a person in pursuing normal goals and would therefore lead to more occasions for painful disengagements. Since timidity, inactivity, and aloofness must have some kind of emotional base, it is possible that being deprived of parents during childhood alters a person's later emotional functioning, making him or her more vulnerable emotionally to normal situations and stresses.

Factors That Dispose People to Give Up

So far, we have considered differences in the way people are constituted to react emotionally, owing to their genetic inheritance and to traumatic early separations from their parents. These are probably not the only reasons that some people become depressed more than others. The theory of the incentive-disengagement cycle allows us to look for other reasons by recasting the question. If people get depressed as a part of disengaging from lost incentives, then if we wish to know why some people are unusually given to depression we should ask why they are unusually likely to give up on their goals. For this question, there are a number of answers.

Unrealistic goals. People are more likely to fail in their undertakings if they persist in committing themselves to unrealistic goals. It is therefore not surprising that clinicians report that depressed patients are more likely than others to set unreasonably high, rigid goals, and to measure their worth against higher standards than those used by others (Beck, 1974; Becker, 1974).

Limited repertory of coping skills. People are more likely to fail if they lack the sheer ability to cope. Among the reasons that bonnet macaque orphans avoid the worst depression is that they can wheedle bonnet adults into adopting them (Kaufman, 1973). People from whom little was demanded in childhood may find themselves without routine skills for maintaining adult relationships (Beck, 1974).

Faint hopes. People vary greatly both in the strength of their hopes that they will succeed and in their faith that they can do something about it. Simply knowing that one has in the past succeeded after long, hard work may help a person persist at unpromising tasks. Rats that have been rewarded irregularly when they work for food persist at their task longer when the experimenter stops rewarding them than rats that have been rewarded every time they respond (Amsel, 1972). Their greater persistence is not due to momentary expectations, as evidenced by the fact that they remain persistent rats even after they have been switched to a long series of frequent rewards and even when they are given tasks unlike the ones they started with. Comparable experiments have not, of course, been performed with humans, but the animal evidence suggests that a person's capacity to persist through severe adversity may be developed through early moderate adversity.

Much also depends on how much influence a person believes he or she has on the success of a project and on whether one attributes success or failure to ability, effort, luck, or the difficulty of the undertaking. People who believe that their own efforts are more important than other factors in determining whether they will succeed or fail at a task persist longer at it (Shepel & James, 1973). People who attribute their failures to not having tried hard enough or to bad luck persist longer than people who attribute their failures to low ability or to the difficulty of the task (Dweck & Reppucci, 1973; Weiner, Heckhausen, Meyer, & Cook, 1972).

People's patterns of expectations and attributions can together constitute a self-perpetuating system (Heckhausen, 1975a). People who believe that their own efforts are important are more likely than others to make those efforts. They are therefore more likely to succeed at the projects they undertake, and they will therefore remain convinced that their efforts count. People who attribute their failures to low ability and who do not believe that trying harder would make much difference are less likely to persist at tasks, are therefore less likely to succeed, and will therefore remain convinced that the outcomes of their undertakings are largely beyond their control. Such persons are likely to choose either very easy tasks, well within their ability as they see it, or very hard, risky tasks, in which success would largely be a matter of good luck. In either case, the person would attribute success to something other than his or her own efforts — either to easy tasks or to good luck — thereby again confirming the conviction that success is beyond his or her control. In this way, people can develop enduring patterns of viewing their worlds that dispose them to give up too soon and therefore to become depressed.

The experimental evidence on which the above conclusions are based comes alive in the deep futility experienced by certain poor children in the Appalachian mountains (Polansky, Borgman, & de Saix, 1972). The mothers of these children themselves chronically feel helpless, hopeless, apathetic, and aloof. They neglect their children, often physically but especially psychologically, simply by not responding to the child's individual requests and initiatives. Eventually, the children learn the lesson that nothing does any good. They then generalize the lesson to their other life settings, such as school, with disastrous consequences that further drive the lesson home. Thus, another generation is infected with its mothers' sense of futility, which, without intervention from outside, is bound to transmit its deadly hopelessness to yet another generation.

Inner Experience and the Incentive-Disengagement Cycle

The inner face of depression is extraordinarily grim. Typically, depressed people feel melancholy or apathetic. They feel beleaguered by the world's demands to do this and accomplish that, demands that they fear they will disappoint because of inadequacy. They notice bodily sensations and fear they may be seriously ill. They cannot concentrate. They are bored with their dull inner life, whose staleness is unpredictably shattered by thoughts of what they have lost and by waves of sorrow in the wake of their remembrances. They mull their responsibility for their predicament with remorse over their guilt or with regret for their limitations. They stand exposed at least to themselves as frail. Will they ever shine again? Can they ever enjoy again? Can they ever again feel a sense of untarnished accomplishment, a pride undemeaned by the pretended admiration of others who are trying to be kind? The world is bleak, the future dark. Oh, for the peace of intactness!

The litany of the depressed is all too familiar to clinicians, but many aspects of it have been poorly understood. Why hypochondria? Why such a boring inner self? Why such persistent hopelessness and self-derogation? Why such difficulty in concentration? When we now merge the theory of the incentive-disengagement cycle with the theories of thought and affect presented in the earlier chapters, the meaning and causes of the symptoms become clear.

How Thought Is Organized during the Cycle

When people become excited or aroused about an incentive, they become unusually attentive to anything associated with it. The usual sensitization to incentive-related cues that occurs during states of current concern becomes greatly heightened. At the same time, however, people become less attentive to other cues (Easterbrook, 1959). They do not notice events as readily if they are unrelated to the pursuit at hand and they make less good use of them.

The phases of the incentive-disengagement cycle are, of course, phases of increased involvement with a blocked incentive. During invigoration, people focus on it harder, work harder, and come to value it more highly. They become more responsive to events related to their efforts, and, at least for the moment, they care less about and attend less to things not related to it.

This pattern of attending and valuing continues through the invigoration and aggression phases of the cycle. It also seems to continue on through the depression phase, but here its meaning and function become drastically altered by changed circumstances. After all, the person has begun to give up, has stopped trying. Events and things related to the lost incentive no longer help achieve it. Instead, they only serve as reminders of the loss. At the same time, other pursuits seem meaningless, and the cues related to them have little appeal and attract little attention. The person's current concerns about them have lost most of their influence on attention, recall, and thought. Thus, virtually the only features of the world that are not blah are painful and accusatory. From this basic configuration flow the characteristics of thought during depression.

Hypochondria. People who are depressed tend to be more than normally concerned with their physical health and more than normally fearful that various physical sensations bode serious illnesses such as heart disease or cancer (Jacobs, Fogelson, & Charles, 1968). The hypochondria of the depressed can be explained as follows. First, depressed people are far less responsive to outside stimulation than before, because they have ceased to care about most of the incentives to which they had earlier been committed. Therefore, they are likely to become more responsive to small pains and bodily sensations. Second, this is likely to be especially the case for the considerable number of depressed individuals who also experience anxiety (Grinker et al., 1961; Claghorn, 1970), since their bodily sensations permit them to attribute their anxiety to something concrete: a physical disorder. Third, depressed individuals typically want help and care; but since their objective circumstances often do not seem to warrant as much care as they would like, they may be reluctant to seek it without a better pretext, and other people often become impatient with them when they try. However, being "sick" provides the necessary pretext. It brings with it special gains of attention, sympathy, tolerance, and care. The role of "being sick" must therefore seem rather attractive to many depressed people, and it may help some of them to adopt and act on bodily concerns.

Pangs. "The most characteristic feature of grief," writes Parkes (1972), "is not prolonged depression but acute and episodic 'pangs'. . . . At such a time the lost person is strongly missed and the survivor sobs or cries aloud for him" (P. 39). In the language of Chapter 2, a pang is a respondent segment of thought and feeling induced by external cues or by the bereaved person's previous thoughts in conjunction with his or her still-alive current concern about the lost loved one. The "pang" is therefore just a special case of respondent thought, distinguished primarily by the strong, painful feelings that accompany it.

Pangs have another special characteristic, one that does not set them apart from other respondent segments but that does affect the way they are regarded by the person having them: They are "senseless," in that they catapult one back into a lost past. That is, of course, inevitable, if the current concern about the lost person is still alive — if disengagement is still incomplete — because the actions appropriate to the concern are continuations of the invigoration and aggression phases, such as searching for and trying to retrieve the thing lost; but the thing lost is past.

How does it happen that people continue to think thoughts that have become clearly outmoded? Pangs are not the only striking instance of this in the bereaved. Widows vividly describe moments when they spontaneously imagine a departed husband to be present, plan to tell him something, watch for his return from work, and fix tea for him (Marris, 1958). Often, these moments become occasions for pangs of grief. They occur for the same reasons they had occurred for years while the husband was still alive: They were habitual ("integrated") modes of thinking and acting, induced jointly by relevant cues and current concerns. Even though those concerns have outlived their appropriateness, the system continues to function. Perhaps the pangs are renewed bereavements over each particular facet of life that the bereaved person discovers must be abandoned. Perhaps, then, disengagement occurs in spurts, each pang helping another obsolete sector of life fade from current concern to fond and painful memory.

Qualities of fantasy. Depressed individuals are relatively indifferent to most of the incentives that remain realistically available to them. Since current concerns govern a person's responsiveness to cues and thereby the content of fantasy, the weakened concerns of the depressed should make them unresponsive to most stimuli. Not only should this unresponsiveness lead people to engage in less goal-directed activity, it should also make their fantasy less varied, more repetitive, and more stale, much of it still focused on their lost incentive, their depression, their resentments, and their bodily concerns.

These conclusions seem to be borne out by the results of a study in which college men and women and a group of prisoners completed a set of questionnaires that assessed depression and daydreaming experiences (Traynor, 1974). There was a tendency for the more depressed respondents to report more daydreaming, which presumably reflects less deliberate problem-solving thought. Taking differences in daydreaming tendencies into account, one of the most consistent findings was that the more depressed subjects were the most bored with their daydreams. They also thought more about their fears of failure, about feelings of guilt, and (in the case of the college men) about aggression. Finally, they found their daydreams less enjoyable and acceptable.

Bereaved widows, too, complain about their thoughts. They "returned in their minds again and again to the events of their husband's death, compulsively reviewing the course of the illness or accident. They did this both in reverie and in conversations with others. Again and again they asked themselves why it had happened. They seemed to have little control over 'dwelling' so on their experience" (Glick, Weiss, & Parkes, 1974, P. 126).

Much the same qualities that characterize the waking fantasy of the depressed also intrude on their dreams. When a large group of psychiatric patients were asked to recall their most recent dream, about 30% of those who were at least mildly depressed reported that their dream included some kind of frustration or harm, as compared with only 11% of the nondepressed patients (Beck & Ward, 1961).[7]

As we saw in Chapter 2, whatever influences the flow of fantasy also alters the flow and efficiency of directed thought. It is therefore not surprising that more than half of a group of recently bereaved widows and widowers reported having difficulty concentrating or suffering from a poor memory (Clayton, Halikes & Maurice, 1971).[8] Depressed individuals do less well than others on most tasks that require concentration or directed thought (Miller, 1975).

Gloomy Views of Self and World

People who are depressed are very likely to be pessimistic as well (Beck, 1974). Aaron Beck speaks of the depressive's "cognitive triad" of negative views of self, of world, and of future. Nor is it just the case that pessimistic people are more likely to get depressed. Beck found that when his patients' depressions lifted, their pessimism tended to dissipate also.

Within the framework of the incentive-disengagement cycle, the depressed person's pessimism is understandable. The person has just sustained a loss of something important. He or she was unable to prevent this loss, which underscores his or her vulnerability to later disasters and vividly demonstrates personal limitations. Failure is thus not only depressing, it also lowers a person's self-esteem (Lewinsohn & Flippo, 1969 [unpublished study cited by Becker, 1974]; Lish, 1969).

Recognizing their real failures, people become depressed and pessimistic. As a result, they underestimate their actual powers, pass up valid opportunities, and become less effective members of society, thereby helping them to confirm their low opinion of themselves. They interpret some things as failures that are not and give up pursuits that were realistically likely to succeed; and these consequences of depression in turn increase the number of their disengagements and therefore the psychological causes of depression.

Both cognitions and affects play a causal role in this chain of events, and together they form a vicious circle. In the swing of theorists toward cognitive views of depression, perhaps primarily influenced by Beck's (1967) important contributions, it is important not to neglect the reciprocal effects of cognitions and feelings on each other. Affect is, as we saw in Chapter 3, evaluative feedback. If the affect is depressed, the feedback is saying that things are going badly. Depressed people, long accustomed to paying attention to their feedback systems, will draw the apparently appropriate conclusions. The gloomy dispositions of people who have been made depressed chemically as a result of drugs or of natural hormone fluctuations serve as cases in point.

Fluctuations and the Stability of Mood

Everyone experiences some ups and downs in their daily moods, although some people are clearly more stable than others (Wessman & Ricks, 1966). Some of the differences are no doubt due to biological factors, but others can be explained by the nature of the incentive-disengagement cycles. To do so requires one important assumption; when a person is in two or more cycles at the same time, the effects on affect summate with each other and with whatever other influences may be operating on mood at the same time. This assumption is supported by the evidence we saw in Chapter 3 that people "add up their pluses and minuses" in arriving at their level of well-being. Thus, if someone has reached the depression phase of a cycle with respect to one incentive, the invigoration phase with respect to a second incentive, and is consummating a third, we would predict a relatively flat level of affect. That is, the person will be neither as depressed about the lost incentive as he or she might have been nor as euphoric about the one achieved.

Most people probably have a number of irons in the fire at a particular moment in time, a variety of projects some of which are going better than others. As long as identical phases of different incentive-disengagement cycles do not coincide in time, mood should remain relatively stable, fluctuating moderately within easily tolerable limits. If, however, a person loses several incentives at about the same time, or loses an incentive of overriding importance, we would predict a massive mood shift in the direction of depression. Depending on the person's personal, social, and material resources for dealing with deep depression and for locating alternative incentives, the depression may or may not require clinical attention.

Correspondingly, if someone experiences a number of triumphs within a short time, mood should become euphoric. Since euphoric moods tend to raise the adaptation level for good feeling, however, we would predict that the aftermath of euphoric periods will be periods of mild depression owing to the loss of euphoria, and these will also be periods of increased vulnerability to depression arising from actual losses.[9]

The Sense That One's Life Is Meaningful

Depressed individuals often complain that their lives have become meaningless. We have confirmed this clinical observation in our own questionnaire research with college students, which is described in

Chapter 1. In fact, the sense that their lives are meaningful was more closely related to two "feeling scales" (Wessman & Ricks, 1966) than to anything else. The first of the two is the scale for "Receptivity towards and Stimulation by the World," which ranges from "Passionately absorbed in the world's excitement. My sensations and feelings incredibly intensified." to "Life is too much trouble. Sick of everything, want only oblivion" (correlation with meaningfulness of .46, $p<.001$). The second scale is for "Elation vs. Depression," which ranges from "Complete elation. Rapturous joy and soaring ecstasy." to "Utter depression and gloom. Completely down. All is black and leaden" (correlation of .42, $p<.001$). Put in other words, of the 38 students who said their life is "full of meaning," only four (10%) felt less than "pretty good. OK," and of those who answered "very meaningful," only 17 of 57 (23%); but, on the other end, 13 of the 35 students (37%) who felt their life was only "somewhat" meaningful and six of the 11 (54%) who felt their life was only "slightly" meaningful felt less than "pretty good" — they felt "a little bit low" or worse.

Probably, the sense of meaninglessness is a part of depression — depressed individuals' recognition of their lack of interest in any incentive other than the one lost.

Clinical Implications of the Incentive-Disengagement Cycle

For reasons that are probably deeply rooted in the North American white culture, being depressed is considered not so much a misfortune, like scraping one's knee, but an abnormality. To be depressed is seen as wrong, as "negative thinking," as a flaw in the depressed person's character. Depression makes other people uncomfortable and it makes the one depressed a "drag." The popularization of Freudian theories has helped people to view depression as pathological, but because those theories have failed to provide a viable explanation of depression, people are hard put to know how to deal with it.

These attitudes, of course, compound the problems of the depressed. They often feel inadequate and ashamed that they cannot act merrier for their friends, and they fear that there is something basically wrong with them to account for their depression. By searching their own characters for fundamental defects, they are often kept from seeing their depression as a current problem that can be solved.

The theory of the incentive-disengagement cycle offers an alternative formulation of their problem and some alternative approaches to treatment. This view recognizes that depressions may sometimes be caused by malfunctions of the brain's biochemistry and physiology, and that some individuals are far more vulnerable to becoming depressed than others. However, this is not the crux of most depressions, anymore than a tense guitar string is enough to produce a tone. Guitar strings must first be plucked. People become depressed when they are giving up something to which they had become committed. In this view, depression is a normal and even adaptive process that accompanies disengaging from an incentive. It may become pathological in some circumstances and in some people, but despite its being a nuisance, in itself it need cause little concern for the psychological viability of the depressed individual. If one were to draw a physical analogy, it is more akin to a painful bruise than to a broken leg or to varicose veins. In severe cases, depression, like a bruise, might call for clinical support, and it also carries an increased risk of precipitating a more serious pathology. Nevertheless, the depressive process as such can be seen as essentially part of recuperating from loss.

If this view is correct, it will be worthwhile to consider a number of ideas that flow from it regarding research, treatment, and education.

Implications for Clinical Research

The account of the incentive-disengagement cycle given above will suggest to the research-minded reader a great variety of researchable problems, and these need not be spelled out here. Every statement concerning this theory is intended to be testable, and a great many need extensive further investigation. There are, however, some further implications which are less apparent and which I shall therefore describe here.

Interpreting manic states. A small proportion of people who become severely depressed are "bipolar," in the sense that their depressions alternate with "manic" states of exaggerated excitement and self-assertion. (Occasionally, people also become manic without experiencing states that are clearly depressed.) Although the affinity of mania and depression has long been recognized, their relationship to each other has not been well understood. It is becoming increasingly apparent that depression and mania are biochemically distinct states (e.g., Goodwin & Bunney, 1973; Gattozzi, 1970). The behavior of a manic is in some respects opposite to that of the depressed. Yet, there seems to be a link between the two, inasmuch as one follows the other with considerable regularity in some patients.

The concept of the incentive-disengagement cycle suggests in general terms what this link might be. We must first consider the nature of mania. Although manic patients often claim to be highly elated while they are manic, both their own later memory of their mania and the impression of observers at the time of their mania agree that they are at best only moderately elated (Platman, Plutchik, Fieve, & Lawlor, 1969). Instead, manic patients are extremely active, impulsive, aggressive, rejecting, and devoid of fear or caution. Manic patients are often quick-tempered and violent, and their manic excitement occasionally exhausts them to the point of physiological collapse. This pattern of manic behavior resembles an invigoration or aggression phase carried on well beyond its usual limits. It is the sort of behavior one might expect without a "stop" mechanism — the sort of outcome against which depression seems to guard.

These considerations suggest that what mania and severe depression have in common is that they are both exaggerated phases of incentive-disengagement cycles. What distinguishes them is that they represent different phases. Perhaps the neural and biochemical mechanisms that underlie the cycle sometimes push the depressed patient into a depressive phase prematurely or too profoundly, and at other times precipitate the patient into an aggressive phase inappropriately. In either case the mechanism is deranged.

If these conclusions are correct, it might pay to examine manic-depressive cycles from the standpoint of the incentive-disengagement theory. Are there events that could account for the transition from mania to depression or from depression to mania, such as renewed encouragements or defeats? Do changes in patients' assessments of their situations precede or follow biochemical changes that govern mood? Are there certain kinds of incentive losses or certain circumstances of incentive loss that distinguish manic from depressive patients? What are the biological signals produced during unsuccessful aggression phases that trigger the downswing into depression, and how may these signals become deactivated in mania and prematurely activated in "endogenous" depressions? And so on.

Disentangling different forms of depression. Depression takes a number of different forms — so many, in fact, that researchers seem unable to agree on what forms there are. It is quite possible that there are several distinct paths to depression. After all, breakdowns can occur at any of the levels of functioning involved in incentive-disengagement cycles, such as losing incentives, brain structures that subserve the disengagement cycle, brain chemistry, and endocrine products that may affect brain function.

Disentangling these various kinds of depression is difficult, and the theory of the incentive-disengagement cycle may help in two different ways. First, it provides a framework for thinking about differences between various forms of depression. Second, because it explicitly ties depression to incentive losses, it provides a way of thinking about the complications of *secondary* depressions. That is, a person may not only become depressed about losing an external incentive, he or she may also become further depressed about having become disabled by depression. For instance, some depressed patients suffer from severe retardation of their motor functions — they move and speak far more slowly than normal. When such patients were given a certain drug (L-dopa), their retardation lifted first and their mood began to improve somewhat later (Goodwin & Bunney, 1973). It is quite possible that at least some of their depression had been about their retardation, or that their physical improvement constituted the kind of success that elevates depressed patients' moods.

It is entirely possible that severe depressions eventually become a mixture of primary and secondary depressions. If that is so, the presence of secondary depressions would tend to blur some of the distinctions among depressions that developed for different reasons. Insofar as all contained some secondary depression, all would appear to the clinician to be more alike than they really are. The concept of the incentive-disengagement cycle may help to separate secondary depression from primary, and therefore to throw into greater relief the distinctions among different basic conditions.

Depression through overwhelming. Sometimes people seem to become depressed before they have actually lost anything, but when they are besieged by a multitude of difficulties that overtax their capacity to respond. That is, when a person is struggling to achieve a number of different objectives or to stave off an array of different disasters, he or she may react to a single further complication by sinking into depression. This cause of depression has not received much attention from theorists or clinicians and it seems to be undocumented in the research literature. It does, however, fit into the theory of the incentive-disengagement cycle, since that theory identifies disengagement with giving up. That is, loss of incentives must be interpreted subjectively from the standpoint of the loser. Being overwhelmed with more challenges than one feels able to master must lead to giving something up, even though an outside observer might not consider any of them insurmountable. From the outside, then, it will appear that the person was striving hard, then became depressed, and therefore lost the struggle, when in fact the depression was a reaction to the person's having subjectively given up.

It would be of considerable clinical interest to discover how often depression results from overwhelming and what kinds of people are especially susceptible to becoming depressed in this way.

Pinpointing sources of depression. Most depressions are about something fairly obvious, such as the loss of a loved one, of a career objective, of a social status, and the like. Others, however, have a source that is often obscure to both the patient and the clinician. Sometimes the patient may have been unaware of having become committed to an important incentive. For instance, a person may have formed unconscious sexual designs on a friend and may then become depressed when the friend marries. In other instances, the incentive may have been "lost" only in the sense that it lost its value, as in the case of a person tiring of an objectively good job. Or a person may defend against admitting that something is important because it would deflate his or her self-esteem. In these cases, the patient may not "know" why he or she is depressed, and the clinician may have to probe for a long time before finding a source or giving the case up as endogenous.

The theory of the incentive-disengagement cycle may help to devise strategies for identifying elusive lost incentives. Since, presumably, the patient's concern about the incentive being given up is still current, it may be possible to monitor the patient's thought content and psychophysiological reactions, such as skin resistance, finger blood volume, blood pressure, pupil size, and heart rate, while presenting a series of stimuli based on events and fixtures of the patient's recent life. Presumably, patients will be most responsive to stimuli that are related to the sources of their depressions, and the images they evoke in the patient will also be those most painful to contemplate.

Depression and disengagement. We have seen that depression seems to accompany the process of disengagement. This raises an interesting question: Is depression *necessary* in order for disengagement to occur? Is depression simply a side-effect of disengagement, or is it crucial to the whole process? These questions suggest the importance of discovering to what extent various pharmacological and electroconvulsive therapies interfere with the patient's disengagement from incentives. Remedies that interfere with disengagement may have either desirable or undesirable effects, such as sending back into contention someone who is too easily discouraged, or reviving a commitment to a goal that were better abandoned.

Implications for Treatment

Much of the work that goes on in psychotherapy can be thought of in terms of clarifying the client's incentives.[10] Whether therapists proceed in the psychoanalytic or in the behavioral tradition, they identify hidden impulses or discover what "reinforcements" are maintaining particular behaviors (that is, they are discovering at which incentives the patient's behaviors are directed) and they unearth defense mechanisms or key aversive stimuli (that is, they discover negative incentives that the patient's behavior is directed at avoiding.) Sometimes this work is explicit, but often it is only implicit.

The theory presented here suggests that therapists should carry out the task of clarifying incentives explicitly when they deal with people who are depressed. If the patient is depressed as a result of a disengagement process, it is up to the therapist to identify the process and help the patient understand what is going on. The therapist can be of considerable help simply by removing patients' sense of mystification about depression, enabling them to view depression as a natural, normal reaction that is usually self-limited in time. The therapist's other objectives, within an incentive-disengagement framework, are to clarify what factors in patients' life styles or decision processes may have made disengagement more likely than it needed to be, to help patients reorder their aspirations and devise strategies to realize them in as satisfying a way as possible, and to help patients form new incentive commitments that will restore a sense that their lives are meaningful. The last of these tasks coincides with the principal mission of logotherapy (Frankl, 1969). Understanding the ins and outs of people's relationships to their incentives may help the therapist to help the patient — the process of disengagement, the changes in the patient's receptiveness to various incentives, sources of pain in contemplating some incentives, the substitution-value of others, the stream of the depressed person's thoughts, and the disruption of the depressed person's resources for coping.

Behavior therapists have begun to develop techniques that should prove useful in helping to reorient depressed patients. For instance, Tharp, Watson, and Kaya (1974) have reported the cases of four depressed college women whom they treated successfully by means of an inexpensive program that is very relevant to the approach taken here. The four women had earlier participated in a course on human adjustment in which they learned and practiced some standard techniques for modifying simple behaviors, such as recording the frequency of behaviors they wished to change and rewarding the more desirable behaviors they wished to adopt in their place. Next, each of the women received some rudimentary forms and instructions to "pay particular attention to the antecedents of depressive feelings, and to consider intervention strategies which would interrupt chains-of-events leading to depressive reactions" (Tharp, Watson, & Kaya, 1974, P. 2). All four of these people substantially eliminated their problems with depression, even though two of them (Cases 3 and 4) were quite seriously depressed at the outset.

One woman discovered, as a result of keeping careful track of her moods, that her depression was only intermittent and that some kinds of activities depressed her whereas others pleased her. This insight apparently permitted her to take hold of her life and greatly reduce the amount of her depression.

A second woman eventually recognized her depression as feelings of loneliness, rejection, and uselessness that were produced by specific events in her life; and she also came to realize that she was made vulnerable to becoming depressed in this way because of her "over-dependence" on others. She set out to gain greater self-reliance by stopping all thoughts about her depression and its antecedents when they started and substituting some pleasant, absorbing activity, such as sewing. Thus, depressive thought about one incentive was cut off by forcing attention to another incentive. She said, "I never thought of my sewing as something I'm really interested in, but I'm beginning to see that it can be those simple things that are good and have meaning" (Tharp, Watson, & Kaya, 1974, P. 5).

The third case was more seriously depressed. She decided that she thought herself into depression by dwelling on unhappy interpersonal relationships or worries about her future. We might infer that she had acquired a pattern of deprecating herself in connection with interpersonal conflicts. To break the downhill chain of thoughts that invariably led her to depression, she worked out a thought-substitution strategy in which she stopped all incipient depressed thoughts and substituted a pleasant fantasy she called "my good dream," which was probably woven around positive incentives. This technique produced dramatic results in reducing her depression.

The fourth case, also seriously depressed, came to realize that she was depressed about her inability to assert her wishes and opinions with others — that she got depressed about not achieving her own goals in her relationships with other people — as a result of which she felt controlled and used. She successfully carried out a plan of systematically rewarding herself for honestly expressing her feelings, thereby bringing her depression down to a normal level.

The four cases do not constitute very rigorous evidence in favor of the methods used. The sample was small, and because there was no untreated comparison group there is no assurance that these students would not have thrown off their depressions even without help. Nevertheless, it is interesting that in each case the apparently effective treatment consisted of an incentive manipulation, involving first identifying the depression with a particular antecedent event and then doing something about that.

Education for Mental Health

Much of the trouble that people have with depression stems not from the inherent quality of depression but from not understanding what it bodes for them or says about them. There may be no way to make depression a pleasant experience but at least it can be a non-frightening, constructive experience. The difference lies in accepting depression as a natural event, as an important source of information, and as a basis for future planning and decision-making. To achieve this understanding ought to be one of the objectives of public education.

Medical practitioners are familiar with the fact that medical patients are often reassured and helped simply by having their physician put a name on their symptoms. Calling a pattern of pains "dysentery" or "ulcers" or "gastritis" signals to the patient that the pains are understandable, predictable, and manageable. As long as depression is regarded as simply a symptom, its meaning is ambiguous and its portents frightening. By referring to depression as part of a known process with a more or less predictable course and predictable consequences, it also becomes something to which a person can relate, for understanding conveys power. Insofar as the present view of aggression and depression is valid, teaching it and its implications may be able to provide a basis for such understanding.

If the incentive-disengagement theory is valid, a program of education for mental health should include two broad areas of discussion. One has to do with the nature of depression itself. The other has to do with managing goals, both of individuals and of organizations.

Education regarding depression. A program should, of course, present certain basic concepts: that incentive-disengagement cycles are reactions to blocked incentives, that their phases include invigoration, aggression, depression, and recovery, and that depression is in most cases a part of giving up incentives. Second, the program should present some of the accompaniments of the cycle: changes in the subjective value of other incentives, unrealistic degrees of pessimism, increased resentment and irritability, self-dissatisfaction, difficulty in concentrating, listlessness and fatigue, and so forth. The emphasis here should probably be placed on the extent to which the person's normal evaluative feedback system becomes distorted during the cycle. People lose perspective on the importance of both the blocked and the other incentives, and they had best allow for this distortion when they make decisions. Third, an educational program should point out the self-diagnostic value of depression. It tells people something about their prior values and goals and about their expectations of what they deserve and what they can achieve.

Rational goal management. Becoming committed to a goal apparently has serious consequences for people. It mobilizes their energies, influences their values after at first merely reflecting them, enables them to experience elation when things are going well, and exposes them to the risk of depression if things go badly. Choosing one's goals, then, becomes a highly consequential act which it is important to perform wisely. There are many considerations in such a choice. Avoiding commitments reduces the chances of being hurt, but it also reduces the chances of feeling elated.[11] Choosing goals that are too difficult unnecessarily lays one open to failure and depression. Overtaxing one's capacities to respond by tackling too many goals may lead to becoming overwhelmed and depressed. Settling for repetitive goals or goals that are too easy may result in diminishing satisfactions if the goals have no strong intrinsic or instrumental value, and may eventually be depressing as the person is forced to give up seeking satisfaction in that kind of activity. There are also the considerations regarding incentive value discussed in the previous chapter.

Insofar as these generalizations are valid, they could be incorporated into an educational program. Furthermore, they should be of concern not only to individuals making their own decisions but also to managers of organizations. The goals managers set for their organizations and the goals that managers encourage their staffs to set for themselves will, according to the view presented here, strongly affect their psychological functioning in the ways already discussed. It should be of considerable interest to investigate the role of goal-setting on organizational behavior.

Summary

There are a number of ways to lose what one has set out to attain or enjoy, such as disillusionment with the goal, exorbitant costs of attaining it, and insurmountable obstacles. People are in important ways organized around their goals, and giving one of them up therefore requires some psychological reorganization, the more drastic as the goal had been involving. Giving up an incentive sets in train a sequence of events that includes invigoration of the person's efforts to attain the goal, aggression and primitivization of those efforts, a downswing into depression, a period of depression, and a gradual recovery. During this sequence, called an *incentive-disengagement cycle*, the person becomes disengaged from the lost incentive, in that the incentive no longer commands much power over the person's thoughts and actions. However, during the cycle itself the lost incentive seems more valuable to the person than before, and other incentives seem less valuable. Thus, the person's values become distorted during disengagement. After the end of the cycle, the lost incentive probably remains valuable but no longer controls much of the person's behavior or inner experience, and other incentives have regained their former value and control. Recovery is hastened if the person has access to attractive alternative incentives.

Depression is a period of sad or apathetic mood, spasmodic pangs of grief and yearning, pessimism, irritability and resentment, indifference to many former pleasures, social withdrawal, and fantasies that are boring, unpleasant, and gloomy. These qualities reflect the heightened concern with something now lost and the diminished concern with incentives still available. Most depressed individuals suffer a loss in self-esteem, and many become hypochondriacal and anxious. In fact, they are more likely than nondepressed individuals to be personally ineffectual, to become ill, and to die. Nevertheless, depression is part of a process that is highly adaptive for individuals and perhaps even necessary for their survival, and there are many reasons to believe that depression has survival value for the species.

People vary greatly in their susceptibility to becoming depressed. They vary partly because they have inherited different tendencies for the neural and humoral mechanisms that underlie the incentive-disengagement cycle to break down. People also seem to be rendered emotionally more vulnerable to depression in adulthood by having lost a parent during their childhood years. Finally, people have developed different repertories of skills for coping with difficulty, different capacities to persist during adversity, and different expectations of how likely their own efforts are to help them succeed.

If this view of depression is valid, therapy for depression should be concerned with identifying incentive losses that may be responsible, helping patients to accept their depression as a natural, adaptive process, alerting them that depression will warp their value judgments, and assisting them to review their incentive commitments to make depression no more likely in their lives than necessary. Similarly, it may be possible to prevent some of the anxiety, distorted judgments, and depressive spirals that accompany depression over lost incentives by educating the public concerning the nature of depression and its expectable accompaniments.

Alienation, Futility, Discontent

Some life situations offer enlivening goals to strive for or powerful pleasures that fill a person's consciousness. In them, people act bouyant and feel a sense of effectiveness and élan. Other life situations are engulfed by major losses — of a loved other, a mode of living, a great plan. They "take the wind out of people's sails." Life seems stagnant and inhospitable. People feel depressed, resentful, and apathetic. In real life, of course, pure types of life situations are uncommon. Most people most of the time live in between these extremes, with a mix of bounties and hardships that produce a mixture of sadness and satisfaction. Nevertheless, imagining pure cases can sometimes be helpful. In this instance, describing two pure cases points to the need to describe a third, one that highlights a third kind of element in less pure life situations.

That is, there are extreme, more or less stable life situations in which people have no very powerful incentives to strive for or to enjoy. They may have had hopes at one time, but these have long since been dashed without ever having been replaced. These people are no longer recovering from a loss. They are chronically deprived. From their vantage point, nothing that they can do is likely to make much difference. Life continues to make certain demands on them. They may still have to put forth efforts to avoid an even worse fate, but they have given up hope of escaping their basic impoverishment.

One can unfortunately find relatively pure instances of this type. One thinks of African hunter-gatherers trapped in an arid preserve by government policy (Turnbull, 1972) or Appalachian whites caught in a social system they are unable to master (Polansky, Borgman, & de Saix, 1972). The impoverishment need not be economic. The world has its Hedda Gablers. Nor need the impoverishment of satisfactions

be total in order to be devastating. The thin maternal satisfactions of a
beset ghetto mother (Rainwater, 1970) and the economic security of
an educated wife with shattered aspirations (Wilson, 1950) are not
enough to fill the void.

Pure cases aside, a great many people live out their years discontent with one or more fixtures in their lives, more or less resigned to
making the best of a bad situation. The problem may be a dull job, a
perfunctory marriage, a prison sentence, or a disabled body. Defeat in
one area of life does not necessarily prevent people from finding
satisfactions in other areas. However, when people must devote
hours each week to the very thing that has ceased to hold much
satisfaction — when the job must still be done, the spouse still related
to, the sentence served, and the body borne with — it can hardly
help but change the tenor of a life.

The ideas we have examined in previous chapters would suggest
that situations of this kind must exercise some rather powerful effects
on the inner experiences of people trapped in them. Suppose someone gives up hope of intrinsic satisfactions in a job while continuing
to perform it for the income or to satisfy other people's expectations.
The job stays the same but not the incentive situation that the job
represents. Performing the job is now no longer aimed at positive,
attractive incentives, such as advancement, glory, stimulation, feeling
effective, or expressing oneself but rather at not losing a paycheck,
not losing the respect of spouse or relatives, or not having to give up
one's house. The incentives have changed from predominantly positive ones to predominantly negative ones. The goal is no longer to get
as much out of the job as possible but rather to do just enough (ultimately, the least necessary) to keep the job. The job feels less and less
like a part of oneself and ever more like an instrument for warding off
losses. Insofar as it seems an inescapable part of one's life, one will
routinize it and think about it as little as possible, in the way that one
routinizes getting home from work through the traffic. Since there are
really no ways for the job to go especially well, it will be the source of
little positive affect such as joy or pride; but since it may be threatened
now and then, and since it will sometimes conflict with other interests
and therefore seem burdensome, it will be the source of occasional
negative affects, such as fear, disgust, and anger. It is likely to become
the focus of an influential current concern only on these latter occasions. Even then the person is likely to be concerned about the form
of the job — keeping it, rearranging it, and so forth — rather than
about its content. The person's respondent processes are therefore

unlikely to reflect the content of the job, and the person is correspondingly unlikely to originate creative thoughts about the objectives of the job itself.

People who feel forced to live with unsatisfactory situations also develop characteristic feelings of discontent. They report themselves to be more or less dissatisfied, and they may feel alienated and futile. These are important feelings, sometimes powerful and often nagging. They clearly color the quality of an individual's life, and they constitute one more way in which people's experiential lives are governed by their relationships to incentives.

The purpose of this chapter, then, is to trace people's alienation from incentives at work, at home, and toward their lives as they age. First, however, we must consider what it means to feel "alienated" from something or someone, and how a social scientist can infer that someone is alienated.

Alienation and Discontent

"Alienation" means "estrangement". To feel alienated from something means, in a literal sense, to regard the thing as alien, as not-me. People make a remarkably clear distinction between what they regard as "me" and what they regard as "not-me." Gordon Allport used to shock his introductory students with the following thought experiment. First, recognize that your mouth continuously accumulates saliva. Every few seconds you swallow some. Although you are usually unaware of your swallowing, you are not put off by becoming aware of it. Now imagine that instead of swallowing, you spit the saliva into a glass. When you have accumulated a glassful, you drink it. Disgusting thought? Of course. But is that not remarkable? What a few moments earlier seemed part of "me" and seemed a perfectly acceptable thing to swallow now seems decidedly "not-me" and becomes a nauseating thing to contemplate swallowing.

Nausea aside, other kinds of things can also switch from "me" to "not-me" or vice versa. I can clearly recall the sudden end of my "honeymoon" period with a certain job. The next time I entered my office building, the building itself — its old Victorian face, its winding, old wooden staircase — seemed strange to me. After months of ascending those stairs, I had become totally familiar with them. Climbing them required no special thought about them. In some sense, they had become a routine part of me, something with which I identified. Now they seemed distinctly foreign. I have experienced that distinctive feeling at other times as well: toward a friend who had betrayed a trust, toward a group whose goals I could no longer reconcile with mine, and, in general, toward people and objects whom I could no longer trust to safeguard my larger interests.

In some sense, of course, it is necessary to distinguish objects from oneself just to think about them. "Philosophy," wrote Kaufmann (1970), "is born of estrangement" (P. xxvii). The modern use of the term "alienation" began with Hegel, however. He described a form of alienation that occurs when people come into conflict with the surrounding culture, lose their tacit identification with it, and come to regard it as something "other" than themselves (Schacht, 1970). To Hegel, this feeling is something much more than an intellectual recognition that something is different from oneself. It has within it elements of *conflict* with social institutions.

The next significant use of the concept was by Karl Marx, from whom it gradually found its way into modern sociology. In its general outlines, Marx's concept of alienation is consistent with Hegel's, but Marx specified the alienating conflicts of interest somewhat differently. Marx's starting point is with the worker's relationship to his or her work. For Marx, work is an intensely expressive activity: It is the way in which people "objectify" or "actualize" themselves (Schacht, 1970). For this reason, workers ideally identify themselves with the products of their labor and look on them as sources of profound satisfaction. In modern industrial society, however, workers are unable to express themselves through their products. Their output is too much coerced and controlled by others; the constraints placed on their efforts prevent any significant sense of workmanship; workers may not even know what the end-product is that they are making; and, in any case, the workers' output enriches the capitalist-owners' wealth and power over against the workers' own. Therefore, Marx reasoned, workers become alienated from their own labor and its products; and since workers see themselves as existing in a mutually exploitative society, they also become alienated from their fellow humans.

Following Marx, the concept of alienation has been used by numerous sociologists and sociologically inclined psychologists and theologians (Schacht, 1970). Most of them have broadened and changed its meaning, until today the term "alienated" has become little more than an epithet with which to label disliked social institutions and their victims (Schacht, 1970). Sometimes "alienation" refers to an affect, sometimes to a cognitive recognition that one's interests are badly served by certain others, and sometimes to social institutions themselves of which the writer disapproves and which he or she therefore assumes must be "alienating." In view of these diverse uses to which the term "alienation" has been put, is there any point in continuing to use it?

It seems likely that when writers use the term "alienation" they are among other things alluding to a distinctive affect, one that people can readily recognize but to which no theorist of emotion seems to have done justice. Possibly, it is not a separate affect but a mixture of affects, such as anger, fear, and cooled love. Its opposites are perhaps easier to describe. For instance, alienation from someone is probably incompatible with romantic love for the same person, since romantic love is characterized by an overwhelming impulse for a merged identity. Alienation can also be opposed to Gordon Allport's (1961) concept of "self-extension" — treating other people or objects for practical purposes as parts of one's own identity — and to Alfred Adler's (1973) concept of *Gemeinschaftsgefühl* (sense of community, commonly translated as "social interest"). Many writers, in fact, have described an affective sense of common destiny, of brotherhood, or of ·generalized love for members of the human community, to which alienation is the opposite number.

Marxist alienation and Adlerian *Gemeinschaftsgefühl* describe feelings whose scope may embrace the whole cosmos, but the affect of alienation also touches much humbler relationships. In my own experience, I feel extremely wary toward and rather alienated from treacherous, swaying little bridges over small streams, for instance, but quite at home on safer ones. For many years I wore ties comfortably and proudly. Then, in the social climate of 1970, I discovered that my tie misrepresented me to some of my students and colleagues and even actually frightened some of them away. Within my academic unit, I gradually became a tie-wearing exception. My tie came increasingly to seem like a foreign growth around my neck. Eventually, I came to regard it as so emphatically "not-me" that I gave up wearing it.[1] These various emotional experiences differed from one another in some ways, of course, but they had in common an aversion and a "not-me" quality that seemed quite distinctive.

Perhaps the many writers who have dealt with alienation in such different ways are all referring intuitively to this common subjective state. Some may explicitly treat its affective character, others may overlook the affective tone and talk only about the thoughts and beliefs that accompany it, and still others may leap directly into dealing with the social arrangements from which they feel intuitively alienated.

To summarize, it may be that alienation represents a particular affect or cluster of affects that people feel toward objects, other people, or institutions from whom they had once expected help or pleasure but who let them down in some major respect. For the emotional tone of alienation to continue, it may also be necessary that the person be trapped into having to continue relating to the alienated object, thereby precipitating an ambivalence. In other words, alienation presupposes a *disillusionment* with something, especially with something from which one cannot get away (Stokols, 1975). There are, of course, many ways in which this disillusionment can occur. First, it may happen suddenly, as when a good friend turns out to be a swindler or when one's company comes under ruthless new management. Alternatively, one's incentive may be gradually leached away, as when one habituates to and grows weary of a job or a spouse, in the manner described in Chapter 4. Third, one's hope for making something gratifying out of a difficult situation may be gradually worn down by repeated failure, leading at last to a new, clear realization that the person or situation is intractable. At the end, the feeling is, among other things, one of alienation.

Problems of Measurement

In order to study alienation scientifically it is necessary to measure it, and in order to measure something one must be able to define it precisely. Since the 1950s, therefore, a number of investigators have tried to clarify meanings and to construct measuring instruments. In probably the most widely cited attempt to clarify the concept of alienation, Melvin Seeman (1959) distinguished five different senses in which previous writers had used it:

1. "Powerlessness" to influence events that bear on one's major interests.
2. A sense of "meaninglessness" in which "the individual is unclear as to what he ought to believe" (P. 48).
3. "Normlessness," a "high expectancy that socially unapproved behaviors are required to achieve given goals" (P. 50) because the society provides inadequate socially approved means for attaining goals that are socially emphasized, such as becoming wealthy.

4. "Isolation," in the sense of not sharing the dominant values and beliefs of the surrounding culture.
5. "Self-estrangement," in which one undertakes work or other activities exclusively to gain approval or rewards from other people, rather than for one's own satisfaction or approval.

None of these senses of alienation refer directly to an affective state. All of them, on the other hand, touch on an individual's relationships to his or her goals. Powerless people are prevented from attaining some of their goals. Insofar as they are confused about their social environments, they are rendered powerless. If they believe that they can attain their goals only by employing unsavory means, they are plunged into conflicts between means and ends, or they may suffer the loss of another goal, self-esteem. If their values and beliefs are at odds with those of their neighbors, they will be less able to form a sense of solidarity with others, and they may have to buck the social system around them to attain some of their goals.

The flavor of these "forms" of alienation is highly cognitive. It is therefore not surprising that the questionnaires devised to measure them ask respondents primarily about their beliefs. People are asked to rate their agreement or disagreement with such statements as, "We are just so many cogs in the machinery of life" (Dean, 1961, P. 756), "I often wonder what the meaning of life really is" (Dean, 1961, P. 756), and "In order to get ahead in the world today, you are almost forced to do some things which are not right" (Middleton, 1963, P. 133). Of course, not every investigator uses Seeman's classes of alienation, and different investigators ask different specific questions.

In general, the various "forms" of alienation tend to be moderately closely related to one another.[2] Perhaps the conditions reflected by one kind of belief (for instance, meaninglessness) produce the conditions for another kind of belief (for instance, powerlessness). On the other hand, it may also be (as Shepard, 1972, said of powerlessness, meaninglessness, and normlessness) that they are all just "factors . . . *associated with* alienation" (P. 163, italics added) rather than aspects of alienation itself. That is, alienation itself may reside not in any of the beliefs tapped by the various scales, but rather in certain affective responses toward particular features of a person's life, responses that are more likely to develop in circumstances that make people feel powerless, confused, and isolated.

If this analysis is correct, the methods that have been used most to measure people's alienation really measure something several steps removed — complex beliefs rather than raw affect. To be sure, there are exceptions. For instance, Keniston (1965) made extensive use of clinical methods to describe a group of highly alienated college students. Interestingly, he wrote of them, "On every level, . . . the alienated refuse conventional commitments, seeing them as unprofitable, dangerous, futile, or merely uncertain and unpredictable" (P. 52). It is reassuring that this description jibes so well with the characteristics listed by Seeman, given that Keniston used methods capable of registering far more affective and complex features of alienated inner experience than methods using simple, belief-oriented questionnaires. The sociologist Kolaja (1961) was also getting close to the core of alienation when he asked workers simply whether they felt as though their factory belonged to them. Another investigator searched through protocols of interviews with a sample of women to find expressions of "futility," which included such highly affective statements as ". . . am not doing anything worthwhile"; ". . . cannot cope with this"; ". . . feel I can no longer go on"; and so on (Wilson, 1950, Pp. 32–33).

There is one further kind of measure that, although imprecise, probably also taps feelings of alienation: questions that simply ask people to express their satisfaction or dissatisfaction with some aspect of their lives. "Satisfaction" is, of course, a very ambiguous term. However, people who are dissatisfied with something or someone of whom they had expected better things, and with whom they must continue to relate, satisfy the basic conditions for feeling alienated (Stokols, 1975).[3] It seems reasonable to expect that dissatisfaction expressed under these conditions will also reflect alienation. Furthermore, when people express dissatisfaction with their careers or with their marriages, it is reasonable to suppose that in most cases they had at one time expected greater satisfaction from these than they found. Therefore, people who remain in jobs and marriages with which they are dissatisfied probably can in many cases also be said to be alienated from them.

One can certainly think of exceptions to these generalizations. For some individuals, the dissatisfactions may be so slight or recent that they merely invigorate the person to improve the situation. Or an unsatisfactory job or marriage may have been merely a stepping stone to some further goal, which the individual is still on schedule to attaining. However, in the absence of better evidence, the many investigations that have asked people about their satisfaction with various aspects of work, marriage, and life in general provide useful information.

Opportunity and Aspiration:
Social Class and Education

Alienation is often a matter of reality not coming up to one's aspirations. People commonly seek out situations they believe present opportunities for realizing some of their aspirations. They willingly meet the demands of these situations insofar as they continue to believe in them. For instance, students work harder if their test grades or other school activities are likely to help them achieve their own longer-range goals (Raynor, 1974; Stinchecombe, 1964). People become alienated when they discover that the promise of opportunity for which they worked was false, especially if they regard themselves as now "stuck" in their barren situations.

If this is the case, then we would expect the relatively less well-advantaged groups in a mobile society to feel more alienated and less satisfied with their lives than the more advantaged. This is clearly so. In the United States, the poor person, the lower-status worker, and the black express more alienation and dissatisfaction than others (Bean, Bonjean, & Burton, 1973; Bradburn, 1969; Dean, 1961; Lystad, 1972; Middleton, 1963; Sheppard & Herrick, 1972). Presumably, that is because their opportunities are on the average less well-suited to their goals.

Opportunity, however, is only a part of the picture. Alienation arises from the relation of opportunities to aspirations. The great sociologist Emile Durkheim (1930/1951) theorized that if society fails to place a lid on people's expectations, their unbridled aspirations might often outrun the means for realizing them; and he proposed that an unresolvable discrepancy between aspirations and means is one factor in promoting suicide.

We would expect that one of the factors that affects (or perhaps reflects) people's aspirations is the level of education they have attained. Most people who attain relatively high levels of education probably either originated in socially well-placed families, and hence apply comparatively high economic standards in judging their lives, or were exceptionally highly motivated to achieve something, whether within their educational institutions or outside. Insofar as they feel that they have invested time and effort, they are likely to

expect commensurate rewards in the form of economic or social success. Consequently, we can infer that education is related to levels of
aspiration in life, and that, for comparable levels of success achieved,
those individuals who have the greater amounts of education will also
be the more alienated and less satisfied.

Again, this is the case. Low-income blue collar workers feel more
dissatisfied with their jobs if they have had college educations (Sheppard & Herrick, 1972) and college-educated white-collar workers feel
more alienated from jobs over which they lack control than do less
well-educated workers (Kirsch & Lengermann, 1972).

Sometimes the opportunity to "improve" one's social status intro-
duces conflicts with other goals and itself promotes alienation. For
instance, among Nigerian Fulani-Hausa youths, education alienates
some even as it reduces the alienation of others. Those whose values
are modern feel less alienated the better their educations; among
those whose values are traditional, it is the better educated individuals
who express greater alienation from their society (Armer, 1970). For
the more traditional youths, modern education calls basic values into
question and inculcates goals such as "getting ahead" that conflict
with more traditional satisfactions such as strong family ties, status,
and so on. Thus, although education helps people with modern out-
looks to achieve their goals, it may actually hinder people with traditional values from achieving theirs and, evidently, leads them to feel
more alienated.

Alienation from Work

There is a long-standing argument among industrial psychologists
and sociologists about whether American workers like their work.
Those who believe that the answer is "Yes" point to the fact that
when workers are simply asked in opinion polls whether they are
satisfied with their work, more than three-quarters typically answer
that they are. Such investigators therefore believe that the supposed
need to "enrich" workers' jobs is a "myth" (Fein, 1973). Indeed,
according to this view, workers do not wish their work enriched,
since enrichment often means complicating jobs and demanding
greater personal involvement.

On the other side, however, stands an impressive array of contrary
evidence. It is hard to say what workers mean in an absolute sense
when they claim to feel satisfied with their work. It is clearer that 93%
of urban university professors, 77% of individually practicing

lawyers, and only 24% of blue-collar workers say that, given a second chance, they would choose their work again; or that, offered a 26-hour day, "Two out of three college professors and one out of four lawyers . . . but only one out of twenty nonprofessional workers would make use of the extra time in work activity" *(Work in America,* 1973, P. 16). It is reasonable to conclude that although workers may be more or less resigned to their jobs, they are not well pleased.[4]

It is possible that work in America has become less enjoyable over the years. Although responses to survey questions concerning overall job satisfaction have remained fairly constant at least since 1958 (U.S. Department of Labor, 1974), analyses of fiction published in American magazines show a distinct trend. In 1890, 27% of the story plots contained work as a source of frustration for characters over the age of 40. In 1955, the figure had risen to 57% (Martel, 1968). Insofar as magazine fiction reflects something of what is on the minds of people at large, work frustrations clearly became a much more prominent factor between 1890 and 1955.

Factors in Satisfaction with and Alienation from Work

What, then, are the incentives in work situations whose presence promotes satisfaction and whose absence alienates the workers? We shall consider them in three groups: power to control one's own work, economic rewards, and pleasures in the work itself.

Control. Perhaps the crucial point in Marx's view of workers' alienation is that industrial workers have lost control over their work. By virtue of the wage system for employing them, Marx observed, they have surrendered all significant control over the manufacturing process to the employer. Within the confines of particular jobs, individual workers have little control over what they produce or over the conditions under which they produce it. Since their products are directed from outside themselves, and since they are themselves merely instruments, they have difficulty in identifying their products with themselves. Therefore, a key factor in worker alienation is the worker's powerlessness in the face of the industrial organization that governs production.

Research results indicate that power and control do indeed play an important role in worker alienation. Workers who hold highly structured, tightly controlled jobs express more alienation than freer workers (Bonjean & Grimes, 1970; Kirsch & Lengermann, 1972). Workers whose jobs involve greater responsibility and autonomy are less likely to quit or be absent from their jobs (Porter & Steers, 1973). Scientists and engineers respond to directive supervision with considerable alienation (Miller, 1967). And in one survey (Sheppard & Herrick, 1972), "[w]ork dissatisfaction (and life dissatisfaction) were practically nonexistent among the self-employed" (P. 12).[5]

It could be argued, of course, that the real determiners of satisfaction or dissatisfaction might have been not powerlessness itself but various other unattractive features that often go with highly structured jobs. However, this objection is blunted by the results of another study (Fried, Weitman, & Davis, 1972). Here, jobs also varied according to whether machine operators could set their own pace and adjust or correct their machines. However, the workers were rotated through work stations containing the different types of jobs. They were part of the same organization and presumably commanded as much personal prestige at one station as at another. Pay scales were controlled. Yet, workers at the more structured stations had higher rates of absenteeism.

Finally, there is the case of workers in Yugoslavia. Since the development of Titoist communism in the early 1950s, Yugoslav enterprises have been under the effective control of elected workers' councils. Theoretically, Yugoslav workers thus collectively retain control over all the basic economic and operational decisions of their work organizations. Asked "How many employees feel that the factory is their property?", a majority of respondents at one factory answered "all" or "many" (Kolaja, 1961). That these responses are not simply a matter of workers parroting a party line is indicated by the fact that Kolaja received quite different responses from Polish workers (Blumberg, 1968). Furthermore, by one estimate (Blumberg, 1968), the Yugoslav Gross National Product nearly tripled from 1954 to 1964 and continued to expand at a rate of 10% per year during the years 1964 to 1966. Yugoslav workers, in substantial control of their enterprises, neither talk nor act very alienated.[6]

Although power and control play an important role in workers' satisfaction or alienation in their jobs, the relevant factors are probably not power and control in and for themselves. Power probably is important insofar as it enables workers to design their work to be as satisfying as possible. For one thing, not all workers are put off by lacking control. Particularly, those workers who most believe in the validity and importance of authority relationships are far less alienated by highly structured and closely supervised jobs (Pearlin, 1962; Sheppard & Herrick, 1972). In general, however, control over one's job is only one feature of work among many. The factors that produce satisfaction or alienation at work vary from one individual to another, depending on his or her values (Mobley & Locke, 1970).

Money. Pay and opportunities for promotion are clearly also incentives that affect job satisfaction. Workers who are relatively well paid express more satisfaction with their jobs overall (Sheppard & Herrick, 1972) and are less likely to quit or be absent (Porter & Steers, 1973). The important factor here is not the worker's objective pay level but how well his or her pay compares with expectation. If the pay level fails to match prior expectations — if it seems unfair — it is likely to alienate the worker (Pearlin, 1962; Porter & Steers, 1973). Workers who do not expect to be promoted tend not to desire promotion, and those who expect promotion want it (Hahn, 1975).

This is not to say that money is necessarily the primary incentive for working, or even that it is necessary. In general, of course, money is most important to those who have the least of it; but the argument often advanced by opponents of "welfare state" liberalism, that without the threat of utter poverty most people would go on permanent vacations, is clearly false. There is, ironically, the evidence of the best-off groups themselves. Most wealthy individuals continue to work despite the fact that they could live comfortably without employment (Macarov, 1970). In one large group of workers, 80% said that if they suddenly became rich they would keep working (Morse & Weiss, 1955).

Even more convincing are the results of the New Jersey Graduated Work Incentive Experiment (U.S. Department of Health, Education, and Welfare, 1973). In this experiment, more than 1200 poor and near-poor families were chosen randomly by a federal agency to receive a guaranteed minimum income. The minimum levels were varied for different families from 50% to 125% of the poverty level, which was $3300 yearly for a family of four at the beginning of the experiment in 1968. If families worked and received earned income above the guaranteed level, a portion of the government support money was withdrawn. Whenever their earnings grew large enough, all federal contributions ceased. This income level ranged for a family of four between about $3000 and $8000 per year, depending on the particular experimental plan the family was selected for. As it turned out, the differences in plans seemed to have no significant effects on the behavior of the families; and 18 months later, as compared with a control group of families that received no benefits, the families receiving the guaranteed income continued to work about as many hours as before. Relative to a control group of families who received no guaranteed income payments, they also continued to earn about as much money from paid employment as before.

Thus, the threat of being without income was unnecessary to motivate these families to work. We may therefore infer that other incentives were sufficient to keep them working: the prospect of higher incomes, recognition, companionship of co-workers, stimulation, and other benefits accorded even by many low-status jobs.

Intrinsic satisfactions. When workers are asked which job facets are "very important" to them, the aspects of work most often described in this way are (in descending order of frequency) as follows: 1. "work is interesting"; 2. "enough help and equipment to get the job done"; 3. "enough information to get the job done"; 4. "enough authority to do my job"; 5. "good pay"; 6. "co-workers are friendly and helpful"; 7. "opportunity to develop my special abilities"; 8. "job security is good"; 9. "can see the results of my work"; and 10. "responsibilities are clearly defined" (U.S. Department of Labor, 1974, P. 16; Sheppard & Herrick, 1972, Pp. 10–11). Most of these aspects of jobs have to do with the work itself — the intrinsic satisfactions to be derived from it or the conditions that help get the job done well. The only two "bread and butter" issues among the top ten job facets, pay and job security, stand fifth and eighth on the list. Among blue-collar workers taken alone, pay is the facet most often described as "very important," but "help and equipment" is a close second and the other items listed above generally also rate high.

Of these various job facets, the one most closely correlated with overall job satisfaction is being "given a chance to do the things I do best," followed by "interesting work"; "good pay" and "opportunity to develop my special abilities" are tied for third (Sheppard & Herrick, 1972, P. 12).

What these workers are telling us, then, is that the possibilities provided by their jobs for self-fulfillment, stimulation, and personal growth are at least as important, on the average, as pay and security. This generalization seems to hold not only for what workers say but also for what they do, since factors intrinsic to the nature of the work also seem to predict employee turnover (Mangione, unpublished, cited by Lawler, 1973). Scientists and engineers who feel that their company unduly restricts their choice of research projects or insufficiently encourages their professional development express significantly more alienation from their work (Miller, 1967). Lawler (1973) concludes from his own research that the intrinsic satisfactions a job promises to bestow on a worker are crucial to the worker's performance: "[a]lthough the difference is small, there is a definite tendency for expectancies concerned with achievement, accomplishment and other growth type outcomes to be the best predictors of work behavior" (P. 10).

Although no one knows whether dissatisfaction with work is really more rampant today than in past periods of history, it is possible that today's emphasis — especially among the educated — on finding intrinsic satisfaction in work may sometimes operate to promote dissatisfaction, or at least expressions of dissatisfaction. Particularly when the intrinsic satisfactions are not basic sensual, social, or other wired-in incentives, and where they are regularly attained, they ought (in accordance with Chapter 4) to habituate. If, however, work is undertaken for relatively enduring extrinsic incentives, ranging from filling basic economic needs to serving a responsive community of others, we should expect people to weary of their careers less quickly.

Perhaps one key change from work in past periods is that work in modern industrial societies often takes place without much sense of it being a contribution to a definable, responsive community, whose social responses can serve as relatively enduring extrinsic incentives. Interestingly, nursing personnel become significantly less alienated from their work, regardless of other aspects of their jobs, if they have close social relationships with other members of their work groups (Pearlin, 1962).

Work Enrichment

It is the current common wisdom that today more people than ever are growing dissatisfied with their jobs and careers. Different writers offer different reasons: Work is more highly structured today, more fragmented, and less personal. People live longer, and therefore more of them have the opportunity to outlive their interest in their vocations. People are better educated and therefore need more stimulation and challenge. The prescription is commonly to make the jobs more stimulating.

Although one might expect dull jobs to pall with time, older workers on the average express greater satisfaction with their jobs than younger workers, not less, and this is furthermore the way it has been as long as investigators have been studying job satisfaction (U.S. Department of Labor, 1974). Although older workers are less sanguine about their chances of professional advancement (Garvey, 1973), they are more pleased with other aspects. Asked "How often do you leave work with a good feeling that you have done something particularly well?", the percentage replying "very often" rises from 23% of blue-collar workers under age 20 to 53% of such workers 65 years old and over (Sheppard & Herrick, 1972).

This, however, is again only part of the story. More older than younger workers say their jobs have little or no variety (40% versus 27%), but of those workers who so describe their jobs, "only 9 percent of the youngest, but 55 percent of the oldest, say the lack of variety bothers them rarely or never!" (Sheppard & Herrick, 1972, P. 124). It appears that the older workers have made their peace with their particular jobs, even though they recognize the defects. Of workers over age 40, 36% had thought at least once in a while about "seriously making a real effort to enter a new and different type of occupation (or had already made such a shift), and also that they would choose a training or education program making it possible to get a promotion or a better job. In the 40–49 age group alone, the proportion is nearly half" (Sheppard & Herrick, 1972, P. 156). These statistics present a striking contrast to the statistics of "satisfaction," which now seem more likely to be statistics of resignation.

The most recent major movement to combat worker alienation has been called "job enrichment." Job enrichment can take as many forms as there are jobs, of course, but the forms have certain important features in common. Most often one enriches a job by reversing its fragmentation — by giving a single worker control over a large enough part of an industrial, clerical, or creative process that he or she can feel a sense of turning out a complete product. For instance, where in one situation a requisition might be typed by one person, proofread by a second, and corrected by a third, an "enriched" job might make one individual responsible for all three operations. A telephone service representative might be assigned a particular group of customers instead of simply responding to the next inquiry and might be given the authority to monitor a complete service procedure through its various steps. Laboratory technicians might be given authority to requisition equipment and services, train their junior staff, and write reports on the research projects for which they had been responsible. The results, in many of the cases reported in print, have been increased quality of work done, usually greater productivity, and occasionally greater job satisfaction as reported in questionnaire responses (Ford, 1973; Paul, Robertson, & Herzberg, 1969; Strauss, 1974).

To be sure, the job enrichment movement has its critics (e.g., Fein, 1973). The successes are often reported by the professionals responsible for them. The reporting is not always objective. The failures are, presumably, rarely reported. Many workers want no part of complicating their jobs.

The limitations of job enrichment can probably be seen best in incentive terms: What is in it for the individual worker? People who have successfully organized their lives around nonjob incentives such as their families, vacation homes, sports, or volunteer activities, and people who have adopted a passive life-style of allowing the mass media to massage their affect systems (see Chapter 7), may be glad to have routinized their job activities to the point of nearly unconscious performance. They may feel as if they have no energy or inclination for getting more involved in their work than they already are. Although a revised job may succeed in enlisting their involvement, their alienation is already virtually complete and their commitments have been placed elsewhere. For job enrichment to involve such workers, the new satisfactions offered would have to outweigh the satisfactions the worker must give up.

It is clearly essential that rewards be tailored to the people they are aimed at. Caplan (1973) reported on the experiences of agency staffers working with street gangs or providing job training to unemployed youths. These programs often succeeded in establishing good relationships with street youths and in eliciting from them an apparent commitment to change their ways, but they too often failed to get their clients over the last hurdle of actually taking and keeping a job, even if the job was by objective standards quite desirable. Even worse, the youths on whom the professional staff spent the most time — the ones who seemed most promising — had the lowest employment rate. They were the boys who had demonstrated the highest-order skills for living and achieving in the inner-city culture. They were better at managing other inner-city people and at marshaling ghetto resources. The manner in which they failed was often spectacular. The job would be arranged, everything would appear to be in order. Then, perhaps the night before the job was to start, the client would do something that made starting the job impossible. One got himself arrested for beating an old man. Another was killed during a restaurant holdup. A third, about to enter college with a scholarship and to appear on a television program as a good example, "withdrew from the college, spent his entire stipend on new clothes, and joined a black militant organization" (Caplan, 1973, P. 57).

Since these setbacks tended to occur on the very threshold of employment, it appeared that the prospect of changing role from a street youth to a jobholder may have been responsible; but why especially for the most capable, promising people? Caplan concluded that the issue was precisely one of relative competencies. A person who is highly competent in a street setting and has a sense of high self-worth there was being asked to enter a setting in which his competencies were at best marginal and his sense of self-worth correspondingly low. The balance of incentives, apart from the relationship with the staffer, was clearly on the side of staying on the street.

We can see, then, that just as job enrichment is likely to be completely irrelevant to one of Caplan's street youths, so is it likely to be a matter of indifference to anyone else whose major incentive commitments are elsewhere. Although the threat of poverty is unnecessary to keep people from loafing, a reformed job structure will not automatically seduce people into becoming emotionally involved in their work. If our analysis is correct, people are likely to become involved in work insofar as they have become socialized into having the necessary competencies and into valuing the incentives available through work, in comparison with competencies and incentives for other spheres of activity. If, then, their jobs use those competencies and dispense those incentives, the worker will be satisfied. If not, the worker will become alienated.

Satisfaction and Dissatisfaction in Marriage [7]

In Western stories of married women, relationships between the spouses almost invariably end badly. One thinks of Madame Bovary, Hedda Gabler, Anna Karénina, Scarlett O'Hara, and many others. Of course, there would be no story line if nothing went wrong and no tragedy if something did not turn out irreconcilable, but it is noteworthy that the trouble in marriage stories is inherent in the partners or in the relationship itself. Western writers in general take an extremely pessimistic view of marriage, as reading through a collection of quotations (Evans, 1968) will reveal. There is wide agreement with Alexander Pope that "They dream in courtship, but in wedlock wake" (Evans, 1968, P. 748), with Ambrose Bierce's definition of marriage as

"The state or condition of a community consisting of a master, a mistress, and two slaves, making in all, two" (Evans, 1968, P. 431), and with La Rochefoucauld's maxim that "There may be good, but there are no pleasant marriages" (Evans, 1968, P. 431).

It might seem hard to explain why the institution has survived were it not for the evident fact that, in reality, many marriages are highly gratifying, and, perhaps more important, the single state is worse. Single individuals express on the average significantly less satisfaction with life than those who are married, primarily because marriage reduces the number of unpleasant factors in peoples's lives, especially for men (Bradburn, 1969).

Perhaps the literary gloom surrounding marriage reflects the euphoria of courtship as much as the realities of marriage. It seems established that as marriages age they become gradually less satisfying, on the average, at least for the first 20 years (Blood & Wolfe, 1960; Hicks & Platt, 1970; Pineo, 1961). In some respects, the drop is on the average quite large, especially in overall adjustment, sharing of interests and activities, frequency of sexual intercourse, love, sense of permanence, and consensus (Pineo, 1961).

The slide in people's satisfaction with marriage does not go on indefinitely, however. Parents whose last children have left home remain about as satisfied as before, on the average (Blood & Wolfe, 1960), and there is some evidence that their satisfaction begins to grow again. Many more people between the ages of 40 and 65 whose last child has left home report that their lives have grown better than report that they have grown worse (Deutscher, 1968). Couples who have retired report more satisfaction with their marriages and lives than couples with children (Rollins & Feldman, 1970). This evidence has its serious weaknesses: It is cross-sectional — different couples are chosen to represent different life stages — and the sample sizes are often rather small. It nevertheless seems safe to conclude that marriages do not seem to become much worse after the years of rearing children.

Factors Related to Marital Satisfaction and Stability

People get married for many different reasons. American college students often wish to marry for love, to form close ties, to have a home and family, and for security (Casler, 1970). No doubt there are also other reasons, including desires to improve or preserve their economic or social status. These reasons constitute the incentives for seeking marriage, and they appear to define to a considerable extent the factors that make marriages satisfying or alienating.

First of all, stable marriages are on the average more "successful" than the unstable ones by conventional socioeconomic standards: husbands' incomes and educations are higher (Renne, 1970), husbands' occupations are more prestigious, and the couple are more likely to own their own home (Levinger, 1965). There is, of course, a serious problem here of determining how these things are related to marital stability. A likely explanation is that economically well-to-do individuals are subjected to fewer economic stresses that can poison a couple's personal relationship. Thus, Levinger (1966) concluded from a study of couples seeking divorce that "spouses in the middle-class marriages were more concerned with psychological and emotional interaction, while the lower-class partners saw as most salient in their lives financial problems and the unsubtle physical actions of their partner" (P. 806). Better-to-do couples also have more resources for solving interpersonal problems: more space for separate bedrooms, more privacy, more opportunities for vacations and other luxuries that can provide positive offsets to interpersonal strains, and so forth. Furthermore, if the family is succeeding economically, its members have more to lose in a material sense from breaking up the unit. Finally, in accordance with Chapter 4, we would expect that people would develop more positive affect toward economically successful than toward economically unsuccessful marriages. It is interesting to note, for instance, that members of experimental work teams like and respect each other more if their teams have been successful than if they have failed (Blanchard, Adelman, & Cook, 1975).

If we are to believe the reasons people give for getting married, the main incentives have to do with being close to someone they love; and attaining these incentives bears most importantly on their happiness with the marriage. Results from a survey indicate that "[p]eople who report very happy marriages are more likely to concentrate on relationship sources of happiness, while those reporting less happiness in marriage tend to concentrate on the situational aspects of marriage (home, children, social life) as sources of their marital happiness" (Gurin, Veroff, & Feld, 1960, P. 98). The wives who are most satisfied with their marriages make family decisions with their husbands jointly, share some household tasks, belong to two or three of the same organizations, get daily reports on their husbands' work lives, go on joint visits with workmates about once a month, and know at least half of their husbands' friends (Blood & Wolfe, 1960).

Perhaps the drastic drop in companionship experiences during the first seven or so years of marriage (Rollins & Feldman, 1970) helps to account for the reduced satisfaction with marriage after those early years; or, conversely, it may itself reflect a lowered value of companionship as romantic love wanes and the relationship becomes mired in the problems of work, children, and changed personal needs.

One of the conditions that affects companionship is the spouses' commitment to work. In general, the more hours wives work outside the home, the less satisfying is the marriage (Hicks & Platt, 1970) and the more likely are the partners to divorce (Levinger, 1965). This, however, depends in part on the wife's reasons for working. Wives in low-income families (Blood & Wolfe, 1960) or wives who work out of economic necessity (Orden & Bradburn, 1969) express less satisfaction with their marriages than wives who stay home, but wives who work by preference are at least as satisfied as those who do not work. Furthermore, the quality of the marriage of a working wife seems to depend in part on her husband. If both members of the couple have strong career commitments, they are less likely to be greatly satisfied with their marriage (Bailyn, 1970). If the working wife has no career commitments, or if the working husband's primary commitment is to his family, it makes little difference to the happiness of the marriage whether the other spouse is committed primarily to a career or to the family (Bailyn, 1970). Finally, marriage partners who work together have the highest average satisfaction in their marriages, at least for the wife (Blood & Wolfe, 1960). In general, then, it seems that a contemporary marriage needs at least one partner willing to give it top priority; otherwise its crucial companionship functions wither, it holds less incentive value for its members, antagonisms become more pronounced, and it is consequently more vulnerable when the partners are faced with attractive alternatives.

Factors Related to Marital Dissatisfaction and Divorce

Marriages may, of course, become unsatisfying simply through the absence of positive incentives — through economic hardship, lack of companionship or personal support, and thwarting of the partners' fulfillment of their personal goals. However, marriages do not depend purely on the number of positive incentives they offer. They may be damaged by unpleasantness and by attractive incentives outside the marriage. On the other hand, they may be held together by outside pressures to preserve the marriage (Levinger, 1965).

One kind of incentive that is restricted in conventional American marriage is the freedom to engage in social and sexual relations with people other than the spouse. For some individuals, this can constitute a serious deprivation. People who looked to their peers before marriage rather than to family or church for basic value judgments are significantly less satisfied with their marriages (Whitehurst, 1968). People who were active sexually before marriage are more inclined than others to engage in extramarital sexual activity (Kinsey et al., 1953). People who do so experience less satisfying sexual relations with their spouses and see more opportunities for sex with others (Johnson, 1970). It is hard to tell what is cause and what is effect. Perhaps, as common sense would suggest, people who are less satisfied with sex in marriage are more inclined to find it elsewhere. On the other hand, it may be that people who have gained the skills or have the desire for more varied social and sexual activities find monogamous marriage more frustrating, recognize or manufacture more extramarital opportunities, and hence assign their marriages a lower relative incentive value.

Somewhat unexpectedly, except perhaps to frazzled parents, another source of dissatisfaction with marriage is having children. School-age children are a greater source of disagreement between parents than any other (Blood & Wolfe, 1960); and couples with children tend to express less satisfaction with their marriages than childless couples (Renne, 1970) and less general well-being in the case of lower-income couples with more than two children (Bradburn, 1969). This negative effect of children is, of course, a broad statistical average. Children provide some parents with their most profound sense of satisfaction. Nevertheless, they also often introduce a sense of strain whose effect, on balance, is to weaken the attractiveness of marriage.[8]

Divorcing parents complain of not getting from their partners the incentives people look for in marriage. They complain of financial problems, neglect of home or children, infidelity, sexual incompatibility, lack of love, physical abuse, verbal abuse, drinking, suspicion, jealousy, untruthfulness, and "vague subjective complaints" (Levinger, 1966, P. 804). For these people, the community of affection seems broken, perhaps beyond repair, and the path toward a satisfying life leads away from the marriage.

Conclusion

People get married to gain certain specific ends, and they remain married and experience satisfaction insofar as their marriages continue to provide these incentives. Running through the great variety of individual experiences is a strong trend for marriages to become progressively less satisfying during at least the first 20 or so years. One of the more powerful incentives for marrying is to act out one's love, with the merging of identities and the sexual impulses that entails. Love is one of the qualities that, over the course of a marriage, most clearly declines (Pineo, 1961). The couples who have become most disenchanted kiss and confide in each other the least.

We are beginning to learn something of the circumstances in which marriages thrive or wither. We can point to objective factors — income, children, occupational activities, and so on — that go with marital happiness or misery, at least in a statistical sense. However, we have little systematic knowledge about the processes involved. We can guess that poverty, crowding, harassment by children, distraction by work, and the irritability produced by frustration would all sap the capacity of a marriage to fulfill its promise. People most often enter marriage hopeful, with faith that they can avoid the pitfalls and often unaware of where those pitfalls are located. When they discover the problems, find them intractable, and disengage from achieving their personal goals within the marriage, the marriage must seem hollow, an alien burden to be shunted aside for the sake of one's own welfare. Certainly, an alienative marriage is a weak competitor for an attractive alternative, such as a new love that once again promises specific fulfillment.

Are these kinds of specific circumstances enough to account for declining satisfaction as marriages mature? One might think so on grounds that, first, there is no place to go after the euphoria of courtship but down, and, second, that the passing of time permits disruptive influences to grow by accretion. However, one could argue on the contrary that since really bad marriages end in divorce during the earlier years, older marriages should on the average be the better ones. Furthermore, with time, the partners to the marriage gain experience in solving problems and also perhaps gain a broader perspective on themselves and each other. Therefore, one could argue that marriages should become *more* satisfying with time. Only with much more focused research shall we be able to assess the relative weight of these various factors. One further possibility remains, however: that just as most incentives lose value through habituation or satiation as they continue to be enjoyed (Chapter 4), so the power of a particular love or of a particular marriage as a whole also declines, simply through being enjoyed, quite apart from other factors.

In all likelihood, then, marriages are subject to all of the various processes that affect the value of incentives. Some of the satisfactions are innate — skin contact, sexual excitement, food, perhaps children, and probably the experience of love itself. Others are learned extensions of these. Insofar as the marriage permits the partners to reach goals that would otherwise be harder or impossible to achieve, it should gain value. Each partner may also discover unexpected satisfactions with the other and therefore value the marriage all the more. If the marriage follows a very barren period of loneliness, it is likely at first to seem especially good. Obstacles to communion between the partners, such as brief separations or passing arguments, may enhance the value of the marriage. On the other hand, however, we expect that the intrinsic satisfactions of love and sex will eventually come to seem relatively commonplace for the partners. With continued good relating, their adaptation levels for interpersonal satisfaction should rise and the satisfaction they have will come to seem correspondingly unremarkable. They may strive for novel variations — in sex, personal expression, scenery, children, and so forth — and we would expect an eventual turning outward from the marriage itself to reach for new experiences. If the marriage is good, the reaching out may take the form of wishing to extend the relationship to encompass more ground, such as children, artistic productions, social action, or bridge. If either partner lacks the flexibility to do this, if their new interests move in different directions, or if they lack the necessary resources, personal or economic, we would expect the marriage to suffer as a result. At the end of deterioration there wait the ultimate ways to turn away: alcohol, television, work, extramarital involvements, and divorce.

Satisfaction and Advancing Age

"Midway upon the journey of our life I found myself in a dark wood, where the right way was lost. Ah! how hard a thing it is to tell what this wild and rough and difficult wood was, which in thought renews my fear! So bitter is it that death is little more" (Dante, 1941, P. 1). So Dante began his journey into Hell at the age of 35. Many others have also arrived at middle age disoriented, no longer excited by the goals of their youth, their personal values in flux, feeling a need to reassess the meaning and direction of their lives. They confront the realization that the years remaining will probably be fewer than the years already gone by, and increasingly they reckon time not in years lived but in years left (Neugarten, 1968).

Throughout life, growth and decline change things. Sometimes the changes are dramatic, but more often they occur gradually. Then, like a geologic fault under stress, the accumulated changes produce a perceptible shift, and the person must come to grips with his or her life again. The important changes during adult aging take place in people's relationships to their incentives: in the values of the incentives, in their social feasibility, and in people's physical capacity to attain and enjoy them. For the average person, though by no means universally, the changes are on balance for the worse.

The Gradual Decline of Happiness

The evidence suggests that people become overall less happy between their 20s and 40s, that they remain approximately equally happy from their 40s to their 60s, and that happiness falls off again during and after their 70s. In the earlier decades, the decline is quite gradual, but it accelerates in the oldest decades. Most of this evidence comes from public surveys comparing people of different ages (Bradburn, 1969; Dean, 1961; Gurin, Veroff, & Feld, 1960). It therefore suffers from the defect that we do not know whether the differences are due to age or to generation. For instance, it is conceivable that the generation born before World War I contains a less happy group of people — for whatever reason — than the people born after World War II, quite apart from the differences in their ages. However, one team of investigators enlisted a group of individuals who were at least 65 years old and followed them for nine years (Britton & Britton, 1972). Satisfaction declined for 60%, stayed about level for 11%, and increased for 29%. Thus, twice as many experienced a loss in happiness as experienced a gain.

When old people are asked to pick the "worst years of a person's life," they tend to pick the later years more often than any other period (Harris, 1975). Thus, of the people in their late 60s who name their worst period, 30% name their 60s; of the respondents in their 70s, 55% name the 60s and 70s; and of the respondents in their 80s, two-thirds name an age over 60 as the worst period. Lest it appear that people feel unhappiest about whatever age they happen to be, people ages 18 to 54 also pick these late years, which they have never experienced, as the worst years, along with their teens.

The slight drop in satisfaction from the 20s to the 40s may actually reflect a larger, somewhat more nearly qualitative change. When people are asked separately about their positive affects (for instance, excitement) and their negative affects (for instance, loneliness), they report considerably less positive affect in their 40s than in their 20s, but they also report somewhat less negative affect (Bradburn, 1969). The two tend to cancel each other out, leaving a small net loss in happiness; but, viewed another way, it is apparent that emotional life from 21 to 49 becomes considerably more serene.

When we look at people strictly according to their ages, our statistics tend to smooth out and mask some important fluctuations. Obviously not every 25-year-old or every 65-year-old is at the same stage of his or her life as every agemate. One 25-year-old is a parent and businessperson, another has just married, yet another is single and finishing graduate school. One 65-year-old is about to swing a major business deal, another is off on a world tour with a new spouse, and yet another has been institutionalized with a terminal illness. Middle and old age can be extremely turbulent. In fact, depression severe enough to be treated clinically is much more common in middle age than earlier. Chiribago and Lowenthal (1974) surveyed people who were in four stressful "transitional" *stages* of their lives, rather than at particular ages: "High school seniors, newlyweds, middle-aged parents whose youngest child was about to leave the home, and people within two or three years of retirement" (P. 1). Among these groups, the high school seniors were the least happy, the newlyweds were the happiest, and the two older groups fell in between.

There is good reason to believe that differences such as these have more to do with being a newlywed or with being a high school senior than with being a particular age. A questionnaire study found that people in love experience their love just about as intensely whether they are adolescents, young adults, middle-aged, or elderly (Neiswender, Birren, & Schaie, 1975). The elderly reported somewhat less physical sex and both they and the adolescent group reported somewhat more fantasy about their love relationships than the other two groups, but in the spheres of feeling, thought, talk, and other behavior these investigators found no significant differences in the love experience with age. Similarly, people who are leaving their families behind and are facing social or economic uncertainties can reasonably be expected to report more distress than usual, whether they happen to be high school seniors or middle-aged individuals getting divorces. The point here is that the changes in people's satisfaction over the life span may well have much more to do with the different situations in which people are likely to find themselves at different ages than with any fundamental change in the way people react.

Individual Differences in Aging

The way in which people age depends, as Kurt Lewin said of all behavior, on the person and on the environment. Both the aging person's body and his or her social environment become more restrictive with age. People who adapt their goals to these changes are therefore likely to be happier than people who cling too rigidly to earlier goals. Thus, among a group of middle-aged and older psychiatric patients, those who were depressed were more often still committed to goals characteristic of younger age groups than were either undepressed patients or people who are not psychiatric patients (Miskimins & Simmons, 1966; Zacher, 1971).

Sometimes, personal attributes that are liabilities in one setting become advantages in another. For instance, adults usually achieve more and adjust better when they believe that they exercise considerable control over what happens to their own lives. However, residents of at least three homes for the aged were found to be better adjusted if they believed that their lives were controlled primarily by people other than themselves (Felton & Kahana, 1974).

Thus, aging in significant part depends on the individual. Neugarten, Havighurst, & Tobin (1968) described eight quite different approaches to aging by individuals in their 70s. Some people come fully to grips with their aging (the "integrated"). They reorganize their lives around new goals, give up some goals in order to focus on others, or largely disengage themselves from most goals and contentedly take the "rocking chair" approach. Others, less accepting of themselves and their aging (the "armored-defended"), either hold on to their vigorous middle-aged life pattern or attempt to do so while restricting social activities and "closing themselves off from experience" (Neugarten, Havighurst, & Tobin, 1968, P. 176). There are individuals who drop many or most activities and retreat into passive dependence on others. Finally, some individuals (the "unintegrated") become disorganized and deteriorate both emotionally and intellectually. Of these groups of people, the integrated groups and the "holding-on" armored-defended group are the most satisfied with their lives, whereas the passive-dependent and the unintegrated groups are the least satisfied. The first four, who are the happiest, are also those who have brought their incentive commitments into closest alignment with their own capacities to fulfill them. From their observations, Neugarten, Havighurst, & Tobin (1968) conclude that in normal men and women, there is no sharp discontinuity of personality with age, but instead an increasing consistency. Those characteristics that have been central to the personality seem to become even more clearly delineated, and those values the individual has been cherishing become even more salient. In the personality that remains integrated — and in an environment that permits — patterns of overt behavior are likely to become increasingly consonant with the individual's underlying personality needs and his desires (P. 177).

The Changing Incentive World

Old people have a well-intact sense of future events and probably a better developed perspective than the young on the interweaving of past events with future ones. Nevertheless, when they are asked to anticipate important events in the future, they describe events closer to them in time, on the average, than do college students (Kastenbaum, 1963). That should not surprise us. The aged are quite well aware of their much shorter life expectancy. In other respects too, however, their future is somewhat emptier. In Vienna, fewer people over the age of 60 than people aged 30 to 60 can name something that makes their life meaningful (Lukas, 1972). From adolescent to old age, the daydreams men report become somewhat less concerned with the future and somewhat more concerned with the past (Giambra, 1974). In fact, from 17 to 23, they remember daydreaming about the future more than about either their day-to-day affairs or the past. From 24 to 64, they daydream most often about current matters. From 65 on, they report daydreaming about the past somewhat more than about the present or future. The changes are not large, but they are significant. Given the theory that daydreams reflect current concerns, we would have to conclude that old people in comparison to the young are committed to fewer goals beyond the immediate future.

Not only is the future on the average shorter and emptier, it is also gloomier. Asked to rate the quality of their lives five years in the past, at present, and as it will probably be five years in the future, a sample of people age 50 and over were notably more pessimistic than younger groups (Bortner, Hultsch, Wiorkowski, & Scott, 1975). In fact, 67% expected their future to be no better than at present, compared with 44% of people in their 40s and 25% of people 18 to 29. Fully 21% of the oldest group expected that their lives would get worse, in contrast to 11% of the people in their 40s and 2% of people 18 to 29.

As people age, their interpersonal incentives change appreciably. We have seen that on the average they become less satisfied with marriage. They also engage in progressively fewer sexual activities (Kinsey, et al., 1948, 1953). Older men report fewer daydreams about sex and also fewer hostile and heroic daydreams (Giambra, 1974). People over 65 participate in fewer of their communities' social, economic, and political activities than younger adults, exercise less leadership there, and spend less time in them (Barker & Barker, 1968). They are much less likely to go to restaurants, movies, parks, sports events, libraries, concerts, and museums (Harris, 1975). From the 50s to the 60s people report a greatly reduced variety of social contacts, and they display less concern with communicating in an orderly or logical fashion or with justifying opinions (Shukin & Neugarten, 1964). On the average, then, older people interact with a more restricted range of people in less demanding ways, and in those interactions they are more idiosyncratic and more careless of other people's needs as listeners.

There is some evidence that as people age their desire for sensory stimulation also declines (Giambra, 1974; Kish & Busse, 1968) and that their mental imagery, especially their auditory imagery, becomes less vivid (Giambra, 1974). However, most of this decline seems to be complete by middle age. There is little further decline after about age 50. It is quite possible that, because they require less external stimulation, a variety of events may lose some incentive value for people between youth and middle age, such as the bustle of a busy social setting, background music, nights on the town, and so forth.

The tenor of inner life changes in another way, this time progressively into the oldest age brackets. Older people report having fewer daydreams, feel less absorbed in them, consider themselves to be less distractible, and yet, despite both reduced daydreaming and reduced activity, they are less often bored (Giambra, 1974).

In interpreting these results concerning the incentive world of older individuals, two persistent questions arise. *First*, to what extent are these changes due to difference in generation rather than to difference in age? For instance, it is quite possible that people born about the turn of the last century have more sexual inhibitions, are accustomed to a lower level of sensory stimulation, and have greater internal resources for entertaining themselves than generations raised with the automobile and the mass media. Present-day surveys may therefore be detecting shifts in the nature of the United States population rather than universal effects of aging as such. *Second*, to what extent have older people curtailed their activities because the activities are less attractive to them rather than because the activities are less available or less feasible for them? Are we looking at differences in value or in access?

In regard to the first question, it seems likely that much of the difference between the young and the old in affect and motivation is due to age rather than to the historical period in which people were born. We have seen that the survey findings of diminishing happiness have been confirmed in a longitudinal study (Britton & Britton, 1972). There is also evidence that not only do older individuals tell stories with less active and less emotional characters in them than the stories told by younger people contain (Rosen & Neugarten, 1964), but their story characters become yet less animated as the same storytellers grow older (Lubin, 1964). In these limited cases, then, longitudinal research that follows the same people over the years has confirmed the earlier evidence from cross-sectional research that made comparisons among different groups of people. The fact that these results agree strengthens confidence that other age differences, found using cross-sectional evidence, also reflect age rather than merely generation. This does not, of course, mean that the changes observed are necessarily biological or inevitable parts of aging. They may rather reflect the peculiarities of age roles in our society. They nevertheless appear to characterize the process of aging as it occurs in this society at this time.

Regarding both the first and the second question, there are further reasons for believing that at least some of the behavior of old people is related to their age rather than to their generation and is not of their free choosing: People in our society have definite conceptions of how old people should act and are willing to put them "in their place;" most older people are happier when they can continue to pursue and enjoy their accustomed incentives than when they give them up; and some of the apparent deterioration of old age can actually be reversed by offering sufficient incentives for behaving competently. To these intriguing aspects of aging we shall now turn.

Social Constraints on the Behavior of Old People

We tend to think of old people as having certain stereotyped traits. Old people are slow, a bit clumsy, slightly irascible, and quaint, and they speak with somewhat tremulous voices. Only 29% of the general public would describe "most people over 65" as "very bright and alert," but more than two-thirds of those over 65 would describe themselves that way. Only 21% of the public would describe "most people over 65" as "very open-minded and adaptable," as compared with the 63% of the over-65 people who describe themselves that way. For "very good at getting things done," the percentages are 35 and 55 (Harris, 1975). In the mass media, the old tend to be eliminated from any active part in family life or plot development, and when they appear they often serve in character roles or as victims of violent crimes.

People have definite ideas concerning the behaviors "appropriate" at different ages (Neugarten, Moore, & Lowe, 1968). For instance, 84% of one middle-aged sample agreed that "most people should be ready to retire" between ages 60 and 65. Age 45 may be too old in many people's eyes for wearing a two-piece bathing suit, having another child, or moving one's family from one town to another to get ahead in one's company. People who continue to exhibit youthful levels of sexual interest are tagged "dirty old men" or "dirty old ladies." Thus, a wide range of expressions and incentives become "disapproved" as people grow older, quite independently of their actual wishes.

Furthermore, these age norms tend to be enforced, usually through low-key expressions of disapproval: looks of embarrassment, smirks, raised eyebrows, surprise, and ridicule. Sometimes the sanctions are applied through ignoring or through harassing. For instance, older university students are sometimes held to stricter standards of evaluation. Job applications from older applicants are sometimes simply ignored.

One writer (Rosow, 1967, 1974) has suggested that old people are given an empty role — one with no specific prescriptions concerning what they should do, in contrast to the much better specified roles of younger adults. It seems more accurate, however, to say that the role assigned by our society to old people is a highly specified role of doing very little. After retirement age, they are expected to engage in light recreational activities, occasional babysitting, and possibly certain volunteer services. They are specifically excluded from active involvement in the major institutions of society, such as its businesses, governments, schools, and churches, except in honorary roles carrying little power to affect decisions. The exclusion is sometimes explicit, as in mandatory retirement regulations. Perhaps even more powerfully, it is conveyed simply by example. People can see what others do, both in mass media depictions and in their first-hand experiences. They have become accustomed through a lifetime's training to discern what behavior is "appropriate" and what behavior is not, and to be guided accordingly. Most older people (like most people generally) would rather not risk the humiliation of seeming to aspire to "inappropriate" goals.

Given that such social pressures exist, it seems superfluous to explain the actions of today's old people as peculiarities of their particular generation. Of course, cultures do change over time, and the social environments of old people also change. No doubt the more liberally educated generations growing up today will create a somewhat different climate for their old age than the generations now old. In the meantime, however, they are themselves contributing the social forces that shape the behavior of their elders. Social systems are much more stable, with much more inertia, than the individuals enmeshed in them. Thus, the "Now Generation" is actually helping to keep the passing generation in its place.

Engagement, Disengagement, and Satisfaction with Life

It has been argued (Cumming & Henry, 1961) that not only do people gradually withdraw from interpersonal relationships, occupational commitments, and other entanglements as they age, they actually become happier as they do so. That they withdraw is indisputable. To assert that they are happier withdrawing is, however, probably misleading. It may be true in the sense that one can reduce frustration and depression by disengaging from goals disapproved of by society or blocked by physical infirmities. That, however, is a very different matter from suggesting that the state of having disengaged from major incentives is in itself attractive, or that achieving that state is good for the person who has disengaged.

People differ, of course, in the extent to which they wish to remain engaged in their old activities. Retirement from one's work, specifically, may be a welcome change. On the average, people are as satisfied with their lives after retirement as before (Streib, 1975). But there is another side to this. Of people over 65, 63% are retired and another 6% are unemployed. Thirty-seven per cent of the retirees had been forced to retire. Fully 31% of the retirees and unemployed workers would like to work again, and 29% would not rule out returning to work if someone offered them a suitable job (Harris, 1975).

Many people resist the condition and the label of being old as long as they possibly can, which suggests something of the attraction with which being old is regarded. One of the paradoxes of aging is that the person who is growing older may not feel older. Aging persons tend to cling to a concept of themselves as middle-aged. At the same time, they maintain a low opinion of old people in general. Thus, in one sample of apartment dwellers over the age of 62 (women) or 65 (men), "[w]hile 83 per cent felt that they were still personally useful, only 37 per cent acknowledged this for the elderly in general. Similarly, while another 83 per cent thought that older people who felt middle-aged were simply deluding themselves, almost one half of the sample insisted that they were personally middle-aged or young" (Rosow, 1967, P. 318).

Most people value at least some of the social roles they play, and they tend to cling to these as long as possible. Healthy adults may continue certain kinds of activities — involving household, relatives, friends, neighbors, church, and so forth — at essentially middle-aged levels into their 70s (Cumming & Henry, 1961), when activity drops off. At whatever age people give up their roles of worker, spouse, and so forth, most of them feel badly about their loss (Havighurst, Neugarten, & Tobin, 1968; Kuhlen, 1968). Identifying oneself as old may, in fact, be something of a capitulation, a concession that one can no longer compensate for the erosion of capacity that comes with age. Thus, those who call themselves "old" are much more likely than their agemates to have already lost two or more major roles (Rosow, 1967), and when people disengage they often do so because of ill health (Maas & Kuypers, 1974).

We might expect that people will choose to stay engaged with their incentives more emphatically if the incentives in their lives are more worthwhile. We do, in fact, find that middle-class old people (up to age 75) are more reluctant to consider themselves old (40% do) than are working-class people (75%) (Rosow, 1967). Middle-class individuals are even more reluctant to associate with other old people, as by living in retirement neighborhoods. It seems likely that the more affluent life of the middle-aged middle class makes them less willing to cash in their status for the social allowances made for the old.

Thus, many people actively resist giving up their major incentives, resist identifying themselves as "old," and feel badly when they are forced to do so. It seems safe to infer that the changed activity patterns that come with age are often not freely chosen.

Incentives and the Psychological Deficits of Aging

People commonly assume that old people deteriorate psychologically for purely biological reasons. Gerontologists speak of age "deficits," by which they have in mind such things as slowed reflexes, mental rigidity, deteriorating intelligence, and perhaps related personality traits such as excessive cautiousness. As psychologists and other scientists study this matter further, however, it is becoming clear that much of the apparent "deficit" is simply the response of the old to their more barren life situations. Of course, people do deteriorate biologically as they age, but that is far less responsible for changes in psychological abilities or in inner experience than one might think.

Ironically, this is one area in which investigators were for some time fooled by generational differences. One team (Nesselroade, Schaie, & Baltes, 1972) gave intelligence tests to a sample of adults age 21 to 70 in 1956 and again in 1963. Looking just at the 1956 results, they found — as had previous investigators — that older people made lower scores on the tests, especially after about age 50. However, when the investigators compared each person's score in 1956 with his or her score in 1963, they found that, in all but one dimension, intelligence had on the average either held steady over the seven-year interval or had actually improved. The one dimension in which scores had declined, which included measures of visual-motor flexibility, probably reflected situational influences or momentary personal states more than long-term changes in ability. Thus, it appears that important intellectual abilities do not necessarily decline with age.

This is not to say that all individuals remain as well informed and intellectually active in their old age as in their younger years. The problem, however, is usually one of circumstances, not of abilities. Mental functions, skills, knowledge, and general activity patterns can atrophy with disuse, and will remain unused unless there are sufficient incentives available to make their use worthwhile. Thus, therapists who apply reward systems systematically can fairly reliably improve the psychological performance of the institutionalized aged (Riedel, 1974). Healthy adults can remain sexually active into extreme old age if they keep performing sexually, but they court serious sexual difficulties if they do not (Masters & Johnson, 1966).

The problem of accounting for the psychological deficits of old age then shifts to finding the reasons that older individuals withdraw from intellectual, sexual, and athletic pursuits. Sometimes, of course , the reason is physical infirmity that interferes with an activity directly. Perhaps more often, however, it has to do with the changed social rewards or incentive values available to old people — for instance, the embarrassment of exercising physically in a society that values good looks, high levels of skill, and heavy contact sports; social disapproval of old people seeking sexual stimulation; boredom with an unvarying sexual routine; intolerance for elders' contributions to public discussions; and so forth.

If "old" behavior is produced simply by the old person's circumstances, the same circumstances should produce the same kinds of behavior in younger people. Robert Kastenbaum (1971) has now shown that this happens. For instance, he had young people "play a game in which they act as advisers to a city government. As the game goes on, conditions in the city change, officials are replaced, and the adviser finds himself treated as an 'oldtimer.' His advice is still requested routinely, but it becomes clear that nobody is paying attention. His role is empty, yet he must continue to go through the motions. Those we have tested in this situation show impotent rage, and preoccupation with bodily discomfort, and tend to go off on tangents about the 'old times' when they were powerful and effective" (Kastenbaum, 1971, P. 54). In another study, Kastenbaum was able to make younger participants as cautious as their elders by putting them in situations in which they were to make decisions on the basis of little relevant information amid social disapproval from others.

It appears that much of what have seemed to be natural psychological deficits of aging are in fact the consequences of the incentive systems with which our modern aged are surrounded.

Conclusions

It seems that we can account for much of what happens during the course of aging in terms of the incentive situations in which aging people find themselves. There is ample evidence to suggest that, as they grow older, most people gradually shed some or all of the incentives and the related patterns of activity that are most important in their younger years: sports, romantic love, various kinds of external stimulation, children, sex, work, positions of power, involvement in community organizations, marriage, and, for those eventually institutionalized, even the simple operations of personal maintenance. It now appears that they do so, on the average, with regret. This is obviously not true in all cases, nor must "giving up" a disliked job or other unpleasant role necessarily be construed as a loss, especially if it is replaced by something that the person has long wanted to substitute. Nevertheless, for most people, giving up activities around which they had organized their lives is indeed experienced as a loss, and they are the less happy for it.

Some of this progressive impoverishment of people's incentive worlds may be necessary and unavoidable. A substantial part, however, can be attributed to the particular social system in which it occurs — the kinds of incentives held out to or withheld from older people by their peers and by the others in our society. As a result, although some middle-aged people may be pushed too hard for their liking, many older individuals are underutilized and undermotivated, with the result that their abilities wither prematurely and they become alienated from themselves and from life itself.

It is worth pointing out that this problem is, from a historical viewpoint, quite new. Since the turn of the last century, the life expectancy of Westerners has increased by about 20 years. Thus, at the age when many of our contemporaries are just getting well into their midlife crises, most of their great grandparents were already dead. Not only do we have an unprecedented number of older people, but the loose and fragmented structure of our families and communities is turning them into a distinct, separate class, few members of which are accorded by their communities a designated place that carries enough respect and is substantial enough to organize a life around. We have simply not yet created the necessary arrangements in our society for coping intelligently with the results of modern longevity.

That is, of course, another way of saying that we have yet to arrange our system of social and material incentives in such a way as to challenge and absorb our old people. Until we do, we shall continue to look upon old age as a period relatively empty of meaningful content, and a good many of the old themselves, when they finally bring themselves so to identify themselves, will continue to agree.

Alienation and Inner Experience

Psychologists and other social scientists have concerned themselves very little with the inner experience of alienation. Yet that inner experience is obviously extremely important to the alienated person and very important to anyone hoping to understand the alienated person's behavior. So far in this chapter, we have dealt in the terms generally used by social scientists in approaching alienation: the beliefs people affirm about their situations and their ratings of how "satisfied" or "dissatisfied" they feel about something. It may, however, be possible to get a somewhat closer look at the experience of alienation.

Affect in Alienation

There is no reason, apart from intuitive conviction, for supposing that the experience of alienation carries with it a particular distinctive affect. Nothing like "alienation" or "satisfaction" appears, for instance, on the lists of emotions investigated by Tomkins, Ekman, Izard, or their associates. It would be possible to argue that alienation is simply a complex mixture of "primary" emotions, such as anger, disgust, and distress, with the notable absence of enjoyment or interest. Then, again, it may have its own properties. There is no way at present of knowing. We may, however, consider the constellation of feelings reported by Wilson's (1950) sample of college-educated women during the 1930s, women selected because of their feelings of "futility." Many of the statements made by these women to indicate futility were, on the surface at least, statements of belief about their life situations, such as ". . . will never be able to" or ". . . my class of women . . . social parasites." Other statements, however, largely conveyed affect: ". . . cannot cope with this"; ". . . feel I can no longer go on"; ". . . lost hope"; ". . . completely discouraged"; ". . . expect nothing"; ". . . disillusioned"; ". . . ineffectual . . . purposeless"; ". . . no future ahead for me"; ". . . nothing to live for"; ". . . everything is wrong"; ". . . my life is a muddle"; ". . . life is so futile"; ". . . life holds nothing"; ". . . like a squirrel in a cage I go on"; ". . . my outlook is bleak"; ". . . at a loss"; ". . . feel starved for opportunities"; ". . . cannot live a complete life"; ". . . felt simply doomed"; and ". . . am just chasing things around" (Wilson, 1950, Pp. 32–33).

No clinician would have trouble identifying these kinds of statements as the kind one expects of people who are depressed. However, these people were not especially depressed by usual standards. Wilson says of them that they "seemed to be leading lives of average normal women, from all indications functioning satisfactorily as active and able persons. Observations of them over a period of time in no way indicated a group of bleak, frustrated lives. But in spite of being above average in appearance, intellectual ability, accomplishment, socio-economic status, income, and objectively measured emotional stability, *they expressed futility*" (Wilson, 1950, P. 30). Their statements were not primarily menopausal or midlife expressions: Although the age range of the women was 20 to 49, their median age was 30. However, the nature of some of these statements and the contexts in which they were made suggest that we are dealing here not with the usual depression phase of an incentive-disengagement cycle but rather with a postcycle phenomenon: a feeling, perhaps following the recovery phase of the cycle, that there are no attractive incentives toward which to turn next. The elements of this feeling seem to go with continued *meaningless* functioning, in the sense that the activity is not advancing goals that the person identifies as most crucial to her or that she sees no concrete goals that she values highly. The statements express a sense of meaninglessness of the present life situation and yet a sense of being trapped in it.

These women were relatively well-to-do and, at their median age, were perhaps still in the process of adjusting their expectations of life from youthful aspirations to middle-aged resignation. In that light, their experience may well be similar to that of young union members described above who were also unusually dissatisfied but, probably, were destined to become resigned and ostensibly "satisfied" (Sheppard & Herrick, 1972). It undoubtedly requires a considerable leap of inference to suppose that their feelings have much in common with those experienced by alienated workers, alienated spouses, and older people dissatisfied with their shrinking lives. Nevertheless, the kind of affect Wilson's women seemed to be communicating may well be like that felt by people in general toward particular alienative aspects of their lives.

Alienation, Attention, and Thinking

We saw in Chapter 2 that people notice, attend to, recall, and think about things related to their current concerns. Some concerns are usually more influential than others in directing a person's thoughts; and, although we have yet to define precisely what factors make a concern influential, they almost certainly have something to do with the "importance" of the incentive to the person, by which we mean the power of the incentive to command the person's emotional reactions. All of these considerations lead us to some predictions about the inner life of the alienated individual.

Alienation from something means that the thing — job, marriage, society, or whatever — has ceased to have much positive incentive value for the person. It may still be instrumental for avoiding certain negative consequences. The disliked job, for instance, may still be useful for fending off poverty, and living in Society X may still be preferable to leaving friends, family, and mother tongue for a society elsewhere. However, the thing the person is alienated from has ceased to be the main focus of a concern, especially if there is no great danger of losing it. A disliked job can be routinized, for instance, and if the person feels fairly secure in it, it may have very little power over the person's respondent processes. On the job, the person may continue to turn in a passably satisfactory performance by virtue of routinely attending to and having the right thoughts about the minimum operations necessary to get by. However, his or her respondent processes will be about something else: about plans for after five o'clock, about the upcoming weekend, about personal involvements, about other employees, and perhaps about finding a different job. Since respondent thought probably plays a large role in creative thinking (Klinger, 1971), such employees are highly unlikely to contribute very creatively to their employers' missions.

There is a good deal of evidence to confirm these notions. A number of studies, most of them involving Melvin Seeman, have shown that people who feel generally powerless to affect their lives (and who are presumably alienated from society) have a poorer command of the facts they need to help themselves out of their oppressive life situations (Lystad, 1972). There is often a problem of determining which is cause and which is effect in such studies: Are the uninformed people driven to feeling powerless by their ignorance? This, however, seems not to be what happened. Participants in psychological experiments take longer at making decisions and keep their thoughts better fixed on the task before them if they believe that their skill makes a difference (Lefcourt, Lewis, & Silverman, 1968). In experimental laboratory situations, people who believe that their lives are controlled by outside forces, rather than by themselves, make less use of available information to get things done (Phares, 1968) and look for less information in the first place (Davis & Phares, 1967; Lefcourt & Wine, 1969).

These laboratory results have been confirmed in a field study (Bickford & Neal, 1969). Here the investigators distributed to participants in a vocational training program a newsletter containing information relevant to their employment opportunities. Later, the participants were tested on their knowledge of their immediate situation in the training program and on their knowledge of their larger work opportunities. The investigators found that the participants who were the most alienated (according to scales of powerlessness, meaninglessness, and normlessness) had learned less from the newsletter than those who were least alienated. In fact, only 14% of the participants who scored low on all three of the scales (and who were therefore least alienated) were unknowledgeable about both their immediate situation and their larger opportunities, as compared with 74% of those who scored high (that is, were most alienated) on all three scales. These differences can not be explained in terms of the participants' backgrounds, since their alienation was unrelated to the number of years of formal schooling, length of previous unemployment, or the desirability of the last job they held.

Of course, people who are alienated about something are unresponsive only to those things they are alienated from. For instance, among better educated workers, those who were more alienated from their jobs much more often (60%) preferred receiving information relevant to changing their jobs over information on sports and leisure than did the less alienated workers (36%) (Seeman, 1972).

There are, of course, situations in which a person is alienated from virtually everything in his or her life. Then there are no influential concerns to direct attention except the concern for changing the life situation itself, which may seem a lost cause. Accordingly, relatively few things would have the power to command attention very strongly, and those few things are likely to be basic bodily urges, body sensations, and cues of potential danger or of potential relief from the present situation. If we can make the assumption that people in that kind of life situation are more likely than others to be bored, then it is interesting to note here that, in Leonard Giambra's (1974) study of daydreaming over the life span, boredom was highly correlated with mindwandering (correlation coefficient of .62) and with distractibility (correlation coefficient of .43). Interestingly, Karstens (1928) also found that, as her experimental subjects began to "satiate" on tasks that they were asked to repeat to the point of futility, they also had serious difficulties with maintaining concentration. These results, then, seem to accord with our expectations based on the theory of current concerns.

To sum up, then, alienated individuals seem to have characteristic feelings: a sense of the meaninglessness or futility of their activities, hopelessness about making the alienative incentive or activity rewarding, resentment, and some low-level depressionlike affect. They are responsive only to the most necessary aspects of their alienative incentives or activities, are highly responsive to escaping them, and, insofar as their alienation is general, have trouble with mindwandering and distractibility.

Personality Dispositions to Become Alienated

To become alienated, people must find themselves in a situation in which they have become disillusioned with an incentive but must continue to live with it. Becoming disillusioned is a process of, first, discovering that for one reason or another the incentive is not providing the value expected, and, second, losing hope of being able to salvage the situation.

Obviously, the objective nature of people's life situations plays an important role in determining whether they will become alienated from something. Some jobs, marriage partners, and governments are almost bound to alienate people from them. Nevertheless, each of the requirements for becoming alienated also incorporates an indispensable personal element. The expectation that an outcome disappoints is the individual's own. The assessment that nothing can be done to salvage a situation is the individual's own. The decision to live with an unsatisfactory situation — despite the feeling of being "trapped" into having to go on living with it — is normally an individual's own decision, arrived at after taking into account all of the gains and losses from continuing or not; and that decision rests on the individual's assessment of what might be done to construct attractive alternative life situations.

People can be expected to differ from one another in the way they arrive at all of these expectations and assessments. We have already seen in Chapter 5 that people with unrealistically high expectations of life or of themselves are more likely than others to become depressed. Presumably, they are also more likely to become alienated. Work by Keniston (1965) with alienated college students, which we shall look at in greater detail later, suggests that this is so. In addition, people can systematically misassess their situations and their own abilities, or limit the range of incentives they are able to enjoy, or become so conflict-ridden as to make enjoyment or attainment of many incentives impossible. To these personal dispositions we shall now turn.

Developing a Sense of Effectiveness

Imagine that you are at a party. Someone brings out one of those games the object of which is to guide a ball down a path that weaves between holes in a board, the player controlling the ball with two knobs that change the tilt of the board. The guests will react to this game in quite different ways. Some will say, "Oh, no! I'm no good at that kind of thing." Others will get a gleam in their eye as they maneuver for a chance to try it out. Some, perhaps under the pressure of friends' expectations, will begin to move the ball along, feel terribly humiliated as it drops out of sight, and quickly give the game to someone else. Others will chuckle as the ball disappears too soon, start over in a determined way, and keep at it until they manage to roll the ball from start to end, at which point they feel immensely good about themselves. What accounts for these different reactions?

First, the different kinds of people described above typically differ in several interconnected ways. They size up the same situations differently, they feel differently about identical outcomes, and they gravitate to different kinds of activities. Specifically, some people, faced with a challenging situation, are not much put off by failures and greatly enjoy success, and they therefore seek out opportunities to meet challenges; whereas others feel badly about failures and are only slightly gratified by successes (Heckhausen, 1973, 1975a). For this second group, the net expected affect from meeting challenges is therefore negative, and they consequently avoid such situations when they can. Furthermore, the people who hope for success are inclined to attribute success to their ability and to blame failures on not having tried hard enough. They can therefore take pride in their successes, and they do not have to interpret failures as reflections on their basic worth. In contrast, people who most fear failure in challenging situations tend to blame their failures on inadequate ability to do the job, but they attribute successes to their having tried especially hard or to good luck. Thus, they do let failures lower their sense of basic worth, and they can take little credit for successes.

Heinz Heckhausen (1972, 1973, 1974a) points out that for a particular person all these events constitute a "self-reinforcing system." The hope-of-success person seeks out challenges to meet, persists at them longer and harder, therefore succeeds more often, and feels ever better about him- or herself. Such a person is likely to view the world as filled with interesting possibilities. The fear-of-failure person, on the other hand, shies away from challenges, or gives up too soon on the unavoidable ones, and therefore experiences little gratification and much pain from them. This person sees little to be gained in meeting challenges, is cut off from an important kind of gratification, and dismisses many opportunities because they carry the risk of pain.

It seems likely that these different ways of approaching challenging situations are life-long patterns. There is some accumulated evidence about how they start (reviewed by Heckhausen, 1972): Hope-of-success people seem to come from families that generate warm, supportive climates. The parents have high standards and applaud success but do not punish failures. The mothers (who are still the primary caretakers of the children) arrange opportunities for the children to encounter challenges but do not interfere with the children's attempts to respond to them. Heckhausen proposes that children get enough innate satisfaction from performing well that they will come to prize their successes even without parents specifically rewarding them. However, if parents take over the children's attempts to perform, they may rob them of the satisfaction of having done it all themselves; and if the parents ridicule or otherwise punish failures so severely as to outweigh the good feelings of success, children will start avoiding the incentives of achievement. Then children are unlikely to grow up viewing themselves as especially effective with challenging situations, and they are unlikely to seize the opportunities that arise. We would expect, therefore, that as adults such people will be unable to find satisfaction in challenging opportunities, will persist less long in difficult situations, and will feel less free to try out alternative jobs or life situations when the ones they are in go sour. The evidence on whether these people are indeed more likely to become alienated is not yet in, but at this point it seems likely that they are.

Becoming Immobilized by Conflict

For people to pursue goals, they must be able to become committed to them. Although this might seem so automatic a process that it can pose no problems for a person, people do, in fact, often suffer from an inability to become committed. They speak then of wanting to find something that might interest them, of wishing to "find themselves," or of seeking to discover who they are. They may well be active people in some sense, going to school or earning a living, perhaps even married — but they do not identify themselves with the pattern of their lives. They are in that sense alienated from much of what they do.

There are no doubt numerous ways to arrive at conflicts that immobilize a person. To consider one way, people may be so unsure of what is right for them that they cannot entrust themselves to any single major course of action. The problem here seems often to be that the person has failed to acquire a firm "identity," to use the concept developed by Erik Erikson (1963). To become committed to something means believing that one wants that goal enough to make the necessary sacrifices and to give up the alternatives with which it is incompatible. Some people, however, are unable to sort out the conflicting demands made of them by themselves and by others. They respond by trying to meet all of these demands or by defaulting from making any major decisions at all. They put off basic decisions such as launching careers and forming intimate personal relationships (Orlofsky, Marcia, & Lesser, 1973). These people are sometimes said to possess "diffused" identities.[9]

Kenneth Keniston (1965) reported on an intensive study of highly alienated male college students. Interpretations of clinical interviews with them and of stories the students wrote about standard sets of pictures (TAT) revealed some personality characteristics very like those of identity diffusion: "On every level . . . the alienated refuse conventional commitments, seeing them as unprofitable, dangerous, futile, or merely uncertain and unpredictable (P. 52). . . . The alienated generally affirm that they have no long-range goals, and indeed believe it impossible to find or create such goals; . . . Long-range planning is impossible, given the uncertainty of the future and the likelihood that things will turn out badly; what remain are the needs of the moment, of the body, the senses, the heart, and the 'humor of the ego'" (P. 56).

Keniston's attempt to explain their behavior, given the nature of the data, is necessarily conjectural. It has the almost allegorical quality of psychoanalytic interpretation. Nevertheless, the argument is revealing.

First, these men had at one time been quite close to their mothers, but not to their fathers, whom they regard as "weak, damaged, phony and unemulable characters" (P. 136). However, they now see their mothers "at best, as controlling and limiting, and at worst, as devouring and murderous" (P. 136). Nevertheless, if we can accept Keniston's analysis, these students remain committed to a state of total dependence, of total fusion with another (originally their idealized mother), that is simply not possible. They sense that, if they achieved it, it would probably destroy them. Because they succeeded in their Oedipal contests with their fathers, they were also left with a dislike of all competitive and rivalrous social situations, and they thus reject most of the American occupational world. Hence, the incentives available to them seem too weak in comparison with what they wish to have, and also too dangerous. They are unable to identify with their fathers, and therefore reject an important role model. Consequently, these people, trusting nothing and no one, remain blocked by conflict, socially isolated, economically unproductive, and largely miserable.

Options for the Alienated

People who are alienated from something in their lives have perhaps five kinds of options.

First, they may settle for more modest returns. Thus, as we have seen, workers still know that certain aspects of their work are unattractive, but they complain about them less, having apparently resigned themselves to the jobs they have. A spouse may lower his or her goals for the marriage and settle for whatever companionship or sexual gratifications remain. An aging individual may disengage from incentives no longer available and focus on those still there. Eventually, the adaptation level should sink, and the formerly despised incentives will seem more attractive.

Second, people may accept the thing from which they are alienated as purely instrumental for achieving other goals. Thus, a worker may routinize a job for the income it provides. A person may put up with a troublesome spouse for wealth, connections, or housekeeping.

Third, alienated people may take drastic action to alter their life situations to rid themselves or to strike back at the thing that has alienated them. Workers quit jobs, spouses divorce each other, and aging individuals may, like Juan Ponce de Leon, search for the fountain of youth in Florida. When the alienation of American young people from their society reached its peak during the Indochina war, thousands of groups tried to construct "alternative life styles" by establishing communes or other new communities whose values would be consistent with their own. Other people, alienated from their old life situations, join the world's emigrants, adventurers, revolutionaries, and drifters. Finally, having no remaining emotional identification with their work or with their society, they may turn to crime. Thus, dissatisfied workers are much more likely to steal from their employers or to commit sabotage (U.S. Department of Labor, 1974). Young men who are alienated from the educational system have a much higher rate of traffic violations (Pelz & Schuman, 1973). Interestingly, only among this group does drinking increase traffic violations. In three Southern U.S. cities, crime committed by blacks declined significantly during periods of major civil rights activity, when blacks presumably felt less alienated from at least some sectors of their society (Solomon, Walker, O'Connor, & Fishman, 1965).

Fourth, individuals bereft of sufficiently satisfying incentives, despairing over the possibility of changing their life situations, may take direct action on the messenger carrying the bad news: They may manipulate their affects by whatever means lie at hand — spectator athletics, the mass media, opera, drugs, and so on.

Fifth, there is suicide. In fact, one of the early major contributions to understanding alienation was part of the first major social-scientific analysis of suicide (Durkheim, 1897/1951).

How people's manipulations of their affects derive from their incentive situations — including the ultimate manipulation, suicide — is the subject of the next two chapters.

Chapter 7

Tampering with the Message System

After work and school activities, the typical cycle of the American day turns toward mind-altering activities that range from drinking alcohol to watching television. Probably every technique for altering the way one feels has at one time or another been regarded as a major social problem, but each has its aficionados. The theoretical argument developed in the previous chapters puts us in a position to understand why these behaviors are so firmly entrenched, and it also helps explain why particular individuals make greater use of them than others do, and in which life situations.

Crucial to this explanation is a proposition argued in Chapter 3: The way in which people evaluate the things that happen to them — the way in which people distinguish among various types of good and bad — is by means of the affects inside of them that are aroused by events: joy, fear, anger, contentment, disgust, and so on. People's affective systems, according to this view, are their evaluative feedback systems, their message systems for telling them how things are going. Accordingly, people perform those actions that they expect will yield them the best harvest of affects.

The business of optimizing affects goes on all of the time. People are constantly working to produce the best readings possible from their message systems, either for the longer run or for the immediate moment. Higher organisms must necessarily do so if they are to survive, because it is ultimately their affect systems that tie them into the realities that govern their existence. Consider an individual whose development is typical for his or her species, and who is facing a situation that is also typical for the species. For that individual, affect identifies which incentives are indispensable for the survival of the individual or of the species, and affect registers the individual's progress in attaining them.

The kinds of events to which the affect system is wired to react have to be specified rather crudely, even though the circuitry must be awesomely complicated. An innate system of this kind must be set to respond to a whole class of possible physical events, the individual forms of which vary unpredictably from one occasion to the next. For instance, newborn infants must be programmed to suck at almost any blunt object around their mouth, because if their brains are programmed too narrowly they would fail to respond to the nipples or nursing techniques of many mothers. Therefore, the wired-in specifications that guide a brain must be loose enough to fit the widely varying environments that the organism might face.

Because organisms make innately programmed responses to rather broad classes of stimuli — at least until they have individually learned to be more discriminating — it is possible to "fool" the affect system by presenting an organism with something only resembling the right schema. For instance, a hungry newborn infant can be induced to suck at a spatula, finger, or rattle, none of which provide milk. A fish, the male three-spined stickelback, can be induced to attack wads of red cloth, even though they do not have the other properties of red-bellied male rivals.

Inside the organism, affective responses depend in significant part on biochemistry. As we saw in Chapter 5, for instance, noradrenaline plays an important role in both agression and depression. Therefore, not only can the affective system be fooled by manipulating external events, it can also be manipulated biochemically. In a natural setting, the system helps an organism get started in dealing with its environment until its behavior can be progressively refined and reshaped by learning; but there are many ways to play on the system so as to render its messages false.

Humankind is, of course, the first species having the technological ability to tamper with the message system on a significant scale, and tamper we have. From opera to beer, from sun dance to stock car race, humans have devised an admirable array of methods for changing their feeling states. These methods have become deeply ingrained aspects of their cultures. To most people, they are as integral and unquestioned a part of living as eating and sleeping.

The reason seems clear enough. With habituation and satiation, many pleasures become less intense (Chapter 4). Losing in one's efforts to get or keep an incentive produces a whole sequence of more or less unpleasant affects (Chapter 5). Being left unsatisfied in a situation one is stuck with leaves people feeling unpleasantly alienated

(Chapter 6). Everyone experiences at least some of these lapses from good feeling, and some people experience them much of the time. Rationally, people may know (although often they do not) that their unpleasant feelings reflect real discrepancies between their wishes and their realities and that changing just the feelings will not improve the realities. However, people do not experience the goodness of their realities directly. What they experience directly are their affects. If something can alter their affects for the better, then they will necessarily value the things that produced the change. Only if people know that feeling better immediately will be more than counterbalanced by feeling worse later is there even a chance of their forgoing the immediate pleasure. Therefore, if manipulating one's message system simply adds good feeling or reduces bad feeling without inordinate cost or pain, the methods of manipulation are bound to join the person's store of valued actions and things. From the standpoint of biological function, the new activity may seem artificial; but from the standpoint of raw inner experience, anything that produces a certain good feeling is just as real and valuable and *meaningful* as any other way of producing it.

Therefore, people and cultures turn to methods for improving their inner experiences just as naturally as they gratify basic biological urges. People may forgo the pleasant affects of sexual arousal if they believe that they will be stricken with relentless guilt thereafter, and they may forgo the euphoria of drinking alcoholic beverages if the firm prospect of social rejection or physical deterioration or roasting in hell for eternity strikes them as distinctly worse. Otherwise, however, it is more likely that they will participate in and help develop cultural institutions for sexual play and drinking.

Methods for Manipulating Affects

Harnessing Natural Incentive Systems

The simplest and most straightforward way to control one's affects is to simulate the situations that elicit affect most naturally. If we assume that every major kind of affect can be elicited by some kind of natural incentive, then one can construct new incentives that contain the same crucial elements. For instance, attacking and vanquishing another organism feels pleasant when the other organism has been blocking some goal-oriented activity of the attacker. Contests of all kinds bring together the essential elements of this situation, and they often add elements of the pride that comes with mastery. The contestants are by definition blocking each other from gaining the social approval and sense of mastery provided by winning. Sometimes the contestants are pitted against each other in only the most thinly veiled fashion, as in such contact sports as boxing, wrestling, football, and basketball. At other times the interaction is much more genteel, as in bridge or chess. Nevertheless, there is no question that people are opposing one anothers' interests, are perhaps enjoying watching one another "sweat it out" in difficult situations, and feel very strong emotions about the outcome. Deep as the depression of losing may be, the thrill of victory makes it all worthwhile.

Physical educators often argue that athletics are really quite different from organized combat — that the two are related only in the minds of deviant athletes or vicious audiences — but the evidence suggests otherwise (Keating, 1972). The reason physical educators must be concerned with "sportsmanship" is that the veneer of friendliness is so easily rubbed off. The most that can reasonably be said is that the trained athlete's aggression is usually impersonal and rarely outlasts the game, when it may be replaced with sympathy. Certainly, good sportsmanship is not a very deeply ingrained norm among some "amateur" sports organizations. In the words of Woody Hayes, Ohio State University's football coach, "We'd rather have an immoral win than a moral victory" (Sports Illustrated, Dec. 6 1971, P. 90).

Another type of natural incentive situation is that which endangers people. With good luck, the unpleasant affect of fear gives way to the pleasure of relief and perhaps to the pride of mastery. There is even some reason to suppose that after repeated encounters with dangerous situations the end of danger may produce strong euphoria (Solomon & Corbit, 1974). Around this basic type of situation, people have organized a variety of adventures. Some are genuinely hazardous, such as exploring jungles or parachuting from airplanes. Others merely simulate danger, such as riding a roller coaster. In each case, participants engage in unnecessary and economically disadvantageous activities in order to produce powerful affects in themselves.

Western society has evolved long-standing traditions for harnessing sexual arousal in noncoital situations. Some circles have developed flirtation to a fine art, and sexual arousal provides an important source of gratification in many kinds of mixed-sex dancing. In recent decades, many married couples have turned to "swinging" as a full-scale, non-simulated sexual activity intended to restore or enhance their pleasure in copulation.

In settings that are usually less organized, people may try to harness a variety of affective systems — aggression, mastery, relief, and sexual arousal — through sadomasochistic acts (Fromm, 1973). Thus, some people experience great pleasure in setting cats on fire, putting out cigarettes on women's breasts, being whipped while nude, or simply maintaining strict, destructive control over someone else's life. Sometimes, of course, sadomasochistic activity becomes organized, as in lynchings, pogroms, officially sanctioned torture, and death camps. There are often many volunteers among the participants in these activities. Some groups, such as school classes, may unofficially designate targets for cruelty, in which many pupils then indulge themselves. Thus, for some individuals, perhaps especially those who feel powerless and isolated, sadomasochistic behavior provides a major source of personal satisfaction (Fromm, 1973).

People can also find ways to harness the kinds of feelings that parents often experience while tending small children. We saw in Chapter 4 that feeling "gooey inside" at the sight of a small baby may somehow be wired in. There may also be other ways in which "nurturant activities" can arouse positive affects. If there are, people can simulate their essential elements (or learned extensions of them) in specially arranged situations. Thus, people can find pleasure in visiting hospital patients, staffing senior citizen centers, and taking retarded groups swimming.

Spiritual Approaches

One of the most prominent directions in which people turn for help with their unsatisfactory feeling states is that of the various religious disciplines. Just which satisfactions an individual finds there depends to a great degree on who he or she is and which religion he or she is turning to. Some religious activities bring quite secular economic and social rewards, such as making advantageous business contacts, getting rid of the children on Sunday morning, maintaining a social position of prestige and influence, and so forth. Other satisfactions may be less instrumental for making extrinsic gains but may nevertheless be a simple harnessing of everyday incentive systems, just like those described in the previous section. For instance, wielding influence in a congregation can serve to affirm one's mastery of power over others, can satisfy needs to nurture, and can bring regard and affection. Losing oneself in a revival meeting can produce a sense of solidarity with others and a sense of acceptance by both the others and God. Conversion to a new religious faith often carries with it a sense of profound euphoria and new-found confidence. This may be because the proselytes have dissolved some old value conflicts by disengaging from certain old goals, with the result that they can now form commitments to crucially important incentives such as self-acceptance, communion, and salvation unhampered by conflicting values. (Actually, remarkably little is known about the psychological processes of religious conversion.)

There are other rewards of religious activity that had until very recently virtually disappeared from the religions of the West but that continue to characterize the religions of the East: states of ecstasy experienced during one or another form of meditation. The meditator may induce a "trance" by whirling, staring at a mandala, chanting a Sanskrit mantra, or repeating a Latin prayer. With the proper concentration, often attained after years of supervised practice, it is possible to achieve brief periods of profoundly altered consciousness, apparently accompanied by characteristic changes in brain waves, whose qualities are claimed by meditative masters to outdo those of any other experience.

Because such meditation requires a highly demanding discipline, especially for those most strongly committed to other incentives, few people achieve mastery, although many gain the benefits of less intense "trance" states. Some individuals abandon worldly pursuits and embrace instead a life largely organized around transformed states of consciousness. Buddhist and Hindu religious forms have institutionalized such life-styles, as had some segments of premodern Christianity. It is interesting that in India, which provides probably the greatest social support for such activity, people typically enter these religious vocations during middle age[1] at a time when other incentive values have often begun to fade (Chapter 6).

Passive Massage of the Affect System

Human spectators often take on the plight of people they observe — feeling their aspirations, suspense, joys, fears, and defeats. There is no need for the spectator to be related to the person observed, to be affected by the same events, or even to have direct sensory contact with the person. A female college professor in Bulgaria can read Arthur Miller's *Death of a Salesman* and emphathize with Willy Loman, and a modern American encyclopedia salesperson can feel wracked by the agony of King Lear.

Not only does this human capacity for empathy contribute profoundly to the possibility of humane social relationships, it also provides the possibility of passive emotional massage.[2] That is, people can arrange to observe the lives of others so as to induce in themselves a wide array of powerful affects. They can listen to gossip, listen to an epic poem, watch an athletic contest, attend an opera, hear a song, watch a dramatic production, read a novel or a comic book, see a film, or experience a comedian's funny insights. They can tune in on nearly the entire range of such presentations on television. As they do, and as they allow themselves to be drawn into the contrived reality of the show, they will feel pride, love, joy, fear, sadness, anger, disgust, vindication, relief, sexual arousal, penitence — in fact, all of the feelings they are capable of experiencing with respect to real situations that might involve them. Presumably, people choose these spectator experiences to supplement their "real-life" experiences and are the more likely to spend time with them the less their actual life situations offer them satisfactions they can accept.

Certainly, spectator satisfactions can be relatively powerful. For instance, people who are alienated from their jobs, who find family life uneventful, who are physically and recreationally too inactive to have developed any other sources of pride, and who lack intimate communication with others, can establish a sense of identification with an athletic team. They thereby gain a series of goals (victories over opponents) and hopes, a sense of vicarious pride in their teams' exploits, and a sense of comradeship with other fans. A whole string of athletic "events" they would not otherwise have cared about are now emotionally meaningful and suspenseful.

There would be no need for spectator athletics if people's lives were filled with less contrived experiences. As Goodhart and Chataway (1968) write, "It is only because millions of people are not effectively involved in the societies in which they live and work that they identify themselves so passionately with the participants in a sporting ritual" (P. 156). Nevertheless, even though the pleasures of passively watching sports or television pale before the experiences of deep love or genuine accomplishment, they are "real" from the standpoint of the affective message system, and their power is bound to seem greater when the person's adaptation level for powerful experiences is low.

There is no intention here to denigrate athletics in comparison to other spectator activities. Watching athletic events can teach spectators techniques for enriching their own participation in sports, just as drama can teach its audiences about the ranges of the human experience. However, audiences generally patronize neither athletics nor drama for their educational benefit. Many "culture vultures" attend plays and operas or read novels for the same reasons that others watch football or soap operas: To stir in themselves more powerful and more satisfying experiences than they can find in their everyday "real" lives.

The only one of these pursuits about which social scientists have collected much evidence is television watching. We shall take a further look at some of this evidence in a later section.

Intervention with Chemicals

The last major class of ways to manipulate the affect system is through the use of chemicals. This method is, of course, far from new. People have used alcohol, opium, peyote, marijuana, and doubtless other substances for so long that their origins are lost in the unrecorded past. Many chemicals have become integrated into ancient religious observances. In fact, the official American prohibition of alcohol early in this century excepted religious uses, such as for the Christian Mass. The blessing for wine is among Judaism's oldest forms. Peyote is divine and legal for the Native American Church. Doubtless, the ritual status of psychoactive chemicals derives from their ability to alter inner experience.

The most prominent uses of psychoactive chemicals are not, however, for ritual purposes but to change moods. People traditionally associate festive occasions with alcohol and, increasingly, with marijuana. Despite the scare tactics used by some leaders of earlier generations, people overdo their use of drugs (including alcohol) and persist in using them not because of a physiological "monkey on their back" but because the drugs improve the way they feel, and because this improvement outweighs for them alternative things they might do with their lives. The choice is complicated, and physiological addiction may somewhat discourage stopping, but for the most part the choice is free. We shall consider the evidence for this, too, in a later section.

Value Judgments

Listing ways to "fool" or "manipulate" the affective message system implies a judgment that experiences arranged in these ways are somehow inferior to "genuine" experiences. That is a judgment in which I concur, but for personal rather than for scientific reasons. Objectively, the *affective* experience is real however it is produced. To impose a judgment of its value, it is not enough to say that it was a response to something contrived, for how can we say that responses to something contrived are necessarily inferior to other responses? Alcohol and the New York Jets may be less "natural" in some sense than fresh apples, but then so is apple pie. Is enjoying apple pie therefore flatly inferior to enjoying fresh apples?

In order to make a value judgment, one must first agree on a criterion for deciding that something is valuable. There are various kinds of criteria that can be applied. One might be biological survival: If watching Hee Haw for an additional five minutes contributes less to the survival of the human species than spending the five minutes planting beans, painting a house, or writing a book, it was an inferior way to spend the five minutes. Another possible criterion might be the larger social good: If the five minutes contributes less to the general social happiness than talking to a friend, picking up litter, or casting steel, the activity was inferior. One might judge an activity according to its contribution to personal growth, to elevated experience, or to glorifying God. Whatever the criteria used, they reflect the prior values of the judge. Absolute inferiority does not exist.

For practical purposes, "values" are a matter of a person's affective responses to the fixtures of his or her world. There is no reason that those responses need be simple or uneducated. A person who is able to experience the humor or pathos of a television program may also feel disgusted with the implications of the human caricatures portrayed there or feel bored with the trivial variations on a repeated unenlightening theme. The boredom may be born of education or insight and is therefore in a sense less direct and more contrived than the person's empathy with the characters in the show. The boredom or disgust may nevertheless outweigh the empathic enjoyment and may therefore deter the person from watching. Or someone may realize that his or her intimate personal encounters have brought more lasting affective satisfaction — have been more "meaningful" — than repeated games of bridge, and he or she may therefore decide to replace bridge playing with more significant relationships. Of course, if playing bridge happened to promise the greater lasting satisfactions, the decision would have gone the other way. In either case, in whichever direction the decision may have been guided by the person's beliefs about the world, the person's affective response system is the ultimate arbiter of value.

Incentives and the Mass Media[3]

Americans spend an enormous amount of their time with the mass media, especially television. A conservative estimate suggests that Americans devote about half of their "leisure" time, or an average of about two and a half hours per day, with one or another mass medium, two hours of it with television (Robinson, 1969).[4] That compares with one-sixth of their leisure time spent visiting with friends or relatives. It is easy, of course, to blame the television industry for having "narcotized" the American public, but there is some evidence that in the case of children, at least, the time spent watching television would in the absence of television have been spent in some other medialike form of entertainment, such as radio, comic books, or pulp magazines (Schramm, Lyle, & Parker, 1961). It therefore seems more likely that television watching simply does a better job of satisfying certain needs than alternative methods.

There is, however, little question that American viewers not only spend a great amount of time with their television sets, they also often develop a strong emotional attachment to them. Asked to state which invention of the "past 25 years or so" has "done the most to make your life more enjoyable, pleasant, or interesting", over 60% of American respondents choose television, more people than choose cars, home laundry equipment, or refrigerators (Steiner, 1963, P. 22). When their television sets break down, people get them repaired or replace them as quickly as possible, nearly half the time within a day.

There is reason to believe that television viewers develop a sense of having personal relationships with the characters of television programs much as they would with people with whom they actually interact. In one survey, "[a]lmost all respondents . . . talked about the characters of the program as if they were real people, in real situations, facing real problems and real predicaments. . . . Many respondents said that one or more of the characters on the program reminded them of a friend or relative. Some told of incidents that they shared in common with plots of the program; as if some comradeship existed between them" (Lichty, 1965). It is therefore not surprising that when the television set breaks down, a viewer might report feeling "like someone is dead" (Steiner, 1963, P. 25). There is here real dependence of viewers on television characters, and losing them un-expectedly can set off real grief.

Functions of Television

Watching television is plugging oneself into an automatic-experience machine. Just as certain "exercise belts" make one's mus-cles contract electrically without having to move about deliberately, so it appears that television, like other such media, sets in motion a train of emotional responses that are in many ways like those that people experience in the course of a relatively exciting day, without the individual having to will anything or to move from his or her chair. Watching the screens of their television sets, people can enjoy the feelings of intimate personal relationships, towering athletic achievements, narrow escapes, lucky wins in parlor-game contests, and great victories over social renegades or over duly constituted social authorities, according to taste. The feelings are there — they move around — while the torso rests and while the whole psychic apparatus for planning, intending, and acting lies dormant. In short, television and other such media provide an emotional massage for an individual who remains in most respects passive. Accordingly, we would expect that people will reach for a television switch when they are unable to produce comparably powerful and pleasant experiences at reasonable cost to themselves in their "real" lives.

That a massage like the one described goes on is fairly clear. Televi-sion viewers seem to identify themselves with the characters they view, and this identification enables them to experience what is hap-pening to the character as though, to some extent, it were happening to them. Happy endings, for instance, leave viewers feeling less emo-tional stress than do sad endings; and, significantly, the viewers are most affected by the fate of a story hero whom they think of as being like themselves (Tannenbaum & Gaer, 1965). As it happens, televi-sion viewers prefer to watch characters whose personalities they be-lieve are like their own (Perrow, 1968). Therefore, viewers are in effect choosing their programs so that they can best share the emotions of the characters they see.

Viewers also choose programs with strong emotional content. Most viewers claim that they select particular favorite programs, rather than just watching anything in order to "escape;" and the programs they choose tend to be those that are emotionally most arousing (Steiner, 1963). Favorite programs are described by such terms as "entertaining," "interesting," "stimulating," "honest," and "exciting." The most popular types are, first, "action" and, second, comedy or variety programs (Steiner, 1963).[5] Thus, in every respect, television viewers act as if they wish to maximize the power of their vicarious experience, provided that it is on balance pleasant for them and provided that they have the capacity to absorb it.

Who Watches Television?

Given our incentive theory, we would also expect that the people who make the most use of television are those whose lives are emotionally most impoverished, and hence who are probably most alienated. This appears to be the case. Children have been found to be heavier television viewers if their parents are relatively restrictive about sexual behavior and spank them a lot (Maccoby, 1954) and if the parents have aspirations for them that disagree with the children's own aspirations for themselves (Schramm, Lyle, & Parker, 1961). Those 10th graders who watch the most television are the most favorable toward antisocial aggression (Schramm, Lyle, & Parker, 1961) and are hence probably frustrated in attaining their own goals. Sometime between about 5th and 10th grades, most of the intellectually more gifted children give up heavy television viewing, whereas most of those with below-average scores remain heavy viewers; and, similarly, the children of white-collar families watch significantly less television than the children of blue-collar families (Schramm, Lyle, & Parker, 1961). Adults who feel confused and powerless about life and who distrust others are more likely to enjoy television's "escape" programs (Pearlin, 1959); and in a street survey in Vienna, the locations at which the fewest people could name something that gave their lives meaning were found at Vienna's famous *Prater* amusement park and at its palace-garden-zoo complex of Schönbrunn (Lukas, 1972). Thus, the people who make the most use of the entertainment media are those who feel their lives to be most empty. "The principle," write Schramm et al. (1961), "seems to be that television is attractive in inverse proportion to the attractiveness of the competition" (P. 30).

It is, of course, not necessary to feel completely deprived or alienated from something in order to enjoy television. A large majority of most American groups watch and value television programs (Steiner, 1963). One possibility is that television and other entertainment media, through their passive emotional massage, extend emotional satisfactions into time periods when people are too fatigued to pursue "real" incentives. Perhaps the most common characterization of television watching is that it is "relaxing" (Lichty, 1965; Steiner, 1963); and the implication is often that viewers who need the relaxation most feel tired or harassed from their working day.

In conclusion, television viewers choose emotionally exciting programs, and they choose them to obtain the best fit between their own personalities and those of the principal characters they watch, thereby maximizing their ability to share the characters' feelings. People thus act as if they intend to obtain from television a passive affective massage. Those whose lives seem to have the least to offer them, or who are too tired to pursue the real possibilities available, reach for this massage most persistently.

Drugs and Life Situations

Nearly as many Americans use various chemical methods to alter their feelings as watch television, and the number is in the same general range as those who watch athletic contests or who attend church. More than two-thirds of all American adults use alcohol (Cahalan, 1970), for instance, and more than half of them are likely to have used it within the past week (National Commission on Marijuana and Drug Abuse, 1973). More than a third smoke tobacco regularly and 8% smoke marijuana (National Commission, 1973). A third of one sample had used marijuana at least every week for some period of time between the ages of 20 and 23 (Drug use still high, 1975). Obviously, using drugs to change feelings is a well established fixture of the American social landscape.

There are, however, innumerable ways to use drugs. People use different substances, different dosages, at different frequencies, in different settings, to accomplish different objectives. There seems to be some agreement that it makes sense to classify users of any particular drug into several types. Keniston (1968), for instance, divided marijuana users into "tasters," "seekers" (irregular users), and "heads" (regular frequent users) in the belief that their motives for using marijuana are distinctly different. Another group divided drug users into those who engage in light experimentation, moderate or short-term heavy use, and long-term heavy use (State Street Center, 1972). The National Commission on Marijuana and Drug Abuse (1973) prefers five classes: experimental use, social or recreational use, circumstantial or situational use, intensified use, and compulsive use. McAuliffe and Gordon (1974) distinguish two types of heroin addicts, "hardcore" addicts who try for a high every day and "weekenders" who take just enough on weekdays to stave off withdrawal sickness. Stimson (1973) divides his British heroin addicts into four groups. Such classifications help one to think about the diversity of drug use patterns, but it should remain clear that people use drugs according to a great variety of individual needs and life situations. To understand how people use drugs, one must understand what benefits drugs have to offer people, which drugs are available to a person and at what cost, how much people know about using various drugs, and what social expectations, pressures or penalties people face with respect to using them.

Drug Use and Social Context

Since people live in a social context, a great deal of their drug use is a matter of engaging in culturally "normal" behavior. Where people are expected to drink alcoholic beverages at cocktail parties, they are very likely to do so simply in order to "fit in." People drink most often with their friends, and half of a group of South Carolina teenagers considered "going along with the group" the most important reason for their drinking (Kimes, Smith, & Maher, 1969, cited by Albrecht, 1973). If a youth can gain a sense of social communion with a group of friends by joining them in marijuana smoking, he or she is then very likely to smoke. In one group of youthful drug users, 48% of the men and 33% of the women said they started using drugs because it was "cool" or because of friends' examples or pressures to conform (State Street Center, 1972). (Most of the others said they started for the "experience" or out of curiosity.) Thus, there is a considerable difference between reasons for starting drug use and reasons for continuing its use later on. Initially, under the aegis of peers, the "individual takes the drug to see for himself what the value of the drug experience is. . . . Later, . . . the tension or anxiety [that underlies drug use] seems to be directly related to conflicts around identity, family, school and interpersonal relationships" (State Street Center, 1972, P. 69). In general, an individual's pattern of drug use represents a variation of whatever the local "normal" pattern is. It is a departure from that pattern, rather than something invented out of whole cloth completely for the individual's idiosyncratic needs.

As one might expect, therefore, one can predict much about an individual's use of drugs from knowing his or her social origins, background, and present associations. For instance, more than two-thirds of middle-class families in which mothers or fathers use alcohol at least once a week have children who are also heavily involved with drugs, as contrasted with drug-using children in less than two-fifths of families whose mothers or fathers use less alcohol (Blum & Associates, 1972). Among a nonrandom sample of New York area college students, 87% of politically left, nonreligious men use marijuana, but only 13% of politically moderate, very religious women do (Johnson, 1973). Clearly, social background and social surroundings have a lot to do with drug use.

People have no choice of their sex, parents, birthplace, or parents' socioeconomic status and culture, but they do have a choice of the people they associate with as adults. Here a question arises: Do people choose friends who fit in with their drug preferences, or do people choose friends on other grounds and then change their own drug habits to suit their friends? The answer is that both happen quite commonly. However, in Johnson's group of New York area students, "more persons gain or give up their friendships to accord with their own marijuana use . . . than shift their marijuana use to accord with their friendships" by a ratio of more than three to one (Johnson, 1973, P. 66). Therefore, not only do individuals' backgrounds go far to determine the kinds of people they are, it is also true that as adults they can often choose the set of social pressures that will continue to govern many of their actions; and they make their choices to suit best their own particular tastes and goals.

Not all individuals place equal value on the approval of those around them, and those that care less about it are then freer to pursue incentives disapproved by the majority culture. In fact, if we judge from scores on personality tests, both users of marijuana, an illicit drug, and alcoholics, who overuse an accepted drug, care less than most people about social criticism and are more assertive than average in pursuing their individual goals (Blake, Wick, Burke, & Sanesino, 1974; Brill et al., 1971; Button, 1956; Goldstein, 1971; Goss & Morosko, 1969; Hinckley, 1970; Hogan, Mankin, Conway, & Fox, 1970; Jones, 1968; Rosen, 1960; McClelland, Davis, Kalin, & Wanner, 1972; Scherer, Ettinger, & Mudrick, 1972). That is, for these people others' disapproval, especially authorities', is a weaker negative incentive than it is for most individuals in our society. Here, then, is a factor in people's personality makeup that influences how closely they are likely to be governed by social expectations in their responses to their individual life situations, to whose powerful influence we turn next.

Drugs and Incentive Impoverishment

Drugs have many uses apart from specific medicinal ones, including some that are quite positive. Some drugs can be used as tools to help people accomplish specific goals. For instance, people most often take amphetamines and physicians sometimes use opiates to provide themselves with energy when they are tired but need to go on (Winick, 1961). Laborers in India and some other parts of the world use marijuana for the same reason (Chopra, 1969). People often take a drink to "calm their nerves" before an unnerving assignment. They may use psychedelic drugs specifically to explore their inner potentialities. And so on.

Drugs also lend themselves to other uses, however. Many psychoactive drugs seem to act directly on brain pleasure centers to produce a sense of well-being. They can therefore be used to manipulate the affect system. People can use them "recreationally" to add to the good feeling states that a person can produce "naturally" with nondrug incentives; or people can use them to replace nondrug incentives when the person's life situation is barren of attractive ones.

Finally, psychoactive drugs can sometimes virtually anesthetize people, disorganizing or clouding their conscious inner experience to provide some relief from intolerable thoughts and feelings.

All of the uses that are aimed directly at manipulating the affective message system presumably take place when people feel cut off from the possibility of finding as much satisfaction in nondrug activities. In point of fact, there is considerable evidence that people take more drugs of several kinds when they feel that their lives have been impoverished. This appears to be true whether incentive impoverishment is inferred from people's socioeconomic status, alienation, depression, or directly from knowledge of their life situations.

Socioeconomic status. In general, as we saw in Chapter 6, poor people are on the average less happy. Presumably, that has something to do with their having fewer resources for finding and achieving enjoyable incentives. Drug use also varies with income level. Although more high-income than low-income people drink alcohol, fewer high-income men get drunk a lot, go on binges, or engage in other kinds of problematic drinking (Cahalan, 1970). Presumably, their drinking is more likely to be recreational. Before the upsurge of marijuana use during the 1960s, there was general agreement that marijuana was used especially often by impoverished or lower-class groups in India (Chopra, 1969), Morocco (Benabud, 1957), and in the United States, where the lower-class users in question were mostly black (Charen & Perelman, 1946; Freedman & Rockmore, 1946; Marcovit & Myers, 1944; Mayor's Committee, 1944).[6] After 1960, the distribution of users in the population gradually changed, at least in the United States, primarily because students began to smoke marijuana in large numbers, beginning with those from upper and upper middle-class white backgrounds with high incomes (Anker, Milman, Kahan, & Valenti, 1971; Chambers, 1971a; Goldstein, 1972; Goode, 1970; National Commission on Marijuana and Drug Abuse, 1973). However, if one excludes students, the people who use marijuana most heavily are the unemployed (Chambers, 1971b; National Commission, 1973). The people least likely to use marijuana include small businesspeople, farmers, and housewives.[7] It is interesting to consider that each of these latter groups enjoys considerable freedom of choice in planning how to spend their working time, and they are more likely to be working for goals that they believe they have chosen themselves.

Alienation. The alienated, on the average, feel more deprived of things they want than other people; and people who feel alienated as measured by alienation questionnaires do have a slight tendency to report more problem drinking (Cahalan, 1970; Jessor, Young, Young, & Tesi, 1970) and to use more marijuana (Horman, 1973; Jessor, Jessor, & Finney, 1973; Knight, Sheposh, & Bryson, 1974). However, the kind of alienation related to marijuana use is apparently of a certain kind: It is alienation from societal institutions and values rather than feelings of isolation, helplessness, or personal futility (Jessor, Jessor, & Finney, 1973; Knight, Sheposh, & Bryson, 1974).

The meaning of this relationship becomes clearer if we consider the case of some students in Rocky Mountain high schools (Jessor, Jessor, & Finney, 1973; Jessor, 1976). Those who used marijuana valued achievement significantly less and valued independence significantly more than the nonusers. Their value system, therefore, was directly contrary to the value system enforced by the school and, in fact, by most of the institutions established in our society for young people. The marijuana users were faced with a system that offered achievement incentives they did not value much and that denied them the independence they did value. As a result, they participated less in the activities established for them and, probably, they received fewer of the rewards. Thus, they achieved poorer grades than the nonusers, participated in fewer extracurricular activities, and less often attended church. On the other hand, they pursued other incentives not under the control of authorities: They were sexually more active than the nonusers and they smoked marijuana. Many of them would probably have resonated to Aldous Huxley's state of mind while he was on mescaline:

> I realized that I was deliberately avoiding the eyes of those who were with me in the room, deliberately refraining from being too much aware of them. One was my wife, the other a man I respected and greatly liked; but both belonged to the world from which, for the moment, mescalin had delivered me — the world of selves, of time, of moral judgements and utilitarian considerations, the world (and it was this aspect of human life which I wished, above all else, to forget) of self-assertion, of cocksureness, of overvalued words and idolatrously worshipped notions (Huxley, 1954, P. 36).

Depression. Depression is related to most kinds of drug use, though at best weakly to marijuana and the psychedelics. For instance, among former soldiers returned from Viet Nam, 63% of those who displayed at least three symptoms of alcoholism had experienced several weeks of depression, as compared with 44% of the heavy drinkers and only 29% of the light drinkers and abstainers. Similarly, those who had experienced at least several weeks of depression constituted 65% of barbiturate users, 63% of narcotics users, 54% of amphetamine users, 42% of those who used only marijuana, and 30% of those who used none of these drugs (Robins, 1974). Several other studies have also found that heavy drinkers are more depressed than others (Goss & Morosko, 1969; Overall & Patrick, 1972; Weingold, Lachin, Bell & Coxe, 1968; Williams, 1966).[8]

Incentive-poor situations and the search for meaning. The military services have long been places where, for many men, little happens to lighten their lives. Early reports of marijuana use in the U.S. military contain a pervading sense of unremitting boredom and dreariness (Freedman & Rockmore, 1946a and b; Marcovitz & Myers, 1944). Much the same is true of the modern army. Soldiers sent to Viet Nam greatly increased their use of drugs there, especially their use of narcotics, as compared with the period before they arrived there. After their return, their use of drugs returned substantially to what it had been before (Robins, 1974).

In the United States, the heaviest use of narcotics is in those slum areas whose residents must put up with terrible living conditions and with a cycle of being trapped in poverty that quickly erodes their hopes of ever leaving the ghetto. Under these conditions, drugs provide a focus of life and thought — and a sense of meaning. The meaning resides not only in the drug itself, although that may be the ultimate objective of each day, but also in the complex chain of activity — of stealing, hustling, copping, and shooting — necessary to maintain a heroin habit. Preble and Casey (1972) say of modern ghetto heroin addicts, "If they can be said to be addicted, it is not so much to heroin as to the entire career of a heroin user. . . . He, too, is driven by a need to find meaning in life which, because of certain deficits and impairments, he cannot find in the normal course of living" (P. 116).

Middle-class people are also more likely to use drugs when their lives are barren of meaningful incentives. Thus, for instance, families whose children are heavily involved in drugs — and whose parents also are likely to drink more — provide emotionally poorer family climates (Blum & Associates, 1972). Comparing three groups of middle-class families that varied in the extent to which their children were into drugs, "[t]he major difference between the three groups was the degree to which they had fun together — not in the strength of the bond (P. 257). . . . Superior parents . . . create so joyous an atmosphere at home that the child learns to expect good from the outside world as well. Their child has no wish to discover within himself the rewards of paradise" (P. 271). Such children therefore become more engaged with the institutions and goals established for them by the larger society, and they experience less desire to manipulate their feelings with drugs.

In our own research, we have found that college students who do not regard their lives as very meaningful are more likely to use alcohol. Among the 106 members of a drug education class, those who reported their lives as only "slightly" or "somewhat" meaningful were more than twice as likely to drink once a week or more often than those who reported their lives to be "full of meaning" (p < .05). In a more heavily drinking sample of 158 students from a number of university classes, we found much the same relationship (p = .05), except that the proportion of frequent drinkers was higher at all levels of meaningfulness.

The issue of meaningfulness — of involvement with incentives — thus becomes a central issue in drug use. The authors of the second report of the National Commission on Marijuana and Drug Abuse concluded that "a sense of purposelessness and meaninglessness in living contributes more to the attractiveness of drug taking than any other single factor" (P. 105). The evidence described above supports at least the conclusion that a sense of meaninglessness contributes a great deal. To understand just how drugs can fill the gap left in people's lives by the absence of incentives that are meaningful to them, and to understand more about the conditions under which people choose particular drugs rather than others, it will be necessary to consider what each kind of drug does to and for the user.

Enhancing the Incentive World: Marijuana and the Psychedelics

The active ingredient in marijuana is tetrahydrocannabinol (THC) — actually a family of compounds. It produces subjective effects rather like those produced by more powerful psychedelics, such as LSD, although the dosage required for THC to approximate LSD effects is much larger (Isbell & Jasinski, 1969). Barber (1970) has summarized the effects of LSD as follows:

1. Somatic-sympathetic effects, such as dilation of the pupils, physical weakness, and dizziness;
2. Changes in the way the body is perceived, such as changed size of limbs;
3. Dreamy-detached feelings;
4. Reduced proficiency in intellectual and motor tasks;
5. Changes in the way time is perceived, time usually seeming to pass more slowly;
6. Changes in visual perception, such as brighter colors, distorted objects;
7. Changes in hearing, smell, and taste, and experience in one sense modality can provoke sensations in another sense modality;
8. Greater responsiveness to suggestions;
9. Changes in moods and emotions, "varying from euphoria and ecstasy to dysphoria and psychotic-like reactions" (Barber, 1970, P. 9).

Some of these changes, such as bodily and visual changes, seem to depend largely on the dosage of the drug, while others, such as changes in mood and emotion, also depend in large part on individual situations and personalities. However, in actual practice, people who are unable to obtain enjoyable effects from psychedelic drugs soon stop using them, and experienced users are generally well acquainted with the kinds of situations they need to find or create in order to obtain the effects they want. Although not all of the effects of psychedelic drugs are sources of pleasure, therefore, a number of the effects constitute for many people powerful incentives. To these effects we now turn.

Pleasure. "Marijuana," states an anonymous writer (1967), "is taken to enhance the enjoyment of any type of entertainment or otherwise enjoyable activity" (P. 126). Her statement meets with wide agreement. Of one group of 150 marijuana users (McKenzie, 1970), 53% gave as a dominant reason for using marijuana that it helped them to "experience things more vividly." Other users report that marijuana enhances people's appetites and heightens their pleasure in music, other sounds, taste, smell, touch, and orgasm (Tart, 1971). Under its influence, users find things funnier and find their ideas more insightful. When people are moderately or highly intoxicated, they also focus more intensely on immediate "here and now" experience, and less on past and future events. Thereby they can better appreciate the qualities of the immediate present. That is, marijuana renews people's sensitivity to colors, sounds, smells, and feelings that they have learned to ignore in the course of automating their lives — the grace of a tree or the splendor of a sky on their way to work, for instance, or the smell of dinners cooking along their way home.

Marijuana, in other words, is a kind of incentive amplifier. It would therefore seem to be the drug of choice in situations where some positive pleasures remain but where these are less than the person would like. This amplification, however, can cut both ways. There is considerable reason to believe that marijuana, like the more powerful psychedelics, can also amplify depression and fear.

Well-being, euphoria, and a sense of worth. The most commonly reported benefit of using marijuana is enjoyment of the "high." American World War II soldiers eulogized the high state: "Makes you feel alive;" "I feel good and don't care;" "I feel drunkified and happy;" etc. (Freedman & Rockmore, 1946b, P. 230). Fully 68% of McKenzie's (1970) student sample gave as a dominant reason for using marijuana to "get high, feel good." Of the users in our own student sample, 74% gave as a reason "to get high or for kicks," 71% "to have a good time or to make a good time better," 37% "as a relaxant, or when nervous," and 36% "when bored." About half used it to be sociable with friends. Only 24% used it when depressed. In some cases, the euphoriant effect of marijuana can overcome bad moods, but sometimes it magnifies them (Tart, 1971).

For many World War II soldiers the euphoria included a feeling of greater self-worth and less alienation. These soldiers, who were in most instances southern blacks, often made comments such as the following (Freedman & Rockmore, 1946b):

"I feel like I own everything; when I get that way I don't like for nobody to talk too loud to me" (P. 229).

"It makes me feel like this Army is mine" (P. 229).

"It makes me feel like I'm a man; it springs me up. Without it I'm beat" (P. 229).

"It makes me feel good, grand. I think everybody is below me. I feel like somebody. Without it I feel like anybody else, I feel pretty low" (Pp. 230–231).

Thus, marijuana imparted to them a sense of ownership, belonging, manliness, worth, strength, and superiority, which these black soldiers probably lacked most poignantly in their time and situation.

Social communion. Marijuana smoking has traditionally been a social act. In fact, during the 1960s marijuana smoking became for many counterculture groups a social ceremony, a kind of ceremonial and experiential "glue" for the hippie movement (Allen & West, 1968). However, apart from ceremonial functions, marijuana users report that it makes them feel more open with others, more genuine and insightful, although at high levels of intoxication they may in fact become withdrawn into themselves (Tart, 1971). Of McKenzie's student users, 13% gave as a dominant reason for using marijuana their wish to "be more friendly, enhance sociability and/or be more loving."

A "personal learning and change tool." Nearly a quarter of student users during the late 1960s were using marijuana to explore themselves and to learn more about themselves (McKenzie, 1970). In our 1973–74 student sample, 32% gave this as a reason. For this purpose, however, many turn to other psychedelic drugs: principally LSD, but also mescaline, peyote, psilocybin, STP, and DMT. Only 20 of our 182 students have used psychedelics, but 17 of them (85%) gave self-exploration as a reason, as compared with 70% who take it, among other reasons, to get high. People's use of psychedelic drugs has been studied intensively by the staff of the State Street Center Number

Nine Youth Crisis and Growth Center of New Haven, Connecticut. They found a distinct pattern. People switched from marijuana to stronger psychedelics when they were dissatisfied with their existing life situations and in a state of great personal flux. They did so to foster greater self-knowledge and personal change. They usually found the experience helpful. After six to eighteen months, however, psychedelic users experienced a sense of diminishing returns in the contribution of the drug to personal change, and they consequently stopped using it, although they may have continued occasionally using marijuana. Hence, psychedelics are a "personal learning and change tool" (State Street Center, 1972, Pp. 144–145) rather than just something used repeatedly for the pleasure of the experience itself.

There is little doubt that changes do occur for the users, at least in State Street's group. When they gave up psychedelics, users were often ready to make some kind of new commitment, such as to religious involvement, work, school, or personal relationships. The fresh commitment often reflected changed goals — increased religiousness, a new kind of work, a different area of study, or a new form of relationship. "For many, psychedelic drugs signalled a major shift in personality orientation, from primarily external, related towards events and success, to internal, related to emotional and spiritual guides" (State Street Center, 1972, P. 138). State Street's psychedelic users made an average of seven significant changes in their lives, such as leaving their parents' home, leaving a mate, or moving into a commune; changing friends or sexual practices; leaving or changing schools; taking or changing a job, or deciding to travel without a job; joining a political movement; adopting a new religion, usually Eastern; and becoming personally more aware, open, honest, present-oriented, independent, or artistic. One might object that the changes could simply reflect the fact that most of these users were young people who are often in great flux anyway, even without psychedelics, but State Street reports "an even greater degree of change among older subjects upon beginning drug use" (P. 143).

What could give psychedelics the power to produce such changes? One possibility is that with them users can experience an order of emotional involvement with their surroundings and with themselves greater than any they have experienced before. They can therefore raise their expectations for themselves. Thus, "[h]igh school students report their use of psychedelics [so] as to experience something real, vivid, exciting, and novel" (State Street Center, 1972, P. 145). One user stated that " '[d]rugs put me in touch with ecstasy' " (State Street

Center, 1972, P. 146A). The sense of ecstasy that users sometimes achieve has much in common with the mystical trance states achieved by masters of meditation or with "peak experiences" at moments of great fulfillment.

Another reason for the power of the psychedelics may arise from the changes they induce in people's sensations, perceptions, and thoughts. Users may discover that they can get along with less conscious control over inner processes, experience the world in new categories, recognize the possibility of experiencing and of thinking in alternative ways, and realize more fully the range of potentialities in their own consciousness. With a present emotionally so powerful, interesting, and direct, the machinations of normal jockeying to impress friends or to land a regimented job, spouse, and house in the suburbs must seem at best misplaced.

Whatever the pleasures of psychedelic states, however, people seem to become habituated to them, and after a while the lessons learned become repetitive. Sometimes people also discontinue use after the panic of a "bum trip." Users rarely continue for more than about two years. Apparently, psychedelics work not so much by enhancing incentives or by providing pleasure directly as by pointing out incentives available to people within themselves; and perhaps they dramatize to people the incentive values most powerful and best suited to their individual selves. In a way, then, psychedelics are drugs for people deeply dissatisfied with what they have and struggling to change it — for people with hope, however diffuse, of finding a meaningful future beyond drugs themselves.

Escape from Unpleasantness: Opiates and Other Downers [9]

Opiates are substances derived from opium poppies and include opium, morphine, and heroin — in ascending order of refinement — and various synthetic versions of these such as demerol and delaudid. They are the original drug food of the "opium eaters." They are the true narcotics. Downers include barbiturates such as nembutal and seconal, synthetic substances that, like opiates and alcohol, depress the central nervous system. They all have in common that they are highly addictive and that they can produce very direct and often very marked changes in the user's feeling state.

Heroin, in the words of one user, is "the mellowest downer of all. You get none of the side effects of speed and barbs. After you fix, you feel the rush, like an orgasm if it's good dope. Then you float for about four hours; nothing positive, just a normal feeling, nowhere. It's like being half asleep, like watching a movie; nothing gets through to you, you're safe and warm. The big thing is, you don't hurt. You can walk around with rotting teeth and a busted appendix and not feel it. You don't need food, you don't need people, you don't care. It's like death without permanence, life without pain" (Luce, 1972, P. 145).

In some respects, opiates and barbiturates are used for purposes opposite to those of psychedelics: They are used to restrict and deaden inner awareness. Thus, another user said that his "life was just 'simpler' while on heroin, 'because you don't have to do any kind of introspection. Everything is outside of you. All of your time is spent gettin' money, and coppin', and doin' it, and noddin''''" (State Street Center, 1972, P. 191).

For some time, social scientists believed that users could achieve euphoria only during their early experiences with heroin, after which the users' increasing tolerance and physical dependence on the drug turns their use into an addiction and their habit from one of achieving euphoria to one of staving off withdrawal sickness (Lindesmith, 1968). However, that appears to be untrue. A careful study of 64 addicts in Baltimore (McAuliffe & Gordon, 1974) revealed that all but one still reported experiencing euphoria, 42% of them at least once each day. Not all addicts sought the same pattern of getting high: Some attempted to get high every day and others saved their highs for weekends. Nevertheless, getting high remained an important, frequently attained incentive for them. They took considerably more heroin (on the average, 2.4 times more) than they needed for avoiding withdrawal sickness, expressly to achieve euphoria. They use those drugs best able to produce it rather than substitutes such as methadone that blocks withdrawal sickness and euphoria. The principal reason they gave for not getting high was lack of money. Getting high was unaffected by how long the person had been addicted. In short, "[a]ddicts *need* a drug that prevents withdrawal sickness, but they *crave* a drug that makes them high" (McAuliffe & Gordon, 1974, P. 811).

It remains true that some addicts maintain their habit most of the time at just the level necessary to feel "normal," with only rare excursions into euphoria. It might seem that would not be worth it, but then one must ask what it means for a heroin addict to feel "normal." Is "normal" what the addict's state would have been without any heroin at all, including the misery or boredom he or she took heroin to escape, or is "normal" a relatively low-key state, not terribly euphoric, but less miserable than their state before using heroin? McAuliffe and Gordon do not address this question. However, since the euphoric effects of heroin are directly proportional to the amount used, it seems likely that even without much actual euphoria, and especially without a rush, the heroin user may still be experiencing some relief from misery.

The nature of the chronic relief provided by heroin can be seen in studies of American military men during the early 1970s. Among soldiers returned from Viet Nam, 43% had used narcotics — mostly heroin — at least once. Of these, 88% reported or agreed that they used heroin to get high (Robins, 1974). However, 82% said it made them feel less bored, 74% said heroin made them "more tolerant of Army rules and regulations," 73% said it made them feel less depressed and made the time seem to pass more quickly, and 46% said it made them less fearful and helped them fit in better with other soldiers. Thus, they confirmed other reports that users value not only the high but also the ability of heroin to deaden their emotional reactions to unpleasant features of their immediate life situations.

Situations that precipitate heroin use. People seem to start using heroin when they feel trapped in a situation that offers them few attractive incentives and some imposing negative ones. Being sent to Viet Nam was certainly such a situation for many soldiers. The percentage of them that used narcotics jumped from 11% before Viet Nam to 43% in Viet Nam. It dropped back down to 10% after their return. Interviews with civilian addicts (Cortina, 1971) provide some insights into statistics such as these. For instance, there is "Pablo," a Chicano epileptic who first gave up at the age of 14:

"These years between fourteen and seventeen they are like years in a dream, I tell you, sir. . . . I stopped going to church, I stopped school, I think I stopped living, really. . . . I have stick of weed and drink. . . ."
. . . "I got no pride left, I don't see no future, at that time I have died. Then, when I am about sixteen and a half, I suddenly think: 'Pablo, six months and you will be seventeen.' Believe me sir, that is like a miracle. Like a shade pulled up on a window. . . . " (Cortina, 1971, P. 24).

Pablo joined the Army, hiding his epilepsy.

"I am a good soldier. Would you believe, sir, that I change? No more marijuana or drink. Would you believe, sir, I got my high school equivalency diploma in five months in the army? . . . And then the crash. Boom!"

He had an epileptic attack and was discharged from the army. With no satisfactory place to live, aware of his family's hardships but unable to bear living with them, he moved in with a sister whose husband pushed heroin, and he became addicted.

Another interviewee was a high school music teacher who also played in music organizations where heroin use was common. He had built himself a good life and used only marijuana. One night his wife passed out.

"She had an incurable disease. The doctors told me it was hopeless. It could be weeks or months . . . in six weeks she was dead. This was . . . you know, I was the kind of fellow . . . I never paid any attention to bills, or what I owed, or what had to be shopped for, or income tax. . . . She was my business manager. . . . It comes back in snatches, that time . . . I recall one afternoon, I had just gotten finished teaching and picked up my two small daughters from their school. I was trying to get something for their supper. I was fiddling around trying to open some cans, and I was trying to get some of their dresses together to take them to be laundered . . . the house was a mess, I never got the dishes washed up . . . it was chaos. . . . And then, right then . . . a fellow I played with, another musician, dropped by the house. He was a heroin user and he asked me if he could fix at my house because he couldn't fix at his house because his wife was giving a cocktail party. I said okay . . . and I don't know . . . I asked him for a bag. . . ." (Cortina, 1971, P. 50).

(Excerpts from Frank Michael Cortina: *Stroke a Slain Warrior*, New York: Columbia University Press, 1971, reprinted with permission of the publisher and author.)

In many such cases, people begin using heroin when they feel overwhelmed by the problems facing them, when the problems are recurrent, and when they see no hope of escaping. Positive incentives either hardly exist or have dried up, and the person faces numerous negative incentives, either because of objective circumstances or because of inner conflicts or inadequacies. That seems to be particularly true if the individual has no long-term goals to provide some acceptable meaning for present hardships. In Robins' (1974) study of returnees from Viet Nam, he found that first-term enlisted men had a higher rate of heroin use than draftees, but the lowest rate was that of career soldiers, who presumably had a long-term commitment to a life in the military for which service in Viet Nam was simply a phase.

Once a person becomes a heroin addict, heroin and the life associated with it in contemporary America provide their own strong meaning. Asked how often they think about wanting to get high, 68% of McAuliffe and Gordon's (1974) addicts replied, "Whenever I am not high." Altogether 90% of them think about it at least once a day. This cannot be simply a preoccupation with the drug itself, because most addicts must work hard, either legally or illegally, to find the wherewithall, and must then track down their connection to obtain their supply — often an extremely demanding and elaborate process (Preble & Casey, 1972). Thus, "the life" and the heroin together provide a powerful incentive, a complex network of subgoals and activities, and hence a kind of meaningful living.

Manufactured Optimism: Alcohol and the Amphetamines [10]

Chemically, alcohol and amphetamines have quite different properties. Alcohol is a central nervous system depressant and amphetamines, such as dexedrine and benzedrine, are stimulants. Alcohol is highly addictive and amphetamines are not, although people develop increasing physical tolerance for both. People often take alcohol to "relax," but they take speed to give them energy. Nevertheless, in different ways they can both foster optimism (Cole, 1967).

Amphetamines. "You don't really have a trip with speed," a young user told the State Street Center staff (1972, P. 187). "It just makes you go faster. More able to do things more efficiently. Like if you want to go and have a good time, drop about six bennies and you'll be able to do anything you want to do. . . . When I was doing a lot of speed, it was more of a hassle than anything else. I got to the point that I had to do speed to have a good time, and that is a drag."

On high doses, people may lose the need to eat or sleep and remain continuously active. Therefore, people often take amphetamines in specific situations that call for more effort than they feel up to, either because they are too tired or, in some cases, too discouraged. (One might add that amphetamines also produce some serious physiological side effects, and the seemingly boundless energy is often accompanied by impaired judgment.)

Alcohol. In some respects, the effects of alcohol are so well known as to require little comment. Small doses relax people and produce a warm, mellow feeling. In this state people feel more sociable and less inhibited. As the dosage increases, judgment and coordination become seriously impaired, and people become more variably emotional in ways that range from sadness to belligerence to euphoria. As people become drunker, their consciousness becomes increasingly dulled in a kind of anesthesia somewhat like that produced by the narcotics, possibly ending with unconsciousness. Although there has been considerable controversy about just which effects of alcohol account for its common use, and particularly for alcoholism, a coherent picture is beginning to evolve.

Anxiety theory of alcohol use. The first notion to gain general support was that people use alcohol to reduce anxiety. This was an attractive idea because there is little question that alcohol indeed does reduce anxiety, and because anxiety is something that everyone wishes to reduce. Experiments with animals have shown them to become less fearful when intoxicated than when sober (Pawlowski, Denenberg, & Zarrow, 1961; Scarborough, 1957). One way of studying this change is to place animals in a conflict between desire and fear, and then to observe how alcohol changes the way the animal resolves the conflict. For instance, hungry animals can be taught to run down an alley to get food at one end. Then they can be subjected to electric shocks there. Animals naturally become rather cautious about approaching the food end of the alley (which is also the shock end) under these conditions. They approach more slowly and often go only part way. However, after they have been injected with alcohol they go faster and farther and more often make it to the food (Barry & Miller, 1962; Freed, 1968).

Not only do animals show less fear under the influence of alcohol, they have also been shown to use more alcohol when frightened. For instance, animals have been taught to expect electric shocks a certain interval of time after a warning signal. Between receiving such a signal and suffering the shock, animals are understandably rather anxious. At those times, they use more alcohol than they do before the warning signal or after the shock (Cicero, Myers, & Black, 1968; Clark & Polish, 1960).

There is some evidence that people also use alcohol to relieve anxiety. Raymond Higgins and Alan Marlatt (1975) recruited college students who were heavy social drinkers to take part in what was billed as a wine-tasting experiment. They were also required to "talk about experiences from earlier periods of their lives." Half of them were led to believe that they were being watched and listened to by girls who would later rate them on desirability. The intent, of course, was to induce in these students fear of being evaluated. All of the students were encouraged to drink as much wine as they wished in order to rate the taste of the wine. The group who thought they would be evaluated drank significantly more than the rest. In our own research, 26% of the students who use alcohol use it sometimes "as a relaxant, or when nervous." Together with some other evidence (e.g., Williams, 1966) and everyday observation, there seems little reason to doubt that people use alcohol to quell fear.

Unfortunately, the explanation that alcohol reduces anxiety does not adequately explain most excessive drinking by humans. First of all, alcoholics are not more fearful than other people. Indeed, they score higher on personality test scales, such as the MMPI Psychopathic Deviate scale, that measure unconcern about punishment and disapproval (Button, 1956; Rosen, 1960). One might argue that alcoholics experience a normal level of anxiety because the alcohol they are already using heavily has driven down their anxiety. However, this seems an unlikely explanation, because when future alcoholics are still children they actually exhibit fewer abnormal fears and have greater confidence in themselves than do future nonalcoholics (McCord & McCord, 1960). Finally, studies that have compared different societies have found no consistent evidence that societies that drink heavily are more fearful than other societies (Barry, Buchwald, Child, & Bacon, 1965; Field, 1962).

Dependency-conflict theory of alcohol use. Another idea proposed to account for alcoholism is that alcoholics are caught in a personal conflict between wishing to be dependent on other people and fearing that such dependency will destroy them (McCord & McCord, 1960). Therefore, they act outwardly very independent while at the same time they indulge their dependency needs by drinking; and they drink alcohol both to shore up their masculine self-image and to reduce the anxiety provoked by their continuing inner conflict. There is some evidence to support this notion. First, the mothers of alcoholics-to-be are unusually inconsistent in their attitudes toward their sons, alternately showing them affection and rejecting them (McCord & McCord, 1960). That kind of behavior is well calculated to produce conflict, since the child cannot continue to depend on his mother without getting hurt, and yet the mother's recurrent affection keeps him from finally disengaging from wanting her love. Furthermore, it is true that prealcoholic junior high school boys exhibit less outward dependency and are more assertive and hostile than others (Jones, 1968). Finally, a comparison among 110 societies around the world showed that those whose parents indulged their children the least consumed the largest average amount of alcohol (Bacon, Barry, & Child, 1965).

However, there is also some contrary evidence. First, whether the parents in a society indulge their children has no bearing on the tendency of the adults to become drunk (Bacon, Barry, & Child, 1965). On the other hand, people tend to get drunk most often in societies in which people are least able to depend on other people for help *as adults*. In other words, problem drinking, as opposed to simply customs involving the use of alcohol, is a matter not of how children are raised but of what happens to them as adults. In a society where people are more likely to be overwhelmed by their adult problems — for instance, in which a sick adult is unable to turn to a neighbor to till the fields or mind the children — people more often drink to excess.

Another bit of evidence against the notion that people drink to satisfy dependency needs is that, while drinking, people think neither more nor less about dependency than when sober, as judged from the stories they tell. Thus, "[t]hough we were coding as carefully as we could the thoughts that went through the drinker's mind while he was drinking, yet we could find no clues that pointed toward 'satisfaction of desires for dependency' or feeling 'warm, comfortable, secure and accepted'" (McClelland, Davis, Kalin, & Wanner, 1972, P. 279).

Power, womanliness, and drinking. McClelland and his colleagues concluded instead that what drinkers think about is power — their ability to have an impact on people and events. They asked men to write dramatic stories about standard pictures shown them, and found that after their storytellers had taken a few drinks they told stories with more characters concerned about having an impact than either these storytellers or other people in similar settings told while sober. It is as if drinking brings out a state of mind in which more things are possible, in which the drinker can afford to think more vigorously about those of his goals that involve making an impact on others. Since it is pleasant to feel effective and powerful, people drink to increase their sense of power.

However, this is a theory of drinking by men. It is based on evidence gathered purely from men, and, as it turns out, does not apply to women. Drinking does, to be sure, also affect women's thoughts. When women have been drinking in a party setting, the stories they tell in response to pictures have fewer unhappy endings, more positive feelings, more pleasure, and less goal-directed activity (Wilsnack, 1974). In these respects the state of mind of these women became more like that of nursing mothers, and hence Wilsnack concluded that alcohol made them feel more "womanly." Furthermore, she found that a group of women who were receiving psychotherapy for alcoholism had suffered a significantly higher proportion of life events that would threaten their sense of womanliness — difficulties in conceiving a child, repeated miscarriages, permanent infertility, and loss of mates — all before they began heavy drinking (Wilsnack, 1973). Wilsnack therefore concluded that women drink to feel more womanly.

Conclusion: Drinking and rose-colored glasses. At this point, it should be apparent that no theory is likely to be adequate that states that all people — or even all members of a particular group — drink for the same reason. What all of the theories have in common is the idea that people drink to feel as if they have more of something they lack — confidence, security, power, womanliness, and no doubt many other qualities and incentives. More generally, it appears that people drink to buttress their hopes that they can achieve their goals. Thus, the worker worn out or humiliated from a day's drudgery, the administrator overcommitted to a host of struggles, the parent driven beyond tolerance, and the individual feeling trapped — all may gain courage and a brighter perspective on themselves by moderate drinking; or, of course, they may seek to drink heavily enough to blot it all out.

The experimental evidence is borne out by the testimony of three alcoholics interviewed on a Pacific Coast skid row (Wiseman, 1970):

"Sober, I'm rather shy and backward, especially around groups. I'm an introvert. When I get to drinking, I enjoy people more."

"When I was a lush, I thought I was the greatest lover in the world, God's gift to women."

"Alcohol is marvelous at removing obstacles for a while. Everyone gets to the point where he is just fed up and scared and worried. He doesn't know where to turn. Alcohol takes care of that. The important becomes unimportant. Your problems aren't anywhere near what you thought." (Wiseman, 1970, P. 15).

The feelings are positive, the messenger is cheerful, and all is therefore better.

Preference versus Addiction

The public image of narcotics addiction and of alcoholism has been very much like an image of demonic possession. The demon theory as popularly held views the chemical substance itself as the demon. People commonly view it as a "monkey on the back" of the person addicted, and they naturally assume that the person must be "cured" by exorcising the demon. "Recovered" alcoholics are believed to be in grave jeopardy of relapse if they take so much as a sip of alcohol. Hosts worry about serving their recovered alcoholic guests food cooked in wine. Old "demon whiskey" plays a prominent part in folk music.

Although no one would dispute that drug addictions are gravely serious problems, the demon theory of addiction is quite erroneous, and it has led to what can objectively only be considered disastrous public policies (Stachnik, 1972). Thus, the full force of police power has at one time or another been directed toward stopping the demon at its source: federal Prohibition early in this century, Operation Intercept in the late 1960s (aimed at marijuana), and the continuing battle against heroin imports today. Yet, all this force may turn out to have made the situation worse. Its chief immediate effect is to restrict the supply of a drug only partially, while driving up the price. To afford high-priced drugs, some users are willing to commit crimes. A 40-month study of Detroit (Silverman, Spruill, & Levine, 1975) concluded that for every rise of 10% in the price of heroin, the overall rate of crimes for money increased 2.9%. Some kinds of crimes increased more than others. Armed robberies, for instance, increased by 6.4%, unarmed robberies and burglaries rose 4%, and simple assault rose 5.6%. That is a high price for society to pay in order to purge a demon. Let us consider the demon theory further.

Withdrawal sickness. The large grain of truth in demon theory is that in the true addictions, such as those produced by long repeated use of tobacco, alcohol, barbiturates, and the opiates, the user becomes physically dependent on continued use. Suddenly to stop use of the drug — "cold turkey" — is often (but not invariably) to invite serious physical illness and, a small proportion of the time, death. In many cases, the "abstinence agony" of withdrawing from alcohol or from heroin is about as unpleasant as a severe case of flu, and the range, which depends on how long and how much the person has been using, runs from mild transient discomfort to fatal convulsions in withdrawal from alcohol. If users have no compelling reason to stop use, withdrawal is simply a needless illness that they have no wish to suffer. In short, ending an addiction to alcohol or to heroin without medical supervision usually involves a very unpleasant and often painful process, but one well within the range of normal experience and one that is quite endurable. To insist that addicts continue to use

their drugs primarily to avoid withdrawal sickness is greatly to over-
state the case.

There is considerable evidence to support this view. First, narcotics
were originally distributed in the United States for their medical help
in relieving pain, and they continue to be used medically without
thereby creating much additional addiction. By 1963, American
physicians were administering over a billion doses of narcotics annu-
ally without any evidence that their patients had subsequently become dependent on them (Blum, 1969). When people either do not
know they are being withdrawn from narcotics or did not intend to
use their narcotics to manipulate their feelings, withdrawal poses
few problems.

Second, when people wish to end their addictions to pursue other
incentives, they seem able to do so. Thus, out of the estimated 34% of
all American soldiers who first began to use narcotics in Viet Nam,
79% stopped use after returning home (Robins, 1974). That is to say,
27% of all American soldiers first tried narcotics in Viet Nam and
stopped after their return, and another 7% of American soldiers first
tried narcotics in Viet Nam and continued use in the United States.
This is, of course, a very high rate of withdrawal from those narcotics,
most of which were heroin. The 7% who continued their narcotics
habit Stateside were, moreover, offset by another 8% who had first
tried narcotics in the United States, continued use in Viet Nam, and
then stopped. Thus, even though 43% of American soldiers were at
some time using drugs in Viet Nam, and about half of these considered themselves addicted, fewer soldiers were using narcotics after
their return home than used them before going to Viet Nam. Most of
those who stopped did so without medical supervision. For them,
withdrawal sickness was apparently not an insurmountable barrier.

Third, avoiding withdrawal sickness is not the principal incentive
for continuing to drink or use heroin. If it were, why should nearly all
addicts who are forced into withdrawal by arrest revert to drinking or
shooting heroin after their release? In fact, alcoholics sometimes deliberately inflict withdrawal symptoms on themselves in the service of
getting sufficiently drunk. Given the opportunity to work for alcohol
by performing a repetitive experimental task, they save up the
"points" they earn until they can buy enough alcohol for a long
binge, even though during the time they are saving they are suffering
withdrawal (Mello & Mendelson, 1972). Clearly, fear of withdrawal
sickness cannot explain this. Nor can one explain this simply in terms
of an irresistible craving, since we have already seen that most per-

sons can in fact resist it. The only plausible explanation is that addicts consider the pleasant effects of alcohol or heroin resistible but preferable to life without them. That would seem to be at least as much a comment on their life situations or on their ability to gain satisfaction from their life situations as on the potency of the drug. If people cannot hope to make themselves feel good through pursuing and consummating nondrug incentives, they are very likely to turn quite voluntarily to drugs to achieve the same experiential end by manipulating the affective message system.

The first sip. Another part of the demon theory, especially as it regards alcoholism, is the idea that even small amounts of the drug can turn an abstinent alcoholic back to drink. Since the root cause of alcohol lies in the devilish power of alcohol, so goes this belief, the first sip of alcohol (or certainly the first drink) is the beginning of the end for recovered alcoholics, since they will then lose control of their drinking and drink until drunk. There are now several grounds for rejecting this belief.

First, we have a series of interesting experiments conducted by Alan Marlatt (1973; Marlatt, Demming, & Reid, 1973). Marlatt recruited a group of alcoholics and social drinkers to participate in what they were told was an experiment to rate the flavors of various beverages. They were encouraged to drink as much as they wished in order to form their judgments. All of the alcoholic participants were active drinkers at the time with no plans to abstain, but they were required to be sober at the time of the experiment. Half of the participants were told that their beverages contained alcohol and half were told they did not. However, half of each of *these* groups actually received alcoholic drinks and half received nonalcoholic drinks. The experimenters then kept track of the number of drinks each participant consumed. Under the "first sip" theory, the alcoholics who received alcohol should have consumed much more than other participants. As it turned out, however, the only factor related to how much the alcoholics drank was whether they were led to *believe* they were drinking alcohol, regardless of whether they were in fact drinking alcohol or not. Those alcoholics who believed they were drinking nonalcoholic beverages drank less, regardless of whether they were actually drinking alcohol. Those who believed they were drinking alcohol, and who in fact were, drank no more than those who believed they were drinking alcohol but were not. Clearly, there was no evidence here for loss of control, but there was evidence that these alcoholics were interested in enjoying the benefits of alcohol.

Another piece of evidence against the "first sip" notion is that some alcoholics can be taught to drink in moderation. One such program (Vogler, Compton, & Weissbach, 1975) provided not only alcohol education and counseling for its alcoholic patients but also helped them to detect the signs that they were drinking too much and coached them in ways to slow down their drinking. Within the year that followed the patients' enrollment in this program, a third remained entirely abstinent and another third engaged in moderate, controlled drinking. Only a third had relapsed.

A large study of treatment programs at 45 alcohol treatment centers confirms in the field what the laboratory studies and experimental treatment programs have reported: 18 months after contact with the center, about a quarter of alcoholic patients have returned to "normal" patterns of drinking moderately (Armor, Polich, & Stambul, 1976). Taken together, the accumulating evidence from laboratory and field investigations (Lloyd & Salzberg, 1975) leaves little doubt that many alcoholics, though not necessarily all, can come to drink moderately.

Finally, there is the clinical evidence from the use of Antabuse (disulfiram). Antabuse is a medication that causes people to become violently ill when they imbibe alcohol. One reason for its effectiveness is that its effects continue for some time — at least several days — after it is taken. It is therefore an excellent guard against impulse drinking and, under the demon theory of alcoholism, should be quite effective in keeping alcoholics dry. Although it is one of the more effective short-term approaches to alcoholism (Wallerstein, 1957; Armor, Polich, & Stambul, 1976), it often fails. Its failures arise when alcoholics decide quite deliberately that they wish to return to drinking, and hence they go off the medication. Thus, "patients with depressive features as prominent aspects of their character patterning . . . did poorly with Antabuse. This was seen very clearly in . . . J. D. . . . His constant alcoholic excess warded off the deep depression underneath. When faced with his inner emptiness and loneliness (via the Antabuse induced sobriety), he could only choose to abandon the attempt at cure" (Wallerstein, 1957, P. 49).

Conclusion: Drugs and Incentives

Affect, incentives, and drug use. The thrust of the evidence, then, is that people use psychoactive chemicals deliberately to improve their feeling states. From among those drugs that they know about and that are available, they choose the particular ones best suited to create the changes they wish to bring about. The kinds of feelings that most often need changing are those that signal to people that their relationships to incentives are either inadequate or disturbed. Thus, the most common psychological complaints of drug users seem to be anxiety, emptiness, boredom, discouragement, futility, frustration, depression, and deprivation. The source of anxiety, presumably, is expecting that something important may go wrong. People feel empty and bored when they are unable to enjoy or work toward significant incentives, either because the incentives are not accessible or because inner conflicts prevent the person from becoming committed to them. The remaining kinds of complaints are all part of the incentive-disengagement process (Chapter 5) or of alienation (Chapter 6). Insofar as different drugs have somewhat different effects, the type of drug people use should depend on the phases of incentive-disengagement cycles in which they find themselves or on their degree of alienation, and thus in turn the type of drugs they use depends on their current relationships to their incentive world.

Thus, for instance, marijuana and the stronger psychedelics should be particularly attractive to people in life situations relatively barren of enjoyable incentives, but not to people who are angry or deeply depressed. Opiates and barbiturates, with their consciousness-dulling effects, should appeal to people whose life situations are not only barren but also cause them frequent psychic pain. Amphetamines should appeal to people with demands on them and who need hope and energy.

Alcohol has such a variety of effects in different dosages that it can serve many functions, which perhaps accounts for its widespread popularity. It can increase optimism, produce euphoria, and, at high enough dosages, anesthetize the consciousness. People might therefore be expected to use it in all phases of the incentive-disengagement cycle. Perhaps, however, one could predict that people would be especially likely to use moderate amounts during the invigoration and aggression phases and heavy amounts during the depression phase.

There is some experimental evidence that people do in fact drink more heavily during aggression phases (Marlatt, Kosturn, & Lang, 1975). Heavy drinkers were experimentally annoyed and criticized by another person. Other heavy drinkers were treated politely. Some of the insulted participants were then given an opportunity to retaliate against their insultors by shocking them electrically, but others were given no opportunity to retaliate. Subsequently, all participants rated the flavors of alcoholic beverages and were encouraged to drink as much as they liked. The participants who had been insulted with no opportunity to retaliate drank significantly more than the participants who had not been insulted, and the insulted participants who had been able to retaliate drank significantly less. Thus, in this situation, being left in an aggressive state fosters drinking. Marlatt also reported on the situations in which a group of relapsed alcoholics had taken their first drink. In nearly a third of the cases, relapses began when the person was "frustrated and angry, usually in an interpersonal context" (Marlatt, 1973, P. 12).

Drug effects on motivation. The view described thus far regards drugs as some among many possible ways to manipulate feeling states. There may, however, be one more way in which drugs bear on incentives: It is possible that some drugs may lessen a person's desire for nondrug incentives by changing their subjective value. In this, drugs are not alone. Anyone who has experienced a powerful satisfaction is for some time likely to view other incentives as rather pale alternatives. People who are in love lose some of their interest in people and pursuits other than the loved one, even to the point of neglecting food, comfort, and rest. People who have experienced great triumphs may find life thereafter somewhat plain. In the same way, people who have experienced great pleasure induced by drugs may have a higher adaptation level than before for worthwhile experiences, and may therefore be even less attracted than before to the other incentives available to them.

There is too little evidence to decide whether drug experiences can, indeed, overshadow and sap other incentives. If they do so, it is possible that they may do so only for a limited time, until the user has become habituated to them or until the user's body has developed too high a tolerance for the drug. In any case, the possibility that some kinds of drug use can temporarily drain away motivation for other activities has theoretical support and is therefore worth pursuing experimentally.

Chapter 8

Self-Annihilation

Among the facts of human life, suicide is one of the hardest for many people to comprehend. In the abstract, people find it eerie. When it happens in one's circle of acquaintances, it produces shock. As a topic of scientific investigation, it was for many years "taboo" (Shneidman, 1963). In short, it is in the biblical sense "unclean."

Nevertheless, suicide is not at all uncommon. Among young men, it is one of the three or four leading causes of death. In Chicago's Cook County, the number of people who each year take their own lives is conservatively about two-thirds as many as die in motor vehicle accidents (Maris, 1969). Officially, about 24,000 Americans kill themselves deliberately each year, and perhaps 200,000 others make the attempt.

The actual count is undoubtedly higher. Very few people are listed officially as suicides if they died by other means, but large numbers of actual suicides go officially unrecognized, for many reasons. Families sometimes go to great lengths to conceal the fact that a member committed suicide. Friendly physicians may overlook suspicious circumstances surrounding a fatal overdose of drugs. Many single-car accidents are actually suicides, but who can know which? A good many murders are provoked by their victims, consciously or unconsciously with self-destructive intent. No one can say precisely how many people deliberately kill themselves each year, but in the United States it is quite likely that the number is double or more the number of cases recognized publicly.

Perhaps one reason that suicide seems so puzzling to so many people is that it runs counter to prevailing conceptions of how human beings function. If, for instance, one believes that humans possess an overriding "survival instinct" or "instinct for life," one cannot explain someone's deliberately destroying that same life, especially for no apparent purpose. If one believes that humans are driven by a desire for pleasure, it seems incredible that a well-to-do person, surrounded by the means to pleasure, would choose to give it up. The purpose of this chapter is to make sense of suicide by applying the theory of incentives and inner experience developed in earlier chapters.

What Kinds of People Are Most Likely to Kill Themselves?

Each year in the United States, 11 people of every 100,000 are officially recorded to have killed themselves. That is neither especially high nor especially low for the world's nations, but more important for our purposes is that in this country as in other countries the suicidal 11 come disproportionately from certain groups; and who those groups are, or in what circumstances they find themselves, can tell us a great deal about the nature of suicide. We shall look first at some of the gross statistics and then examine more closely the patterns they make.

Group Statistics

In general, people are more likely to kill themselves as they age, men more than women, single individuals more than married ones, and seriously ill individuals more than healthy ones.

More specifically, for instance, the number of American men per 100,000 who killed themselves in 1959 was 7.4 between the ages of 15 and 24, 20.5 between the ages of 45 and 54, and 45.5 between the ages of 65 and 74. The comparable suicide rates for women were 2.1, 6.9, and 9.7 (Maris, 1969). Taking just the 65 to 74 age group, as a further example, the suicide rate per 100,000 was 33.6 for married men, 82.0 for single men, and 152.5 for divorced men; and the rate was 7.5 for married women, 9.6 for single women, and 25.8 for divorced women. To put these figures somewhat differently, about one out of 656 divorced men between ages 65 and 74 committed suicide in 1959, as compared with only one out of 58,824 single women between the ages of 15 and 24. If one out of 656 per year still seems a modest number, one must remember what it means: As a particular group of 100,000 divorced men ages the ten years from 65 to 74, one out of about 66 kills himself.

People who have at some time become psychiatrically seriously disturbed also have a very high suicide rate. A follow-up of Texas veterans produces the following conservative estimates (Pokorny, 1964): As compared with the suicide rate of Texas veterans in general, which was 22.7 per 100,000, the rate for alcoholic patients was 133, for schizophrenics 167, and for depressed patients 566 per 100,000. Figures from a variety of sources suggest that of people who have suffered from serious depressive or manic disorders, one of six or seven eventually commits suicide (Pitts & Winokur, 1964). When researchers at the Los Angeles Suicide Prevention Center compared callers who later killed themselves with callers who did not, the single item that best distinguished them was age, but the second best was alcoholism (Litman, Farberow, Wold, & Brown, 1974).[1]

The great French sociologist Durkheim, who launched the modern scientific study of suicide, found that Protestants killed themselves at a greater rate than Catholics and that the more highly educated classes in general killed themselves more often than those less advantaged (Durkheim, 1930/1951). The reason, however, was to Durkheim not the fact of being Protestant or of being educated as such, but rather that in 19th century Europe Protestants and better-educated individuals were on the average less well integrated into encompassing communities that enfolded and constrained them than were Catholics and the less educated. Since the community characteristics of social classes and religious groups change somewhat across the world and through history, it is not surprising that modern U.S. investigators have not found the same relationships as Durkheim. If anything, in fact, the relationships in the U.S. are opposite: The lowest occupational and social strata may well be the likeliest to commit suicide (Dublin, 1963). In Chicago's Cook County, for instance, the suicide rate for male laborers is more than three times that for male professional and technical workers (50.6 versus 14.8 per 100,000) (Maris, 1969).

Special Conditions That Affect Suicide

Durkheim (1930/1951) found that in 19th century Europe the suicide rates of several countries dipped during revolutions, election crises, and wars that excited people's passions. During wars in the present century, the suicide rates of the U.S., Japan, and the European belligerents also fell (Dublin, 1963). On the other hand, events that Durkheim interpreted as signs of prosperity, such as falling food prices, world expositions, and the unification of Germany and Italy, were accompanied by rising suicide rates.

Suicide is more common during late spring and early summer in most of Europe (Durkheim, 1930/1951) and the United States (Maris, 1969). Interestingly, suicide does not vary significantly with the seasons in Los Angeles (Shneidman & Farberow, 1961/1970), where seasonal changes are relatively slight.

Patterns

Although the groupings and conditions described above may seem rather diverse, they all make a difference in people's relationships to their incentive worlds. We saw in Chapter 6 that people experience less satisfaction on the average as they age, that married individuals are on the average happier than divorced, widowed, or single individuals, and that people in low-status jobs derive less satisfaction from their work than people with higher-status jobs. Obviously, the psychiatrically disturbed are less happy than the psychiatrically well. In each of these respects, the statistics on satisfaction parallel those of suicide, sometimes in considerable detail.

Other differences are somewhat harder to cast in terms of people's relationships to their incentives, but by no means impossible. For instance, although women kill themselves far less often than men do, an American survey found that U.S. women describe themselves as on the average only very slightly happier (Bradburn, 1969). However, the same survey also found that wives of wage earners are affected emotionally much less adversely by their husbands' employment problems than are the husbands themselves (Bradburn, 1969). Furthermore, their occupational aspirations for themselves are on the average much more modest than those of men (Barnett, 1973). Although American women have their own significant problems, relatively few of them are their families' chief wage earners, whereas they are more consistently involved with their children and are more likely to be the family's agent in relations with the extended family, the neighborhood, and community organizations. Therefore, they lead on the average lives with closer personal ties, more stable incentives, and fewer possibilities of irretrievably dashed hopes. To some extent, therefore, their lives are on the average better buffered from the emotional shocks of the economic system, and are better centered on interpersonal rewards, than those of men.

It is important to maintain perspective on these sex differences. Despite their lower rate of completed suicides, young women *attempt* suicide far more often than do men, and at all ages women are a sizable majority of people treated for depression. A surplus of uncompleted attempts may well signify that the suicidal act serves as a desperate "cry for help," one which assumes some degree of hope that others will hear and respond. Thus, it seems quite likely that although U.S. women are on the average spared some of the miseries that afflict men, they suffer more from other kinds of miseries, including perhaps those of frustrated careers and artificially curtailed sources of self-esteem; but in their particular forms of unhappiness, they are more likely to call out to a surrounding network or personal relationships for help. Therefore, their unhappiness is less often than men's reflected in the suicide statistics.

How can we account for Durkheim's finding that suicides dip during national conflicts and rise during periods of prosperity? Durkheim himself attributed these phenomena to changes in the solidarity of the societies involved. Thus, nations at war become better integrated societies, but nations in the throes of rapid progress weaken their traditions and disorder their social fabric. Since well-integrated societies are better able to call on their members to make personal sacrifices for the common good, and since they can more effectively moderate their people's aspirations and restrain their actions, fewer of their members commit suicide.

There is no reason to doubt that members of well-integrated societies are less likely to commit suicide. Insofar as societies are strongly integrated, it is because they offer powerful incentives for behaving in traditionally sanctioned or consensually agreed on ways. To put this another way, strongly integrated societies must arrange their incentives in such a way that their members care strongly about one another or at least about their joint projects. Furthermore, to be effective the incentives must be attainable. Therefore, well-integrated societies can be expected to foster relationships between people and their incentives that are relatively benign. If suicide grows out of disturbed relationships of people to their incentives, strongly integrated societies should give rise to few suicides.

However, one may question whether societies indeed become better integrated during, for instance, political revolutions. The critical factor that reduces suicides during revolutions and wars may rather be something other than social integration: It may be that revolution or war creates a set of new incentives — to win, to avoid losing, to better one's lot. These incentives carry in their wake others, such as new personal relationships or new group goals. Taken together, these new incentives may have the power to revivify inner life — to provide a new sense of meaningfulness — in people whose lives had become stagnant and poor. Then, finally, there is the remaining fact that revolutions, wars, and political struggles make lively spectator sports, and they may thereby work results on emotionally impoverished lives similar to the other means of emotional massage described in the previous chapter.

How can we reconcile an apparent paradox, that national progress is often reflected in rising suicide rates, with an incentive interpretation of suicide? First, this generalization does not seem to apply very well to 20th century America. From 1910 to 1931, the U.S. suicide rate was correlated *negatively* with business activity, rising during economic depression and falling in times of prosperity (Dublin, 1963). Second, we must recognize that the kinds of progress described by Durkheim — falling food prices, world expositions, and national mergers — do not have a uniformly enriching effect on all parts of society. When food prices fall, the producers of the food may suffer gravely, and in the 19th century the producers of food still constituted a large part of the population. When independent states become unified, large shifts in power invariably take place, with the result that some individuals and some communities suffer an absolute loss. Economic advances, which in 19th century Europe generally involved industrialization, create great personal dislocation as people lose their farms and independent trades for wage employment, or are forced to change accustomed modes of work to stave off being economically engulfed by the new order. Furthermore, with the changing social scene, many kinds of incentives such as attachments to particular places, people, customs, and ways of relating to others are lost. There is therefore no reason to take at face value Durkheim's optimistic assumption that the kinds of national progress he describes are unmixed blessings for the nations undergoing them.

Nevertheless, it is possible to accept the notion that rapid progress has a disordering effect on societies, and that as a result of the turbulence many people lose satisfactions to which they had become accustomed or fail to cash in on their opportunities as grandly as they had hoped. Insofar as that happens, more people will become depressed or alienated than would have in better regulated societies. People's inability to satisfy their unbridled aspirations was the cause of suicide in Durkheim's original explanation, which we can now tie to individual inner experience by means of the incentive-disengagement cycle (Chapter 5) and the concept of alienation (Chapter 6).

Finally, why should people be more likely to kill themselves in late spring and early summer? There are two possible explanations. First, these times of the year are popular vacation periods. It may be that while away from their work people with few other sources of satisfaction experience their vacation periods as periods of deprivation. Alternatively, their large amount of free time provides them with opportunities to brood at the same time it weakens the restraints of schedule and habit. However, this vacation-time explanation seems unsatisfactory. First, late summer is if anything an even more popular vacation time. Second, Los Angeles workers also often take their vacations in the summer, when their children are out of school, and yet the most suicide-prone month in Los Angeles is February. There is, however, yet another explanation. It rests on the assumption that most people enjoy spring for its warmth and for the resurgence of life it brings. The depressed, however, are likely to find themselves unable to enjoy spring as much as before. The missed enjoyment of spring therefore becomes another loss, one more contribution to depression, but coordinated in such a way that this loss is reflected in seasonal fluctuations of the suicide rate.

Events That Precipitate Suicide

The previous section shows that it is possible to explain the gross statistics of suicide by arguing that suicide becomes more likely as people derive less satisfaction from their relationships with incentives. The lack of satisfaction could arise either from want of adequate incentives to enjoy or from loss of incentives previously enjoyed or coveted. This explanation is very imprecise, and it is by no means the only explanation that these gross data could suggest. It says nothing about the point at which a person may translate dissatisfaction into suicide, or why it is that there are so many people who appear dissatisfied with their lives but do not kill themselves. To sharpen the argument, it is necessary to move to a more psychological level of evidence: In individual lives, what are the events that precipitate suicide, and what is going on in the mind of the person preparing to do it?

In traditional societies, people often committed suicide as a point of honor (Durkheim, 1930/1951). For some, ritual suicide conferred prestige. Many ancient peoples "considered it a disgrace to die in bed" (Durkheim, 1930/1951, P. 217) and therefore killed themselves when they weakened or tired of life. Durkheim believed these forms of suicide to be characteristic of tightly knit societies in which individual personalities were valued far less, even by their possessors, than is true in the contemporary West. Durkheim thought he detected a holdover of this kind of society, and of this form of suicide, in the 19th century European military, where "the soldier kills himself at the least disappointment, for the most futile reasons, for a refusal of leave, a reprimand, an unjust punishment, a delay in promotion, a question of honor, a flush of momentary jealousy or even simply because other suicides have occurred before his eyes or to his knowledge" (Durkheim, 1930/1951, Pp. 238–239). Granted that Durkheim exaggerated his case and was forced to work with very primitive anthropological data, it is no doubt true that suicide has in some times and places been positively valued and carried out with social sanction. These "altruistic" forms of suicide, however, are not characteristic of modern society and contribute little to its problems.

One source of information about the events that precipitate modern suicide is the set of reasons suicidal individuals write down in the notes they leave. Summarizing a great many such notes, together with police and coroners' reports, Shneidman and Farberow (1961/ 1970) write that "among men who commit suicide, ill health, marital difficulties, and psychological depression, the latter of which might well cut across the first two, are given as the three main reasons. Among women who commit suicide, physical ill health, mental ill health, and depression are given. . . . Among attempted suicides ill health does not rank high (except for males), but rather such causes as marital difficulties and depressions are given most often for both sexes and financial and employment difficulties are added for men" (Pp. 217–218). Shneidman and Farberow are not very comfortable with this information. They write that "the reasons for suicide derived in this manner at best reflect only the more superficial, precipitating causes for suicidal behavior," and they add, "What the police and the coroner have told is almost a tautology; namely, that persons who hurt (are in pain) and who are depressed are suicidal" (P. 217).

Nevertheless, it now seems likely that it is precisely these qualities of being in "pain" that appear best to predict suicide. What we must do next, then, is to establish what kinds of pain lead people to kill themselves and under what conditions.

First, people who attempt suicide have on the average suffered through much more difficult life situations than have others. In one study (Paykel, Prusoff, & Myers, 1975), the investigators interviewed a group of 53 people who had attempted suicide and two other groups — depressed but nonsuicidal patients and normal community residents — carefully matched with the first for age, sex, marital status, social class, and race. They tabulated the number of significant events that had occurred in the life of each person, such as job or marital changes, court appearances, illnesses, deaths, and so on, during the previous six months. They found that the suicide attempters had experienced a mean of 3.3 such events each, as compared with 2.1 events for the depressed but nonsuicidal patients and 0.8 for the community residents. Furthermore, whereas the community residents had experienced their events evenly spaced over the previous six months, the depressed patients and especially the suicide attempters had suffered a large part of them in a bunch during the month before becoming depressed or attempting suicide. The kinds of events that especially distinguished the suicide attempters from the others were unpleasant events beyond the individual's control, such as serious illnesses of close family members, serious personal illness, and court appearances for legal offenses. They were also involved much more often than the others in serious arguments with their spouses.

Sometimes the things that go wrong are bunched up in such a way that they keep adding to the burden of despair. They may not seem as important to outsiders as they do to the victim, but their cumulative effect gradually undermines hope until the person sees suicide as the sensible way out. People are often especially bewildered when they read that prominent, successful people have committed suicide at the height of their fame. Consider three such cases. Vincent Van Gogh shot himself to death in 1890 at the age of 37 just as he was gaining his first recognition as a great artist. Sylvia Plath gassed herself in 1963 at the age of 30 on the heels of acclaim for her novel *The Bell Jar*. Ernest Hemingway shot himself in 1961 at the age of 61 amid general recognition that he was one of the world's greatest novelists. What could have prompted them to take their lives? In each case there was an accumulation of factors that seemed to deny them a livable future.

Van Gogh lived for his work. Of course he liked to draw and paint, but his art also served other important needs. He was a cantankerous man with a violent temper, who was unable to get along with anyone and had difficulty seeking friends. For long periods, his only major source of human contact was with the people who served as his models (Nagera, 1967); and when he felt desperately lonely, as he often did, he deliberately lost himself in his work. He was personally so unhappy that for years he periodically drank enough absinthe to "stun" himself. During this time, he became a foremost master of his art. He depended on his work. Then, after about 1888, a number of things happened to him. He was losing his sexual potency, but more important his work was threatened as never before. He was a man deeply afraid to exhibit his work for fear of criticism. The fame he began to acquire in his last year or so filled him with fear that he would now be held by his public to a standard higher still, one he was not sure he could meet. There is some evidence that he was losing his eyesight: His late paintings had in them the rainbow halos around lights that occur naturally in glaucoma, and he sought out sunnier places in which to paint (Maire, 1971). But one more factor is certain. He was threatened with losing his income, without which he could not paint. Since his paintings never sold well enough to pay his expenses, he had from the beginning received most of his income from his brother Theo. Furthermore, Theo had become an important art dealer who pushed Vincent's art. His brother, however, had married, and supporting Vincent became a burden. In 1890, Vincent was hospitalized for depression. And then Theo, long sickly, became gravely ill. It seemed likely that he would soon die, thereby taking from Vincent Van Gogh his main source of emotional, financial, and professional support. At that point, Vincent shot himself.

Sylvia Plath was torn between two selves, a "white plaster" self that presented a winning conventional image to the world and a "yellow," "hairy" self that represented her deep needs for emotional support and sensual adventure. She demanded from her friends absolute devotion, and she set up ways to test their devotion, often by using medical emergencies (Steiner, 1973). In 1962, her husband became interested in another woman and, by fall, they had separated. She, who so abhorred being deserted, was left alone with two small children. "The loneliness here now," she wrote in October, "is appalling" (Plath, 1975, P. 467). And, "I've had nothing to look forward to for so long!" (P. 468). When she moved into a new London apartment, her spritis revived briefly. Her friends came to her aid. "I have never been so happy in my life" (Pp. 488, 491). But she was sick with a severe flu and soon acted beset by her many responsibilities for work, child care, and upkeep of the apartment. On February 4, 1963, she wrote, "[T]he upheaval over, I am seeing the finality of it all, and being catapulted from the cowlike happiness of maternity into loneliness and grim problems is no fun" (Plath, 1975, P. 498). The literary success that fed her white plaster self could not sufficiently nourish the yellow, hairy one. Eight days later she stuck her head into an oven.

In 1959, Ernest Hemingway had begun to slide into fear and obsession (Hotchner, 1966). He had a lingering kidney infection, once complicated by a severe cold. He was obsessed with concern about his blood pressure. He seemed hypochondriacal. He became uncharacteristically cautious about taxes, customs, and safety. A bullfighting circuit in Spain was further dampened by disagreements with his wife Mary. In general, he seemed to have lost some of his elan and self-confidence. He had lived for 20 years in Havana, but in 1960, life in Castro Cuba became unbearable to him. One day, soldiers clubbed his old, beloved Black Dog to death. He left the Havana house, yacht, and life he loved and moved to Ketchum, Idaho, now more fearful than ever. He was convinced that the FBI was out to "get him" for imaginary tax evasion. The idea became a full-blown psychotic delusion. Everywhere he went he knew that he was being "bugged" and spied on by people he saw in the street or in bars. He became afraid to hunt for fear of being shot for trespassing. He took daily statistics on his blood pressure. Worst of all, he could no longer write, could no longer complete a nearly finished book. He was persuaded to enter Mayo Clinic for treatment in 1960 and again in 1961 after his depression over this situation led to attempts at suicide. While there in early June he told his good friend and biographer Aaron Hotchner (1966), "It doesn't matter that I don't write for a day or a year or ten years as long as the knowledge that I can write is solid inside me. But a day without that knowledge, or not being sure of it, is eternity" (P. 298). And again, "What does a man care about? Staying healthy. Working good. Eating and drinking with his friends. Enjoying himself in bed. I haven't any of them" (P. 229). After his discharge from Mayo at the end of June, he returned home to Ketchum, where early the next morning, at his first good opportunity, he shot himself.

There is firm evidence, then, that people who commit suicide are on the average under severe personal duress. There is also other evidence, of course. For instance, one group of investigators (Farberow, Shneidman, & Leonard, 1970b) matched a group of cancer patients who had committed suicide with a group of 32 nonsuicidal patients whose cancers were similar in kind and degree. Of these nonsuicidal patients, 30 died and two were discharged when the hospital could do nothing further to help them. It is clear that the patients who had killed themselves had been desperately ill.

Even when the circumstances are objectively less disastrous, one can often find precipitating events that may very well have been "last straws" for the suicide victim. In the practice of psychotherapy, for instance, "suicide of persons who were in therapy tended with great regularity to occur at a time of separation between patient and doctor. Frequently the separation was caused by an absence of the doctor due to travel or vacation, or it was brought about by an interruption or termination of treatment. . . . That patients feel abandoned by their therapists is well known to the staff of the Suicide Prevention Center. Of approximately 1,700 night calls in 1963, almost a third were from persons who had a therapist" (Litman, 1965/1970, P. 300). Some schizophrenic patients who feel comfortable in hospital but upset outside commit suicide when faced with discharge (Farberow, Shneidman, & Leonard, 1970a). Of people who have been psychiatrically hospitalized and who later commit suicide, more than a third do so within the first month after discharge (Pokorny, 1964).

Despite the fact that people who kill themselves are typically under great stress, it is nevertheless true that the majority of people who suffer similar stresses do not commit suicide. What factors make the difference?

A series of studies of suicides in hospitals reveals a clear pattern (Farberow, Shneidman, & Leonard, 1970a,b; Farberow & McEvoy, 1966/1970; Farberow, McKelligott, Cohen, & Darbonne, 1966/1970; Farberow, Shneidman, & Neuringer, 1966/1970). Whether the patients are suffering from cancer, heart and lung disease, anxiety and depressive disorders, or other neuropsychiatric difficulties, one constellation of factors seems to provoke suicide in large numbers: the patient is dissatisfied with what the hospital is doing for him or her, but is also at odds with his or her home environment. Such a patient has no place to go that provides a feeling of support or help. In contrast, equally ill or disturbed patients who were not suicidal had either developed a good working relationship with their hospital staffs or enjoyed the support of their families, whether in the hospital or during visits home.

There was also another pattern that seemed to cut across types of hospitalization: The more prominent were the signs of incentive-disengagement cycles, the more likely were patients to commit suicide. Cancer patients, for instance, "are subjected to severe if not total disruption of their life pattern, a slow dissolution of their body image, a frontal attack on their self-concept, and a tremendous strain on their interpersonal relationships" (Farberow, Shneidman, & Leonard, 170b, P. 341). Some such patients, who have had a history of exercising tight control over their lives, cling to their long-standing concepts of themselves to the end by deciding their end. Patients of all kinds were more likely to become suicidal if they were unusually hostile or severely depressed. Psychiatric patients were more likely to kill themselves if they were excessively restless or agitated, withdrawn, or violent, or if they were concerned about impending divorces, separations, infidelity, retirement, business failure, and other such "losses" (Farberow & McEvoy, 1966/1970). On the other hand, those with plans for the future, who presumably remained committed to (and could look forward to) enjoying important incentives in the future, chose to remain alive.

Taken together, the evidence suggests that a patient's decision to live or die depends on the same factors that determine the richness of a person's incentive world, factors that also determine a person's sense that his or her life is meaningful. Even a terminal cancer patient may still have the capacity to enjoy the warmth of good human relationships, and these may keep life from becoming a net negative experience even when balanced against the horrors of the disease. When a hospitalized patient perceives — often correctly — that the hospital staff have become indifferent or hostile, and that family and friends have nothing meaningful to offer, the balance can easily swing the other way. In emotional disorders such as severe, long-term anxiety or depression, the individual's affective feedback system for enjoying incentives is itself to some degree incapacitated. It may be that the more severe these disturbances are the more personal support the individual needs to keep the balance from swinging toward self-destruction.

States of Mind at the Point of Suicide

So far we have considered primarily the life situations of people who decide to kill themselves — the circumstances that seem to go into making the decision. At some point, however, these circumstances must be translated into specific thoughts and actions. Discovering the mental state of someone who has killed himself presents unusual difficulties, of course, but a good deal of evidence has accumulated from the reports of people who survived their suicide attempts and from notes left by those who died. To this evidence we now turn.

The Wish to Change Events

Many people who kill themselves fully intended that they should die. That is probably especially true of the hopelessly ill and of many older individuals. However, there is much reason to believe that most suicidal acts are performed very ambivalently as a way to change a desperate situation. Consciously or unconsciously, many of them are actually intended to end short of death. As it happens, the over-whelming majority do, and probably many people who die in suicide die in a sense accidentally.

The irresolute nature of most suicidal behavior is apparent in some of the facts of the behavior itself. First of all, for every completed suicide an average of about eight stop short of death. It would be a sad commentary on the competence of the species if all of these failed attempts had been whole-heartedly sincere. Furthermore, it is esti-mated that 60 to 75% of people who attempt suicide give warning (Stengel, 1964) and 24% act as their own rescuers (Shneidman & Farberow, 1961/1970). Indeed, almost 7% of the calls received by the Los Angeles Suicide Prevention Center are placed by people in the midst of their own suicide proceeding (Farberow, Heilig, & Litman, 1968/1970). Five years after a group of 128 British individuals had attempted suicide, a quarter had died of natural causes but only one of suicide (Stengel, 1964). (However, 80% of a group of male U.S. veterans who killed themselves had a history of previous attempts or threats of suicide [Shneidman & Farberow 1961/1970]. Thus, insofar as these figures are representative, few attempters go on to commit suicide, but most of the individuals who do take their own lives were once among the attempters and threateners. It is therefore important to take any suicidal threat or attempt seriously.

Erwin Stengel (1964) argues that many suicide attempters quite reasonably aim to improve their treatment at the hands of the people around them. People who attempt suicide do in fact guarantee them-selves a greatly improved prospect of professional attention and are often greeted by an "upsurge of love" from those around them. Stengel also suggests that some people go through a suicidal act as a trial by ordeal — as a way of reading their worth or their fate. Of course, attempts made with these aims make sense only in reasonably benign environments, since otherwise they would fail to achieve their aims in their nonsuicidal respects. Stengel reports that, indeed, pris-oners in concentration camps, prisoner-of-war camps, and civilian prisons make few suicide attempts after their beginning adjustment period.

From a purely mechanical standpoint, the reason that so many suicide attempts are stopped in time is that they are performed so that detection and rescue are likely. Barbiturates and slashed wrists are often used in such a way as to make dying a slow process with a correspondingly good chance of detection (Shneidman & Farberow, 1961/1970). The great majority of people who attempt suicide do so with others either present or nearby (Stengel, 1964). In a large Los Angeles sample of suicide attempters, only 29% said afterward that they had wanted unequivocally to die (Shneidman & Farberow, 1961/1970).

The statistics and forms of attempted suicide therefore argue strongly that most people who commit suicidal acts are at least ambivalent about dying and in many cases actively prefer to live. Their suicidal actions are desperate attempts to create changes in their interpersonal environments — to get people to pay more attention to their needs and to be more supportive.

There is further evidence from suicide notes that even in death the suicide often intends to remain related to life. First, there is the fact of suicide notes themselves: In a large Los Angeles sample of completed suicides, 35% of the men and 39% of the women left notes behind. Second, suicide notes contain a remarkably large number of statements "giving instructions and admonitions and sometimes . . . lists of things to do" (Shneidman & Farberow, 1957/1970). In another large sample, at least 37% were written to produce strong effects on someone else, presumably someone close: 21% expressed deep hatred and 16% unworthiness to live (Farberow & Shneidman, 1957/1970). Thus, at the moment of their suicide, many people continue preoccupied with the business of living.

Clearheadedness

People who actually kill themselves typically reach the moment of suicide clearheaded and resolute. Thus, cancer, heart, and lung patients tend to kill themselves during periods of mental alertness, and, indeed, "quiet confusion" is considered to offer a certain protection against suicide (Farberow, Shneidman, & Leonard, 1970b; Farberow, McKelligott, Cohen, & Darbonne, 1966/1970).

Furthermore, suicide notes tend to be extremely concrete and specific, dwelling not so much on larger issues or vague experiencing as on the details of financial transactions, disposal of the remains, care of loved survivors or exclusion of unloved ones, and assorted errands. They have many of the properties of preparing to leave on an extended trip.

Finally, suicide notes contain an aura of certainty, of minds made up (Ogilview, Stone, & Shneidman, 1966/1970). They also tend to make more sweeping assertions, using many "allness" terms such as "forever," "never," "everything," and so on (Osgood & Walker, 1959). Thus, individuals who complete the act of suicide behave consciously as if their decisions are behind them.

Meaninglessness

Although many people express fierce hatred of others or of themselves in their suicide notes, a significant portion express simply the wish to die, often on grounds that life has ceased to offer anything positive to make it worth living. This reason for suicide occurs in less than a quarter of the suicide notes left by people under age 40 but in 57% of men's notes and 75% of women's notes left by people age 60 and over (Farberow & Shneidman, 1957/1970). One investigator (Breed, 1972) reported evidence that major goals had lost meaning for 98% of men and 37% of women suicides. In Los Angeles County, writers of such notes come disproportionately from the most advantaged suburbs: "In their suicide notes they more often than other Area Types give reasons for their suicide, and these reasons are not concerned with ill health or rejection or finances, but rather with such reasons — in this wealthy group — as 'tired of life,' 'as a way out,' 'no point in living,' 'can't go on' — almost as though, to stretch a point, they were surfeited with life itself" (Shneidman & Farberow, 1960/1970).

At the opposite end of the socioeconomic scale, a sense of meaninglessness also contributes to suicide. Here the suicide notes are fewer and less articulate, and they are more often preoccupied with the shocks and suffering that go with being poor. What the notes fail to express is that the sense of meaninglessness robs these people of a positive counterforce to their misery. Thus, in an interview study of 100 poor suicide attempters, Von Andics (1947) concluded that the critical factor for suicide was not economic privation, even though that was the reason most commonly expressed, but "chiefly the uncertainty and lack of aim for the future as well as the impossibility of seeing any way ahead" (P. 181).

Sometimes people have already lost the ability to find anything of value in their lives by the time they enter adolescence. Ringel (1959) concluded that of 136 girls 14 to 20 years old who had attempted suicide, 39 lacked any meaningful emotional focus in their lives. They engaged in many of the usual adolescent activities and relationships, but they regarded none of them as especially important. Close clinical examination and observation revealed in these patients "a complete inner void. One searches in vain for something that fills them up, that truly engages them, that sustains them. There is no foundation upon which to build their existence. They go through the day without plans or goals, simply waiting for what the hours bring without any firm idea of their future" (Ringel, 1959, Pp. 41–42, my translation). When they one day suddenly recognized their emptiness, they impulsively attempted suicide.

A firm vision of one's future — and presumably therefore of the incentives one will be engaged with — seems to be an important sustaining force in people's lives. Thus, among patients hospitalized for depression, the individuals who appeared most suicidal had the dimmest, vaguest idea of their own future (Yufit, Benzies, Fonte, & Fawcett, 1970; Yufit & Benzies, 1973).

One writer on suicide (Stengel, 1964) disputes that people kill themselves out of "pure weariness of life. . . . Whenever it is given as motive it proves to be either a manifestation of depressive or some other mental illness, or secondary to some loss, frustration, or affliction" (P. 114). That, however, is precisely the point. Losses and frustrations, often begotten by afflictions, give rise to depression or alienation and thereby also to a sense of meaninglessness. They and other factors, such as habituation, undermine the person's capacity to value incentives, and they thereby erode the motivational basis for pursuing incentives and enjoying them.

The Decision for Suicide: Conclusions

In view of the evidence, suicide becomes understandable as a clearheaded choice. The individual weighs the satisfactions and miseries he expects to experience while alive against those he or she expects to reap after death. For individuals who believe that death ends an individual's existence, the expected value of death is zero and the expected value of life must exceed zero to make life worthwhile.[2] For individuals who believe in an afterlife, the expected value of life necessary to prolong it may be either greater than zero or less, depending on the person's hopes and fears for the afterlife.

This choice is in most cases not "rational" in the sense of being carefully thought out in mathematical detail. Rather, it results from an affective calculation — the resultant affect the individual has for whatever future he or she can extrapolate from the present. As a consequence, decisions for suicide or against depend on individuals' beliefs about the future and on the affective values they attach to what they see there. Reflective individuals who can distinguish future opportunities and envision future solutions in fine detail may therefore arrive at more optimistic assessments of their future than people who construe their futures more globally; and people with a lively affective response to the pleasures of this world are more likely to arrive at a positive assessment of their futures than those whose values have been dulled by depression or habituation.

The decision for or against *attempts* at suicide is more complicated still. To the relative expected value of life and death one must now add the individual's assessment of the likelihood that he or she will be rescued and treated better by others as a result of the attempt. If the person expects no change or a change for the worse, or if the person is unable to appreciate whatever changes may occur, then the decision process is the same as that for suicide. If, however, people expect a suicide attempt to produce some favorable changes in those around them, and if they are capable of appreciating those changes affectively at the time of the decision, we can expect a higher frequency of suicide attempts designed for rescue. Of course, the individual's assessment of his or her future life must still be fairly close to the indifference point for him or her to gamble it in a suicide attempt, and it must be lower the larger the person regards the risk of dying.[3]

As in the case of suicide, there is no reason to suppose that the decision is based primarily on rational considerations. Rather, it is again likely to be an affective assessment, a matter of doing what "feels" as if it is the best course — an assessment in which actual suicide and mere "attempt" are likely to be indistinguishably intertwined in the person's mind.

Putting the decision in these terms, it is easy to see that it is affected by all of the factors that enter into the incentive-disengagement cycle. People ought then to be least inclined to kill themselves during periods when their net affective tone is invigoration, since then the incentives about which they are invigorated seem more valuable; but they should become increasingly suicidal as they disengage from major incentives during depression.

Since people are often in various phases of different disengagement cycles at the same time, it is apparent that the effect of any one cycle can be altered, deepened, or outweighed by others. For most people, the balance of enjoyment, anticipated enjoyment, invigoration, aggression, and depression remains sufficiently above the critical point that they do not actively contemplate committing suicide. In fact, to many people, valuing the things of this world less than death seems completely alien, and the prospect of suicide, abhorrent. That, however, is most likely due to the fact that they cannot empathize with the debased values of many candidates for suicide — they respond too heartily and too spontaneously to the incentives in their lives to imagine the bitter hollowness of values leached out.

For some individuals, the future seems so clearly hostile that they decide irrevocably to end their lives. People who are terminally ill and desolate, people too sick or incapacitated or tired to go on trying, aging individuals with long histories of interpersonal failure — some of these may at some point make a cool-headed judgment that their futures hold nothing to balance their misery.

For most suicidal individuals, however, there are positive factors favoring life as well as negative factors favoring death. When the balance of positive and negative factors sinks to the critical point of being about equal, the situation becomes unstable. At that juncture, small changes can swing the decision toward life or death. A new opportunity or a ray of hope such as an appointment to see a psychotherapist may temporarily turn the person from a suicide attempt, and a new small frustration may firm up a decision to go ahead with it. Therefore, much suicidal behavior is impulsive — a hasty reaction to a last straw. By the same token, however, most suicidal individuals can be saved if they are reached in time. As one prominent training manual states (Farberow, Heilig, & Litman, 1968/1970), "It is the fact of ambivalence that makes suicide prevention possible" (P. 274).

Chapter 9

Conclusions and Implications
for the Social Sciences

We have come a long way since the "Primitive Law of Incentive" of Chapter 1. We have seen repeatedly that the incentives in people's lives account for a large part of their outward behavior and inner experience, but we have also seen that the impact of the incentive world is often indirect and complex. People's relationships to their incentives ramify into so many psychological processes that little in human nature remains unshaped by them. For this reason, their effects can be seen not only in individual behavior and experience, but also throughout the social relationships that make up the human community; and therefore people's relationships to incentives form a basic core — a point of origin and of departure — for all of the social sciences. This chapter brings together the most basic conclusions about the role of incentives in human life, reflects on the nature of human nature that this view compels, and examines the way in which this analysis of humankind can form for the social sciences a unifying central core.

Incentives, Inner Experience, and Behavior

The Linkages between Incentives and Behavior

One of the most basic lessons we have learned is that incentives do not exert simple, direct effects on behavior. That is, if we now define as incentives all objects and events toward which a person might react affectively — by which he or she feels attracted or repelled — then it becomes clear that not all incentives necessarily exert much influence. People become committed to pursuing certain incentives, however, and then they are very likely to act so as to attain them and very likely to think about them and experience more or less strong feelings about them. For instance, a man might be aware of many attractive women at the same time. He might explore in his fantasies the possibilities for him with each of them. In the same way, a woman might be aware of many attractive career possibilities, and she might "try on" each one in fantasy or in deliberate thought for the purpose of making a decision — tacit or explicit — about which one to pursue. Up to that point, the commitment was to exploring possibilities. After that point, when the decision is made, the commitment is to forming a friendship with particular women or to undertaking a particular career. It now preempts thought. Unless it turns out to be disappointing in some way, the other women or the other careers will no longer have much impact on the person's behavior or thought, even though their objective value as incentives remains unchanged. It is the event of commitment that launches the internal state we have called a "current concern" about the incentive. It is commitment that marks the beginning of an incentive's significant influence over a person's behavior, even when the incentive is not physically present and even when its attainment is a long time away.

If incentives influence people strongly mainly after people have become committed to them, then incentives might not seem to dictate people's behavior very rigidly. After all, "commitment" sounds as if it is a matter of individual choice. However, people's commitments, too, obey certain laws. Commitment can be predicted.

Given a choice of alternative goals to strive for, people tend to prefer those that they value and that they believe they have a reasonable chance to attain. Intuition and everyday observation suggest that this is usually true, and theorists of human motivation have expressed this in a simple formula: the attraction of something for someone equals the value of that thing for the person *times* the apparent probability ("expectancy") that it can be attained (Chapter 1). For instance, a man is unlikely to seek out a woman who will certainly rebuff him, however alluring, or a completely repulsive woman, however available. (That is, unless being hard-to-get itself makes the first one more valuable to him — a potentially self-defeating bent!) A woman, in the same way, is likely to seek a career to which she is to some extent attracted and in which she has a reasonable chance of succeeding. The "Expectancy X Value" formula has been used with some success to predict people's preferences for tasks, games, jobs, and politicans. In order to predict which of these things people will become committed to, one must first know three kinds of things: the *value* of each alternative object or event for a person, the person's beliefs about his or her *chances* of attaining each such possible goal, and the *price* in time, effort, and resources the person believes he or she would have to pay for each one. Of course, these beliefs and values are to a large extent built up through experience with the incentives in one's world, and people are rather unlikely to form commitments to incentives that are clearly unavailable. Therefore, a person's behavior and inner experience does ultimately depend overwhelmingly on his or her incentive world, past, present, and anticipated. One must bear in mind, nevertheless, that between the incentives and their effects stands a complex network of beliefs, values, affects, thoughts, and all the other parts of the biopsychological machinery that keeps organisms related to their incentives.

Incentives and Thought

Thoughts are about incentives — about selecting them, about the gains and losses to be expected from pursuing them, about the means for attaining them, about hopes and fears regarding them, and about the pleasures of savoring them or the pain of surrendering them. The prime condition for thinking about anything is that it be an incentive — or something associated with an incentive, or something instrumental to obtaining an incentive — which the individual has become committed to pursue or enjoy. "Incentive," as defined here, includes two kinds of events that one does not ordinarily think of as being incentives, but which fit the specifications nonetheless: first, determining the incentive value of something new, of something newly noticed, or of something changed in the individual's environment, including assessing the seriousness of a threat or assessing the likely fruitfulness of an opportunity; and, second, making a choice to pursue or to forgo an incentive. In order to determine the incentive value of something one must first investigate it, either motorically or mentally, either by doing or by wondering; and making a choice requires at least a tacit decision process. This assumes that nailing down the value of an ambiguous or "collative" stimulus is more pleasant than leaving it uncertain; and it assumes further that having decided which actions to take is more pleasant than continued inner conflict.

An incentive becomes a goal when the person has become committed to pursuing it. The commitment is the onset of an inner state — a "current concern" about the incentive — which remains until the person has reached the goal or abandoned it. During the state of current concern about the goal, the individual is especially responsive to anything having to do with pursuing it. He or she is more than before inclined to notice cues that bear on it, to remember them, to think about them, and to think about other aspects of the pursuit after having been reminded of it. Each thought cued off in this way relates the cue to the corresponding concern. In other words, the specific content of each thought *bridges* the stimulus and the concern in the sense that it combines elements they have in common (the *Induction Principle*).

The cues that trigger people's attention, memorization, and thoughts can arise either in the external world — for instance, in conversation, during reading or watching television, in the behavior of other people, and so on — or in the person's own flow of thought. Some concerns influence thought more than others — probably especially when the person feels strongly about the incentive in question and has to do something about it soon. When a concern is very influential, the individual's own thoughts keep triggering new thoughts about the same incentive or about things related to it. Then we speak of the person being preoccupied, worried, or obsessed with the incentive.

Cues that bear on incentives spur thoughts in this way without any special effort on the part of the individual having the thoughts. This is the case in most dreams, daydreams, reveries, and mind-wandering. I have called these "respondent" thinking because the thoughts are simply responses to incentive-related cues.

When people wish to work for something in the immediate present, they can, of course, direct their thoughts to some extent, thus rendering the thought "operant." They do this by controlling their attention to keep it focused on the task at hand, and they also guide their behavior according to the feedback they get about how well they are doing. To obtain this feedback they must evaluate the success of each step they take according to how effectively it advanced them toward their goal.

The factors that control thought during respondent periods such as mind-wandering probably operate as usual even when people are trying to apply their thoughts to particular problems. Therefore, in order for people to direct their thoughts, they must override these respondent processes. However, the overriding can rarely be complete, especially when a problem requires the thinker to come up with fresh ideas. In this case, when the thought process needs to be creative, its success depends on the thinker letting his or her thoughts go freely within certain limits.

Whether a thought will be useful depends partly on whether it is relevant to the problem and partly on whether it is guided by the requirements of a good solution. If the thinker pays attention to cues that are irrelevant to solving the problem, the thoughts will be off-target or irrelevant. Here, then, the respondent effects of current concerns will be felt with special force. Creative thought is most likely to occur when the thinker is deeply concerned about solving the problem, since he or she is then attentive to the appropriate cues and likely to respond to them with ideas related to the problem. However, having major concerns about incentives other than finishing the task at hand sensitizes the thinker to cues irrelevant to the task, which disrupts thoughts and distracts the thinker. One may also be so concerned with a problem that one exercises too much operant control over one's thought. Then one may dismiss cues that seem only remotely related to the problem and screen out potentially creative ideas before they have a chance to form.

Operant thinking is most likely to be disrupted under certain specifiable conditions. The thinker may fear the loss of something or be depressed about something other than the problem at hand. Or the thinker may be excited by the prospect of a different goal than the one he or she is working on at the moment. Or, perhaps, the thinker is alienated from the task but is working at it for reasons that have little to do with the problem as such. For instance, a student is most likely to have trouble writing an essay while deeply anxious about the possibility of failing, depressed about a broken love relationship, excited about a vacation due to start the following day, or fed up with essay writing but unwilling to give up the life of a college student.

Incentives and Affect

Organisms come equipped with tendencies to react to certain specific kinds of situations with some specific kinds of behavior that need not be learned. Both the eliciting situations and the behavioral responses are specified only very schematically, providing only the most general outlines of the interaction. For instance, finding one's efforts to do something blocked leads the individual to repeat the behavior with greater force. Each of these behavioral tendencies incorporates some elements that at the level of human inner experience we recognize as affects. Each type of affect is normally accompanied by characteristic physiological changes, postures, and facial expressions, whose recognizability across the world's cultures argues strongly for their status as inborn reaction tendencies.

Most of the affects that have been identified as probably innate are responses to particular kinds of incentive situations. For instance, joy or enjoyment accompanies consummating an incentive or mastering a challenge. Fear follows certain innately frightening stimuli or the threat of experiencing them or things associated with them. Anger follows interferences with one's goal striving, especially those not anticipated. Depression, or at least those components of it that have been called "distress" or "sadness," follow loss of an incentive. And so on.

Affect, which is a component of probably all activities, provides people with a code for interpreting the value of what they are doing. Having only sensory feedback from one's actions is by itself useless, since it provides no information concerning what it signifies for the person receiving it, and therefore no basis for reacting to it. Even comparing an immediate situation with some ideal situation does no better if one does not know whether the ideal situation is ideally favorable or the height of tragedy. In order to provide this kind of information, a person needs evaluative feedback to add to the sensory feedback. The evaluative feedback is provided by one's affective states, which provide an efficient code for interpreting one's perceptions and cognitions. Affective reactions not only signal their evaluations along a dimension of good versus bad. They also communicate several key varieties of good and bad and suggest certain rudimentary ways to react. Affects thus also form a system for classifying and organizing the events a person encounters, a system that undoubtedly has great survival value in ordinary situations, although it also clearly oversimplifies and misrepresents some situations that arise in the complex social world of the human.

It follows further that people value objects and events insofar as these can arouse affect. We have talked about the influences of current concerns on behavior. Now we see that those same behaviors are started and guided on the basis of affect. However, neither affects nor current concerns are dispensable constructs. Both are necessary to describe a functioning organism. Affects establish the value of an incentive, both in anticipation of attaining the incentive and in enjoyment of the incentive after it has been attained. Furthermore, affect also signals the extent to which the individual is on course toward attaining the incentive during the pursuit of it. However, it is logically impossible for affect to signal how well someone is moving toward a goal if the goal is not represented continuously in the brain from start to finish. And that therefore requires something like a current concern about the goal. Thus, affects evaluate incentives and provide evaluative feedback regarding actions or thoughts aimed at incentives, but current concerns — or, rather, the processes presumed to go on during them — provide goal-striving with its organization and persistence.

To speak of "affect" in these general terms is not, of course, to deny that affects come in a variety of forms. It may be that the kinds of affect that evaluate incentives (we might call them "consummatory affects") are systematically different from the kinds that signal progress or failure ("appetitive affects"). That possibility, however, must here remain an interesting problem for future research.

Value

In its role of providing evaluative feedback, affect is the human's ultimate arbiter of value. It therefore forms the basis for all human values. Since affects are aspects of inborn reactions to certain kinds of events, part of the human's value system is innate. However, since affective responses can be conditioned to new classes of events, many of the adult human's values are learned. Nevertheless, this learning proceeds on the basis of an innate tendency to value certain events, a basis that provides, within the limits of biological variation, a starting point of universal values for the human species.

Just what these universal values are has not yet been clearly defined. However, they probably include innate affective reactions to some or all of the following: Certain aromas and flavors; certain fear-provoking sensations, such as those produced by falling, by seeing something looming, by being at the edge of a cliff, and, at certain ages, by darkness; orgasm; certain skin and kinesthetic sensations, such as warmth and coolness (depending on body conditions), stroking, cuddling, rocking, and maybe some textures; pain; elimination of wastes; certain visual configurations that correspond to schematic representations of people's smiles and of infants; some forms of human interaction, such as dependent attachment, romatic love, and attack when angry; certain kinds of alterations in the stimulus field, such as sheer change in stimulation, benign surprises, and seeing or thinking of a familiar thing in a new way; completing an action once it is launched; and exercising skills and capacities to master challenges.

Although people come into the world prepared to value certain kinds of experiences, the realm of experiences valued quickly grows through several forms of learning. First of all, objects and events that regularly accompany or precede the things already valued take on value themselves. This occurs through a process of affective conditioning. Second, values change with familiarity. Strange new objects or events become less frightening and more pleasant as the person first becomes more familiar with them.[1] When the person becomes so familiar with something that it becomes "integrated" into the person's activity patterns, it arouses progressively less attention and affect. In some cases it may still be valued, however, in the sense that the person would experience strong affect over its loss. Third, things gain value as a result of their being instrumental for attaining other things that are already valued. Unless the person finds something intrinsically satisfying in the instrumental object or action, its value rises or falls according to the value placed on whatever it is instrumental for attaining.

The value attached to something is never absolute. Events are judged in the context of what we are used to or of what we expect. How pleasant something is — a given meal or a given income, for instance — depends on whether we have become accustomed to better or to worse. Furthermore, goals come to seem more attractive than before if one encounters an unexpected obstacle to attaining them. Depressed moods lower the value of virtually everything other than the lost incentive the person is depressed about. Finally, the value attached to an incentive generally decreases after one has attained and consummated it, especially if one has done so repeatedly. The loss in value may result simply from disillusionment with something that fails to live up to expectation; but repeated experiences with most incentives, even ones that at first delight a person, diminish the pleasure to be found in them. This phenomenon is probably for instance of habituation or satiation — a process that dulls the reactions of organisms to most kinds of repeated stimuli. Sensory pleasures that have lost value through habituation can be revived to some extent by consciously focusing attention on them after they have become automatized.

Some kinds of incentives are more resistant to habituation than others. Incentives whose value is laid down innately in the nervous system probably do not habituate to zero value but plateau at some nonzero level. Things that derive their value purely because they are instrumental for achieving something else seem to keep their value so long as the ultimate incentive they serve remains valuable. From these facts we can deduce two further conclusions. First, we can infer that the incentives least likely to lose value are those that are either very remote, such as the Nobel Prize for a young scientist, or perhaps unattainable in this world, such as salvation. The various incentives that are subsidiary to these ultimate ones — such as publishing scientific findings, for instance, or proselytizing unbelievers — will retain their value just so long as the person still values the ultimate one and retains sufficient faith that it can still be attained.[2] Second, the incentives most likely to lose their value are those that are not in themselves innately satisfying, that are not subsidiary to a remote but apparently achievable goal, and that are attained and consummated. These latter incentives include many of the occupational and status-seeking incentives of modern industrial society.

Reactions to Loss and Impoverishment of Incentives

Becoming committed to pursuing an incentive changes the person's behavior and inner experience, often profoundly. So do miscarriages of the person's concerns produce changes of their own. When the pursuit is unexpectedly hampered or blocked, there follows a sequence of events (an *incentive-disengagement cycle*) which, if it runs its course, has the effect of reorganizing the person's commitments. The person first tries harder, uses more force or speed, and may try alternative paths to the goal. If these efforts fail, the person is likely to become angry, and his or her efforts become more primitive and aggressive. Eventually, with continued frustration, the person becomes depressed and gives up trying. The depression then gradually dissipates, leaving the person substantially recovered and resigned to the loss of the original incentive. Thus, in the end, the original commitment has been for most practical purposes terminated and the concern is no longer current, although it continues to exercise certain circumscribed effects on inner experience.

In this view, depression is a normal, adaptive process of personal reorganization following a significant loss or defeat. Since the biological machinery of depression can also become disordered through organic pathology, not all depressions necessarily fit this model, but it seems likely that most depressions do. If so it is important that therapy and counseling with depressed individuals take this etiology fully into account and that an understanding of the causes and functions of depression become part of mental health education.

Sometimes people's life situations prevent them from finding the satisfactions they desire. For instance, workers may chafe in jobs over which they have little control or that provide few intrinsic satisfactions of pride in performance or sense of contribution. Marriage partners may be disappointed in the economic and social success of their family or in its ability to provide companionship and love. People entering their later years may lose hope in their ability to accomplish once cherished goals, may experience disillusionment with what they have attained, and may experience progressively tighter limitations on the incentives to which they may aspire, either because of social pressures or because of their own physical infirmities. Members of socially disadvantaged groups, such as the poor, the racial minorities, and, in many cases, women, may lose faith in their society's willingness to give them an equal chance to attain their goals. When people are not only dissatisfied with aspects of their life situations but also feel trapped in them, they experience a pattern of affects, thought, and behaviors characteristic of *alienation*.

Alienated individuals typically believe themselves to be powerless with respect to the things they feel alienated from, see a discrepancy between their legitimate aspirations and the behavior conventionally expected of them, and are often confused by the problems they face. They feel not only dissatisfied with the alienated aspect of their lives, but also that it is futile and meaningless, and somehow "not me." Under these circumstances, people dissociate themselves from the alienating situation as much as possible. The alienating job or marriage, for instance, ceases to be a positive current concern. Only escape from it may be attractive, and if the individual feels trapped by his or her circumstances, the concern of escape may exert little influence on inner experience. Such people no longer pay much attention to cues related to the alienating activity, as for performing a job well or for maintaining a pleasant relationship. If alienation has engulfed much of their lives, they become bored and easily distractible. They withdraw from participation beyond the minimum necessary, and their skills in the alienating area may wither. They are more inclined to engage in actions hostile to the alienating institutions and individuals, including criminal acts.

People undoubtedly vary greatly in their susceptibility to becoming alienated. Those whose life options are restricted by their own internal conflicts are more likely to develop a sense of being trapped. So are those who lack faith in their own ability to influence events. Individuals with authoritarian personalities are less put off by working under another's control, and individuals with modest aspirations are less likely to find them blocked.

This view of alienation has a number of implications for social policy. For instance, work enrichment may prove a valuable method for pleasing those workers still concerned with obtaining intrinsic satisfactions from their jobs, but it is likely to meet resistance from those who have dissociated themselves from their work, automatized its essential operations, and invested their energies in the pursuit of other incentives. A part of the crime rate is attributable not so much to objective deprivations but to subjective alienations. The psychological distinction between these is large, and social programs aimed at ameliorating the one may have little bearing on the other. Finally, social policy for the aged must recognize that a large part of the more problematic behavior and inner experience of old people — withdrawal from participation in the community, intellectual decline, overcaution, and physical inactivity — can be traced to social pressures on the aged to do little and to aspire to little. There is strong evidence that the old prefer younger roles until such time as their physical state prevents filling them. People first accept the deisgnation "old" after they have surrendered important social roles and aspirations, largely under the force of health or social circumstances. Rearranging these social circumstances can greatly increase the satisfaction of many older individuals and at the same time increase the human resources available to the community at large.

People trapped in unsatisfying life situations have a number of options. One is simply to resign themselves to a low level of satisfaction. By abandoning inaccessible incentives, letting the incentive-disengagement cycle take its course, and waiting for their adaptation levels to sink, they may find an increased sense of satisfaction without significantly altering their lives. A second option is to focus on extrinsic incentives that their present bleak lives may be instrumental in helping them gain. A third option is to take drastic action, such as to change jobs or spouses, to emigrate, to become criminal, and so on. Fourth, since the message of bleakness is conveyed through people's affect systems, they may launch a direct assault on their own feelings. Fifth, they may kill themselves.

There are several ways to manipulate one's own affects. People can expose themselves in play to kinds of situations similar to those that influence affects in "real" life, such as flirtation and sports. They can cultivate spiritual practices. They can allow their affects to be manipulated vicariously, as through spectator athletics and the media of entertainment and culture. Finally, they can alter their affects directly by the use of chemical agents. Thus, people tend to choose television programs that are highly arousing (without, however, arousing undue amounts of anxiety or guilt), and the groups that have the most reason to feel alienated in their life situations watch the most television. People are more likely to use chemicals of several kinds if their lives are impoverished, whether the impoverishment takes the form of low socioeconomic status, alienation, depression, or other features of individuals' life situations.

Each variety of drug used improves the person's affective responses in those situations in some way. Many commonly used drugs — alcohol, marijuana, and heroin, for instance — produce a euphoric "high" that serves as a pleasant state valued for itself. Marijuana additionally appears to enhance the incentive value of most sensory experiences, such as pleasant sights, sounds, flavors, and sexual sensations. It is therefore able to improve the enjoyability of many life situations that are not already marked by anxiety or severe depression, which it can also amplify. It and, especially, other psychedelics also open up a range of possible new sensory experiences and even "peak" emotional experiences that many users regard as important tools for self-learning and personal change. Heroin, following the initial "rush," induces a state in which physical and emotional pain are far less disturbing than before. It therefore acts as a buffer against suffering in life situations that offer few satisfactions and many sources of pain. Amphetamines generate energy and alertness, and also a sense of confidence and optimism. At probably all dosages alcohol reduces anxiety, and at moderate dosages it also manufactures a sense of optimism. Its ability to counter depression and despair by increasing optimism and a sense of effectiveness, together with its "high," probably accounts for its widespread, nearly all-purpose use as a consciousness-altering drug.

These uses of drugs to improve affect in bleak or painful life situations appear to be far more important factors in addictions than withdrawal sickness or other physical properties of drugs. There is strong evidence that alcoholics and heroin addicts choose to continue using their drugs because of the positive emotional values they gain from them, rather than because they are in any sense the drug's prisoner. Their drug experiences come to serve as a focus of their lives that provides a sense of meaningfulness where meaning was otherwise lacking. As with other such foci, people are likely to resist strongly having to give them up in the absence of another compelling source of meaning in their lives. It is still an open question whether extended drug use also impairs the individual's valuation of alternative incentives.

Here, too, there are important implications for social policy: Treatment of drug use as primarily a medical problem is mistaken. Treatment that focuses on eliminating the drug, as if the drug were responsible for its use, misses the point. Effective control of drug use must tackle the knotty question of what to do when individuals find life in the drug culture more attractive than life outside it, or when the benefits of drinking outweigh the benefits of staying sober. Such questions go to the heart of social organization in the society affected.

When other solutions to an individual's plight fail, there is always the possibility of suicide. Probably a majority of suicide attempts are carried out as desperate assaults on the feelings and attitudes of others, with the hope of being stopped short of death. Most suicidal acts take place amid strong ambivalence about dying. However, completed suicides often seem to arise out of relatively clear-headed judgments that whatever possibilities remain for future satisfaction and meaning in life are outweighed by prospects of pain and suffering. Frequently, the precipitating event is one that confirms this judgment.

Meaning and Void

When people say their life is meaningful, they generally mean they are involved emotionally with personal relationships, gratifying experiences, or important undertakings. In the language of this book, they derive their sense of meaningfulness from involvements with significant incentives, incentives that are still fresh and powerful enough to command affective responses. In contrast, people become unhappy in various ways when their life situations fail to provide them with these sources of meaning, either because people lack the necessary personal relationships, goods, abilities, or freedoms, or because the incentives available to them have lost their power to command affect. Thus, when someone repeats a satisfying activity to the point of satiation and it leads to no further goals beyond itself, it comes to feel futile. When jobs and marital relationships cease to be satisfying in themselves, they begin to be valued mainly according to their usefulness for attaining incentives outside of themselves. People may make their peace with a dull job or a lifeless marriage, but their emotional investments tend to go elsewhere. There is reason to believe — though the evidence is indirect — that, on the average, jobs and marriages do become less potent sources of meaning with time, and that people trapped in unsatisfying jobs and marriages who have little recourse to alternative satisfactions develop a sense of alienation, futility, and meaninglessness. In the extreme cases in which habituation or psychological depression has robbed most incentives of their subjective value, or when infirmity or other barriers have placed them out of reach, life itself comes to feel meaningless.

In modern industrial society, lack of a sense that one's life is meaningful has taken on the proportions of a major social problem. Viktor Frankl (e.g., 1967) calls it "noögenic neurosis" and has argued eloquently for its growing prevalence and importance in psychiatric practice. Dealing with it presents a problem of affective engineering — of finding ways to rearrange people's lives or the way they view their lives so as to restore to them a sense of meaningfulness.

Frankl's approach is typically to help people discover ulterior purposes which their life patterns might serve. People are encouraged to make their seemingly meaningless activities or suffering subsidiary to some further goal, one they may never before have considered. That goal may be a personal one, such as one's own learning and deepening; or it may be interpersonal, such as maintaining vital emotional support for one's children. It may also be spiritual, such as affirming one's relationship to God.

The thrust of Frankl's approach to meaninglessness, which he calls "'logotherapy," is entirely consistent with what we have discovered about the sources of meaning and void. However, it must not be — and is not intended to be — applied mechanically or rigidly in every case. We have seen that there is a variety of causes for the sense of meaninglessness. They range in seriousness from a passing depression to a personality so hemmed in by psychological conflict that all feasible incentives are disqualified as goals. In the first case, simply accepting that the depression will pass and that the world will once again take on color and zest may help the individual ride out the storm. In the latter case, it may be necessary to help the individual reconstruct his or her personality. In still other cases, psychological treatment may merely ameliorate the person's distress unless it is accompanied by a drastic change in the individual's life situation itself. In every case, competent psychological therapy requires that the therapist bring to bear on a problem all that is known about the many facets of human functioning.

This book has focused on the problem of life's meaning only from the psychological viewpoint: What are the factors that make life *feel* meaningful or empty? It has avoided the philosophic and theological questions of whether in fact human life as such serves a higher purpose. However, many people plainly feel the need to view their lives as being purposeful in this larger philosophic sense. To what can we ascribe this need?

There appear to be no systematic data with which to answer this question. It is an area ripe for research. However, the argument developed in this book suggests some likely answers. First, as we have seen, higher purposes — ulterior goals — transform the psychological nature of immediate activities and short-range goals. If these are intrinsically unsatisfying or are sources of suffering, they cannot by themselves make life seem meaningful. People whose lives are meaningless for reasons such as these can transform their emotional lives here and now, without any change in the objective facts of their life situations, simply by viewing their present misery as serving a higher, perhaps other-worldly goal. They need only believe that they will later benefit in some significant way, such as through eternal tranquility, merging with godhead, or Nirvana; for if they can believe their daily suffering or their everyday activities advance them toward this destiny, their suffering and activities will now evoke not merely pain and boredom but also the powerful positive affects, such as serenity and joy, that accompany being on course toward one's objectives. Furthermore, once an individual has experienced such a transformation of his or her inner life through faith in higher purposes, that faith takes on value of its own. The believer can be expected to hold on to it as firmly and as long as possible — unless, of course, powerful new incentives of this world come along that make faith in the other-worldly ones unnecessary.

Societies that are organized at least partly around a system of religious beliefs may unwittingly produce faith in this way. The children of such societies are early taught the importance of following certain rituals and life patterns, many of which seem to the children unduly restrictive or onerous. Yet, everyone in such social groups is under pressure to perform the prescribed acts on pain of social rejection. Thus, in tightly knit communities, Catholics attend mass, Jews fast on Yom Kippur, and Muslims pray facing Mecca. Furthermore, much of daily life is formed and, to some extent, encumbered by the demands of religious tradition. These religion-based activities evoke a sense of futility and irritation in the unbelievers, but a sense of comfort, warmth, and rightness among the believers. To believe, then, is greatly to improve the emotional tone of one's life — a powerful incentive. Thus, social conventions derived from religious beliefs in turn lay the emotional foundation for perpetuating the system of beliefs: Belief transforms the meaning of the activities one performs perforce, and all of life feels better for it.

There is a further possible basis for needing to believe in a higher purpose. Child-rearing sometimes inculcates in children a sense that any enjoyment of something for its own sake is wicked and the actor correspondingly unworthy. Thus, simple sensory pleasures and even pride in one's accomplishments become conditioned stimuli for feelings of guilt. However, if the individual can find a higher purpose to which to dedicate the pleasant activity, the guilt is assuaged and the enjoyment accordingly enhanced. Thus, people raised in the relatively puritanical traditions of the Victorian and post-Victorian era, but faced with the increasing liberalization of sexual mores in the decades since, may often need to think of sexual activity as sanctified in order to enjoy it free of guilt. Others, raised under demands for both accomplishment and self-effacement, can find gratification in achievement and power by dedicating it to political, social, or religious service. People such as these, too, place great value on the higher purposes to which they dedicate their satisfactions, at least until their guilt reactions have had opportunities to be extinguished, since it is the higher purposes that make enjoyment possible.

Thus, the analysis of meaning and void presented here suggests ways of understanding some of the dynamics of religious faith and some of the conditions that govern conversion and apostasy.

The Nature of Human Nature

Every psychological theory incorporates certain far-reaching assumptions about the nature of human nature. Sometimes these are shared universally and escape notice. For instance, most modern theories of scientific psychology assume that mental processes are at root also physical ones — that mind has no existence independent of the body within which it resides. The view presented here certainly shares this assumption. However, there are other issues in the nature of human nature, issues that have persisted since the dawn of philosophy, on which different theories disagree sharply. Concerning three of these the theory of this book takes a definite position: To what extent are humans rational beings, and to what extent are they controlled by

irrational forces? To what extent or in what sense are humans motivated purely by hedonism? Do humans possess "free will"? Without
attempting to sketch out the history of these issues, this section states
a position with respect to each of them.

Human Rationality

There are several ways of construing rationality. One refers to intellectual powers as such — for instance, the human capacity to deduce
consequences from given premises. Another, which has occupied a
more prominent place in the debate over human rationality, refers to
the capacity of individual humans to order their lives so as to secure
for themselves the greatest measure of good. "Good" may in turn be
defined quite variously: conforming to conventional standards of
value and morality; furthering the biological survival of oneself, one's
family, or one's species; fostering social harmony; and maximizing
feelings of well-being.

Regarding people's ability to order their lives rationally, theorists
have disagreed sharply. Early Enlightenment thinkers, such as John
Locke, believed that given appropriate education, people are capable
of ordering their lives through reason to secure conventionally defined prosperity in conformity with higher morality. Sigmund Freud,
on the other hand, viewed the power of reason as at best a small force
in human life, overshadowed by the need to gratify or defend against
primitive instinctual urges. In the Freudian view, humans are well
equipped for survival as a species, or at least were before the age of
modern technological war. But left to themselves, people slight their
individual survival and are set by nature against enduring social harmony.

The theory presented here views people as operating in an essentially rational manner within certain important boundaries. These
boundaries are of three kinds: values, limitations of intellectual skill,
and interference of respondent thought processes with operant thinking.

The value boundary. People direct their thoughts and actions toward
valued goals, and both their affective life and their undirected
thoughts reflect this pursuit. For most people, however, the values
on which they act are laid down by biology and conditioning, not by
reason. People, indeed, rarely examine their own values spontaneously. Those who do are generally impelled to do so upon finding

themselves in a conflict between incompatible values or upon being confronted by challenges to their values, as in the process of liberal education. In the latter case, most individuals end up with their most basic values intact but with a greatly refined ability to defend them against intellectual assault. We can conclude that the most important influences in determining what directions human behavior will take are established by nonrational means.

Limitations in intellectual skill. Given a set of values, people clearly intend to think and act so as to attain the goals that correspond to them. How effectively people can act depends, of course, on the methods they use to attain their goals — the technology of techniques, implements, and thoughts. All three are to some degree given by society. Just how much individual skills for thinking depend on education, whether formal or not, has yet to be established, but it seems likely that a very great part is determined socially. People seem much more concerned with examining the correctness of their thoughts than with the validity of their values, to such an extent that modern Western philosophy has largely dedicated itself to this single task. Nevertheless, the modes of thought that are considered correct and efficient in this society by no means exhaust the universe of correct and useful thought modes. Rather, they rest on a basis of linguistic structure and intellectual tradition, both of which are typically handed down to new generations without benefit of rational inquiry.

Respondent interference. Even skilled thinkers must conjure up their operant thoughts into consciousness segment by segment. We have seen that this conjuring up of thoughts is a process of an induction by cues and current concerns. When the thinker is unfamiliar with the material he or she is thinking about, when the situation is ambiguous, or when there are several thoughts all of which are formally correct, current concerns are likely to play an unusually prominent role in determining the thinker's conclusions. To that extent, they exert an essentially nonrational influence on the course of apparently rational thinking. If the thinker is overly fatigued, sleepy, drugged, or psychotic, the form of thought itself may become nonrational.

What emerges from these considerations, then, is a picture of humans who tend to think rationally as they strive for values that they find intuitively compelling. They are likely to think that their most basic values are ordained by the natural order of things; they are unlikely to notice the extent to which their forms of thought are limited by language and culture; and they are likely to accept formally correct conclusions as absolutely correct if those conclusions serve their current concerns. This is, then, a picture of a species whose members behave rationally within concrete limits.

This view holds important implications for education. If one's objective is to maximize the rationality of one's people, the way to do so is to engage them in intensive examinations of their most basic values in light of the alternatives, to teach them alternative modes of thought drawn from all of the world's cultures, and to educate them in the influences exerted selectively on their own conclusions by their current concerns.

Hedonism

Views of human nature have diverged widely on the question of whether people are strictly and exclusively motivated to seek pleasure and avoid pain. Traditional Western philosophy and theology have insisted that people are capable of acting for other reasons, such as morality, sympathy, and altruism. Freud and most subsequent psychologists have maintained that behavior is motivated directly or indirectly to strive for one or another form of pleasure, such as gratifying instinctual needs, reducing or optimizing tension levels, or, in psychological theories based on the concept of reinforcement, reducing drive. There have, to be sure, been significant dissents from the hedonistic point of view. For instance, Viktor Frankl argues that people are motivated most powerfully by the search for meaning in their lives, and other "humanistic" theorists such as Abraham Maslow and Carl Rogers have argued for the importance of other seemingly abstract goals such as "self-actualization."

The position of this book embraces both the hedonistic view and that of the dissenters from hedonism. It accomplishes this reconciliation by arguing that the immediate motivating principle is never pleasure or pain defined in purely sensual terms — not flavor, fondling, or elimination of pain as such nor their behaviorist stand-ins such as drive- or tension-reduction as such — but rather the pleasant affects that the sensory pleasures evoke, or the unpleasant affects evoked by pain or loss. Although people come into the world programmed with some definite connections between sensory experiences and affects, the relationships between them are by no means invariable, and with each person's accumulation of life experiences they may diverge widely. Furthermore, this position maintains that the wired-in connections between affects and sensory events probably extend well beyond the obvious ones to include good feelings associated with personal attachments, attack when angry, certain kinds of insights, and so forth. Thus, the theory presented here constitutes a form of what might be called *general affective* hedonism, to distinguish it from the more common *sensual* hedonisms or *tension-reduction* hedonisms that have been most commonly at the focus of debate.

It is interesting to note that the general affective form of hedonism advanced here corresponds in certain respects, though by no means in all, with the later development of Greek hedonism as professed by Theodorus, Annicerus, and Epicurus, particularly with regard to the idea that not only grossly sensuous experiences but also social and intellectual ones are capable of arousing pleasant affects (Windelband, 1901/1958). With certain exceptions, these qualifications were also accepted by later hedonistic philosophers, such as the nineteenth century British Utilitarians. Neither the Freudian psychologists nor the behaviorists adopted this broadened view, however. Within the Freudian system or within such neobehavioristic psychologies as that of Dollard and Miller (1950), the only ways to explain socially enlightened, moral, or self-denying behavior are to view it as associated with instinctual gratification or reduction of drives or else to regard it as learned in order to avoid anxiety. This great restriction on the possible bases of human motivation made explaining much distinctively human behavior cumbersome and intuitively unpalatable. An array of psychological theorists such as David McClelland, Carl Rogers, Abraham Maslow, Viktor Frankl, and numerous others, many of them in the forefront of the movement for a "humanistic" psychology, were in part moved in their theoretical directions by their rejection of the psychoanalytical and drive-oriented psychologies. The view of affect presented here offers a conceptual framework for regarding human motivation more broadly and yet still quite systematically.

Another important characteristic of the present view, that affect serves as evaluative feedback regarding an individual's progress toward goals, rescues it from another criticism that has been leveled at hedonistic philosophies. If one's actions are predicated purely on the desire for pleasure, it has been argued, how can one explain the fact that people sometimes undergo years of hardship to attain distant goals? The argument becomes especially compelling when one recognizes that the distant goals are often ones such as social reforms or personal salvation that seem rather remote from sensuous pleasure. The latter notion, that pleasure needs to be sensuous, however, we have already disposed of. Religious or social-service goals *can* be affectively powerful. The more general criticism, that hedonism cannot explain striving for distant goals if they entail hardship now, assumes that pleasant affect can only arise when goals are reached and the incentives consummated. That, however, is clearly not the case. If affects provide evaluative feedback regarding *progress* toward goals, they begin to operate and to provide pleasure or disappointment from the beginning of striving. Furthermore, giving up a goal is affectively noxious. Therefore, the affect system influences behavior and inner experience throughout the period of a current concern, and is in principle capable of outweighing the hardship and self-denial taken on instrumentally in the course of striving for the goal.

"Free Will"

When people make choices, they normally do so with a sense of being the agents of their choices. When they see alternative paths of action before them, they believe that they could choose any of the alternatives, even though they recognize that choosing some of the alternatives would be foolish or even suicidal. Many philosophers — the Greeks Socrates, Plato, Aristotle, and Epicurus, for instance, and the philosophers of the Christian Church beginning with Plotinus, Origen, and Augustine — affirmed that at least in areas about which people have some knowledge their choices are genuinely "free." This freedom of the will became the philosophic basis for ethics and morality, since ethics and moral choice become irrelevant when choices are predetermined.

The belief in "free will" conflicts, however, with the notion that the world is governed completely by natural law, as maintained by the Greek Stoics and by modern scientists. If all existence is lawful, then everything that happens in it is predetermined, including human choices. Since the view of human nature presented here falls clearly within the scientific tradition of determinism, does it imply that humans lead a robotlike existence with only the illusion of freedom?

Human freedom can be thought of as occurring on at least three levels. First, at the lowest level, people can be thought of as acting independently of their momentary drives and of the immediate stimuli that surround them. Second, they can be thought of as acting independently of their rearing during childhood or of the cultures in which they live. Third, their actions can be thought to be free of any natural law. It seems fairly clear that people do not, in fact, achieve any of the three forms of independence completely. According to the theory of this book, momentary cues do influence thoughts quite profoundly. Values and intellectual skills are imparted through cultural influences. Finally, the existence of such regularities means that human behavior and inner experience are at least partially governed by natural law. However, the fact that this is true does not mean that people are shunted from one action to the next by momentary drives and stimuli. Let us consider the extent to which the theory argued here provides people with spheres of freedom.

First, this theory portrays people as being to a considerable extent free within their immediate situations. Since people are organized around the pursuit and enjoyment of incentives, their actions and inner experience are largely dependent on whatever factors determine the incentives to which they become committed. These factors prominently include relatively enduring characteristics of individuals, such as their values and their expectancies of success, the latter of which in turn depend on the competencies they know they have acquired. Given their current concerns, the hold of situations on people is considerably loosened. People *select* (and often manufacture) the cues to which they respond according to their concerns and they *employ* situations to advance them toward preselected goals. Thus, immediate situations determine human behavior in the sense that a person's behavior must accommodate itself to the cues and opportunities presented by each situation, but that accommodation frequently takes place in the service of a purpose imported into the situation from outside. Furthermore, people often pursue their goals in a way that ignores momentary fluctuations in their drive states, such as hunger, thirst, and sexual arousal. Thus, the future-oriented view of human action presented here is far from a simple unfolding of mechanically conditioned, shaped, and driven responses.

Second, the main psychological determiners of human behavior — value and competence — can themselves be shaped to a significant extent by the individual who holds them. Obviously, someone who wishes to pursue a goal can often choose to learn how. In this way, people can increase their chances of succeeding in their pursuits. Those individuals who are well aware that they can improve their skills are therefore more likely to become committed to incentives on the basis of their values rather than of their competencies.

Moreover, people can also make major changes in their values. It is true, on the one hand, that values come partly innate and partly formed through culture and through the accidents of an individual's life history. On the other hand, people who are aware of the ways in which values can be changed can greatly modify the values with which they find themselves endowed. Through investigation and reflection, they can conclude that certain of their values conflict with others, and they may then deliberately disengage themselves from the less preferred incentives. A person's affective response to something may change as fear, contempt, disgust, or anger comes to overlie the original positive feeling. People can instate new incentives through the symbolic means of reading about them, hearing of them, or deducing that they might be pleasant on the basis of other information. People can also create ideas for new incentives through the same respondent processes of creativity that induce creative solutions to problems.

In each of these cases, new values must branch out from older ones. They cannot be instated whole and unconnected. The prospect of lying on a bed of nails, for instance, is unlikely to attract an ordinary American college sophomore, however much the account he or she reads tells of someone else's devotion to it. If, however, the same sophomore becomes interested in achieving ecstasy through meditation as an outgrowth from enjoyment of other ecstatic or euphoric states, or becomes interested in body control through previous enjoyment of athletics or to gain relief from bodily tension states, and if the same individual gains pride in successful competition with others, it is conceivable that he or she might end up becoming committed to lying on a bed of nails. Thus, branching out from existing values is probably necessary, but the branching process can extend a very long distance in the course of a lifetime. It can lead a young person whose youth was sensuous and who supported one war effort to become chaste, abstinent, and pacifistic in middle age, as in the case of Mohandas Gandhi.

An individual's capacity to make such changes in values depends partly on having a repertory of thinking skills adequate for the task. The individual needs a set of mental algorithms for recombining the diverse elements of his or her experiences, for extrapolating from the incentives that are already familiar to new incentives not yet experienced, and for imagining the possible consequences of consummating these untried incentives. To some extent, furthermore, the degree to which people can transform their own values depends on how abstractly they can view their own experiences. For instance, imagine a person who has discovered pleasure in creating or trying out one or more new ideas. If the person forms the generalization that creating or trying out new ideas is fun, he or she can become committed to the very general goal of exploring as many new ideas or ways of living as possible. Such a current concern (or series of current concerns) must exercise a truly liberating effect on the person choosing it, one which can lead to a far greater enlargement of his or her repertory of values than nature, local culture, and parents are likely in most cases to bestow.

Because of capacities such as these, people are not necessarily constrained just by their immediate social roles, nor are they entirely prisoners of their past actual experiences. They can to some extent recreate themselves and redirect their lives. Their acts are predetermined insofar as their intellectual repertories, their starting values, and the raw data of their life situations are determined, but the sphere of their freedom is still considerable.

Insofar as one wishes to create individuals with the largest possible sphere of inner freedom, the way to do so is to teach people quite explicitly the techniques they might use to free themselves. Such education would acquaint them with the widest possible array of human possibilities, train them in the capacity to analyze and to think through the consequences of their value choices, and teach them to teach themselves the skills for goal-striving that they may need later but cannot anticipate now. This, of course, describes the traditional purposes of liberal education, despite the poor, unfocused manner in which they have often been pursued. Liberal education is in this framework by no means ideally suited to all educational purposes. Ideologues who wish to inculcate particular values have no reason to assume that a truly liberal education will produce graduates faithful to any particular mold. But those who prize the creative ferment of diversity and who fear the fads and cruelties of ideological despotism should find a principled liberal education the method of choice.

How free, then, is humankind? One must distinguish freedom as seen prospectively from freedom seen retrospectively. At a given moment in time, human individuals facing the future can bring to bear a considerable repertory of means for shaping their destinies to their values and for reshaping their values themselves. In that sense, each individual chooses freely within the options recognizably available. The choice is individual in the sense that it is not just like the choice anyone else would make, and it is deliberate in the sense that for the individual the choice was not a foregone conclusion: It entailed a decision process. Prospectively, there appeared to the decision-maker to be a great deal of freedom. After all, it was necessary to make a choice — individually and sometimes effortfully. Retro-spectively, or in the God's-eye view of a universe unfolding over time, it is equally clear that the choices were inevitable. After all, the individual's repertories of skill and value, and all of their many in-teractions among themselves and with the world around, were them-selves ultimately determined by a matrix of forces beyond individual control, because individual control was *it*self determined by them. Thus, from the broadest possible perspective of the cosmos as a whole, everything is determined; but from the viewpoint of the indi-vidual decision-maker, determinism is irrelevant, and the "will" is "free."

Implications for the Social Sciences

The chapters of this book have surveyed the impact of people's com-mitments to incentives. The purview has been wide, and the impact of incentives has been found to be diffused throughout behavior and inner experience. We have seen that people's commitments to incen-tives determine not only actions but also attention, and therefore the world as perceived; recall, and therefore the world as remembered; thought and affect, and therefore the content of inner experience and the stuff of creativity; satisfaction and alienation, and therefore the bonds that bind people to one another and to their groups and societies; and people's sense that their lives are meaningful. Through the medium of altered inner experience, commitments to incentives — or the lack thereof — further lead people to alter their life situations, to engage in crime, to manipulate their experiential life through vicarious experience and chemicals, and to take their lives. Values determine incentive choices, but the vicissitudes of incentive pursuit change values in turn. There is thus no sphere of the social sciences that remains altogether untouched by people's relationships to their incentives, whether we speak of psychology, anthropology, sociology, economics, political science, or historical interpretation.

The sections that follow explore some implications for particular issues in the social sciences that can be derived from the theory presented above. There is no intention here to treat any issue exhaus-tively. That would clearly be impossible within the confines of one book. Rather, the purpose is to point out ways of thinking and directions that research might fruitfully take as a result of applying the theory of this book to problems not only in psychology, where the implications seem plain, but especially in other social scientific fields.

Innate Symbols and Universal Meanings

We have seen that certain incentives are valued innately, in the sense that people seek them or reject them without the benefit of any previous experience with them. Thus, hungry newborn infants turn their mouths toward touches on their faces and spit out foods having strong sour or bitter tastes. There is reason to believe that other, more complicated stimuli are also recognized and responded to innately. If there are innately valued incentives, it follows that there must be an innate basis for recognizing them. That is, the brain must contain a code for identifying each such incentive and some kind of link that translates recognition into response. The brain thus contains representations, at least in a very schematic form, of innately valued stimuli and of the innately appropriate responses to them, including affective responses.

There is no reason to believe that the representation of an incentive in the brain need sit there passively, to become activated only when the incentive is encountered. On the contrary, as I have argued elsewhere (Klinger, 1971), perceptual images are a form of internal act, an "efferent process," which can readily be performed in the absence of the thing it represents. If that is so for images in general, why should it not also apply to the innate brain representation of an incentive? It is thus quite possible that such representations may occur as images in the flow of inner experience. These images are possibly very schematic. Work on lower species indicates that innately prescribed stimuli ("sign" stimuli) are often defined as blobs of a certain color, as two circles approaching, and so on. If such a representation were to occur as an image in inner experience, it would, in a sense, "stand for" the class of incentives it represents, and would therefore constitute an innate symbol. It would be shared by virtually all members of the same species, and would therefore constitute a universal symbol. Finally, it would evoke in each member of the species a tendency toward a particular kind of response, including probably a particular kind of affect. Therefore, such a symbol can be said to have for that species a universal meaning.

The question of whether some aspects of human thought are determined innately has occupied scholars for thousands of years. Some believed that certain concepts are innate, such as the idea of God.

Others, especially in recent centuries, have rejected this possibility. Sigmund Freud and Carl Jung, although they disagreed about many basic aspects of psychology, both believed in one or another form of innate symbolism. Freud (e.g., 1920/1949) argued that certain shapes of imagery contain a certain innately given meaning — that, for instance, elongated objects such as trees and shovels symbolize the human phallus. He became convinced of this in the course of analyzing patients' dreams, when he could frequently find evidence to support, for instance, a phallic interpretation of elongated dream images. Jung (1973) wrote of humankind's "collective unconscious," a kind of rudimentary knowledge expressed in certain universal "archetypes," each of which is an innate primordial image of something fixed and important in the human experience. The archetypes include a female and male component of the "soul image" (called the "anima" and "animus"), the "old wise man," the "earth mother," and so forth. Jung arrived at his theory not only through dream analysis but also through investigations of the art and lore of cultures throughout the world. He kept seeing these classes of imagery emerging in quite diverse societies, and they seemed to have some meanings in common wherever they occurred.

Neither Freud nor Jung used methods that permit a scientific decision concerning the existence of innate symbols or universal meanings. Most psychologists and other social scientists have rejected their ideas. Although Freud and Jung may well have been mistaken in the details of their thinking, however, it seems not only possible but probable that they were correct in the broadest outlines of their ideas.

Assuming that innate universal symbols exist, they are no doubt so schematic that if they occurred to an adult without elaboration, the adult might very well not be able to articulate what they mean, even though they would carry at least a vague affective tone. However, it seems likely that as people respond to the real-life incentives these symbols represent, the symbols themselves become fleshed out with the sensory characteristics of the incentives actually encountered. Thus, from the beginning of actual experience with the incentives in a class, any innate representation of them quickly becomes overlaid with the specifics dictated by a particular time, place, and culture. They come to act like other images and like them, probably, occur in consciousness in accordance with the Induction Principle.

Just what the universal symbols are, precisely how their meaning is defined within the human organism, and what laws govern their occurrence in inner experience all remain to be specified through basic research. The implications for the fields of aesthetics, fine arts, communication, and cultural anthropology are, of course, immense.

Commitment and the Impact of Incentives on Behavior

Expectancy X Value theories try to predict what people will do about incentives according to (1) how likely it seems that they will succeed and (2) how much value they place on the incentive. Expectancy X Value theorists have supposed that their formulations apply to a wide variety of psychological phenomena. They have tried to apply their theories not only to people's choices of tasks, objects, jobs, and so on, but also to the amount of effort people expend in working on them and to the quality of those efforts. In each case, the theories predict that those undertakings that are both most highly valued and most attainable will be most attractive to people and will be worked for hardest and best. The view we have presented here, however, throws serious doubt on this global prediction.

There is no reason to doubt that the Expectancy X Value rule applies at least in a rough way to people's choices of incentives to pursue. Even though experimenters have often used extremely crude techniques for ascertaining the values of particular incentives for their individual research participants, we have seen that they have usually been able to predict better than chance the participants' preferences for particular prizes, tasks, occupations, political positions, and so on. However, after people have become committed to pursuing something, the situation changes. Now the Expectancy X Value formulas most probably stop working as good predictors of what people will do. For most goals, people are likely to exert just enough effort to succeed. Only if attaining goals requires large sacrifices are people likely to put forth much more effort for more valuable than for less valuable goals. Furthermore, it is not necessarily true that they will work hardest for the goals that they are most assured of achieving. On the contrary, we have seen that people increase their efforts for a while when they encounter obstacles that make attaining the goal more difficult and hence less likely. Finally, to complicate matters still further, obstacles seem to make the incentives they block even more valuable than before. Therefore, within certain limits, goals become more attractive and stimulate more effort when something happens to make them less accessible than before.

These considerations make it plain that the Expectancy X Value approaches to human behavior hold some promise for predicting

people's preferences and choices of goals to pursue, but not for predicting people's behavior after they have chosen. To explain the behavior of people already committed to pursuing a goal requires three
kinds of departures from the Expectancy X Value approach. First, the
value of an incentive for someone tells us little in most situations
concerning how much effort the person will exert to attain it. Effort
will usually depend far more on the requirements of the task. Second,
the chances of succeeding at the undertaking may affect a person's
efforts in opposite directions, depending on the circumstances. There
are important instances in which events that make attainment of a
goal less likely make it more attractive. Unelaborated Expectancy X
Value theories seem to make no provision for these instances except
in the restricted case of achievement incentives. (If one has trouble
winning what had looked like an easy game, the game becomes more
challenging and therefore sometimes more appealing.) Third, this fact
indicates the importance of considering the history of an action. The
unelaborated Expectancy X Value model is static. It views the value of
something and the likelihood that it can be attained as fixed quantities
at one moment in time, independent of their history. The theory
presented here requires taking into account not only the momentary
probability of attaining the goal, but also whether that probability
represents a decrease from an earlier probability; and, of course, it
requires knowing whether the individual is committed to pursuing
the incentive.

One highly elaborated Expectancy X Value model (Atkinson &
Birch, 1970) spells out ways in which present tendencies depend on
past events, shows how various factors that affect behavioral tendencies interact with one another, and derives complicated formulas for
predicting rates of change in the tendency to do something. It can
account for the persistence of unsatisfied striving and for the in-
vigorating effect of frustration. However, it makes no provision for
aggression or disengagement or, for that matter, for commitment as
such; and it is subject to the first weakness of other Expectancy X
Value theories described above.

Social Organization and Role Theory

During the late 1940s and early 1950s, a number of workers in social
psychology, anthropology, and sociology became excited over a new
set of ideas that came to be known as "role theory." They took cogni-
zance of the fact that everyone has certain expectations of the people

around him or her, and that people in general act to meet those expectations. Just what the expectations for a particular person entail depend on the person's "position" or "status" in the group. For instance, if the status is that of a physician, the person who holds the status is expected to behave in certain specific ways — to act authoritatively and assertively, to carry out certain kinds of examinations, to appear objective, to avoid using medical interviews for sexual or business purposes, and so on. The status of being a patient also entails particular kinds of behavior, such as to appear somewhat debilitated, to submit to the recommendations of physicians and other authorities, to act somewhat dependent on others, and so on. The sum of the expectations held for someone as a result of that person's status is called the person's *role*, and the person's behaviors in meeting those expectations are referred to as *role behavior* or *role enactments*.

The original formulators of role theory (for instance, Linton, 1945; Newcomb, 1950) were excited by it for two reasons. First, it promised to provide a better way to think about the organization of social groups. This it did by providing a new unit of analysis — the role — for describing and analyzing the workings of groups both large and small. Second, it provided a conceptual link between sociology and psychology, in that roles are at the same time components of social systems and patterns of individual lives.

Role theory left a permanent impress on the science of sociology and on certain areas of social psychology. For instance, it became possible to trace the behavior of people differing in social status toward one another, to explore the unsettling effects on a person of having to enact two or more roles whose requirements conflict with each other, to study how groups react to members who fail to enact their roles properly, and so on. The terminology of role theory also sifted into some other areas of psychology, such as personality, but by and large its impact on the mainstream of research and theory in psychology has been disappointing. One likely reason is that workers outside of social psychology had difficulty seeing the relevance of roles in explaining the processes of motivation, learning, perception, and so on.

That social roles — that is, the consensus of others' expectations — influence individual behavior is beyond question. What is becoming clearer is the extent to which individuals cling to their roles and the vigor with which people often keep others in their roles. One interesting example of people hanging on to their roles was provided in an experiment by Burnstein and Zajonc (1965). They formed college students into four-person groups and arranged that some members of each group were elected to perform more "important" roles in a work task than other members. The members of the groups received regular reports regarding the quality of their performances on the task. However, the experimenters sometimes falsified the reports. If they made it appear that the performance of a high-status member was dropping off, the member's actual performance tended to improve, as if to compensate for the deterioration. Even more interesting, if the experimenter made it appear that a low-status member of the group was performing better, the member tended to respond by performing worse, as if to compensate for performing above the level appropriate to the person's status. In a different experiment (Klinger & McNelly, 1976), boy scout troops were divided into four-person game teams, one member of which was randomly selected as the captain. Boys who were not regular leaders in their troops reported feeling less sociable and less leaderlike when they were selected to be captains than when they remained followers.

One reason people stick to their roles so assiduously is that they have been taught the ill consequences of departing from them. Whyte (1943), who observed the activities of a street gang in Boston, found that the higher the status of a boy within the gang, the better his bowling scores tended to be. However, this was not simply a matter of good bowling scores earning someone high status. Whyte describes vividly the hazing and sabotage faced by gang members who out-bowled people above them in status. U.S. teachers tend to give more attention and praise than usual to pupils who they believe have higher ability — if the pupils are white. They give *less* attention and praise to black students they believe have high ability than to black low-ability students (Rubovits & Maehr, 1973). The message is clear: Stay in your place.

Thus, people are continually being rewarded for playing their roles well and punished for neglecting them. Some of the returns for obedient role playing are easily visible, such as getting credit from a bank or not getting arrested. More often, however, they blend into the fabric of life, such as staying on good terms with one's family, friends, and co-workers, with the regular flow of everyday satisfactions and protections that these relationships confer. Not only are many of the important gains for role playing undramatic, each individual is also exposed to a steady stream of signals as to how he or she is doing with respect to them — smiles, stiffening of the face, positions of the eyebrows, postures, inflections of the voice, movements, gazes, and so forth. People learn the meaning of these ubiquitous signals through long experience, to the point where a person can contemplate doing something and immediately imagine how it would be received by various others if they were there. These imaginings and cues, and the rewards or punishments they portend, guide our behaviors from moment to moment, overridden or ignored only when they are outweighed by conflicting interests.

It is a mistake to think of role behavior as something separate from the rest of life — as a special compartment of activity necessary to placate the busybodies. Nor is good role enactment directed at a special class of incentives. Roles prescribe the ways in which people may pursue their goals, and they also prescribe the goals appropriate for them to pursue. However, the incentives for playing one's role well are in most cases precisely the same incentives that people think of themselves as pursuing in life, often without thinking of them in connection with roles. Thus, to speak of role enactments is really just to take a social perspective on striving for incentives in general. Most incentives, after all, involve other people. Whether one speaks of success, power, love, sex, aggression, admiration, doing the laundry, or having enough to eat, others are likely to be involved in setting the standards, serving as the partners or objects, making the tools, or selling the supplies. Thus, roles link individual humans to their social groups; but the link, as properly conceived, resides in the fact that roles provide orderly social channels for pursuing incentives, and commitments to incentives, as we have seen, determine much of individual behavior and inner experience.

Viewing roles in this way tells us a good deal about them and about the way they affect the people in them. Because roles are maintained by incentives, they are reflected in the behaviors and inner experiences of their occupants. Their fantasies about achievement, for instance, reflect the social status they have attained (Klinger & McNelly, 1969). Thinking of roles in incentive terms makes it clearly understandable why people resist being deprived of the roles they have chosen and become used to and why they become angry and depressed when roles are lost. From the standpoint of a social reformer or revolutionary, social changes are likely to improve the objective living standards of most citizens in the nation. Yet, the proposed social changes are often rejected by many of the people they are designed to help. This phenomenon often baffles the agents of social change, and it often leads planners of reform or revolution to overestimate the amount of support they can gather by means of reasoned persuasion. When one recognizes that changes in roles often set in motion incentive-disengagement cycles, the hostility with which proposals for social change are often greeted becomes more readily comprehensible.

To speak of people playing social roles often evokes an image of people acting out parts artificially, unspontaneously, and involuntarily. That, however, is in general a misconception. People retain a significant element of individual choice, in that they respond to the incentives offered by a particular role in a particular group according to their individual values. People generally are in a position to choose among alternative roles, and they make their choices according to the positive and negative incentives offered by each. Thus, they need not feel cast in a role or even that they are choosing a role as such. People choose from among the incentives available and, having become committed to them, they behave in the ways necessary to obtain them. Those ways are usually kept fairly consistent within a social group. When they are viewed from the standpoint of social structure, the fact that they are stable over time and independent of the particular individuals performing them makes it clear that they are not simply an individual matter and can legitimately be considered stable social roles. That realization, however, is not usually part of the inner experiences of the role occupants.

Sometimes, however, people do become aware of being coerced. That seems to happen most commonly when the incentives that maintain a role are predominantly negative rather than positive, or when the requirements of a role prevent a person from doing something he or she very much wishes to do.[3] For instance, the roles of slave, of citizen under martial law, or of conscriptee are often experienced as coerced. Citizens of totalitarian countries may become restive when they become aware of more attractive alternatives to their lives, particularly if they have become habituated to the positive incentives offered them or if the restraints under which they live are especially harsh.

It may be that people's sense of being free depends not on the amount of control they are actually subject to but on the relative balance of positive versus negative incentives that maintain them in their roles.

Role systems. Roles never come one at a time in isolation. Because roles always involve interactions between two or more individuals, they are defined in relation to one another. We may therefore speak of role *systems* to describe the stable relationships among the members of a social group. A change in one role, for instance that of pastor, can take place only with changes in other roles, such as that of parishioner or church councilperson. However, each of these roles is maintained by someone striving for incentives that are controlled by someone else. Since, at a psychological level, people are most basically pursuing incentives rather than filling roles, there is nothing mechanical about their role behavior. There are no guarantees that a particular role will remain fixed. Rather, role systems are dynamic systems, the resultants of a continuous tug-of-war among the members of a group, each ready to adjust his or her role so as to provide the greatest possible return.

Roles generally drift somewhat over time. Occasionally, they may also shift suddenly, as happened to professors and students on college campuses rather frequently during the 1960s. The fact that people tend to test the limits of their roles is reflected in the countless minor irritations, squabbles, and discontents that crop up even in placid interpersonal relationships. Most often, however, each role is part of a large, complex web of roles, so that a change in one involves the personal interests of many people. They tend to resist infringements on the positive aspects of their roles, and they therefore effectively block significant changes in any single role. When circumstances force changes in a part of a role system, the rest of the system often applies gradual pressure that eventually rolls back the change when circumstances ease. Thus, many of the changes wrested by academic reformers in the 1960s, such as pass-fail grades and "relevant" courses, are gradually succumbing to the pressures of employers, graduate admission committees, and faculty members. Systems tend to reassert themselves over the deviations of their parts.

Role systems generally stabilize at some point beyond which the efforts of people to make changes are overridden by others' resistances to change. Presumably, that point occurs when the relative satisfactions of the members reach some optimum distribution. The distribution is no doubt affected by the power of different members to dispense or withhold satisfactions: Those who have the most power over reward and deprivation can use them more decisively to encourage or discourage changes in the social system.

Inasmuch as all of the relevant variables in such a system can be quantified — initial incentive values, habituation, incentive-disengagement reactions, quantity of each kind of incentive controlled by each role, and so on — it should be possible in principle to write simultaneous differential equations, to build a computer model of a role system, or to devise laboratory simulations of role systems by which the dynamics of role systems can be studied objectively. The units of analysis in such a study would be incentives, and the incentive variables would be their type, size, value, value changes, accessibility, changes in accessibility, instrumental relationships among them, and so forth, according to the principles of incentive motivation and incentive effects that have begun to emerge in the preceding chapters of this book.

Theory of organizations. Just as an incentive view of role systems leads to some interesting insights, it is also possible to derive a theory of the way particular organizations function. Such a theory, then, would permit one to describe conditions necessary for various kinds of organizations to function. One early attempt in this direction was made by Barnard (1938), whose focus was primarily on business organizations. Barnard pointed out that people join organizations in the first place when a particular organization offers to help them meet their objectives more effectively than alternative organizations. They stay in the organization as long as it brings them a net return — as long as it provides them with incentives they cannot attain as well without it, and as long as the value of what it provides is more than the value of what it demands of its members. Barnard cautioned readers to distinguish between the official purposes of the organization and the incentives it provides for its members. It is the incentives for members, not official goals, that most immediately determine the success and the form of the organization.

Other writers have tried to extend Barnard's ideas, for instance to spell out better the kinds of incentives provided by different kinds of organizations, such as business, fraternal, and political ones (Clark & Wilson, 1961). However, these attempts, like Barnard's, are phrased in very general, abstract terms. The broad view they permit of the way in which incentives govern organizational life is extremely vague, and they provide almost no view of the fine grain. One likely reason for their lack of incisiveness is that at the time they were written psychological incentive theory was still in a very early state of development. Its development is, of course, still very far from completed, but it should now be possible to attempt detailed, quantitative incentive models of organizational behavior. It should be possible to predict the viability of a particular kind of organization in a particular setting, the effects of different administrative structures and styles, later changes in the way it is administered, turnover, loyalty, cooperativeness among the various subunits, the kinds of official goals set (according to what is necessary to placate the various constituencies of the organization, such as officers, directors, stockholders, and employees or members), morale (depending on the ability of the organization or of each unit to realize its goals, and the amount of strain required, which govern incentive-disengagement phenomena), and creativity (depending on the ability of the organization to harness and foster the respondent processes of its members). It should further be possible to predict something about the degree of personal warmth, sociability, and mutual support shared by the members. After all, these depend in large part on the members' beliefs that they have common goals and have incentives or help to give one another as individual persons, not merely as impersonal cogs. Thus, it ought to be possible to develop ways of predicting and therefore of creating different organizational "climates."

Social movements. The incentive view presented here permits some insights into the dynamics of social movements, such as those interested in ending a particular war, legalizing or prohibiting abortion, procuring a veterans' bonus, or protecting the wilderness. At any given time, most people's lives fall short of perfection in a variety of ways. People may or may not be aware of the shortfalls, and they may or may not be committed to doing something about them if they are. Awareness generally requires that a person realize that things could be better, and commitment to improvement requires believing that improvement is possible at reasonable cost. These perceptions vary from person to person, with the result that, in a large population, someone is usually committed to doing something about almost every conceivable problem.

Into a population prepared in this way comes an idea for action on some problem, one that may mobilize a few people to address themselves to it seriously. For instance, in the early 1960s certain professors became aware that the Indochina war was not as the U.S. government represented it to be, and they thought of the teach-in as a way to combat it. If the costs of action are not too high and the likelihood of the action's succeeding grows, more people will become committed to doing something about the problem, as the products of value and expectancy rise above each individual's critical level for becoming committed. For this group, the newly established concern begins to change the way they see their world, begins to form a new basis for friendship and cooperation, and begins to modify the roles people are willing to play with one another. Thus, the movement not only becomes institutionalized into one or more formal organizations but also brings into being an extensive network of informal organizations and networks.

As the movement grows, however, it undergoes some inevitable changes. The people who join it do so not simply because of its official goal but because it meshes with their individual goals, and these are likely to vary greatly. Thus, participation in the antiwar movement of the 1960s was motivated variously by compassion for the Indochinese, a sense of guilt over complicity in their destruction, a desire to keep governmental violence under control, the wish to preserve the liberty of others in order to ensure one's own, anger at having been deceived, the wish to avoid being inducted into the military or to protect someone else from induction, a desire for recognition, a chance to establish a positive personal identity, a desire for companionship, the wish to be needed, the need for a socially acceptable excuse for leisure and travel, and the need to maintain one's personal integrity. Ending the war in Indochina, or, more accurately, taking part in the effort to end the war, could serve any of these purposes and more. The personal philosophies, social ideals, and life-styles of the members varied drastically. Inevitably, then, as a movement draws on people with such varied personal concerns, the movement as a whole becomes less clearly defined. It may broaden its goals in some respects and blunt them in others in order to avoid alienating its central support. Or it may spawn a whole spectrum of splinter groups, each serving a particular subset of the membership's goals.

Since movements begin with people's awareness of shortcomings, they probably are most apt to arise either when times become worse, since then the problem is clearly set off from people's adaptation levels, or when people begin to notice significant contrasts between their lot and that of others. The spread of the movement presumably depends on the distribution of the problem in the population, as well as the estimated likelihood that something can be done about it.

In this connection there are some interesting recent data concerning the dynamics of nineteenth-century French revolutions, such as those of 1830 and 1848.[4] The common image of such revolutions is that a period of increasingly widespread revolutionary activity at length topples the government, after which the revolution is soon over. The new historical evidence shows, however, that on the contrary most of the revolutionary violence came *after* the old governments had fallen or become ineffectual (see especially Bezucha, 1975; Koepke, 1973; Rule & Tilly, 1975). The theory presented here can account for these findings if we can suppose that the fact of revolutionary activity changed people's expectations of what could be done about their life situations and thereby recruited them into the revolution.

Movements presumably decline as members' problems are ameliorated or as members become disillusioned with their effectiveness. Thus, the antiwar movement lost much of its vigor on college campuses after the closely spaced invasion of Cambodia and the shootings of Kent State and Jackson State University students in 1970. The mood on the campuses that autumn was clearly one of depression and increasing withdrawal. The beliefs of the movement had by that time, however, engaged the support of large segments of the noncollege population, who diverted their energies into the political campaigns of 1972, and lost. The subsequent Christmas bombing of Hanoi that year elicited only the most feeble protests. The movement had succeeded in turning public opinion nearly 180 degrees, but as a movement it had all but disintegrated.

Political Theory

Political science is the science of social power, especially as it is expressed in governmental institutions and, more broadly, in the authority patterns of a society. It is concerned with the ways in which rewards and punishments are dispensed through more or less enduring, more or less acknowledged organs of government.

Power is influence in social relations, but this is ultimately reducible to control over incentives. We are not, of course, speaking here only of the grossest material incentives, but of all the means for influencing people's affects. People must be able to recognize and appreciate the incentives for them to take effect. Therefore, the detailed sources of power depend heavily on the culture of a particular time and place and, at the psychological level, on people's cognitive processes. That, however, is true of incentives in general. One may also derive power from having the techniques or information for changing the way people view their incentives, but this, in effect, also manipulates incentives. Ultimately, therefore, power means having control over other people's incentives.

Consequently, the psychological theory of power has direct applications in politics, whether defined broadly or narrowly. We have already seen that individuals are organized around the incentives to which they have become committed, and that they are apt to resist obstacles to attaining them. It follows that individuals seek to keep control of their incentives and, circumstances permitting, to expand their control over incentives; and it therefore follows that individuals in that sense seek power. In a social context, that means power over others, or, depending on the individual's goals, at least increased freedom from the power of others. These desires then form the psychological basis for political action in the broadest sense, and because they are so much a part of each individual, they constitute a constant tendency for power in a society to become dispersed.

However, power is generally dispersed rather unevenly in any group; and those who are already relatively powerful are not only equally eager to retain their power but are also better equipped to protect and expand it. Furthermore, there is a point beyond which dispersing power interferes with the ability of the group to achieve its members' ends, with the result that individual members may identify their separate interests with continuing an unequal distribution of power. Therefore, there is in any group a tendency for power to become concentrated.

Inherent in any human group, then, are two continuously opposed tendencies. Political science is the science of their dynamics. Those dynamics are inescapably affected by all of the conditions that affect the value of incentives and the striving for them, including habituation, enhancement through difficulty, invigoration in the face of obstacles, aggression, depression and surrender, and alienation; and they are affected ultimately, if less immediately, by all of the effects of people's relationships to incentives, such as initiativeness, ambition, creativity, addictions to the recreational mass media, drug use, and suicide. These kinds of factors play an important role at several different levels — in the mood and effectiveness of individual powerful politicians, in the dynamics that operate inside governing groups, in the kinds of demands made on the political system, in the ease with which political institutions can recruit help and support, and in the human resources available to political organs within the society. Thus, the concepts of incentive motivation and the things known to depend on people's relationships to their incentives provide important analytic tools for political theory.

One attempt to use this tool took the form of interviewing politicians in a number of different countries to ascertain their chief motives for being in politics. Payne (1972; Payne & Woshinsky, 1972) found seven incentives emerging in their interviews: adulation by others in face-to-face contacts, status in the eyes of a mass public, solving problems through political programs, carrying out a religious or ideological mission, maintaining or restoring moral standards in government, playing the game of political strategy and tactics, and engaging in the conviviality of working and relaxing with other people. Payne concluded from his interviews that any one politician is motivated by only one of these incentives and that the importance of the different incentives varies greatly from one country to another. Thus, U.S. politicians seem to strive most often for programmatic problem solving and for the enjoyment of the political "game," Dominican and Brazilian politicians for adulation, and French deputies for carrying out ideological missions and solving problems programmatically. These differences must arise out of the cultural differences among the U.S., Latin America, and France. They are associated with profound differences in the tone of politics in the different countries and in the things required to get something political accomplished. Because of the methods used and the relatively small samples interviewed, these findings are best taken not as definitive data but as an interesting indication of the possibilities offered by an incentive-theory approach to political science.

Economic Theory

As people interact with one another, they do so in ways that provide them with incentives or advance them toward goals. They may enjoy one another's sharing of experiences, expressions of affection, and so on; or they may feel benefited by one another's help. In the working out of role systems, there occurs what one might describe as a continuing exchange of things valued (Homans, 1961). One person does something another wishes done in exchange for approval, money, goods, or work. Thus, in all social relationships one can discern a very real economy of incentives. This system of exchange is implicitly or explicitly, in one form or another, the subject matter of all social sciences. When the incentives exchanged are material goods and services, it forms the subject matter of economics.

From the standpoint of an individual, material goods and services are incentives like others and, in general, they have the same kinds of effects on the individuals who become committed to them. They differ chiefly in that they are relatively easy to measure against common standards of exchange value, especially money. In a monetary economy, transfers of wealth become so easy and flexible that the process of mutual exchange takes on complex patterns whose laws can to some extent be studied en masse. This is the science of macroeconomics, which thus investigates certain important parts of the larger system for exchanging incentives.

When the subject matter of economics is described in this way, it becomes apparent that, like some other social sciences, economics studies the mass outcomes of the incentive-related processes that govern the actions of millions or even billions of individuals. Its laws can therefore be regarded as in part emergent regularities that derive, though by no means simply, from the regularities of individual behavior. However, in restricting its purview purely to actual exchanges of goods and services, especially as these can be expressed monetarily, it neglects important factors that influence the economic process. Much economic behavior depends on events that such a restricted purview leaves out but which are quite susceptible to measurement by methods developed and accepted in psychological research. These have been surveyed by George Katona (1975), and they include some of the factors described in the earlier chapters of this book.

For instance, one of the best predictors of economic recessions is the public's buying plans, as summarized in the University of Michigan's Index of Consumer Sentiment. Thus, the 1958 recession occurred during what had seemed a firm economy, except that the Index of Consumer Sentiment had started to slump in 1957. With little purely economic reason, therefore, changes in consumer buying plans seem to have presaged and perhaps precipitated a relatively steep recession. Those individual buying plans, as *plans*, are psychological events, involving commitments to incentives. Why should the collective mass of such plans change in the country as a whole? Katona makes some observations that correspond quite clearly to the present view of incentive motivation.

Newfound prosperity is a time of relative optimism and euphoria. More goals therefore seem reachable than otherwise would appear so. Consequently, people raise their levels of aspiration and become committed to goals they might otherwise let go. Since these goals are often objectively difficult to attain, commitments to them yield general invigoration in the face of the new obstacles encountered. The general euphoria helps people to resist becoming depressed in the face of obstacles. Thus, early prosperity feeds on itself.

However, there are also other forces at work during prosperity.

People gradually adapt to their prosperity, with the result that it takes continuing rapid progress, and perhaps an acceleration of progress, to sustain the euphoria. People habituate to economic good news and pay less attention to it than before. As the mood of the country sinks, it becomes more vulnerable to depression and fright. Unfavorable events are now more likely to reduce people's assessment of their chances with risky ventures, and are more likely to cause people to take actions that will protect them against reverses. Thus, they venture less, commit themselves to more modest economic goals, plan to buy less, save more, and hence remove some of the monetary stimulus to economic activity. For instance, Katona suggests that the success of the Soviets' Sputnik rocket in 1957 may have contributed to the mood of pessimism and caution that triggered the 1958 recession, and the mood produced by the Watergate scandal during 1972 through 1974 may have contributed to the recession of 1974–75.

Mass moods and attitudes are, of course, not the only essentially psychological contributors to economic activity. The motives, skills, and expectations of managers play an important role in economic events just as those of individual politicians do in political ones. For instance, whereas the managers of one company seem predominantly committed to achievement incentives, those in another company are predominantly committed to power incentives (Andrews, 1967). Such differences have a significant impact on the modes and efficiency of production and on other economic decisions. The many firms that form the units of an economic system obey the same laws of social organization as other kinds of organization, and these, we have seen, ultimately involve the relationships of individuals to their incentives.

This is not to suggest that the only psychological factors of interest to economics are the motivational and emotional factors described here. A great deal also depends, of course, on the knowledge and skills of the individual decision-makers and producers. As Katona points out, much apparently irrational behavior can be attributed to "habit" — which presumably means that the decision-maker is either ignorant of the alternatives or finds the effort of learning about them or of adjusting to them psychologically too costly to undertake. However, behavior that seems "irrational" on purely economic grounds may in fact be quite rational when other forms of incentives, such as the approval of family and friends, personal integrity, and so forth, are taken into account.

The Concept of Incentive in the Social Sciences: Conclusion

The sketchy suggestions ventured above indicate that thought about problems in virtually all of the social sciences can be enriched and enlivened when they are reconceived in the terms of an elaborated incentive theory. Insofar as incentive values, concerns, moods, thoughts, expectancies, and the various other parts of the theory presented here can be specified and measured, incentive relationships can serve as a unifying conceptual theme for the social sciences, much as evolution or the cell serve in biology. Incentive relationships offer the social sciences a common coin of terminology and focus, and they offer all of them a linkage with processes that appear to be crucial to the organization, to the inner experience, and, indeed, to the essence of living human organisms.

NOTES

Notes

Chapter 1

1. I am indebted to Mary K. Martin for most of the creative work that went into devising this second questionnaire and to her and Tony Palmer for some of the data-processing steps necessary for analyzing the responses to it.

2. The phrase "significant beyond the .001 level" is statistical terminology for stating that a difference (or other result) that large could be expected to arise by chance less than once in a thousand such investigations. In other words, the chance of this result being a fluke is less than one in a thousand. Similarly, significant beyond the .05 level means that the chance of the result being a fluke is less than one in 20.

3. The Purpose in Life Test (Crumbaugh & Maholick, 1964, 1969) is a 20-item paper-and-pencil test in which the respondent rates him- or herself on 20 seven-point scales for variables such as "completely bored" to "exuberant, enthusiastic," "My life is: empty, filled only with despair" to "running over with exciting good things," and so forth. The test is an attempt to measure Viktor Frankl's concept of meaning versus existential vacuum. Although the test has undoubtedly proven useful, it is defective in one significant respect: By including items that measure the individual's feeling states, such as depression, it measures not only the sense of meaningfulness as such but also some of its consequences. Thus, it may be a useful clinical instrument, but for certain kinds of incisive research uses it casts too wide a net.

4. The expression "p<.001" is statistical shorthand for the statement, "significant beyond the .001 level." See description in note 2 above.

5. The argument concerning the role of consciousness in human functioning is, of course, much more complicated than this, and a full exploration would go well beyond the purpose of this book. Nevertheless, the experiments by Mischel et al. provide perhaps the clearest experimental evidence on the matter to date. Their 1972 report actually included three experiments, each of which was more complex than I have indicated, and they effectively ruled out, for instance, the possibility that the observed effects can be attributed simply to the experimenter having given some of the children instructions on how to fill the time or simply instructions to think about something. Beyond this series of experiments, there is amazingly little evidence that can be considered persuasive. For instance, there is considerable evidence that people are unable to learn most kinds of responses unless they are conscious of what they are learning (Spielberger & DeNike, 1966); but these experiments merely demonstrate that learning and consciousness go together. One could still argue that consciousness has no role in promoting learning but that whatever does promote learning also promotes consciousness of the thing learned. We know that informing people how to solve a problem is usually a much more efficient way of teaching than the method of successive approxi-

mations, in which the teacher rewards people each time they come a little closer to the correct solution; and we know also that how people construe a situation or themselves heavily influences what they will do about it (Heckhausen & Weiner, 1972). In both cases, however, one could still argue that what made the difference was the information being conveyed by the teacher or by the person's own cognitive process quite apart from consciousness as such. The fact that people can memorize lists much more effectively if they use mnemonic tricks that depend on imagery (Norman, 1969) is somewhat more convincing that a conscious event as such had an effect. Taken together, this evidence does seem rather compelling.

6. Watson's and Guthrie's theories are examples of theories which, as applied to motivation, have virtually disappeared from view. It is interesting to note that to account for observations of behavior, Guthrie found it necessary to invent a construct that he called "maintaining stimuli" — that is, internal or external stimuli that persist and hence continue to influence behavior over long time intervals. For practical purposes, as Guthrie recognized, a well-hedged, ambiguous construct such as "maintaining stimulus" becomes theoretically indistinguishable from "drive." Its creation virtually concedes the point. However, because it is basically a "push" conception of motivation, in which organisms react to antecedent stimuli instead of selecting the stimuli to respond to on the basis of their goals, it differs significantly from the term introduced in the next chapter, "current concern."

7. This has necessarily been an extremely brief, oversimplified sketch of an involved, interesting history of the psychology of motivation. For a more extended treatment, readers may wish to consult the excellent accounts by Atkinson (1964) and Bolles (1975).

8. These are important effects, of course. Dennet (1975) points out that any form of learning requires an organism capable, first, of generating a variety of responses and, second, of testing them out against some standard of success, so that it may discard ineffective responses and repeat effective ones. In its broadest outlines, this is the way the Law of Effect describes organisms as operating, which is why, Dennet points out, "the Law of Effect will not go away" (P. 169). However, Dennet was referring to the Law in its very broad, schematic outlines.

9. That, at least, is true for very hungry animals whose access to food is severely limited — the kind with which most experiments on animal drive have been done. However, recent work with animals allowed to feed relatively freely shows that if the amount of food or water available for a certain unit of work goes down, animals will work harder to increase the number of food rewards they receive, thereby continuing to fulfill their nutritional requirements (Moran, 1975). Work along these lines has produced another interesting observation that bears on drive theories of motivation: Many species of animals feed at such frequent intervals that they rarely become deprived enough to enter a "drive" state in the classical sense. Clearly these organisms must find a source of motivation elsewhere.

10. The passages that follow are heavily indebted to Mitchell (1974).

11. In its more extended derivations, Atkinson's theory has met with more limited success. Thus, predictions that people who fear failure shrink from tasks that are of intermediate difficulty for them have succumbed to data indicating that this is not so — that even fearful competitors choose tasks of intermediate difficulty, as if to gain the most information they can about their abilities (Meyer, 1973; Meyer & Hallermann, 1974, 1975; Meyer, Folkes, & Weiner, 1975). Evidence that people who fear failure increase their efforts after reverses at least as much as others (Schneider, 1975; Schneider & Eckelt, 1975) also contradicts derivations from Atkinson's model. The model leaves out a number of important constituents that, when they are employed, help to explain preferences for achievement tasks that the original model leaves unexplained (Heckhausen, in press and in preparation). Thus, the model cannot be taken as a valid general statement. Much of the data collected under the influence of this theory

can also be interpreted to reflect the achiever's social status and role conflicts (Klinger & McNelly, 1969). However, it cleared the ground conceptually for dealing with achievement motivation, and it has engendered a number of useful approaches to the problem.

Chapter 2

1. Actually, thoughts about an action may also be accompanied by minute activation of the muscles that would have been involved in the action, activity that can be detected with an electromyograph (Jacobson, 1932). Highly verbal, problem-solving thought or silent reading may produce detectable muscle activity in the lips, tongue, chin, and larynx (McGuigan, 1970; Sokolov, 1972).

2. For arguments and evidence to support the assertions in this paragraph, see my previous book (Klinger, 1971), especially Chapters 4 and 6.

3. This is not as self-contradictory as it may seem. The kinds of questions that researchers have asked marijuana users are not refined enough to tease apart all of the nuances of inner experience while stoned. However, what seems to happen is that while people who are high on marijuana are open to new stimulation, as in conversation, their thoughts are more likely to drift in accordance with the flow of new cues. Additionally, they experience some impairment of short-term memory, with the result that they often forget beginnings of thoughts they are still thinking. In these senses, therefore, marijuana intoxication makes people distractible. Nevertheless, while people are stoned particular stimuli often capture their attention more forcefully, temporarily shutting off openness to the flow of other external or internal cues and riveting attention to a single narrow focus.

There is some electrophysiological evidence to support this notion, but the same evidence also poses some problems. There is a brain wave event called "contingent negative variation" (CNV) that appears to correspond to close attention (Tecce, 1972). CNV is larger than normal during states of medium marijuana intoxication (Low, Klonoff, & Marcus, 1973; Braden, Stillman, & Wyatt, 1974). However, it is not larger and may even be smaller during very high levels of intoxication (Braden, Stillman, & Wyatt, 1974), when blank periods are more common (Tart, 1971). This discrepancy poses some problem for the theory that blank periods during marijuana use arise from narrow focusing on particular stimuli. It is possible, of course, that CNV is not a linear indicator of attentiveness in the staring-at-details sense that characterizes the stoned marijuana user.

4. The advantages of thinking-out-loud procedures are considered by DeGroot (1965), Klinger (1971), and Newell & Simon (1972).

5. For many years psychologists believed that "daydreaming" was an unhealthy activity, the amount of which indicated something about an individual's tendencies toward neurosis or psychosis. In fact, a great many introductory textbooks in psychology still write about fantasy as primarily a "defense mechanism," thus overlooking more than 15 years' accumulating evidence to the contrary. This evidence indicates that probably all people spend large amounts of time in respondent thought, and recent evidence indicates that psychotic patients daydream no more than others and that, in fact, daydreaming is unrelated in any way to degree or type of disturbance, except that the daydreams of depressed patients are less pleasant than average (Starker & Singer, 1975).

6. The fact that the meaning (or, more precisely, the associative value) of something depends on the person's current goals has been noted most forcefully by Kurt Lewin (1917, 1928), who in turn credits Poppelreuter (1913) and Ach (1910). Lewin's "dynamic" psychology is based on the concept that incentives set in motion psychic "forces" that propel people toward attaining the incentives. His students have shown that when people encounter obstacles to completing tasks they are more likely to remember the tasks than if they had completed them (Zeigarnik, 1927; but see also

Butterfield, 1964) and they often resume work on them when they get the chance (Ovsiankina, 1928). Furthermore, if subjects are asked to perform tasks similar to the interrupted ones, they are less likely to return to the interrupted tasks (Lissner, 1933) — that is, outcomes similar enough to the original goals are effective substitutes for them, a fact which can account for some instances in which people forget to carry out something they had intended to do (Birenbaum, 1930). These kinds of evidence make it clear that recall and action depend on continuing, internal goal-related processes, a thesis that was at the heart of Lewin's program.

7. The construct "commitment" is formally somewhat similar to Lewin's (1928) concept of *Vornahme*, which is generally translated as "intention." These terms, however, imply a property of being conscious which I do not wish to stipulate. Furthermore, Irwin (1971) attributes intentionality to those acts which a person expects will bring about a specific preferred outcome, when he or she also expects different acts to lead to nonpreferred outcomes. Since intentionality here remains a property of the entire action sequence, the concept lacks the temporal specificity of the commitment construct as the onset of a state. It seems best to distinguish the two concepts by using different terms.

That commitment is a crucial factor in explaining behavior, over and above the presence of incentives, is shown in an experiment by Locke, Bryan, and Kendall (1968). Although incentives obviously have an important bearing on whether people can become committed to them, Locke et al. found that the size of incentives adds nothing to one's ability to predict behavior once one has already taken account of the person's stated intentions and goals.

8. The concept of current concern is, at this time in our theory building, a provisional, heuristic, nonmentalistic construct devised to label a discrete state: the state of the organism between the time of commitment and the time of consummation or disengagement. The influence that states of concern exert on behavior depends on a number of variables that can be investigated empirically, but these are not part of the concern construct itself. After commitment the existence of a concern does not depend on arousal by cues, and it has no dimension of "strength" that depends on situational factors, although the behavior that arises during the state is, of course, affected by an array of moderator variables. The concept of current concern is theoretically compatible with a number of other concepts, but it is formally different from all of them in one or more respects, and it performs different functions theoretically and heuristically.

It may be helpful in clarifying the concept of current concern to contrast it with some other concepts. It bears some resemblance to the Freudian concept of wish, but it also differs in certain important respects. A wish in Freud's psychoanalytic system is derived directly from an instinctual drive. Although the object of a wish may reflect past learning, the onset and termination of a wish theoretically depends on the existence of the physiological states that activate drives. The wish originates unconsciously in the id and is itself unrefined through such "ego processes" as the weighing of expected gains and losses, although their manifestations may be altered through defense mechanisms. None of these descriptions of the wish construct is true of current concern.

The concept of current concern resembles Lewin's (1928) concept of "quasineed," but it does not share the distinction between quasineeds and "genuine needs." It implies narrower classes of satisfiers that "need" (Murray, 1938) or "motive" (McClelland, Atkinson, Clark, & Lowell, 1953). A need or motive such as "achievement" or "affiliation" can subsume a wide range of possible concrete goals, any one of which may be the focus of a current concern. Thus, someone with a high "need to achieve" may have separate current concerns about setting a new sales record, beating his or her tennis partner, and patenting a new design for a mousetrap. On the other hand, someone interested in setting a new sales record may be doing it for the money, not because of a need to achieve. The underlying reason does not alter the fact of the concern, but it does drastically change the nature of the need or motive as defined by McClelland, et al. Concerns *may* encompass broader classes of outcomes than a single outcome event, depending on what it is the person has become committed to. Conceivably some individuals may be committed, for instance, to entering any competition against a standard of excellence they encounter, in which unlikely event their concerns would be coextensive with a "need" or "motive" in the sense of McClelland et al. The boundaries of the need and motive constructs are defined arbitrarily by the investigators that have constructed them. The boundaries of a current concern, on the other hand, are best defined by the range of alternative outcomes that the individual would find acceptable substitutes for one another. (I am indebted to a private 1976 communication from Heinz Heckhausen for the latter suggestion.) As employed by various investigators (Atkinson & Birch, 1970; Heckhausen, in press), "motive" has come to refer to the stable subjective incentive values that a class of incentives has for an individual. In this usage, it is only a matter of convention that the boundaries of motives are defined as arbitrarily wide. Nevertheless, notwithstanding the fact that motives could be defined in terms of narrower boundaries, the incentive value of members of a class remains conceptually something different from the fact of commitment to pursuing a member of the class. Thus, motives and concerns remain fundamentally separate constructs.

Current concerns also differ from the concept of "action tendency" (Atkinson & Birch, 1970), again despite some similarities. Like current concerns, action tendencies persist after they are aroused. However, in the Atkinson and Birch system, there is no point at which anything comparable to commitment occurs, and there is no provision for disengagement. Action tendencies rise from zero strength according to the extent to which they are "instigated" by certain cues, after which they persist at the level to which they had been raised by the latest instigation unless their strength is reduced through consumption of the tendency. There is thus no distinction between incentive and goal, in the sense of that distinction here. Furthermore, "action tendencies" have a dimension of strength, which can be raised situationally through cues that possess instigating force. Current concerns, as used here, can be said to exert varying degrees of "influence" on behavior according to specifiable conditions, but, as they are now conceived, they do not themselves carry a dimension of "strength."

The concept of current concern differs from "drive" and older uses of "need" in eliminating connotations of both tissue deficits and of activity in neural circuits commonly identified with consummatory behavior or reward sites. Finally, it differs from "central motive state" (Bindra, 1974; Morgan, 1943) in referring in each usage to a potentially enduring state rather than to one elicited by situational cues. Current concerns are conceived here to persist even during intervals when the organism is engaged in behavior irrelevant to the concern, although they continue to influence behavior in more subtle ways.

The concept of current concern also offers certain other special advantages over competing concepts. First, it is nomothetic in form but idiographic in content. Thus, it escapes the formlessness of purely idiographic characterizations, but is nevertheless capable of recognizing the idiosyncratic realities of individual organisms in ways that concepts of drive, common traits, etc., cannot. It is specific to particular incentives, but, unlike the concept of incentive value, it can predict particular contents of thought. The time span of a concern can range from moments to decades, depending upon the psychological realities of the individual in question. It is thus capable of spanning longer time intervals than the concepts of wish, quasineed, and central excitatory state, but also shorter time spans than the concepts of psychological need and motive. It thus fills a gap — that of the intermediate-range motivational force — left empty by the particular definitions of other constructs. (I am again indebted to Heinz Heckhausen for this latter observation, in a 1975 private conversation.)

9. There is a good deal of evidence that current concerns also affect the way in which people perceive their world (reviewed briefly in Klinger, 1975, from the perspective of this theory, and extensively by Erdelyi, 1974, and Jenkin, 1957). In general, stimuli

related to one's current concerns are perceived as more prominent than others. For instance, they look larger and brighter. It is not possible to know from the evidence what produces these effects — whether, for instance, there is some direct effect of concerns on the perceptual experience or whether the perceptual effects are secondary to the effects of concerns on attention. Conceivably, paying closer attention to visual cues makes them look larger — a possibility that has been raised in conjunction with perceptual changes in schizophrenics — and the fact that pleasant cues dilate one's pupils could possibly account for the fact that the stimuli look brighter. Future research on the "New Look" approach to perception must examine these possibilities.

10. There is considerable evidence (Byrne, 1964) that people's responsiveness to concern-related cues depends on two kinds of factors: first, whether the concern is about a threatening, negative incentive, and, second, how the individual characteristically copes with threatening stimuli. Some individuals ("repressors" or "inhibitors") are less likely to perceive or recall stimuli related to threatening incentives than stimuli related to positive incentives, whereas other people ("sensitizers" or "facilitators") are more likely to respond to threatening than to nonthreatening stimuli. These individual differences are interesting and important. For our present purposes, however, it is important to note than the so-called repressors are not generally less responsive to threatening stimuli than to truly neutral stimuli, contrary to the usual interpretation of these results. What are called neutral stimuli in the repression-sensitization literature are actually nonthreatening stimuli the experimenter has asked the experimental subjects to perceive or recall, and the subjects have agreed to do so. This arrangement ensures that the experimental stimuli become the focus of a concern. The fact that the "repressor" subjects are trying to and, in fact, do perceive and recall threatening stimuli nearly as well as they perceive and recall nonthreatening stimuli indicates that neither kind of stimulus is truly neutral (in the sense that subjects are more responsive to both kinds than they would be to truly neutral stimuli). In our own "thought-sampling" research (see this chapter, further below) we have found no systematic differences in subjects' responsiveness to cues related to positive versus negative incentives.

11. These results firmly establish some of what had been inferred from the older "New Look in Perception" and TAT results. Compared with the TAT work they have certain important advantages. In both the TAT and the dichotic listening experimentation, experimenters confront their subjects with cues that are at least potentially relevant to individual concerns: pictures in one case and tape-recorded narrations in the other. However, in the latter case the subjects are under only one instruction that might affect their reception of the cues — to listen with moderate attention — whereas the TAT experimenters ask subjects to view the pictures for purposes of working them into creative stories. These different instructions undoubtedly affect the way the cues are experienced. Furthermore, the only instructions for reporting thoughts in our dichotic listening research are to describe one's free thoughts accurately and to rate them according to certain dimensions. Subjects are trained to do this retrospectively and to avoid anticipating the questionnaire in their thoughts. Thus, the dichotic listening data reflect specific moment-to-moment influences on thought as veridically as trained self-observation permits. In the older TAT work, by contrast, subjects' thought "reporting" is really storytelling according to a format prescribed by the experimenter. The dichotic listening studies investigate influences on the flow of respondent thought, whereas the TAT work investigates influences on respondent portions of a largely operant thought process. The dichotic listening experiments are also able to rule out some alternative explanations that have been applied to the older results. They rule out drive states or drive stimuli as the effective motivational factor, because most of the incentives employed for embedding cues in the tapes are irrelevant to drives as conventionally conceived. The design also rules out the possibility that the results reflect simply the operation of discriminative stimuli, since it was clear to the subjects that

they could not work on achieving their incentives or obtain the actual rewards in the experimental situation.

12. Hyperenergization, of course, has the theoretical status of a construct. There is no way to measure it directly except perhaps through assessing the person's subjective sense of trying. The fact that operant thought, especially operant thought requiring high levels of concentration, raises the thinker's tension level, both experientially and physiologically (Bloom & Broder, 1950; Klinger, Gregoire, & Barta, 1973), and the fact that such thought is more difficult for relaxed thinkers (Bloom & Broder, 1950), is suggestive but hardly conclusive evidence in favor of the construct. At this point, therefore, and until we can find some independent way of measuring hyperenergization, the term merely *summarizes* the circumstance of a person both trying and thinking thoughts predominantly about what he or she is trying to do; strictly speaking, hyperenergization does not *"explain"* either trying or keeping one's thoughts on the task at hand.

Chapter 3

1. There are, broadly, two ways to treat affect. Behavioristically, it can be treated as a construct to be inferred from behavioral observations. Phenomenologically, it can be treated as a reportable facet of inner experience, one that involves no sensory modality. The latter is a legitimate scientific approach, just as it is legitimate to study sensory experience. If two people can agree that they are both experiencing something they call anxiety, this formally has the same validity as two people agreeing that they are experiencing something they call a chair. The fact that you as a third observer can also see the chair does not alter the case qualitatively, since in the case of the chair it only adds a third subjectivity that agrees with the two others. The fact that you agree does not further objectify *their* observations. Furthermore, one can show experimentally that there exist situations in which people agree they experience anxiety, and into which you can place yourself and also experience it. Thus, the phenomenological route gains a certain validity by virtue of the fact that it produces observers' reports that vary lawfully with specifiable conditions.

A difficulty arises when one asks how it is the two (or more) people know how to label their anxiety experience. After all, a person can no more communicate the raw experience of anxiety than one can communicate the raw feel of red. However, one can learn this labeling by three kinds of comparison: (1) One can observe how others behave motorically when they use an affect label — their facial movements, postures, motions — and compare their behavior with one's own; (2) One can compare physiological reactions; and (3) One can compare the eliciting situations in which others use the label. It is probably the confluence of movements (especially facial expressions) and situations that educates children in how to label anxiety (or any other affect).

2. There is no reason to suppose that every kind of emotion involves facial expressions. Presumably, facial correlates of emotion evolved as a form of communication among people that helped groups to survive. The survival value of communicating emotion no doubt varies from one kind of emotion to another. One might suppose that it might be less crucial to communicate a feeling of reverence, for instance, than a feeling of fear. The differences in the extent to which emotions are expressed in the face deserves serious investigation. (I am indebted to Lynn E. Bush II for this insight.)

3. Parts of its repertory will not come into play until well after birth. Its repertory may fail to protect the individual from destruction — it must merely succeed in enough cases so that the species to which the individual belongs can survive. Whether some parts of the repertory become operational may depend on certain environmental events or on opportunities for practice. There are many qualifications one would wish to add in this complicated area, but none of them significantly changes the main points made here.

The term "instinct" fell into disrepute because it was used illegitimately to "explain" behavior. One must remember that to call a behavior "instinctive" is not to explain it at all, but merely to say that it is characteristic of a species and that it is not altogether learned. By implication, it is innately encoded in the brain more specifically than are learned aspects of behavior. In higher animals, most behavior depends both on innate dispositions and on learning. Therefore it would be more accurate to speak of degrees of instinctiveness or, better still, to describe precisely the interactions between brain specifications and environment that produced each particular behavior. For the sake of conciseness, however, I shall continue to use the term "instinct."

4. I am heavily indebted to conversations and correspondence with Lynn E. Bush II during 1976 for the insights described in this section. My conclusions differ from his in emphasis, especially with regard to the usefulness of considering emotions within the framework of instinct.

5. It is still possible that the adrenaline may have produced physical effects too gross to mimic natural emotions experientially, in which case the Marañon findings would be irrelevant. This, however, seems unlikely to explain his results.

6. Some of Hohmann's patients report having lost all sense of sexual excitement. However, sexual excitement is a somewhat different kind of system from fear and anger, and its decline may reflect the declining incentive value of sexual activity. The before-and-after comparisons made by these patients sometimes spanned many years, and Hohmann employed no control group against which to compare the men's decrease in sexual interest.

7. The term "value" has no precise general meaning in psychology. The phrase "incentive value" generally refers either to the physical amount of a reward or punishment or to the effectiveness of an incentive in influencing some organism's behavior. The second of these uses, despite its potential circularity, is closer to the meaning of "value" used in this book. Value is in general a way of describing the thing valued in some other set of terms. Most commonly, it is described in terms of exchange — how much the valueing individual is willing to give up to obtain the thing valued in terms of money, work, or other sacrifices. That is also the meaning intended here. As the following discussion indicates, the position of this book is that the relative value assigned to an incentive depends on an implicit calculation whose terms are the affects aroused by the incentive in question.

8. Barry & Miller found a similar increase in approach speeds to a conflict point after administering amobarbital sodium. However, they did not find the effect with chlorpromazine, a failure that lacks a ready explanation.

9. The position described here has much in common with that of Magda Arnold (1960), who has summarized her position (1973) as follows: "I consider emotion a felt action tendency toward anything intuitively appraised as good, or away from anything appraised as bad for me here and now. . . . Emotion is always an urge to a specific kind of action" (Pp. 15–16). In her system, appraisal is an unconscious, intuitive process whose outcome arouses appropriate emotions. Richard Lazarus (e.g., Lazarus & Averill, 1972) holds a similar view that through appraisal of a situation one forms a judgment of how the situation bears on one's life and then responds to this judgment with corresponding affect. The present position states that the cognitive appraisal process yields an objective prediction of where the situation is likely to lead, rather than an evaluation of good or bad, and that it is this objectively viewed, anticipated outcome that arouses the emotion directly, the emotion thus embodying the evaluative judgment. In the terms of Chapter 2, people respond to situational cues with trains of thought that sometimes imaginally carry situations to their likely outcomes. The noticing process and the direction of the thoughts is, naturally, related to the person's current concerns. Any outcome that falls in a class the person recognizes as bearing on the fate of a concern automatically triggers affect. Thus, there are two kinds of coding processes. The cognitive one finds links between circumstances and concerns, thus reducing the enormous flow of cues to a much smaller number of critical consid-

erations. The emotional one further reduces these inferred outcomes to an even smaller number of evaluative classes, corresponding to the emotion aroused. Of course, certain kinds of cues, including those innately coded and those commonly enough encountered to have become conditioned, elicit affect directly without the need for the longer appraisal process.

The innate behavior sequences that ethologists have called "fixed action patterns" have been found to be far more flexible than originally supposed — so flexible that it is unlikely that they unfold automatically as a rigid unit. Perhaps the process that guides them — the innately specified process responsible for their instinctive quality — is affect, performing its homing function with regard to innately valued incentives. (I am indebted to Lynn E. Bush II for this suggestion.)

The notion of affect as a guiding force was developed extensively by Mowrer (1960), whose thinking in this regard has greatly influenced mine.

10. These findings held true for the men in the sample but were not significant for the women. Dienstbier and Munter attributed this inconsistency to a higher anxiety level on the part of women. It is also possible that decisions of these women to cheat depended more on factors other than anxiety, which the experimental manipulations failed to affect.

11. For a further analysis of this problem and additional arguments, see Harris & Katkin, 1975.

12. The correlation coefficient is an index of how closely two characteristics are associated with each other. When two characteristics are perfectly associated — for instance, heights of people measured in units of centimeters and their heights measured in units of inches — the correlation coefficient reaches its highest value of 1.0. When two characteristics are perfectly associated, but inversely — for instance, the amount of soda pop that people have drunk from a 16 ounce bottle and the amount left in it — the correlation coefficient reaches its lowest value of -1.0. When two characteristics have no relationship to each other — for instance, the temperature outside and my luck at poker — the correlation coefficient is 0.0. In-between degrees of association, such as between a child's IQ and its parent's IQ, produce intermediate coefficients.

Chapter 4

1. There is other experimental evidence to buttress these results, but most of it is less direct and requires more use of inference. For instance, Silverstein (1973) asked college students to learn to pair up nonsense syllables and photographs, in such a way that when shown the nonsense syllable the subject could predict the photograph that went with it. Some of the photographs were very pleasant, others were very unpleasant. Next, the subjects were asked to pair up a new set of nonsense syllables with the old ones, such that when faced with one of the new syllables the subject could predict which of the old syllables went with it. Silverstein found that subjects learned most easily to predict those of the old syllables that had been associated with the pleasant photographs. He also presented some evidence that this easier learning may have occurred because the subjects paid more attention to the syllables that had been associated with pleasant photographs and spent more time rehearsing the syllable pairs that contained them. One could infer that this occurred because these syllables had gained greater value for the subjects — that is, to use the ideas of Chapter 3, that the subjects found them emotionally a bit more rewarding to deal with.

2. It is also an idea that provides an innate foundation for the development of achievement motivation. It fits especially well into Heckhausen's (1972, 1975a) conceptual framework. It articulates nicely with much recent work on achievement motivation in adults (e.g., Atkinson & Raynor, 1974). However, it also suggests that the boundaries of "the achievement motive" as conceived in the tradition of McClelland et al. (1953) may have to be reconsidered.

3. Conversely, people who commit themselves to an unattractive task for what they

know is insufficient compensation are likely to exaggerate the attractiveness of the task, or at least to minimize its tiresomeness (Gerard, Conolley, & Wilhelmy, 1974).

4. In the same way, rats seem to average their past rewards in arriving at an expected reward. When rats have been running a runway for one size reward and are suddenly shifted to smaller rewards, they temporarily run less fast than before. The greater the drop in size of reward, the greater the drop in running speeds. The "negative contrast effect" can therefore serve as a measure of the extent to which the new, smaller reward size departs from the rat's expectations. When rats have been accustomed to running the runway for rewards that vary in size (for instance, 20 pellets of rat chow on half of the runs and 4 pellets on the other half, intermixed) and are then switched to consist-ently small rewards, the drop in running speeds is about as much as one would expect if the earlier rewards had all been as large as the average of those actually dispensed (Peters & McHose, 1974). Thus, the adaptation level principle applies at least roughly to expectations of incentive value.

5. An experiment by Phares (1971) might seem to contradict this generalization. Phares had subjects rank and rate four tasks, similar to those used in intelligence tests, according to how much the subjects "would like to succeed on them (assuming that success was equally possible on each)" [P. 387]. Subjects were then made to fail on the two they initially had preferred most to succeed on, and then they were asked to rank and rate the four tasks according to their preferences again. Subjects now expressed significantly less preference for the tasks they had preferred and failed than they had before.

Although the results are interesting, they probably serve to indicate some of the limits of generalization rather than to invalidate the generalization that blocked incen-tives gain value. First, the tasks used by Phares probably had little intrinsic incentive value for Phares's subjects at the start of the experiment, and the "preferences" ex-pressed by the subjects may well have been rather arbitrary, given that subjects proba-bly did not have very strong preferences and that they were forced by the experimenter to choose. Thus, subjects' failures on their preferred tasks probably represented not so much a blocking of incentives as attaching bad feeling to something of fairly neutral value. That is, the real incentive in this situation, apart from pleasing the experimenter, was probably to make a good showing at these "intelligence test" tasks, and failure at particular tasks would merely make them negatively instrumental to achieving the real incentive. This might be expected to turn the prospect of working at those tasks into a negative incentive, a change reflected in subjects' changed ratings of their desire to succeed at them. Therefore, it seems likely that the results of the experiment are irrelevant to the conclusions stated in this section.

It is important for a person to have become genuinely committed to something in order for obstacles to increase in value. For instance, if experimental subjects choose a certain task and fail on it, they prefer it even more than before, but if the task is arbitrarily assigned to the subject, failure reduces its attractiveness (Greenbaum, Cohn, & Krauss, 1965; Heckhausen, 1970). If the experimental subjects are poorly motivated to do well (as measured by TAT measures of Hope of Success and Fear of Failure), then even the tasks they chose lose value after failure (Heckhausen, 1970). It must be re-membered, of course, that an experimental subject *must* choose one or another task in order to stay in the experiment. The latter subjects may have preferred to choose no task at all but went through the motions to placate the experimenter.

6. This supply-and-demand proposition was recently tested quite directly by an ex-periment in which the commodity was chocolate chip cookies and the subjects were college women (Worchel, Lee, & Adewole, 1975). When the cookies were made to appear in short supply, subjects liked them better, especially when they were led to believe that the scarcity resulted from high demand from other participants, rather than by accident, and especially when the scarcity increased during the experiment.

7. The theory of Atkinson and Birch (1970) has the concept of satiation built into it

directly in the form of "consummatory force." The theory asserts that every activity generates some consummatory force — that is, some reduction in the tendency to continue performing the activity. The amount of consummatory force depends on the kind of activity, since activities vary widely in their "consummatory value," and on the intensity of the activity.

Although not crucial to this discussion, it may be useful to distinguish satiation from habituation in the following fashion. Satiation (in Karstens's sense) represents decreasing satisfaction (or increasing dissatisfaction) with a repeated ideational or motor response. It is in this sense akin to Hullian reactive inhibition. Habituation, on the otherhand, is commonly described in conjunction with decreasing response to a stimulus. Satiation tends to be applied to operant acts and habituation to respondent ones. However, usage is not always consistent in this regard.

8. When male mice who have been living with one female are presented with a different female, their testosterone level rises within 30 to 60 minutes (Macrides, Bartke, & Dalterio, 1975). This does not happen if the new animal introduced is male. The change occurs even though no sexual activity takes place.

Chapter 5

1. Two kinds of objections can be raised to this kind of evidence. First, it has been objected that not all investigations have found differences in upsetting events between depressed patients and others. Especially, a study by Hudgens, Morrison, and Barchha (1967) is often cited. However, there are a number of problems with this study. First, the comparison group consisted of patients from medical and surgical services. Since the kinds of life events studied by Hudgens et al. have been shown to produce medical disorders as well as depression (e.g., Holmes & Masuda, 1973), the comparison group is not fully appropriate. Second, Hudgens et al. defined the upsetting life events as stresses, not just losses. They included events in the distant past (for instance, "arrest or prison ever") and recent events that would not usually be construed as losses (for instance, birth of child). If one looks at recent losses on their list, such as deaths in the family, loss of close relationships, quitting jobs, changes of dwelling, or discord at home or work, there are differences in the expected direction, although in any given category they are unlikely to be statistically significant because of their low overall frequency in these samples.

A second kind of objection is that incentive losses produce forms of disturbance other than depression, such as medical disorders (Holmes & Masuda, 1973) and schizophrenia (Brown & Birley, 1968). However, this need not be an objection. There is no reason to suppose that severe incentive losses might not produce other effects of stress. In any case, people report medical disorders and schizophrenic episodes far more rarely in response to losses than they report depressed mood. Although it must be conceded that the effects of incentive losses are not restricted to invigoration, aggression, and depression, the incentive-disengagement cycle does appear to be their characteristic consequence.

2. Lewinsohn and his colleagues have documented the fact that depressed individuals engage in fewer pleasant activities (Lewinsohn & Graf, 1973; MacPhillamy & Lewinsohn, 1974). In these studies, subjects check their activities on a long list of 320 ordinary events, such as laughing, sitting in the sun, wearing clean clothes, having a lively talk, and so on. Neither mood nor number of pleasant activities predicts the other better from one day to the next. Rather, they go together. Lewinsohn interprets these findings to support the notion that depression is caused by too small amounts of reinforcement, but, in fact, the data merely document the clinically observed impression that mood and activity are associated. The findings that a dip in "reinforcements" on one day does not predict mood on the next better than mood predicts "reinforcements" tends, furthermore, to shed much more doubt on the behavioristic approach

than on an incentive-loss approach, since the dip is probably due in large part to the individual's free choices at each moment, and choosing to engage in fewer activities does not constitute thwarting. Therefore, the dip in activities does not constitute loss of incentives in the sense intended here. However, the behavioristic theory clearly interprets it as a reduction in reinforcers, and it should therefore have some power to predict later mood and not just be associated with mood at the same time.

3. One study (Hammen & Glass, 1975) tried to improve subjects' "reinforcements" by instructing them to increase the number of pleasant activities they engage in. The group's mood did not improve relative to that of various control groups; in fact, it worsened slightly. It should be pointed out, however, that the subjects were relatively depressed members of an otherwise normally functioning college class, and they were already engaged in a normal number of pleasant activities (Lewinsohn, 1975).

4. Students moods can also be raised or lowered by having them read prepared first-person statements that praise or derogate the reader; for instance, "I am a likeable person" or "I can't seem to do anything right" (Coleman, 1975, P. 694). Moods in general seem capable of being induced in such ways. Learning lists of aggressive words ("fist," "punch," and so on) makes students readier to deliver electric shocks to others (Turner & Layton, 1976).

5. Additional evidence for the role of norepinephrine in depression and in reward mechanisms is discussed by Stein (1969) and Seligman (1975). However, precisely how norepinephrine is related to aggressive or depressive behavior is still far from clear. As investigators test the "catecholamine hypothesis" in its many ramifications, the evidence they are accumulating has become rather murky (Mendels, 1975). The problems may be due to the fact that it is hard to assess or to affect norepinephrine directly in a living organism without involving reactions with its biochemical precursors or metabolites, which have their own roles to play. It is also still possible, of course, that norepinephrine plays only an incidental role in depression, but the weight of evidence implicating it so far makes this seem unlikely.

6. I am indebted to Ernest D. Kemble for drawing this material on the amygdala to my attention and for interpreting it in the framework of the incentive-disengagement theory.

7. The method used in this and some other studies suffers from relying on dreams recalled hours or days after the fact, thereby confounding the tendency to have certain kinds of dreams with the tendency to recall them. What is needed, of course, is research that examines the content of dreams obtained with systematic awakenings and REM-EEG techniques. Beck and Ward's (1961) generalization that dreams during depression are more "masochistic" (i.e., more filled with events unfavorable to the dreamer) is partly contradicted by a more recent study using similarly flawed methods (Miller, 1969) which suggests that severely depressed patients' dreams are "pleasant or bland" whereas the dreams of depressed patients who are improving are "troubled and troubling" (P. 561). However, this investigator used a very small sample, and, in any case, it is impossible to disentangle whether the differences reside in dream content or in dream memory.

8. Unfortunately, the investigators provide no information concerning what proportion of a comparable nonbereaved sample would also report these problems. Such a comparison is always essential, but it becomes unusually germane in this case, since more than half of the sample is over 60 years of age. The results are cited here in the faith that the respondents were describing changes traceable to their bereavement and that the rate of complaint is higher than that expectable from a comparable nonbereaved sample.

9. The same prediction would also be made by the theory of opponent processes (Solomon & Corbit, 1974; see also Chapter 4) without reference to adaptation-level theory. It may also appear that opponent-process theory could serve as a general theory of depression. Certainly, the aggression and depression phases and probably the invigoration phase of the incentive-disengagement cycle are accompanied by nega-

tive affect, which is what opponent-process theory would predict would happen when an incentive that has been producing positive affect is removed. There are, however, two problems with opponent-process theory as a theory of depression. First, it cannot explain the cycle of activity changes that occur during disengagement. Second, it requires that the incentive whose absence causes the unhappiness has already been enjoyed for a period of time; it therefore does not address itself to the problem of frustration and thwarting before the incentive has been acquired. It might be possible to extend the theory to such cases. One would have to assume that any time thwarting a pursuit causes depression, the incentive that was pursued was of the same kind (in some way) that the person had enjoyed enough on earlier occasions to desire more. This "craving" for the incentive would then form the motivational base for pursuing the incentive at the next opportunity. The stimuli associated with the new incentive would anticipatorily activate the positive emotional process that had been part of enjoying the incentive the previous time. This process would in turn evoke the negative opponent process, which would become manifest when the pursuit failed. Such an explanation makes a number of untested assumptions; but these are testable in principle.

10. Of course, incentives are not the only things that need to be clarified in psychotherapy, and clarifying incentives entails clarifying associated processes such as values. Focusing on incentives, however, and especially on the subset of incentives to which the patient is committed (goals), has certain advantages over focusing on certain other concepts, such as needs. One advantage derives from the status of incentives and of the current concerns that ensue as the pivotal factors in people's thoughts, feelings, and actions. Needs and other such concepts, as these are ordinarily used in psychology, are somewhat more artificial constructs devised by people other than the patient for classifying behavior. They may bear only the roughest correspondence to the functional relationships between the patient and his or her world of concrete incentives. Another advantage of focusing on incentives derives from being able to use in diagnosis and treatment the specific relationships that this theory presents as obtaining between incentive-related events and thoughts, feelings, and actions.

11. It is an interesting sidelight that meditative practices are aimed at exalted feeling without commitment to material incentives. In fact, many oriental religions — Buddhism, Hinduism, early Christianity, and others — preach lifestyles designed quite specifically to eliminate the consequences of commitment to and disengagement from material incentives. The four cardinal vices of Buddhism are Lust, Pride, Anger, and Avarice (Schopenhauer, 1962). The path to really profound meditation — to the loss of ego boundaries — requires renouncing worldly goods and pleasures. This requirement makes sense within the theoretical framework of this book: Successful meditation entails eliminating respondent thought content of the kind induced by current concerns and concern-related cues, something made much more difficult in the presence of powerful concerns.

Chapter 6

1. In the social climate of 1976 my alienation from ties has waned. Alienation, it seems, is reversible!

2. For instance, in three investigations of relationships among Powerlessness, Normlessness, and Social Isolation (Dean, 1961; Middleton, 1963; Simmons, 1966), the correlations among them ranged from .33 to .67, with a median of .53. Since each of these questionnaire scales contained very few questions, sometimes only one, the scale scores must be relatively unreliable, in which case even the low correlations obtained may indicate a substantial degree of relatedness among the underlying dimensions of alienation. There is therefore evidence that the various kinds of belief represented by the different scales have some basic things in common.

3. That is, a subset of dissatisfaction constitutes alienation. Dissatisfaction and alie-

nation are not equivalent concepts, because alienation is subject to conditions that do not apply to dissatisfaction. Also, those conditions color alienated people's cognitions and perhaps also the mix of emotions they feel about their situations.

4. Although there is considerable evidence of widespread dissatisfaction with work, simple questionnaire measures of job satisfaction do not seem to be very sensitive to it. Despite the evident weaknesses of "job satisfaction" as an *absolute* measure of how well people like their jobs, it does, however, have some value as a measure of relative liking. A wide-ranging review of research on employee absenteeism and turnover — two rather unequivocal behavioral indexes — found both of these related to the satisfaction employees expressed with their pay, with supervision, with the particular content of their jobs, and with overall job satisfaction in a variety of different occupations (Porter & Steers, 1973). Much of the evidence described below rests on measures of relative job satisfaction.

5. This is not an invariable finding. Bonjean and Grimes (1970) compared samples of managers, plant workers, and independent businessmen from the same southern community. Like the managers, the independent businessmen regarded their jobs as relatively free of bureaucracy and they scored fairly low in powerlessness on the alienation scale, but they resembled the workers and differed from the managers in isolation, normlessness, anomia, and general alienation.

6. Recent results (Tannenbaum et al., 1974) indicate that Yugoslav workers are no more satisfied with their jobs and are psychologically less well adjusted than U.S. workers. In view of the problems of comparing expressions of satisfaction or adjustment across cultures, and in view of the many factors that affect both satisfaction and adjustment (including, for instance, level of aspiration), the Tannenbaum results need not be interpreted as conflicting with those of Kolaja.

7. I am indebted to Susan Benham and to James S. Morrison for helping to review the literature for this section. In addition, articles by Hicks and Platt (1970) and Levinger (1965) were more helpful than the references to them in the text might indicate.

8. Blood & Wolfe (1960) found results contrary to these: the childless couples in their sample expressed less marital satisfaction than the parents. However, I found no indication that the differences were statistically significant, and the samples of childless couples, matched for life cycle against the parents, were extremely small. For preschool, preadolescent, and adolescent stages, the sample sizes of childless couples were 9, 28, and 9, respectively. It seems best to accept the large-sample survey results collected by Renée and Bradburn.

9. The central role of blocked incentive commitments in identity theory is revealed by the questionnaire and interview instruments recently developed for measuring identity diffusion. These probe for indications that people are blocked from their goals — indications such as their inability to plan or to finish projects (Henry & Sims, 1970). Instruments for measuring identity diffusion also include questions about the respondents' alienation from socially typical values and activities.

Chapter 7

1. Dennis R. Templeman, personal communication, 1971.

2. The concept of communication "massaging" the receiver of the communication was used extensively by Marshall McLuhan (1967). McLuhan, however, focused on the impact of the *method* of communication, whereas the treatment here is concerned with the thematic *content* of the messages. McLuhan's point that the two cannot be neatly separated in practice is well taken. The use of the term "massage" here was, however, adopted independently.

3. For this section I am heavily indebted to Carol Tester Meyer's (unpublished) capable review of the relevant literature.

4. They spend an average of three and one-half hours each week in front of their

televisions sets, but for about one and one-half hours of that time their attention is focused primarily on something else, such as eating, reading, and sewing.

5. Interestingly, appetites for action are much less keen in the age groups over 54, and preference for news, information, and public affairs programming rises there. This parallels other findings, described in Chapter 6, that older people feel less desire for stimulation.

6. The evidence on which these writers' conclusions are based is quite uneven. Chopra (1969) fails to make clear the basis for his assertion that marijuana use is primarily a lower-class phenomenon. Goldberg (1968) and Benabud (1957) reported that the marijuana users among their psychiatric patients or prisoners came disproportionately from the lower classes, but they failed to report the social-class distribution of their nonusers. Charen and Perlman (1946), Freedman and Rockmore (1946 a and b), and Marcovitz and Myers (1944) reported data from selected United States armed forces personnel during World War II. However, given the similarity of their findings and the degree of consensus, it seems reasonable tentatively to accept their conclusion.

7. For other occupational groups the situation is much more ambiguous. Thus, Chambers (1971b) reported that marijuana use by New York professionals and technical workers was among the lowest rates, whereas the National Commission's (1973) survey suggests that it is among the highest. Both surveys reported a relatively high rate for sales personnel (8.6% and 10%, respectively), but the composition of this category is too mixed to permit any clear conclusions for our purposes. It is likely that patterns of marijuana use among nonstudent adults have been changing rapidly since the late 1960s, and that recreational use among several sectors of the public has begun to increase.

8. We would presume that the reason for this relationship is that depressed people turn to drugs in order to change their inner state. Certainly, that is the reason alcoholics often give for starting a drinking bout. However, two experiments brought groups of alcoholics into a hospital laboratory and, over a period of days or weeks, enabled them to work at a routine experimental task for payment in alcohol (Nathan, Titler, Lowenstein, Solomon, & Rossi, 1970; Ryback, 1969). In this way, the investigators could observe these men during an actual drinking spell. One of their findings, paradoxically, is that as the men became extremely intoxicated, they became more, not less, depressed, and their depression gradually declined as they sobered up. How can we account for these results, which fly in the face both of theory and of the statements that alcoholics make about themselves after the fact?

One possibility is that the alcoholic subjects did indeed feel as depressed as they reported at the time but that they experienced something else in their advanced drunkenness that they valued. Another possibility is that the sterile setting of the hospital laboratory, where they had to perform a meaningless task for alcohol and had to submit to numerous tests, depressed them during their intoxication in ways that skid row would not. Finally, it is possible that there comes a point in alcoholism at which alcohol is no longer capable of improving feeling states (Williams, 1966). There is some support for this idea from another such observational study that did not, however, require its drinkers to work for their alcohol (Alterman, Gottheil, & Crawford, 1975). Some of their hospitalized alcoholics decided to drink alcohol offered them on the ward and others in the same program decided not to. Those that drank were on the average less depressed than those that stayed sober during the first week of the program but then grew more depressed in later weeks, while the nondrinkers grew gradually less depressed. The huge quantities of liquor consumed would then constitute heroic efforts to attain a relief experienced before but now no longer possible, and the depression may represent the beginning of disengagement from alcohol. Certainly, the depressed moods of these people are quite contrary to the experiences of lighter drinkers.

In our own questionnaire research with college students, we have found no relationships between feeling depressed on the day of the questionnaire (using the Wessman-

Ricks Personal Feeling Scales) and how often the person reports using alcohol, even though persistent low-order relationships do occur between alcohol use and the sense that life is meaningful.

9. I am grateful to Sheldon M. Bey for reviewing the literature on motivation for narcotics use up to 1972.

10. I am grateful to Rachel Froiland Quenemoen for reviewing the literature on motivation for alcohol use up to 1972.

Chapter 8

1. Apparently, this generalization holds for alcoholism, when defined as alcohol use that seriously interferes with major life activities such as jobs and marriages, but not for milder uses of alcohol or other drugs. Neuropsychiatric patients who committed suicide while hospitalized were *less* often found to be "under the influence of" alcohol and drugs than a nonsuicidal control group (Farberow & MacKinnon, 1974). Probably, the ability to alter mood states with alcohol can stave off suicidal behavior for a time. However, when continued heavy use of alcohol itself becomes a liability, it may join the factors that promote suicide.

2. Few societies regard suicide as a completely neutral act. Some prize it, at least for certain social classes and under certain conditions, and accord it high prestige. Other societies, probably a majority, condemn suicide and shame both the victim's memory and his or her survivors. No doubt the values assigned by the suicide candidate to the act itself plays a role in the decision equation. Presumably, it takes a less miserable outlook than zero to provoke a suicide that will bring prestige, and more miserable outlook to provoke one that will reap shame. I know of no data on this matter.

There is one further qualification. To assert that death without afterlife has zero incentive value assumes that one considers only the event of death itself. Obviously, even for individuals who foresee no afterlife, the prospect of losing one's earthly pleasures — terminating personal relationships, giving up professional aspirations, ending sensory enjoyment, and so forth — can be extremely distressing, assuming that the individual still thinks that these pleasures remain to be enjoyed. In this analysis, however, the value of death is considered separately from the various consequences of death.

3. It is possible to put all of these considerations quantitatively into a type of Expectancy X Value model recently devised by Heckhausen (in press) and still being elaborated (Heckhausen, unpublished). The model as applied to suicide can serve not only to formalize a means of predicting suicide, but also to suggest additional variables, problems, and derivations. Heckhausen distinguishes among three kinds of "valences": outcome valences, action valences, and situation valences. In each case, a valence expresses the degree to which a person is attracted to something — to a particular kind of action outcome, to a particular action, or to a particular situation. In the case of suicide, for instance, the situation may be spending the evening alone in one's apartment, the action may be turning on the gas, the outcome may be death by asphyxiation, and one perceived consequence may be personal obliteration. The valence of an action outcome (V_0) is a function of the summed products of the incentive value (I_k) of each possible consequence of the outcome multiplied by the person's expectancy that the outcome will lead to the consequence ($E_{0 \to c}$). The valence of an action is a function of the product of the valence of the outcome multiplied by the person's expectancy that the action will produce that outcome. The valence of the situation is a function of the product of the valence of the outcome multiplied by the person's expectancy that the situation will produce that outcome without the person having to do anything about it. Finally, Heckhausen defines a further variable, the "action tendency," which in the case of suicide would be the strength of the person's tendency to undertake a suicidal act. An action tendency (T) is a function of the product of the valence of the action outcome times the difference between the person's expectancy that his or her action

will produce the outcome and the expectancy that the situation will produce it without intervention. Algebraically, $T = f [V_0(E_{A\to o} - E_{S\to o})]$.

For purposes of considering suicide, there are two salient kinds of outcomes: dying and continuing to live. There are many kinds of possible actions, these comprising all of the ways one might go about committing suicide plus the fortunately large class of nonsuicidal alternatives. The possible consequences of dying by suicide or surviving are also extremely large and variable from one person to the next. They include, depending on the individual's beliefs, personal obliteration, going to a pleasant afterlife such as heaven, going to an unpleasant afterlife such as hell, going to a mixed afterlife such as purgatory, visiting certain effects on one's survivors such as grief or joy, suffering grief over the loss of earthly pleasures, receiving a good or bad reputation posthumously as a result of having committed suicide by the particular method used, giving up one's earthly current concerns, and, in the event that the suicide is stopped short of completion, the favorable or unfavorable reactions of others toward oneself as a result of having attempted suicide by the particular method used. Algebraically, therefore, we can write the valence of dying by a particular method of suicide as follows:

$$V_{OD} = f(\sum_k I_k \times E_{D\to I_k})$$

where the symbol Σ stands for "sum of"; I_k is the incentive value of the kth of many possible consequences, such as hellfire, the grief of one's widowed spouse, revenge on one's creditor, etc.; and $E_{D\to I_k}$ represents the person's expectancy that his or her dying will indeed produce that consequence. For instance, if I_k were joy at one's spouse's grief, $E_{D\to I_k}$ would be the prospective suicide's assessment of how likely it is that the spouse will indeed grieve, rather than for instance, be overjoyed. In this model, it is possible for some I_k to be negative, as when the thought of one's spouse's grief is distressing. It is also possible for $E_{D\to I_k}$ to be negative, if dying were to hinder the realization of an incentive. For instance, it would be negative if D stood for dying and I_k stood for continuing to work for one's life goals. Therefore, it is also possible for V_{OD}, the outcome valence of dying, to be negative, as, indeed, it is for the overwhelming majority of people who assiduously avoid dying.

Once the valence of dying has been calculated, it is possible to calculate the valence of each possible way of bringing it about:

$$V_{AS_i} = f(V_{OD} \times E_{S_i \to D})$$

Here, V_{AS_i} represents the action valence of the ith method of committing suicide. A person will presumably choose the method that yields the highest valence, or will decide against suicide if all of the methods that occur to him or her yield valences lower than continuing to live.

In most cases, the action valence will be approximately equal to the action tendency. Only when situations inherently endanger the individual's life is the action tendency different. For instance, standing outside during a bombing raid carries a finite risk of being killed and will, according to the formula for action tendencies, reduce the attraction of doing oneself in deliberately. One may speculate that this aspect of the Heckhausen model can account in part for the reduced rate of suicide during wars and other emergencies. However, we have seen that there are also other explanations for this phenomenon that can be applied more generally, for instance to noncombatant parts of the warring population.

It may be useful to illustrate the use of this model by an example. In what follows, incentive values will arbitrarily be allowed to vary between + 10 and − 10 and expectancies between +1.00 and −1.00. The accompanying table depicts an individual suffering from intractable pain who has no belief in an afterlife, an insufferable creditor, weak attachments to spouse, job, and a club, and a family that takes a dim view of suicide.

Type of Incentive	Incentive Value	Expectancy that Dying by Gunfire Will Attain the Incentive	V × E
Relief of intractable pain	+6	+1.00	+6.00
Personal obliteration	0	+1.00	+0.00
Heaven	+10	0.00	0.00
Hell	−10	0.00	0.00
Purgatory	−5	0.00	0.00
Spouse's grief	−2	+0.20	−0.40
Creditor's anger	+3	+1.00	+3.00
Keeping job	+1	−1.00	−1.00
Club membership	+1	−1.00	−1.00
Disparagement of suicide by family	−6	+1.00	−6.00
Sum of products = V_{OD}			+0.60

Assuming that no other incentives operate in this individual's life (a poor assumption, given the small number of incentives listed), the valence of dying by shooting himself or herself is slightly positive. Since the expectancy that shooting oneself will be fatal is also positive, and assuming that no other methods of suicide are preferable, one would predict that the individual will probably shoot himself or herself if nothing in the situation improves. Note, however, that a slightly strengthened concern for the spouse's feelings, an increased estimate of the spouse's probable grief, or increased rewards from job or club could tip the balance the other way. So, of course, could the emergence of a new positive relationship, for instance, with a therapist.

Chapter 9

1. There are limits to this generalization. For instance, if something is inherently dangerous, such as a tornado, an individual may become more frightened of it as he or she learns more about it. As used in this connection, however, "familiar" means to gain experience with perceiving or acting on the thing itself, rather than gathering information about it indirectly. Another limitation is that very strong or painful stimuli sensitize the person to them — the person reacts more sharply than before — rather than habituating. People who have been through a tornado are often more, not less, afraid of tornadoes than before. However, for inherently innocuous stimuli that are not so strong as to engender sensitization, the generalization holds.

2. There are also other factors, of course, that enter into the matter of whether someone remains committed to a very long-term goal. For instance, the person might decide that the accumulating sacrifices are too high. The long-term goal might have been set to satisfy neurotic needs that have meanwhile been eliminated or satisfied more easily. The person might discover a particularly alluring shorter-term goal that diverts the person and causes him or her to give up the long-term goal. Certainly, the temptations of love or immediate gain often take their toll of long-term plans for both achievement and salvation!

3. In recent research (Jellison & Harvey, 1976) people felt that they had the greatest amount of choice when they were faced with many positive, rather than negative, incentives of about equal attractiveness. If the number of alternatives grew too large, however, the result was a sense of confusion rather than of free choice.

4. I am indebted to Truman Driggs for bringing these findings to my attention.

REFERENCES

References

Ach, N. *Ueber den Willensakt und das Temperament*. Leipzig: Van Quelle & Meyer, 1910.

Adamson, R. Contrast effects and reinforcement. In M. H. Appley (Ed.), *Adaptation level theory*. New York: Academic Press, 1971. Pp. 159–168.

Adler, A. *Superiority and social interest: A collection of later writings*. (H. L. Ansbacher and R. R. Ansbacher, Eds.) New York: Viking, 1973.

Albrecht, G. L. The alcoholism process: A social learning viewpoint. In P. G. Bourne & R. Fox (Eds.), *Alcoholism: Progress in research and treatment*. New York: Academic Press, 1973. Pp. 11–42.

Allen, J. R., & West, L. J. Flight from violence: Hippies and the green rebellion. *American Journal of Psychiatry*, 1968, 125, 364–370.

Allport, G. W. *Personality: A psychological interpretation*. New York: Holt, 1937.

Allport, G. W. *Pattern and growth in personality*. New York: Holt, Rinehart and Winston, 1961.

Alterman, A. I., Gottheil, E., & Crawford, H. D. Mood changes in an alcoholism treatment program based on drinking decisions. *American Journal of Psychiatry*, 1975, 132, 1032–1037.

Americans' view of life's satisfactions charted in new volume on social indicators. *ISR Newsletter*, Spring 1976, 4 (2), 6–7.

Amsel, A. The role of frustrative nonreward in noncontinuous reward situations. *Psychological Bulletin*, 1958, 55, 102–119.

Amsel, A. Frustrative nonreward in partial reinforcement and discrimination learning: Some recent history and a theoretical extension. *Psychological Review*, 1962, 69, 306–328.

Amsel, A. Behavioral habituation, counterconditioning, and a general theory of persistence. In A. H. Black & W. F. Prokasy (Eds.), *Classical conditioning II*. New York: Appleton-Century-Crofts, 1972, Pp. 409–426.

Andrews, F. M., & Withey, S. B. *Social indicators of well-being: The development and measurement of perceptual indicators*. New York: Plenum, 1976.

Andrews, J. D. W. The achievement motive and advancement in two types of organizations. *Journal of Personality and Social Psychology*, 1967, 6, 163–168.

Anker, J. L., Milman, D. H., Kahan, S. A., & Valenti, C. Drug usage and related patterns of behavior in university students: I. General survey and marijuana use. *Journal of the American College Health Association*, 1971, 19, 178–186.

Anonymous. The use of marijuana and LSD on the college campus. *Journal of the National Association of Women Deans and Counselors*, 1967, 30, 124–128.

Appley, M. H. (Ed.) *Adaptation-level theory*. New York: Academic Press, 1971.

Archibald, H. C., & Tuddenham, R. D. Persistent stress reaction after combat: A 20-year follow-up. *Archives of General Psychiatry*, 1965, 12, 475–481.

367

Armer, M. Formal education and psychological malaise in an African society. *Sociology of Education*, 1970, 43, 143–158.

Armor, D. J., Polich, J. M., & Stambul, H. B. *Alcoholism and treatment*. Santa Monica, California: Rand, 1976.

Arnold, M. B. *Emotion and personality* (2 vols.). New York: Columbia University Press, 1960.

Arnold, M. B. Historical development of the concept of emotion. Paper presented at the annual meeting of the American Psychological Association, Montreal, 1973.

Atkinson, J. W. *An introduction to motivation*. Princeton, New Jersey: Van Nostrand, 1964.

Atkinson, J. W., & Birch, D. *The dynamics of action*. New York: Wiley, 1970.

Atkinson, J. W., & Raynor, J. O. (Eds.) *Motivation and achievement*. Washington, D.C.: Winston, 1974.

Atkinson, R. C., & Wickens, T. D. Human memory and the concept of reinforcement. In R. Glaser (Ed.), *The nature of reinforcement*. New York: Academic Press, 1971, Pp. 66–120.

Averill, J. R. Grief: Its nature and significance. *Psychological Bulletin*, 1968, 70, 721–748.

Bacon, M. K., Barry, H., III, & Child, I. L. A cross-cultural study of drinking: II. Relations to other features of culture. *Quarterly Journal of Studies on Alcohol*, 1965, Supplement, 3, 29–48.

Baier, K. *The meaning of life*. Canberra: Australian National University Press, 1957.

Bailyn, L. Career and family orientations of husbands and wives in relation to marital happiness. *Human Relations*, 1970, 23, 97–113.

Baker, J. W., II, & Schaie, K. W. Effects of aggressing "alone" or "with another" on physiological and psychological arousal. *Journal of Personality and Social Psychology*, 1969, 12, 80–86.

Bandura, A. Behavior theory and the models of man. *American Psychologist*, 1974, 29, 859–869.

Barber, T. X. *LSD, marijuana, yoga, and hypnosis*. Chicago: Aldine, 1970.

Bardwick, J. M. *The psychology of women*. New York: Harper & Row, 1971.

Barker, R. G., & Barker, L. S. The psychological ecology of old people in Midwest, Kansas, and Yoredale, Yorkshire. In B. L. Neugarten (Ed.), *Middle age and aging: A reader in social psychology*. Chicago: University of Chicago Press, 1968. Pp. 453–460.

Barker, R. H., Dembo, T., & Lewin, K. Frustration and regression: An experiment with young children. *University of Iowa Studies in Child Welfare*, 1941, 18 (1).

Barnard, C. I. *The functions of the executive*. Cambridge, Mass.: Harvard University Press, 1938.

Barnett, R. C. The relationship between occupational preference and occupational prestige: A study of sex differences and age trends. Paper presented at the annual meeting of the American Psychological Association, Montreal, 1973.

Barry, H., III, Buchwald, C., Child, I. L., & Bacon, M. K. A cross-cultural study of drinking: IV. Comparisons with Horton ratings. *Quarterly Journal of Studies on Alcohol*, 1965, Supplement No. 3, 62–77.

Barry, H., III, & Miller, N. E. Effects of drugs on approach-avoidance conflict tested repeatedly by means of a "telescope alley." *Journal of Comparative and Physiological Psychology*, 1962, 55, 201–210.

Barta, S. G., Kemble, E. D., & Klinger, E. Abolition of cyclic activity changes following amygdaloid lesions in rats. *Bulletin of the Psychonomic Society*, 1975, 5, 236–238.

Bass, B. M. The substance and the shadow. *American Psychologist*, 1974, 29, 870–886.

Beamer, W., Bermant, G., & Clegg, M. T. Copulatory behavior of the ram, *Ovis aries*. II: Factors affecting copulatory satiation. *Animal Behavior*, 1969, 17, 706–711.

Bean, F. D., Bonjean, C. M., & Burton, M. G. Intergenerational occupational mobility and alienation. *Social Forces*, 1973, 52, 62–73.

Beck, A. T. *Depression: Clinical, experimental, and theoretical aspects*. New York: Harper & Row, 1967.

Beck, A. T. The development of depression: A cognitive model. In R. J. Friedman & M. M. Katz (Eds.), *The psychology of depression: Contemporary theory and research*. Washington, D.C.: Winston, 1974.

Beck, A. T., & Ward, C. H. Dreams of depressed patients. *Archives of General Psychiatry*, 1961, 5, 462–467.

Becker, J. *Depression: Theory and research*. Washington, D.C.: Winston, 1974.

Benabud, A. Psycho-pathological aspects of the Cannabis situation in Morocco: Statistical data for 1956. *U.N. Bulletin on Narcotics*, 1957, 4, 1–16.

Berger, D. F. Alternative interpretations of the frustration effect. *Journal of Experimental Psychology*, 1969, 81, 475–483.

Berger, R. J. Experimental modification of dream content by meaningful verbal stimuli. *British Journal of Psychiatry*, 1963, 109, 722–740.

Berkowitz, L. *Aggression: A social psychological analysis*. New York: McGraw-Hill, 1962.

Berlyne, D. E. Arousal and reinforcement. In D. Levine (Ed.) *Nebraska symposium on motivation*. Lincoln: University of Nebraska Press, 1967. Pp. 1–110.

Berlyne, D. E. *Aesthetics and psychobiology*. New York: Appleton-Century-Crofts, 1971.

Berman, P. W. Attraction to infants: Are sex differences innate and invariant? Paper presented at the annual meeting of the American Psychological Association, Chicago, 1975.

Bezucha, R. J. The revolution of 1830 and the city of Lyon. In J. M. Merriman (Ed.), *1830 in France*. New York: Franklin Watts, 1975. Pp. 119–138.

Bickford, H. L., & Neal, A. G. Alienation and social learning: A study of students in a vocational training center. *Sociology of Education*, 1969, 42, 141–153.

Bindra, D. Neuropsychological interpretation of the effects of drive and incentive-motivation on general activity and instrumental behavior. *Psychological Review*, 1968, 75, 1–22.

Bindra, D. A motivational view of learning, performance, and behavior modification. *Psychological Review*, 1974, 81, 199–213.

Birenbaum, G. Das Vergessen einer Vornahme. *Psychologische Forschung*, 1930, 13, 218–284.

Blake, B. F., Wick, E., Burke, W., & Sanesino, A. The early adolescent's personality and his style of marijuana usage. Paper presented at the annual meeting of the American Psychological Association, New Orleans, 1974.

Blanchard, F. A., Adelman, L., & Cook, S. W. Effect of group success and failure upon interpersonal attraction in cooperating interracial groups. *Journal of Personality and Social Psychology*, 1975, 31, 1020–1030.

Bleuler, M. *Die Depressionen in der arztlichen Allgemeinpraxis*. (2nd Edition.) Basel: Benno Schwabe, 1948.

Blood, R. O., Jr., & Wolfe, D. M. *Husbands and wives: The dynamics of modern living*. New York: Free Press, 1960.

Bloom, B. S., & Broder, L. J. *Problem-solving processes of college students: An exploratory investigation*. Chicago: University of Chicago Press, 1950.

Blum, R. H., & Associates. *Society and drugs*. San Francisco, California: Jossey-Bass, 1969.

Blum, R. H., & Associates. *Horatio Alger's children*. San Francisco, California: Jossey-Bass, 1972.

Blumberg, P. *Industrial democracy: The sociology of participation*. London: Constable, 1968.

Bolles, R. C. Reinforcement, expectancy, and learning. *Psychological Review*, 1972, 79, 394–409.

Bolles, R. C. *Theory of motivation*. (2nd Edition.) New York: Harper & Row, 1975.

Bonjean, C. M., & Grimes, M. D. Bureaucracy and alienation: A dimensional approach. *Social Forces*, 1970, 48, 365–373.

Bortner, R. W. Systems implications of improvements in adult learning. In D. F. Hultsch & R. W. Bortner (Eds.) *Interventions in learning: The individual and society*. A symposium presented at the 27th annual meeting of the Gerontological Society, Portland, Oregon, 1974. Offset. Pp. 36–64.

Bortner, R. W., Hultsch, D. F., Wiorkowski, J. J., & Scott, D. T. A taxonomy of patterns of personal time perspective and subjective deprivation. Unpublished paper, 1975.

Bowlby, J. Grief and mourning in infancy and childhood. In R. E. Eissler et al. (Eds.), *The Psychoanalytic Study of the Child*, 1960, 15, 9–52.

Bowlby, J. *Attachment and loss*. Vol. 2. *Separation*. New York: Basic Books, 1973.

Bradburn, N. M. *The structure of psychological well-being*. Chicago: Aldine, 1969.

Braden, W., Stillman, R. C., & Wyatt, R. J. Effects of marihuana on contingent negative variation and reaction time. *Archives of General Psychiatry*, 1974, 31, 537–541.

Breed, W. Five components of a basic suicide syndrome. *Life-Threatening Behavior*, 1972, 2, 3–18.

Brehm, J. W. *Responses to loss of freedom: A theory of psychological reactance*. Morristown, N.J.: General Learning Press, 1972.

Brewer, W. F. There is no convincing evidence for operant or classical conditioning in adult humans. In W. B. Weimer & D. S. Palermo (Eds.), *Cognition and the symbolic processes*. Hillsdale, N.J.: Erlbaum, 1974. Pp. 1–42.

Brill, N. Q., Crumpton, E., & Grayson, H. M. Personality factors in marijuana use. *Archives of General Psychiatry*, 1971, 24, 163–165.

Britton, J. H., & Britton, J. O. *Personality changes in aging: A longitudinal study of community residents*. New York: Springer, 1972.

Brown, G. W., & Birley, J. L. T. Crises and life changes and the onset of schizophrenia. *Journal of Health and Social Behavior*, 1968, 9, 203–214.

Bull, N., & Strongin, E. The complex of frustration: A new interpretation. *Journal of Nervous and Mental Disease*, 1956, 123, 531–535.

Burnstein, E., & Zajonc, R. B. Individual task performance in a changing social structure. *Sociometry*, 1965, 28, 16–29.

Bush, L. E., II. Individual differences multidimensional scaling of adjectives denoting feelings. *Journal of Personality and Social Psychology*, 1973, 25, 50–57.

Butterfield, E. C. The interruption of tasks: Methodological, factual, and theoretical issues. *Psychological Bulletin*, 1964, 62, 309–322.

Button, A. D. A study of alcoholics with the MMPI. *Quarterly Journal of Studies on Alcohol*, 1956, 17, 263–281.

Byrne, D. Repression-sensitization as a dimension of personality. In B. A. Maher (Ed.), *Progress in experimental personality research* (Vol. 1). New York: Academic Press, 1964. Pp. 169–220.

Cahalan, D. *Problem drinkers*. San Francisco, California: Jossey-Bass, 1970.

Calder, B. J., & Staw, B. M. Self-perception of intrinsic and extrinsic motivation. *Journal of Personality and Social Psychology*, 1975, 31, 599–605.

Campbell, D., Sanderson, R. E., & Laverty, S. G. Characteristics of a conditioned response in human subjects during extinction trials following a single traumatic conditioning trial. *Journal of Abnormal Social Psychology*, 1964, 68, 627–639.

Caplan, N. Competency among the hard-to-employ youths. Springfield, Va.: National Technical Information Service, U.S. Department of Commerce, 1973.

Casler, L. Marriage motives in two college populations. *Personality*, 1970, 1, 221–229.

Cattell, R. B., & Nesselroade, J. R. Likeness and completeness theories examined by 16 personality factor measures on stably and unstably married couples. *Journal of Personality and Social Psychology*, 1967, 7, 351–361.

Chambers, C. D. *An assessment of drug use in the general population*. Albany, New York: Special New York State Narcotic Addiction Control Commission, 1971. (a)

Chambers, C. D. *Differential drug use within the New York State labor force*. Albany, New York: New York State Narcotic Addiction Control Commission, 1971. (b)

Charen, S., & Perelman, L. Personality studies of marijuana addicts. *American Journal of Psychiatry*, 1946, 102, 674–682.

Cherry, E. C. Experiments on the recognition of speech with one and two ears. *Journal of the Acoustical Society of America*, 1953, 25, 975–979.

Chiriboga, D. A., & Lowenthal, M. F. Psychological adaptation in later life: A dual model. Paper presented at the annual meeting of the American Orthopsychiatric Association, San Francisco, 1974.

Chopra, G. S. Man and marijuana. *The International Journal of the Addictions*, 1969, 4, 215–247.

Cicero, T. J., Myers, R. D., & Black, W. C. Increase in volitional ethanol consumption following interference with a learned avoidance response. *Physiology and Behavior*, 1968, 3, 657–660.

Claghorn, J. The anxiety-depression syndrome. *Psychosomatics*, 1970, 11, 438–441.

Clark, P. B., & Wilson, J. Q. Incentive systems: A theory of organizations. *Administrative Science*, 1961, 6, 129–166.

Clark, R., & Polish, E. Avoidance conditioning and alcohol consumption in Rhesus monkeys. *Science*, 1960, 132, 223–224.

Clayton, P. J., Halikas, J. A., & Maurice, W. L. The bereavement of the widowed. *Diseases of the Nervous System*, 1971, 32, 597–604.

Clayton, P. J., Halikas, J. A., & Maurice, W. L. The depression of widowhood. *British Journal of Psychiatry*, 1972, 120, 71–78.

Cole, S. O. Experimental effects of amphetamines: A review. *Psychological Bulletin*, 1967, 68, 81–90.

Coleman, R. E. Manipulation of self-esteem as a determinant of mood of elated and depressed women. *Journal of Abnormal Psychology*, 1975, 84, 693–700.

Condry, J. The role of initial interest and task performance on intrinsic motivation. Paper read at the annual meeting of the American Psychological Association, Chicago, 1975.

Corteen, R. S., & Wood, B. Autonomic responses to shock-associated words in an unattended channel. *Journal of Experimental Psychology*, 1972, 94, 308–313.

Cortina, F. M. *Stroke a slain warrior*. New York: Columbia University Press, 1971.

Costello, C. G. Depression: Loss of reinforcers or loss of reinforcer effectiveness? *Behavior Therapy*, 1972, 3, 240–247.

Crumbaugh, J. C., & Maholick, L. T. An experimental study in existentialism: The psychometric approach to Frankl's concept of noögenic neurosis. *Journal of Clinical Psychology*, 1964, 20, 200–207.

Crumbaugh, J. C., & Maholick, L. T. *Manual of instructions for the Purpose-in-Life test*. Lafayette, Indiana: Psychometric Affiliates, 1969.

Cumming, E., & Henry, W. E. *Growing old: The process of disengagement*. New York: Basic Books, 1961.

Daly, H. B. Learning of a hurdle-jump response to escape cues paired with reduced reward or frustrative nonreward. *Journal of Experimental Psychology*, 1969, 79, 146–157. (a)

Daly, H. B. Is instrumental responding necessary for nonreward following reward to be frustrating? *Journal of Experimental Psychology*, 1969, 80, 186–187. (b)

Dante Alighieri. [*The divine comedy of Dante Alighieri*] (C. E. Norton, Trans.). Boston: Houghton Mifflin, 1941.

Davis, D. R. Recovery from depression. *British Journal of Medical Psychology*, 1952, 25, 104–113.

Davis, M. Effects of interstimulus interval length and variability on startle-response habituation in the rat. *Journal of Comparative and Physiological Psychology*, 1970, 72, 177–192.

Davis, W. L., & Phares, E. J. Internal-external control as a determinant of information-seeking in a social influence situation. *Journal of Personality*, 1967, 35, 547–561.

Davis, W. L., & Phares, E. J. Parental antecedents of internal-external control of reinforcement. *Psychological Reports*, 1969, 24, 427–436.

Dean, D. G. Alienation: Its meaning and measurement. *American Sociological Review*,
1961, 26, 753–758.

De Charms, R. *Personal causation: The internal affective determinants of behavior*. New York:
Academic Press, 1968.

DeGroot, A. *Thought and choice in chess*. The Hague: Mouton, 1965.

Deikman, A. J. Deautomatization and the mystic experience. In C. T. Tart (Ed.), *Altered
states of consciousness*. New York: Wiley, 1969. Pp. 23–43.

DeKoninck, J.-M., & Koulack, D. Dream content and adaptation to a stressful situation.
Journal of Abnormal Psychology, 1975, 84, 250–260.

Dembo, T. Der Ärger als dynamisches Problem. *Psychologische Forschung*, 1931, 15,
1–144.

Dennet, D. C. Why the Law of Effect will not go away. *Journal of the Theory of Social
Behavior*, 1975, 5, 169–187.

Deutscher, I. The quality of postparental life. In B. L. Neugarten (Ed.), *Middle age and
aging: A reader in social psychology*. Chicago: University of Chicago Press, 1968. Pp.
263–268.

Dienstbier, R. A., & Munter, P. O. Cheating as a function of the labeling of natural
arousal. *Journal of Personality and Social Psychology*, 1971, 17, 208–213.

DiLollo, V., Davidson, R. C., Hammond, G. R., & Donovan, R. J. The relative effects of
nonreward and response thwarting on the frustration effect. *Psychonomic Science*,
1968, 10, 31–32.

Doerries, L. E. Purpose in life and social participation. *Journal of Individual Psychology*,
1970, 26, 50–53.

Dollard, J., Doob, L. W., Miller, N. E., Mowrer, O. H., & Sears, R. R. *Frustration and
aggression*. New Haven: Yale University Press, 1939.

Dollard, J., & Miller, N. E. *Personality and psychotherapy*. New York: McGraw-Hill, 1950.

Drug use still high among American youths, latest findings from longitudinal study
show. *ISR Newsletter*, Summer 1975, 3.

Dublin, L. I. *Suicide: A sociological and statistical study*. New York: Ronald, 1963.

Durkheim, E. [*Suicide: A study in sociology*] (G. Simpson, Ed. and Trans., J. A. Spauld-
ing, Trans.). New York: Free Press, 1951. (Originally published, 1930.)

Dweck, C. S., & Reppucci, N. D. Learned helplessness and reinforcement responsibility in children. *Journal of Personality and Social Psychology*, 1973, 25, 109–116.

Easterbrook, J. A. The effect of emotion on cue utilization and the organization of
behavior. *Psychological Review*, 1959, 66, 183–201.

Eden, D. Intrinsic and extrinsic rewards and motives: Replication and extension with
kibbutz workers. *Journal of Applied Social Psychology*, 1975, 5, 348–361.

Edwards, W. The theory of decision making. *Psychological Bulletin*, 1954, 51, 380–417.

Eibl-Eibesfeldt, I. *Ethology: The biology of behavior* (E. Klinghammer, Trans.). New York:
Holt, Rinehart, and Winston, 1970.

Eisenberger, R. Explanation of rewards that do not reduce tissue needs. *Psychological
Bulletin*, 1972, 77, 319–339.

Ekman, P. Universals and cultural differences in facial expressions of emotion. In J.
Cole (Ed.), *Nebraska Symposium on Motivation, 1971*. Lincoln: University of Nebraska
Press, 1972. Pp. 207–283.

Ekman, P., Sorenson, E. R., & Friesen, W. V. Pan-cultural elements in facial displays of
emotion. *Science*, 1969, 164, 86–88.

Erdelyi, M. H. A new look at the new look: Perceptual defense and vigilance. *Psychological Review*, 1974, 81, 1–25.

Erikson, E. H. *Childhood and society*. New York: Norton, 1963.

Ervin, F. R., Mark, V. H., & Stevens, J. Behavioral and affective responses to brain stimulation in man. In J. Zubin & C. Shagass (Eds.), *Neurobiological aspects of psychopathology*. New York: Grune & Stratton, 1969.

Estes, W. K. Reward in human learning: Theoretical issues and strategic choice points. In R. Glaser (Ed.), *The nature of reinforcement*. New York: Academic Press, 1971. Pp. 16–36.

Evans, B. *Dictionary of quotations*. New York: Delacorte, 1968.

Fantz, R. L., Fagan, J. F., III, & Miranda, S. B. Early visual selectivity. In L. B. Cohen & P. Salapatek (Eds.), *Infant perception: From sensation to cognition*. Vol. 1: *Basic visual processes*. New York: Academic Press, 1975. Pp. 249–345.

Farberow, N. L., Heilig, S. M., & Litman, R. E. Evaluation and management of suicidal persons. In E. S. Shneidman, N. L. Farberow, & R. E. Litman (Eds.), *The psychology of suicide*. New York: Science House, 1970. Pp. 273–291. (Reprinted from *Techniques in crisis intervention: A training manual*. Los Angeles, California: Suicide Prevention Center, 1968.)

Farberow, N. L., & MacKinnon, D. A suicide prediction schedule for neuropsychiatric hospital patients. *Journal of Nervous and Mental Disease*, 1974, 158, 408–419.

Farberow, N. L., & McEvoy, T. L. Suicide among patients with anxiety or depressive reactions. In E. S. Shneidman, N. L. Farberow, & R. E. Litman (Eds.), *The psychology of suicide*. New York: Science House, 1970. Pp. 345–368. (Reprinted from *Journal of Abnormal Psychology*, 1966, 71, 287–299.)

Farberow, N. L., McKelligott, J. W., Cohen, S., & Darbonne, A. Suicide among cardiovascular patients. In E. S. Shneidman, N. L. Farberow, & R. E. Litman (Eds.), *The psychology of suicide*. New York: Science House, 1970. Pp. 369–384. (Reprinted from *Journal of the American Medical Association*, 1966, 195, 422–428.)

Farberow, N. L., & Shneidman, E. S. Suicide and age. In E. S. Shneidman, N. L. Farberow, & R. E. Litman (Eds.), *The psychology of suicide*. New York: Science House, 1970. Pp. 164–174. (Reprinted from E. S. Shneidman & N. L. Farberow (Eds.), *Clues to suicide*. New York: McGraw-Hill, 1957.)

Farberow, N. L., Shneidman, E. S., & Leonard, C. V. Suicidal risk among schizophrenic patients. In E. S. Shneidman, N. L. Farberow, & R. E. Litman (Eds.), *The psychology of suicide*. New York: Science House, 1970. Pp. 307–324. (a)

Farberow, N. L., Shneidman, E. S., & Leonard, C. V. Suicide among patients with malignant neoplasms. In E. S. Shneidman, N. L. Farberow, & R. E. Litman (Eds.), *The psychology of suicide*. New York: Science House, 1970. Pp. 325–344. (b)

Farberow, N. L., Shneidman, E. S., & Neuringer, C. Case history and neuropsychiatric hospitalization factors in suicide. In E. S. Shneidman, N. L. Farberow, & R. E. Litman (Eds.), *The psychology of suicide*. New York: Science House, 1970. Pp. 385–402. (Reprinted from *Journal of Nervous and Mental Disease*, 1966, 142, 32–44.)

Fein, M. The myth of job enrichment. *The Humanist*, 1973, 33 (5), 30–32.

Felton, B., & Kahana, E. Adjustment and situationally-bound locus of control among institutionalized aged. *Journal of Gerontology*, 1974, 29, 295–301.

Fernandez, R. In *American Report*, 1973, 4 (6), 19.

Ferster, C. B. Behavioral approaches to depression. In R. J. Friedman & M. M. Katz (Eds.), *The psychology of depression: Contemporary theory and research*. Washington, D.C.: Winston, 1974. Pp. 29–45.

Festinger, L. A theoretical interpretation of shifts in level of aspiration. *Psychological Review*, 1942, 49, 235–250.

Field, P. B. A new cross-cultural study of drunkenness. In D. J. Pittman & C. R. Snyder (Eds.), *Society, culture, and drinking patterns*. New York: Wiley, 1962. Pp. 48–74.

Fisher, A. E., Effects of stimulus variation on sexual satiation in the male rat. *Journal of Comparative and Physiological Psychology*, 1962, 55, 614–620.

Fitzgerald, R. C. Reactions to blindness: An exploratory study of adults with recent loss of sight. *Archives of General Psychiatry*, 1970, 22, 370–379.

Ford, R. N. Job enrichment lessons from AT&T. *Harvard Business Review*, 1973, 51 (1), 96–106.

Forehand, R., & Baumeister, A. A. Rate of stereotyped body rocking of severe retardates as a function of frustration of goal-directed behavior. *Journal of Abnormal Psychology*, 1971, 78, 35–42.

Fowler, H. Implications of sensory reinforcement. In R. Glaser (Ed.), *The nature of reinforcement*. New York: Academic Press, 1971. Pp. 151–195.

Fowler, H., & Whalen, R. E. Variation in incentive stimulus and sexual behavior in the male rat. *Journal of Comparative and Physiological Psychology*, 1961, 54, 68–71.

Frankl, V. E. *Man's search for meaning: An introduction to logotherapy*. New York: Washington Square, 1963.

Frankl, V. E. *Psychotherapy and existentialism: Selected papers on logotherapy*. New York: Simon and Schuster, 1967.

Frankl, V. E. *The will to meaning: Foundations and applications of logotherapy*. New York: New American Library, 1969.

Freed, E. X. Effect of alcohol on conflict behaviors. *Psychological Reports*, 1968, 23, 151–159.

Freedman, H. L., & Rockmore, M. J. Marijuana; a factor in personality evaluation and army maladjustment. Part I. *Journal of Clinical Psychopathology*, 1946, 7, 765–782. (a)

Freedman, H. L., & Rockmore, M. J. Marijuana; a factor in personality evaluation and army maladjustment. Part II. *Journal of Clinical Psychopathology*, 1946, 8, 221–236. (b)

Freud, S. *Civilization and its discontents*. [1930] (J. Strachey, Trans. & Ed.) New York: Norton, 1961.

Freud, S. [*A general introduction to psychoanalysis.*] (J. Riviere, Trans.) New York: Perma Giants, 1949. (Originally published, 1920.)

Freud, S. Instincts and their vicissitudes. In *Collected papers* (Vol. 4). London: Hogarth, 1953. (Originally published, 1915.)

Fried, J., Weitman, M., & Davis, M. K. Man-machine interaction and absenteeism. *Journal of Applied Psychology*, 1972, 56, 428–429.

Friedman, A. S. Hostility factors and clinical improvement in depressed patients. *Archives of General Psychiatry*, 1970, 23, 524–537.

Fromm, E. *The anatomy of destructiveness*. New York: Holt, Rinehart and Winston, 1973.

Gallup, G. G., Jr., & Altomari, E. Activity as a postsituation measure of frustrative nonreward. *Journal of Comparative and Physiological Psychology*, 1969, 68, 382–384.

Garcia, J., Hankins, W. G., & Rusiniak, K. W. Behavioral regulation of the milieu interne in man and rat. *Science*, 1974, 185, 824–831.

Gartlan, J. S., & Brain, C. K. Ecology and social variability in *Cercopithecus aethiops* and *C. mitis*. In P. C. Jay (Ed.), *Primates: Studies in adaptation and variability*. New York: Holt, Rinehart and Winston, 1968. Pp. 253–292.

Garvey, A. J. Age and social class differences in values, interests, and job satisfaction. Paper presented at the annual meeting of the American Psychological Association, Montreal, 1973.

Gatchel, R. J., & Proctor, J. D. Physiological correlates of learned helplessness in man. *Journal of Abnormal Psychology*, 1976, 85, 27–34.

Gattozzi, A. A. *Lithium in the treatment of mood disorders* (NIMH, National Clearinghouse for Mental Health Information Publication No. 5033). Washington, D.C.: U.S. Government Printing Office, 1970.

Gentry, W. D. Sex differences in the effects of frustration and attack on emotion and vascular processes. *Psychological Reports*, 1970, 27, 383–390.

Gerard, H. B., Conolley, E. S., & Wilhelmy, R. A. Compliance, justification, and cognitive change. In L. Berkowitz (Ed.), *Advances in experimental social psychology* (Vol. 7). New York: Academic Press, 1974. Pp. 217–247.

Giambra, L. M. Daydreaming across the life span: Late adolescent to senior citizen. *International Journal of Aging and Human Development*, 1974, 5, 115–140.

Gilbert, D. H. Reward expectancy strength as related to the magnitude of frustration in children. Unpublished Ph.D. dissertation, University of Southern California, 1969.

Glick, I. O., Weiss, R. S., & Parkes, C. M. *The first year of bereavement*. New York: Wiley, 1974.

Glickman, S. E. Responses and reinforcement. In R. A. Hinde & J. Stevenson-Hinde (Eds.), *Constraints on learning: Limitations and predispositions*. New York: Academic Press, 1973. Pp. 207–241.

Glickman, S. E., & Schiff, B. B. A biological theory of reinforcement. *Psychological Review*, 1967, 74, 81–109.

Goldberg, L. Drug abuse in Sweden. *U.N. Bulletin on Narcotics*, 1968, 20, 1–31.

Goldstein, J. W. Motivations for psychoactive drug use among students. Department of Psychology Report No. 71–15. Pittsburgh: Carnegie-Nellon University, 1971.

Goldstein, J. W. On the explanation of student drug use. In E. Goode (Ed.), *Marijuana*. (2nd Edition.) Chicago: Aldine-Atherton, 1972.

Goode, E. *The marijuana smokers*. New York: Basic Books, 1970.

Goodenough, F. Expressions of the emotions in a blind-deaf child. *Journal of Abnormal and Social Psychology*, 1932, 27, 328–333.

Goodhart, P., & Chataway, C. *War without weapons*. London: Allen, 1968.

Goodman, D. A., & Weinberger, N. M. Habituation in "lower" tetrapod vertebrates: Amphibia as vertebrate model systems. In H. V. S. Peeke & M. J. Herz (Eds.), *Habituation*. Volume 1. *Behavioral studies*. New York: Academic Press, 1973. Pp. 85–140.

Goodwin, F. K., & Bunney, W. E., Jr. Psychobiological aspects of stress and affective illness. In J. P. Scott & E. C. Senay (Eds.), *Separation and depression: Clinical and research aspects*. Washington, D.C.: American Association for the Advancement of Science, 1973. Pp. 91–112.

Goss, A., & Morosko, T. E. Alcoholism and clinical symptoms. *Journal of Abnormal Psychology*, 1969, 74, 682–684.

Gouaux, C. Induced affective states and interpersonal attraction. *Journal of Personality and Social Psychology*, 1971, 20, 37–43.

Graham, F. K. Habituation and dishabituation of responses innervated by the autonomic nervous system. In H. V. S. Peeke & M. J. Herz (Eds.), *Habituation*. Vol. 1. *Behavioral studies*. New York: Academic Press, 1973. Pp. 163–218.

Gray, J. *The psychology of fear and stress*. New York: McGraw-Hill, 1971.

Greenbaum, C. W., Cohn, A., & Krauss, R. M. Choice, negative information, and attractiveness of tasks. *Journal of Personality*, 1965, 33, 46–59.

Greenberg, D., Uzgiris, I. C., & Hunt, J. McV. Attentional preference and experience: III. Visual familiarity and looking time. *Journal of Genetic Psychology*, 1970, 117, 123–135.

Greene, D., & Lepper, M. R. An information-processing approach to intrinsic and extrinsic motivation. Paper presented at the annual meeting of the American Psychological Association, Chicago, 1975.

Greeno, J. G. The structure of memory and the process of solving problems. In R. L. Solso (Ed.), *Contemporary issues in cognitive psychology: The Loyola Symposium*. Washington, D.C.: Winston, 1973. Pp. 103–133.

Grinker, R. R., Miller, J. Sabshin, M., Nunn, R., & Nunnally, J. C. *The phenomena of depressions*. New York: Harper & Row, 1961.

Gurin, G., Veroff, J., & Feld, S. *Americans view their mental health*. New York: Basic Books, 1960.

Guthrie, E. R. *The psychology of learning*. New York: Harper & Row, 1935.

Hahn, D. K. Why don't workers want to be promoted? Paper presented at the annual meeting of the American Psychological Association, Chicago, 1975.

Hammen, C. L., & Glass, D. R. Depression, activity, and evaluation of reinforcement. *Journal of Abnormal Psychology*, 1975, 84, 718–721.

Harris, L., & Associates. *The myth and reality of aging in America*. Washington, D.C.: National Council on the Aging, 1975.

Harris, V. A., & Katkin, E. S. Primary and secondary emotional behavior: An analysis of the role of autonomic feedback on affect, arousal, and attribution. *Psychological Bulletin*, 1975, 82, 904–916.

Harrison, A. A., & Crandall, R. Heterogeneity and homogeneity of exposure sequence and the attitudinal effects of exposure. *Journal of Personality and Social Psychology*, 1972, 21, 234–238.

Harrison, A. A., Tutone, R. M., & McFadgen, D. G. Effects of frequency of exposure of changing and unchanging stimulus pairs on affective ratings. *Journal of Personality and Social Psychology*, 1971, 20, 102–111.

Havighurst, R. J., Neugarten, B. L., & Tobin, S. S. Disengagement and patterns of aging. In B. L. Neugarten (Ed.), *Middle age and aging: A reader in social psychology*. Chicago: University of Chicago Press, 1968, Pp. 161–172.

Heath, R. G. Electrical self-stimulation of the brain in man. *American Journal of Psychiatry*, 1963, 120, 571–577.

Heath, R. G. (Ed.) *The role of pleasure in behavior*. New York: Hoeber, 1964.

Hebb, D. O. *The organization of behavior*. New York: Wiley, 1949.

Heckhausen, H. Achievement motive research: Current problems and some contributions toward a general theory of motivation. In W. J. Arnold (Ed.), *Nebraska Symposium on Motivation* (Vol. 16). Lincoln: University of Nebraska Press, 1968. Pp. 103–174.

Heckhausen, H. Change in attractiveness of task after failure: Cognitive dissonance theory versus achievement motivation theory. In J. Linhart (Ed.), *Proceedings of the International Conference on Psychology of Human Learning* (Vol. 1). Prague: Institute of Psychology, Czechoslovak Academy of Sciences, 1970. Pp. 191–203.

Heckhausen, H. Die Interaction der Sozialisationsvariablen in der Genese des Leistungsmotivs. In H. Thomae (Ed.), *Sozialisation*. (Vol. 7 of *Handbuch der Psychologie*.) Göttingen: Hogrefe, 1972.

Heckhausen, H. Intervening cognitions in motivation. In D. E. Berlyne & K. B. Madsen (Eds.), *Pleasure, reward, preference*. New York: Academic Press, 1973. Pp. 217–242.

Heckhausen, H. Fear of failure as a self-reinforcing motive system. In I. G. Sarason & C. Spielberger (Eds.), *Stress and Anxiety* (Vol. 2). Washington, D.C.: Hemisphere, 1975. Pp. 117–128. (a)

Heckhausen, H. Effort expenditure, aspiration level and self-evaluation before and after unexpected performance shifts: The role of motive constructs and of task-related cognitions. Unpublished paper, 1975. (b)

Heckhausen, H. Ein kognitives Motivationsmodell und die Verankerung von Motivkonstrukten. In H. Lenk (Ed.), *Handlungstheorien in interdisziplinärer Perspektive*. In press.

Heckhausen, H. Motivation and its constructs: A cognitive model. In preparation.

Heckhausen, H., & Weiner, B. The emergence of a cognitive psychology of motivation. In P. C. Dodwell (Ed.), *New horizons in psychology (Vol. 2). London: Penguin, 1972*.

Heinicke, C. M. Parental deprivation in early childhood: A predisposition to later depression? In J. P. Scott & E. C. Senay (Eds.), *Separation and depression: Clinical and research aspects*. Washington, D.C.: American Association for the Advancement of Science, 1973. Pp. 141–160.

Heinicke, C., & Westheimer, I. *Brief separations*. New York: International Universities Press, 1966.

Helson, H. *Adaptation-level theory: An experimental and systematic approach to behavior*. New York: Harper & Row, 1964.

Henke, P. G., & Maxwell, D. Lesions in the amygdala and the frustration effect. *Physiology and Behavior*, 1973, 10, 647–650.

Henry, W. E., & Sims, J. H. Actors' search for a self. *Trans-action*, 1970, September, 57–62.

Hess, E. H. Ethology and developmental psychology. In P. H. Mussen (Ed.), *Carmichael's manual of child psychology* (3rd Edition, Vol. 1). New York: Wiley, 1970. Pp. 1–38.

Hicks, M. W., & Platt, M. Marital happiness and stability: A review of the research in the sixties. *Journal of Marriage and the Family*, 1970, 32, 553–574.

Higgins, R. L., & Marlatt, G. A. Fear of interpersonal evaluations as a determinant of alcohol consumption in male social drinkers. *Journal of Abnormal Psychology*, 1975, 84, 644–651.

Hinckley, R. G. Nonmedical drug use among college student psychiatric patients. *Journal of the American College Health Association*, 1970, 18, 333–341.

Hinton, B. L. Environmental frustrations and creative problem-solving. *Journal of Applied Psychology*, 1968, 52, 211–217.

Hiroto, D. S. The relationship between learned helplessness and locus of control. Unpublished Ph.D. thesis, University of Portland, 1971.

Hirschman, R., & Brumbaugh-Buehler, B. Electrodermal habituation and subjective response. *Journal of Abnormal Psychology*, 1975, 84, 46–50.

Hoffman, H. S., & Solomon, R. L. An opponent-process theory of motivation: III. Some affective dynamics in imprinting. *Learning and Motivation*, 1974, 5, 149–164.

Hogan, R., Mankin, D., Conway, J., & Fox, S. Personality correlates of undergraduate marijuana use. *Journal of Consulting and Clinical Psychology*, 1970, 35, 58–63.

Hohmann, G. W. Some effects of spinal cord lesions on experienced emotional feelings. *Psychophysiology*, 1966, 3, 143–156.

Hokanson, J. E., & Burgess, M. The effects of three types of aggression on vascular processes. *Journal of Abnormal and Social Psychology*, 1962, 64, 446–449.

Hokanson, J. E., Burgess, M., & Cohen, M. Effects of displaced aggression on systolic blood pressure. *Journal of Abnormal and Social Psychology*, 1963, 67, 214–218.

Holmes, T. H., & Masuda, M. Life change and illness susceptibility. In J. P. Scott & E. C. Senay (Eds.), *Separation and depression: Clinical and research aspects*. Washington, D.C.: American Association for the Advancement of Science, 1973. Pp. 161–186.

Holton, R. B. Amplitude of an instrumental response following the cessation of reward. *Child Development*, 1961, 32, 107–116.

Homans, G. C. *Social behavior: Its elementary forms*. Harcourt, Brace & World, 1961.

Honorton, C. Psi-mediation and the regulation of sensory input. Paper presented at the annual meeting of the American Psychological Association, New Orleans, 1974.

Honorton, C. "Error some place!" *Journal of Communication*, 1975, 25, 103–116.

Horman, R. E. Alienation and student drug use. *The International Journal of the Addictions*, 1973, 8, 325–331.

Hotchner, A. E. *Papa Hemingway: A personal memoir*. New York: Random House, 1966.

Hsiao, S. Effect of female variation on sexual satiation in the male rat. *Journal of Comparative and Physiological Psychology*, 1965, 60, 467–469.

Hudgens, R. W., Morrison, J. R., & Barchha, R. G. Life events and onset of primary affective disorders. *Archives of General Psychiatry*, 1967, 16, 134–145.

Hull, C. L. *A behavior system*. New Haven: Yale University Press, 1952.

Hutchinson, R. R. The environmental causes of aggression. In J. K. Cole & D. D. Jensen (Eds.), *Nebraska Symposium on Motivation, 1972*. Lincoln: University of Nebraska Press, 1973. Pp. 155–181.

Huxley, A. *The doors of perception*. New York: Harper & Row, 1954.

Irwin, F. W. *Intentional behavior and motivation: A cognitive theory*. New York: Lippincott, 1971.

Isbell, H., & Jasinski, D. R. A comparison of LSD-25 with $(-)$ $-\Delta^9$-transtetrahydrocannabinol (THC) and attempted cross tolerance between LSD and THC. *Psychopharmacologia*, 1969, 14, 115–123.

Izard, C. E. *The face of emotion*. New York: Appleton-Century-Crofts, 1971.

Izard, C. E. *Patterns of emotions: A new analysis of anxiety and depression*. New York: Academic Press, 1972.

Jacobs, T. J., Fogelson, S., & Charles, E. Depression ratings in hypochondria. *New York State Journal of Medicine*, 1968, 68, 3119–3122.

Jacobson, E. The electrophysiology of mental activities. *American Journal of Psychology*, 1932, 44, 677–694.

Jacobson, E. *Depression*. New York: International Universities Press, 1971.

James, W. *The principles of psychology*. [1890] New York: Dover, 1950.

Jellison, J. M., & Harvey, J. H. Why we like hard, positive choices. *Psychology Today*, March 1976, 47–49.

Jenkin, N. Affective processes in perception. *Psychological Bulletin*, 1957, 54, 100–127.

Jessor, R. Predicting time of onset of marijuana use: A developmental study of high school youth. *Journal of Personality and Social Psychology*, 1976, 44, 125–134.

Jessor, R., Jessor, S. L., & Finney, J. A social psychology of marijuana use: Longitudinal studies of high school and college youth. *Journal of Personality and Social Psychology*, 1973, 26, 1–15.

Jessor, R., Young, H. B., Young, E. B., & Tesi, G. Perceived opportunity, alienation, and drinking behavior among Italian and American youth. *Journal of Personality and Social Psychology*, 1970, 15, 215–222.

Johnson, B. D. *Marijuana users and drug subcultures*. New York: Wiley, 1973.

Johnson, R. E. Some correlates of extramarital coitus. *Journal of Marriage and the Family*, 1970, 32, 449–456.

Jones, M. C. Personality correlates and antecedents of drinking patterns in adult males. *Journal of Consulting and Clinical Psychology*, 1968, 32, 2–12.

Jung, C. *The portable Jung*. (R. F. C. Hull, Trans.) New York: Viking, 1973.

Kagan, J. *Change and continuity in infancy*. New York: Wiley, 1971.

Karstens, A. Psychische Sättigung. *Psychologische Forschung*, 1928, 10, 142–254.

Kastenbaum, R. Cognitive and personal futurity in later life. *Journal of Individual Psychology*, 1963, 19, 216–222.

Kastenbaum, R. Age: Getting there ahead of time. *Psychology Today*, 1971, 5 (7), 53–54, 82–84.

Katona, G. *Psychological economics*. New York: Elsevier, 1975.

Kaufman, I. C. Mother-infant separation in monkeys: An experimental model. In J. P. Scott & E. C. Senay (Eds.), *Separation and depression: Clinical and research aspects*. Washington, D.C.: American Association for the Advancement of Science, 1973. Pp. 33–52.

Kaufmann, W. The inevitability of alienation. In R. Schacht, *Alienation*. New York: Doubleday, 1970. Pp. xv–lviii.

Keating, J. W. Paradoxes in American athletics. In A. Flath (Ed.), *Athletics in America*. Corvallis, Oregon: Oregon State University Press, 1972. Pp. 17–31.

Kelly, J. F., & Hake, D. F. An extinction induced increase in an aggressive response with humans. *Journal of the Experimental Analysis of Behavior*, 1970, 14, 153–164.

Kemble, E. D., & Beckman, G. J. Escape latencies at three levels of electric shock in rats with amygdaloid lesions. *Psychonomic Science*, 1969, 14, 205–206.

Kemble, E. D., & Beckman, G. J. Runway performance of rats following amygdaloid lesions. *Physiology and Behavior*, 1970, 5, 45–47.

Kemble, E. D., & Schwartzbaum, J. S. Reactivity to taste properties of solutions following amygdaloid lesions. *Physiology and Behavior*, 1969, 4, 981–985.

Keniston, K. *The uncommitted: Alienated youth in American society*. New York: Dell, 1965.

Keniston, K. Heads and seekers. *American Scholar*, 1968, 38, 97–112.

Kety, S. S. Neurochemical aspects of emotional behavior. In P. Black (Ed.), *Physiological correlates of emotion*. New York: Academic Press, 1970.

Kinsey, A. C., Pomeroy, W. B., & Martin, C. E. *Sexual behavior in the human male*. Philadelphia: Saunders, 1948.

Kinsey, A. C., Pomeroy, W. B., Martin, C. E., & Gebhard, P. H. *Sexual behavior in the human female*. Philadelphia: Saunders, 1953.

Kirsch, B., & Lengermann, J. J. An empirical test of Robert Blauner's ideas on alienation in work as applied to different type jobs in a white-collar setting. *Sociology and Social Research*, 1972, 56, 180–194.

Kish, G. B., & Busse, W. Correlates of stimulus-seeking: Age, education, intelligence, and aptitudes. *Journal of Consulting Psychology*, 1968, 32, 633–637.

Klein, D. C., & Seligman, M. E. P. Reversal of performance deficits and perceptual deficits in learned helplessness and depression. *Journal of Abnormal Psychology*, 1976, 85, 11–26.

Klein, D. F. Endogenomorphic depression: A conceptual and terminological revision. *Archives of General Psychiatry*, 1974, 31, 447–454.

Klerman, G. L. Pharmacologic aspects of depression. In J. P. Scott & E. C. Senay (Eds.), *Separation and depression: Clinical and research aspects*. Washington, D.C.: American Association for the Advancement of Science, 1973. Pp. 69–90.

Klinger, E. Modeling effects on achievement imagery. *Journal of Personality and Social Psychology*, 1967, 7, 49–62.

Klinger, E. *Structure and functions of fantasy*. New York: Wiley, 1971.

Klinger, E. Utterances to evaluate steps and control attention distinguish operant from respondent thought while thinking out loud. *Bulletin of the Psychonomic Society*, 1974, 4, 44–45.

Klinger, E., Barta, S. G., & Kemble, E. D. Cyclic activity changes during extinction in rats: A potential model of depression. *Animal Learning and Behavior*, 1974, 2, 313–316.

Klinger, E., Barta, S. G., Mahoney, T. W., et al. Motivation, mood, and mental events: Patterns and implications for adaptive processes. In G. Serban (Ed.), *Psychopathology of human adaptation*. New York: Plenum, 1976.

Klinger, E., Gregoire, K. C., & Barta, S. G. Physiological correlates of mental activity: Eye movements, alpha, and heart rate during imagining, suppression, search, concentration and choice. *Psychophysiology*, 1973, 10, 471–477.

Klinger, E., & McNelly, F. W., Jr. Fantasy need achievement and performance: A role analysis. *Psychological Review*, 1969, 76, 574–591.

Klinger, E., & McNelly, F. W., Jr. Self-states and performances of preadolescent boys carrying out leadership roles inconsistent with their social status. *Child Development*, 1976, 47, 126–137.

Knight, R. C., Sheposh, J. P., & Bryson, J. B. College student marijuana use and societal alienation. *Journal of Health and Social Behavior*, 1974, 15, 28–35.

Knott, P. D. Frustration in relation to primary and conditioned incentive value: Effects on verbal evaluation, selective attention, size estimation, and reward expectancy. Unpublished Ph.D. dissertation, Vanderbilt University, 1967.

Knott, P. D., Nunnally, J. C., & Duchnowski, A. J. Effects of primary and conditioned incentive value. *Journal of Experimental Research in Personality*, 1967, 2, 140–149.

Koepke, R. Charles Tanneguy Duchatel and the Revolution of 1848. *French Historical Studies*, 1973, 8, 236–254.

Koestler, A. *The act of creation*. New York: Macmillan, 1964.

Kolaja, J. A Yugoslav workers' council. *Human Organization*, 1961, 20, 27–31.

Kruglanski, A. W., Riter, A., Amitai, A., Margolin, B-S., Shabtai, L., & Zaksh, D. Can money enhance intrinsic motivation?: A test of the content-consequence hypothesis. *Journal of Personality and Social Psychology*, 1975, 31, 744–750.

Kuhlen, R. G. Developmental changes in motivation during the adult years. In B. L. Neugarten (Ed.), *Middle age and aging: A reader in social psychology*. Chicago: University of Chicago Press, 1968. Pp. 115–136.

Kurtz, K. H., & Jarka, R. G. Postion preference based on differential food privation. *Journal of Comparative and Physiological Psychology*, 1968, 66, 518–521.

Laird, J. Self-attribution of emotion: The effects of expressive behavior on the quality of emotional experience. *Journal of Personality and Social Psychology*, 1974, 29, 475–486.

Lanzetta, J. T., Cartwright-Smith, J., & Kleck, R. E. Effects of nonverbal dissimulation on emotional experience and autonomic arousal. *Journal of Personality and Social Psychology*, 1976, 33, 354–370.

Latané, B., & Schachter, S. Adrenalin and avoidance learning. *Journal of Comparative and Physiological Psychology*, 1962, 65, 369–372.

Lawler, E. E., III. What do employees *really* want? Paper presented at the annual meeting of the American Psychological Association, Montreal, 1973.

Lazarus, R. S., & Averill, J. R. Emotion and cognition: With special reference to anxiety. In C. D. Spielberger (Ed.), *Anxiety: Current trends in theory and research* (Vol. 2). New York: Academic Press, 1972, Pp. 241–283.

Lefcourt, H. M., Lewis, L., & Silverman, I. W. Internal versus external control of reinforcement and attention in a decision-making task. *Journal of Personality*, 1968, 36, 663–682.

Lefcourt, H. M., & Wine, J. Internal versus external control of reinforcement and the development of attention in experimental situations. *Canadian Journal of Behavioural Science*, 1969, 1, 167–181.

Leff, M. J., Roatch, J. F., & Bunney, W. E., Jr. Environmental factors preceding the onset of severe depressions. *Psychiatry*, 1970, 33, 293–311.

Lepper, M. R., & Greene, D. Turning play into work: Effects of adult surveillance and extrinsic rewards on children's intrinsic motivation. *Journal of Personality and Social Psychology*, 1975, 31, 479–486.

Levine, M. Hypothesis theory and nonlearning despite ideal S-R reinforcement contingencies. *Psychological Review*, 1971, 78, 130–140.

Levinger, G. Marital cohesiveness and dissolution: An integrative review. *Journal of Marriage and the Family*, 1965, 27, 19–28.

Levinger, G. Sources of marital dissatisfaction among applicants for divorce. *American Journal of Orthopsychiatry*, 1966, 36, 803–807.

Levitt, E. E., & Lubin, B. *Depression: Concepts, controversies, and some new facts*. New York: Springer, 1975.

Lewin, K. Kriegslandschaft. *Zeitschrift für angewandte Psychologie*, 1917, 12, 440–447.

Lewin, K. Wille, Vorsatz, und Bedürfnis. *Psychologische Forschung*, 1928, 7, 330–385.

Lewin, K. *A dynamic theory of personality: Selected papers*. New York: McGraw-Hill, 1935.

Lewin, K. *The conceptual representation and the measurement of psychological forces.* Durham, North Carolina: Duke University Press, 1938.

Lewinsohn, P. M. A behavioral approach to depression. In R. J. Friedman & M. M. Katz (Eds.), *The psychology of depression: Contemporary theory and research*. Washington, D.C.: Winston, 1974, Pp. 157–178.

Lewinsohn, P. M. Engagement in pleasant activities and depression level. *Journal of Abnormal Psychology*, 1975, 84, 729–731.

Lewinsohn, P. M., & Graf, M. Pleasant activities and depression. *Journal of Consulting and Clinical Psychology*, 1973, 41, 261–268.

Lewis, M., & Brooks, J. Infants' social perceptions: A constructivist view. In L. B. Cohen & P. Salapatek (Eds.), *Infant perception: From sensation to cognition*. Vol. 2: *Perception of space, speech, and sound*. New York: Academic Press, 1975. Pp. 101–148.

Lichty, L. W. "The Real McCoys" and it's [sic] audience: A functional analysis. *Journal of Broadcasting*, 1965, 9, 157–166.

Lindesmith, A. R. *Addiction and opiates*. Chicago: Aldine, 1968.

Linsky, A. S. Community structure and depressive disorders. *Social Problems*, 1969, 17, 120–131.

Linton, R. *The cultural background of personality*. New York: Appleton-Century-Crofts, 1945.

Lish, J. A. The influence of oral dependency, failure, and social exposure upon self-esteem and depression. Unpublished Ph.D. dissertation, New York University, 1969.

Lissner, K. Die Entspannung von Bedürfnissen durch Ersatzhandlungen. *Psychologische Forschung*, 1933, 18, 218–250.

Litman, R. E. Suicide as acting out. In E. S. Shneidman, N. L. Farberow, & R. E. Litman (Eds.), *The psychology of suicide*. New York: Science House, 1970. Pp. 293–304. (Reprinted from L. E. Abt & S. L. Weisman (Eds.), *Acting out*. New York: Grune & Stratton, 1965.)

Litman, R. E., Farberow, N. L., Wold, C. I., & Brown, T. R. Prediction models of suicidal behaviors. In A. T. Beck, H. L. P. Resnik, & D. J. Lettieri (Eds.), *The prediction of suicide*. Bowie, Maryland: Charles, 1974. Pp. 141–159.

Lloyd, R. W., Jr., & Salzberg, H. C. Controlled social drinking: An alternative to abstinence as a treatment goal for some alcohol abusers. *Psychological Bulletin*, 1975, 82, 815–842.

Locke, E. A. Toward a theory of task motivation and incentives. *Organizational Behavior and Human Performance*, 1968, 3, 157–189.

Locke, E. A., Bryan, J. F., & Kendall, L. M. Goals and intentions as mediators of the effects of monetary incentives on behavior. *Journal of Applied Psychology*, 1968, 52, 104–121.

Loeb, A., Beck, A. T., & Diggory, J. Differential effects of success and failure on depressed and nondepressed patients. *Journal of Nervous and Mental Disease*, 1971, 152, 106–114.

Logan, F. A. Frustration effect following correlated nonreinforcement. *Journal of Experimental Psychology*, 1968, 78, 396–400.

Logan, F. A. Incentive theory, reinforcement and education. In R. Glaser (Ed.), *The nature of reinforcement*. New York: Academic Press, 1971. Pp. 45–61.

Low, M. D., Klonoff, H., & Marcus, A. The neurophysiological basis of the marijuana experience. *Canadian Medical Association Journal*, 1973, 108, 157–165.

Lubin, M. I. Addendum to Chapter 4. In B. L. Neugarten and Associates, *Personality in middle and late life: Empirical studies*. New York: Atherton, 1964. Pp. 102–104.

Luce, J. End of the road: A case study. In D. E. Smith & G. R. Gay (Eds.), *"It's so good, don't even try it once": Heroin in perspective*. Englewood Cliffs, N.J.: Prentice-Hall, 1972. Pp. 143–147.

Ludwig, L. D. Intra- and interindividual relationships between elation-depression and desire for excitement. *Journal of Personality*, 1970, 32, 167–176.

Lukas, E. S. Logotherapie als Persönlichkeitstheorie. Unpublished Ph.D. dissertation, University of Vienna, 1971.

Lukas, E. S. Zur Validierung der Logotherapie. In V. Frankl, *Der Wille zum Sinn: Ausgewählte Vorträge über Logotherapie*. Bern: Huber, 1972. Pp. 233–266.

Lundberg, U., & Ekman, G. Emotional involvement while anticipating an examination: A psychophysical study. *Perceptual and Motor Skills*, 1970, 31, 603–609.

Lundberg, U., Ekman, G., & Frankenhaeuser, M. Anticipation of electric shock: A psychophysical study. *Acta Psychologica*, 1971, 35, 309–315.

Lundberg, U., von Wright, J. M., Frankenhaeuser, M., & Olson, U.-J. Involvement in four future events as a function of temporal distance. *Scandinavian Journal of Psychology*, 1975, 16, 2–6.

Luria, A. R., & Vinogradova, O. S. An objective investigation of the dynamics of semantic systems. *British Journal of Psychology*, 1959, 50, 89–105.

Lykken, D. T. A study of anxiety in the sociopathic personality. *Journal of Abnormal and Social Psychology*, 1957, 55, 6–10.

Lystad, M. H. Social alienation: A review of current literature. *Sociological Quarterly*, 1972, 13, 90–113.

Maas, H. S., & Kuypers, J. A. *From thirty to seventy: A forty-year longitudinal study of adult life styles and personality*. San Francisco: Jossey-Bass, 1974.

Macarov, D. *Incentives to work*. San Francisco: Jossey-Bass, 1970.

Maccoby, E. E. Why do children watch television? *Public Opinion Quarterly*, 1954, 18, 239–244.

MacPhillamy, D. J., & Lewinsohn, P. M. Depression as a function of levels of desired and obtained pleasure. *Journal of Abnormal Psychology*, 1974, 83, 651–657.

Macrides, F., Bartke, A., & Dalterio, S. Strange females increase plasma testosterone levels in male mice. *Science*, 1975, 189, 1104–1106.

Maire, F. W. Van Gogh's suicide. *Journal of the American Medical Association*, 1971, 217, 938–939.

Mandler, G. The interruption of behavior. In D. Levine (Ed.), *Nebraska Symposium on Motivation, 1964*. Lincoln: University of Nebraska Press, 1964, Pp. 163–219.

Marañon, G. Contribution à l'étude de l'action émotive de l'adrénaline. *Revue française d'Endocrinologie*, 1924, 2, 301–325.

Marcovitz, E., & Myers, H. J. The marijuana addict in the army. *War Medicine*, 1944, 6, 382–391.

Maris, R. W. *Social forces in urban suicide*. Homewood, Ill.: Dorsey, 1969.

Mark, V. H., & Ervin, F. R. *Violence and the brain*. New York: Harper & Row, 1970.

Marlatt, G. A. Determinants of alcohol consumption in a laboratory taste-rating task: Implications for controlled drinking. In *Can alcoholics learn to control their drinking?* Symposium presented at the annual meeting of the American Psychological Association, Montreal, 1973.

Marlatt, G. A., Demming, B., & Reid, J. B. Loss of control drinking in alcoholics: An experimental analogue. *Journal of Abnormal Psychology*, 1973, 81, 233–241.

Marlatt, G. A., Kosturn, C. F., & Lang, A. R. Provocation to anger and opportunity for retaliation as determinants of alcohol consumption in social drinkers. *Journal of Abnormal Psychology*, 1975, 84, 652–659.

Marris, P. *Widows and their families*. London: Routledge & Kegan Paul, 1958.

Martel, M. U. Age-sex roles in American magazine fiction (1890–1955). In B. L. Neugarten (Ed.), *Middle age and aging: A reader in social psychology*. Chicago: University of Chicago Press, 1968. Pp. 47–57.

Maslow, A. H. *The farther reaches of human nature*. New York: Viking, 1971.

Masters, W. H., & Johnson, V. E. *Human sexual response*. Boston: Little, Brown, 1966.

Mayor's Committee on Marihuana. *The marihuana problem in the City of New York*. Lancaster, Pennsylvania: Jacques Cattell, 1944.

Mazies, M. B. Antipollution measures and psychological reactance theory. *Journal of Personality and Social Psychology*, 1975, 31, 654–660.

McAuliffe, W. E., & Gordon, R. A. A test of Lindesmith's theory of addiction: The frequency of euphoria among long-term addicts. *American Journal of Sociology*, 1974, 79, 795–840.

McClelland, D. C., Atkinson, J. W., Clark, R. A., & Lowell, E. L. *The achievement motive*. New York: Appleton-Century-Crofts, 1953.

McClelland, D. C., Davis, W. N., Kalin, R., & Wanner, E. *The drinking man: Alcohol and human motivation*. New York: Free Press, 1972.

McCord, W., & McCord, J. *Origins of alcoholism*. Stanford, California: Stanford University Press, 1960.

McDougall, W. *An introduction to social psychology*. London: Methuen, 1921.

McGuigan, F. J. Covert oral behavior during the silent performance of language tasks. *Psychological Bulletin*, 1970, 74, 309–326.

McKenzie, J. D. Trends in marijuana use among undergraduate students at the University of Maryland. Counseling Center Research Report #3-70. College Park: University of Maryland Counseling Center, 1970.

McKinney, W. T. Jr., Suomi, S. J., & Harlow, H. F. Depression in primates. *American Journal of Psychiatry*, 1971, 127, 1313–1320.

McKinney, W. T., Jr., Suomi, S. J., & Harlow, H. F. New models of separation and depression in rhesus monkeys. In J. P. Scott & E. C. Senay (Eds.), *Separation and depression: Clinical and research aspects*. Washington, D.C.: American Association for the Advancement of Science, 1973. Pp. 53–66.

McLuhan, M., & Fiore, Q. *Medium is the massage*. New York: Random House, 1967.

Mello, N. K., & Mendelson, J. H. Drinking patterns during work-contingent and non-contingent alcohol acquisition. *Psychosomatic Medicine*, 1972, 34, 139–164.

Melvin, K. B., & Anson, J. E. Image-induced aggressive display: Reinforcement in the paradise fish. *Psychological Record*, 1970, 20, 225–228.

Melvin, K. B., & Cloar, F. T. Habituation of quail (*Colinus virginianus*) to a hawk (*Butes swainsoni*): Measurement through an 'innate suppression' technique. *Animal Behaviour*, 1969, 17, 468–473.

Mendels, J. (Ed.) *The psychobiology of depression*. New York: Spectrum, 1975.

Mendels, J., & Cochrane, C. The nosology of depression: The endogenous-reactive concept. *American Journal of Psychiatry*, 1968, 124, 1–11.

Mendelson, J. Role of hunger in T-maze learning for food by rats. *Journal of Comparative and Physiological Psychology*, 1966, 62, 341–349.

Meyer, W.-U. Anstrengungsintention in Abhängigkeit von Begabungseinschätzung und Aufgabenschwierigkeit. *Archiv für Psychologie*, 1973, 125, 245–262.

Meyer, W.-U., Folkes, V., & Weiner, B. The perceived informational value and affective consequences of choice behavior and intermediate difficulty task selection. Unpublished paper, 1975.

Meyer, W.-U., & Hallermann, B. Anstrengungsintention bei einer leichten und schweren Aufgabe in Abhängigkeit von der wahrgenommenen eigenen Begabung. *Archiv für Psychologie*, 1974, 126, 85–89.

Meyer, W.-U., & Hallermann, B. Intended effort and informational value of task outcome. Unpublished paper, 1975.

Middleton, R. Alienation, race, and education. In S. S. Guterman (Ed.), *Black psyche: The modal personality patterns of black Americans*. Berkeley, California: Glendessary, 1972. (Reprinted from *American Sociological Review*, 1963, 28, 973–977.)

Miller, G. A. Professionals in bureaucracy: Alienation among industrial scientists and eingineers. *American Sociological Review*, 1967, 32, 755–768.

Miller, J. B. Dreams during varying stages of depression. *Archives of General Psychiatry*, 1969, 20, 560–565.

Miller, N., & Stevenson, S. S. Agitated behavior of rats during extinction and a curve of spontaneous recovery. *Journal of Comparative Psychology*, 1936, 21, 205–231.

Miller, N. E. Experimental studies of conflict. In J. McV. Hunt (Ed.), *Personality and the behavior disorders* (Vol. 1). New York: Ronald, 1944. Pp. 431–465.

Miller, W. R. Psychological deficit in depression. *Psychological Bulletin*, 1975, 82, 238–260.

Miller, W. R., & Seligman, M. E. P. Depression and learned helplessness in man. *Journal of Abnormal Psychology*, 1975, 84, 228–238.

Mischel, W., Ebbesen, E. B., & Zeiss, A. R. Cognitive and attentional mechanisms in delay of gratification. *Journal of Personality and Social Psychology*, 1972, 21, 204–218.

Mischel, W., & Masters, J. C. Effects of probability of reward attainment on responses to frustration. *Journal of Personality and Social Psychology*, 1966, 3, 390–396.

Miskimins, R. W., & Simmons, W. L. Goal preference as a variable in involutional psychosis. *Journal of Consulting Psychology*, 1966, 30, 73–77.

Mitchell, T. R. Expectancy models of job satisfaction, occupational preference and effort: A theoretical, methodological, and empirical appraisal. *Psychological Bulletin*, 1974, 81, 1053–1077.

Mitchell, T. R., & Biglan, A. Instrumentality theories: Current uses in psychology. *Psychological Bulletin*, 1971, 76, 432–454.

Mobley, W. H., & Locke, E. A. The relationship of value importance to satisfaction. *Organizational Behavior and Human Performance*, 1970, 5, 463–483.

Moore, B. S., Underwood, B., & Rosenhan, D. L. Affect and altruism. *Developmental Psychology*, 1973, 8, 99–104.

Moran, G. Severe food deprivation: Some thoughts regarding its exclusive use. *Psychological Bulletin*, 1975, 82, 543–557.

Moray, N. Attention in dichotic listening: Affective cues and the influence of instructions. *Quarterly Journal of Experimental Psychology*, 1959, 11, 56–60.

Morgan, C. T. *Physiological psychology*. New York: McGraw-Hill, 1943.

Morse, N. C., & Weiss, R. S. The function and meaning of work and the job. *American Sociological Review*, 1955, 20, 191–198.

Mowrer, O. H. *Learning theory and behavior*. New York: Wiley, 1960.

Moyer, K. E. *The physiology of hostility*. Chicago: Markham, 1971.

Murray, H. A. *Explorations in personality*. New York: Oxford, 1938.

Nagera, H. *Vincent Van Gogh: A psychological study*. London: George Allen & Unwin, 1967.

Nathan, P. E., Titler, N. A., Lowenstein, L. M., Solomon, P., & Rossi, A. M. Behavioral analysis of chronic alcoholism. *Archives of General Psychiatry*, 1970, 22, 419–430.

National Commission on Marijuana and Drug Abuse. *Drug use in America: Problem in perspective*. Washington, D.C.: U.S. Government Printing Office, 1973.

Neisser, U. *Cognitive psychology*. New York: Appleton-Century-Crofts, 1967.

Neiswender, M., Birren, J. E., & Schaie, K. W. Age and the experience of love in adulthood. Paper presented at the annual meeting of the American Psychological Association, Chicago, 1975.

Nesselroade, J. R., Schaie, W. K., & Baltes, P. B. Ontogenetic and generational components of structural and quantitative change in adult behavior. *Journal of Gerontology*, 1972, 27, 222–228.

Neugarten, B. L. The awareness of middle age. In B. L. Neugarten (Ed.), *Middle age and aging: A reader in social psychology*. Chicago: University of Chicago Press, 1968. Pp. 93–98.

Neugarten, B. L., Havighurst, R. J., & Tobin, S. S. Personality and patterns of aging. In B. L. Neugarten (Ed.), *Middle age and aging: A reader in social psychology*. Chicago: University of Chicago Press, 1968. Pp. 173–177.

Neugarten, B. L., Moore, J. W., & Lowe, J. C. Age norms, age constraints, and adult socialization. In B. L. Neugarten (Ed.), *Middle age and aging: A reader in social psychology*. Chicago: University of Chicago Press, 1968. Pp. 22–27.

Neuringer, A. Pigeons respond to produce periods in which rewards are independent of responding. *Journal of the Experimental Analysis of Behavior*, 1973, 19, 39–54.

Newcomb, T. M. *Social psychology*. New York: Dryden, 1950.

Newell, A., & Simon, H. A. *Human problem solving*. Englewood Cliffs, N.J.: Prentice-Hall, 1972.

Nickel, T. W. The attribution of intention as a critical factor in the relation between frustration and aggression. *Journal of Personality*, 1974, 42, 482–492.

Nisan, M. Evaluation of temporally distant reinforcements. *Journal of Personality and Social Psychology*, 1973, 26, 295–300.

Norman, D. A. *Memory and attention: An introduction to human information processing*. New York: Wiley, 1969.

Nunnally, J. C., Duchnowski, A. J., & Parker, R. K. Association of neutral objects with rewards: Effect on verbal evaluation, reward expectancy, and selective attention. *Journal of Personality and Social Psychology*, 1965, 1, 270–274.

Nunnally, J. C., & Faw, T. T. The acquisition of conditioned reward value in discrimination learning. *Child Development*, 1968, 39, 159–166.

Nunnally, J. C., Stevens, D. A., & Hall, G. F. Association of neutral objects with reward: Effect on verbal evaluation and eye movements. *Journal of Experimental Child Psychology*, 1965, 2, 44–57.

Nuttin, J., & Greenwald, A. G. *Reward and punishment in human learning*. New York: Academic Press, 1968.

Office of Economic Opportunity. *Further preliminary results of the New Jersey graduated work incentive experiment*. Washington, D.C.: Office of Economic Opportunity Pamphlet 3400-4, 1971.

Ogilvie, D. M., Stone, P. J., & Shneidman, E. S. A computer analysis of suicide notes. In E. S. Shneidman, N. L. Farberow, & R. E. Litman (Eds.), *The psychology of suicide*. New York: Science House, 1970. Pp. 249–256. (Reprinted from P. J. Stone, D. C. Dunphy, M. S. Smith, & D. M. Ogilvie (Eds.), *The General Inquirer: A computer approach to content analysis*. Cambridge, Mass.: M.I.T. Press, 1966.)

Olds, J., & Milner, P. Positive reinforcement produced by electrical stimulation of septal area and other regions of the rat brain. *Journal of Comparative and Physiological Psychology*, 1954, 47, 419–427.

Orbach, C. E., & Sutherland, A. M. Acute depressive reactions to surgical treatment for cancer. In P. H. Hoch & J. Zubin (Eds.), *Depression*. New York: Grune & Stratton, 1954. Pp. 237–252.

Orden, S. R., & Bradburn, N. M. Working wives and marriage happiness. *American Journal of Sociology*, 1969, 74, 392–407.

Orlofsky, J. L., Marcia, J. E., & Lesser, I. M. Ego identity status and the intimacy versus isolation crisis of young adulthood. *Journal of Personality and Social Psychology*, 1973, 27, 211–219.

Osgood, C. E., May, W. H., & Miron, M. S. *Cross-cultural universals of affective meaning*. Urbana: University of Illinois Press, 1975.

Osgood, C. E., & Walker, E. G. Motivation and language behavior: A content analysis of suicide notes. *Journal of Abnormal and Social Psychology*, 1959, 59, 58–67.

Oswald, I., Taylor, A. M., & Treisman, M. Discriminative responses to stimulation during human sleep. *Brain*, 1960, 83, 440–453.

Overall, J. E., & Patrick, J. H. Unitary alcoholism factor and its personality correlates. *Journal of Abnormal Psychology*, 1972, 79, 303–309.

Overmier, J. B., & Seligman, M. E. P. Effects of inescapable shock upon subsequent escape and avoidance responding. *Journal of Comparative and Physiological Psychology*, 1967, 63, 28–33.

Ovsiankina, M. Die Wiederaufnahme unterbrochene Handlungen. *Psychologische Forschung*, 1928, 2, 302–379.

Parkes, C. M. The first year of bereavement: A longitudinal study of the reactions of London widows to the death of their husbands. *Psychiatry*, 1970, 33, 444–467.

Parkes, C. M. *Bereavement: Studies of grief in adult life*. New York: International Universities Press, 1972.

Pascal, B. *Pensées; The provincial letters* (W. F. Trotter & T. M'Crie, Trans.). New York: Modern Library, 1941.

Patterson, C. J., & Mischel, W. Effects of temptation-inhibiting and task-facilitating plans on self-control. *Journal of Personality and Social Psychology*, 1976, 33, 209–217.

Paul, W. J., Robertson, K. B., & Herzberg, F. Job enrichment pays off. *Harvard Business Review*, 1969, 47 (2), 61–78.

Pawlowski, A. A., Denenberg, V. H., & Zarrow, M. X. Prolonged alcohol consumption in the rat: II. Acquisition and extinction of an escape response. *Quarterly Journal of Studies on Alcohol*, 1961, 22, 232–240.

Paykel, E. S., Myers, J. K., Dienelt, M. M., Klerman, G. L., Lindenthal, J. J., & Pepper, M. P. Life events and depression. *Archives of General Psychiatry*, 1969, 21, 753–760.

Paykel, E. S., Prusoff, B., & Klerman, G. L. The endogenous-neurotic continuum in depression: Rater independence and factor distributions. *Journal of Psychiatric Research*, 1971, 8, 73–90.

Paykel, E. S., Prusoff, B. A., & Myers, J. K. Suicide attempts and recent life events. *Archives of General Psychiatry*, 1975, 32, 327–333.

Payne, J. L. *Incentive theory and political processes: Motivation and leadership in the Dominican Republic*. Lexington, Mass.: Heath, 1972.

Payne, J. L., & Woshinsky, O. H. Incentives for political participation. *World Politics*, 1972, 24, 518–546.

Pearlin, L. I. Social and personal stress and escape television viewing. *Public Opinion Quarterly*, 1959, 23, 255–259.

Pearlin, L. I. Alienation from work: A study of nursing personnel. *American Sociological Review*, 1962, 27, 314–326.

Peeke, H. V. S., & Peeke, S. C. Habituation of conspecific aggressive responses in the Siamese fighting fish (*Betta splendens*). *Behaviour*, 1970, 36, 232–245.

Pelz, D. C., & Schuman, S. H. Drinking, hostility, and alienation in driving of young men. Paper presented at the Third Annual Alcoholism Conference of the National Institute of Alcohol Abuse and Alcoholism, Washington, D.C., 1973.

Perrow, M. V. A description of similarity of personality between selected groups of television viewers and certain television roles regularly viewed by them. Unpublished Ph.D. dissertation, University of Southern California, 1968.

Peters, D. P., & McHose, J. H. Effects of varied preshift reward magnitude on successive negative contrast effect in rats. *Journal of Comparative and Physiological Psychology*, 1974, 86, 85–95.

Petrinovich, L. A species-meaningful analysis of habituation. In H. V. S. Peeke & M. J. Herz. (Eds.), *Habituation*. Vol. 1. *Behavioral studies*. New York: Academic Press, 1973. Pp. 141–162.

Phares, E. J. Differential utilization of information as a function of internal-external control. *Journal of Personality*, 1968, 36, 649–662.

Phares, E. J. Internal-external control and the reduction of reinforcement value after failure. *Journal of Consulting and Clinical Psychology*, 1971, 37, 386–390.

Piliavin, I. M., Hardyck, J. A., & Vadum, A. C. Constraining effects of personal costs on the transgressions of juveniles. *Journal of Personality and Social Psychology*, 1968, 10, 227–231.

Pineo, P. C. Disenchantment in the later years of marriage. *Marriage and Family Living*, 1961, 23, 3–11.

Pitts, F. N., Jr., & Winokur, G. Affective disorder. III: Diagnostic correlates and incidence of suicide. *Journal of Nervous and Mental Disease*, 1964, 139, 176–181.

Plath, S. *Letters home: Correspondence 1950–1963* (A. S. Plath, Ed.). New York: Harper & Row, 1975.

Platman, S. R., Plutchik, R., Fieve, R. R., & Lawlor, W. G. Emotion profiles associated with mania and depression. *Archives of General Psychiatry*, 1969, 20, 210–214.

Pokorny, A. D. Suicide rates in various psychiatric disorders. *Journal of Nervous and Mental Disease*, 1964, 139, 499–506.

Polansky, N. A., Borgman, R. D., & de Saix, C. *Roots of futility*. San Francisco: Jossey-Bass, 1972.

Poppelreuter, W. Ueber die Ordnung des Vorstellungsablaufes. *Archiv für die gesamte Psychologie*, 1913, 3, 208–349.

Porter, L. W., & Steers, R. M. Organizational, work, and personal factors in employee turnover and absenteeism. *Psychological Bulletin*, 1973, 80, 151–176.

Posner, M. I., & Boies, S. J. Components of attention. *Psychological Review*, 1971, 78, 391–408.

Preble, E., & Casey, J. J., Jr. Taking care of business: The heroin user's life on the street. In D. E. Smith & G. R. Gay (Eds.), *"It's so good, don't even try it once": Heroin in perspective*. Englewood Cliffs, N.J.: Prentice-Hall, 1972. Pp. 97–118.

Prechtl, H. F. R. The directed head turning response and allied movements of the human baby. *Behavior*, 1958, 13, 212–240.

Price, J. S. Genetic and phylogenetic aspects of mood variation. *International Journal of Mental Health*, 1972, 1, 124–144.

Racinskas, J. R. Maladaptive consequences of loss or lack of control over aversive events. Unpublished Ph.D. dissertation, University of Waterloo, 1971.

Rainwater, L. *Behind ghetto walls: Black families in a federal slum*. Chicago: Aldine-Atherton, 1970.

Ratner, S. C. Habituation: Research and theory. In J. Reynierse (Ed.), *Current issues in animal learning*. Lincoln: University of Nebraska Press, 1970. Pp. 55–84.

Raynor, J. O. Future orientation in the study of achievement motivation. In J. W. Atkinson & J. O. Raynor (Eds.), *Motivation and achievement*. Washington, D.C.: Winston, 1974. Pp. 121–154.

Rees, W. D., & Lutkins, S. G. Mortality of bereavement. *British Medical Journal*, 1967, 4, 13–16.

Reiss, S., & Sushinsky, L. W. The competing response hypothesis of decreased play effects: A reply to Lepper and Greene. *Journal of Personality and Social Psychology*, 1976, 33, 233–244.

Renne, K. S. Correlates of dissatisfaction in marriage. *Journal of Marriage and the Family*, 1970, 32, 54–67.

Riedel, R. G. Experimental analysis as applied to adulthood and old age: A review. Paper presented at the annual meeting of the American Psychological Association, New Orleans, 1974.

Ringel, E. Ueber Selbstmordversuche von Jugendlichen. *Internationales Journal für Prophylactische Medizin und Social-hygiene*, 1959, 2, 39–44.

Robins, L. N. *The Viet Nam drug user returns*. Washington, D.C.: U.S. Government Printing Office, 1974.

Robinson, J. P. Television and leisure time: Yesterday, today, and (maybe) tomorrow. *Public Opinion Quarterly*, 1969, 33, 210–222.

Rollins, B. C., & Feldman, H. Marital satisfaction over the family life cycle. *Journal of Marriage and the Family*, 1970, 32, 20–28.

Rosen, A. C. A comparative study of alcoholics and psychiatric patients with the MMPI. *Quarterly Journal of Studies on Alcohol*, 1960, 21, 253–266.

Rosen, J. L., & Neugarten, B. L. Ego functions in the middle and later years: A thematic apperceptive study. In B. L. Neugarten and Associates, *Personality in middle and late life: Empirical studies*. New York: Atherton, 1964. Pp. 90–101.

Rosenblatt, P. C., Walsh, R. P., & Jackson, D. A. *Grief and mourning*. New Haven: Human Relations Area Files Press, 1976.

Rosenfeld, H. M., & Franklin, S. S. Arousal of need for affiliation in women. *Journal of Personality and Social Psychology*, 1966, 3, 245–248.

Rosenhan, D. L., Underwood, B., & Moore, B. Affect moderates self-gratification and altruism. *Journal of Personality and Social Psychology*, 1974, 30, 546–552.

Rosenthal, D. *Genetic theory and abnormal behavior*. New York: McGraw-Hill, 1970.

Rosow, I. *Social integration of the aged*. New York: Free Press, 1967.

Rosow, I. *Socialization to old age*. Berkeley, California: University of California Press, 1974.

Roth, S., & Bootzin, R. R. Effects of experimentally induced expectancies of external control: An investigation of learned helplessness. *Journal of Personality and Social Psychology*, 1974, 29, 253–264.

Roth, S., & Kubal, L. Effects of noncontingent reinforcement on tasks of differing importance: Facilitation and learned helplessness. *Journal of Personality and Social Psychology*, 1975, 32, 680–691.

Rubovits, P. C., & Maehr, M. L. Pygmalion black and white. *Journal of Personality and Social Psychology*, 1973, 25, 210–218.

Rule, J., & Tilly, C. Political process in revolutionary France, 1830–1832. In J. M. Merriman (Ed.), *1830 in France*. New York: Franklin Watts, 1975. Pp. 41–85.

Ryan, T. J., & Watson, P. Frustrative nonreward theory applied to children's behavior. *Psychological Bulletin*, 1968, 69, 111–125.

Ryback, R. S. Alcohol the euphoric agent? *Psychology*, 1969, 6, 7–12.

Salisbury, H. E. *The 900 days: The siege of Leningrad*. New York: Harper & Row, 1969.

Scarborough, B. B. Lasting effects of alcohol on the reduction of anxiety in rats. *Journal of Genetic Psychology*, 1957, 91, 173–179.

Schacht, R. *Alienation*. New York: Doubleday, 1970.

Schachter, S. *Emotion, obesity, and crime*. New York: Academic Press, 1971.

Schachter, S., & Latané, B. Crime, cognition, and the autonomic nervous system. In D. Levine (Ed.), *Nebraska Symposium on Motivation, 1964*. Lincoln, Nebraska: University of Nebraska Press, 1964. Pp. 221–273.

Schachter, S., & Singer, J.E. Cognitive, social, and physiological determinants of emotional state. *Psychological Review*, 1962, 69, 379–399.

Scherer, S. E., Ettinger, R. F., & Mudrick, N. J. Need for social approval and drug use. *Journal of Consulting and Clinical Psychology*, 1972, 38, 118–121.

Schildkraut, J. J., & Kety, S. S. Biogenic amines and emotion. *Science*, 1967, 156, 21–30.

Schneider, K. Die Wirkung von Erfolg und Misserfolg auf die Leistung bei einer visuellen Diskriminationsaufgabe und auf physiologische Anstrengungsindicatoren (Pulsfrequenz und Hautwiderstand). Unpublished paper, Psychologisches Institut, Ruhr University, Federal Republic of Germany, 1975.

Schneider, K., & Eckelt, D. Die Wirkungen von Erfolg und Misserfolg auf die Leistung bei einer einfachen Vigilanzaufgabe. *Zeitschrift für experimentelle und angewandte Psychologie*, 1975, 22, 263–289.

Schopenhauer, A. *The will to live: Selected writings* (R. Taylor, Ed.). New York: Doubleday, 1962.

Schramm, W., Lyle, J., & Parker, E. B. *Television in the lives of our children*. Stanford, California: Stanford University Press, 1961.

Schreiner, L., & Kling, A. Behavioral changes following rhinencephalic injury in cat. *Journal of Neurophysiology*, 1953, 16, 643–659.

Schreiner, L., & Kling, A. Rinencephalon and behavior. *American Journal of Physiology*, 1956, 184, 486–490.

Schwartz, G. E., Fair, P. L., Salt, P., Mandel, M. R., & Klerman, G. L. Facial muscle patterning to affective imagery in depressed and nondepressed subjects. *Science*, 1976, 192, 489–491.

Scott, J. P., Stewart, J. M., & DeGhett, V. J. Separation in infant dogs: Emotional response and motivational consequences. In J. P. Scott & E. C. Senay (Eds.), *Separation and depression: Clinical and research aspects*. Washington, D.C.: American Association for the Advancement of Science, 1973. Pp. 3–32.

Seay, B., & Harlow, H. F. Maternal separation in the rhesus monkey. *Journal of Nervous and Mental Disease*, 1965, 140, 434–441.

Seeman, M. On the meaning of alienation. In A. W. Finifter (Ed.), *Alienation and the social system*. New York: Wiley, 1972. (Reprinted from *American Sociological Review*, 1959, 24, 783–791.)

Seeman, M. Alienation and knowledge-seeking: A note on attitude and action. *Social Problems*, 1972, 20, 3–17.

Seligman, M. E. P. Depression and learned helplessness. In R. J. Friedman & M. M. Katz (Eds.), *The psychology of depression: Contemporary theory and research*. Washington, D.C.: Winston, 1974. Pp. 83–113.

Seligman, M. E. P. *Helplessness: On depression, development, and death*. San Francisco: Freeman, 1975.

Seligman, M. E. P., & Hager, J. L. (Eds.). *Biological boundaries of learning*. New York: Appleton-Century-Crofts, 1972.

Shepard, J. M. Alienation as a process: Work as a case in point. *Sociological Quarterly*, 1972, 13, 161–173.

Shepel, L. F., & James, W. H. Persistence as a function of a locus of control, task structure and reinforcement schedule. Paper delivered at the annual meeting of the American Psychological Association, Montreal, 1973.

Sheppard, H. L., & Herrick, N. Q. *Where have all the robots gone? Worker dissatisfaction in the '70's*. New York: Free Press, 1972.

Shneidman, E. S. Suicide as a taboo topic. In N. L. Farberow (Ed.), *Taboo topics*. New York: Atherton, 1963.

Shneidman, E. S., & Farberow, N. L. A psychological approach to the study of suicide notes. In E. S. Shneidman, N. L. Farberow, & R. E. Litman (Eds.), *The psychology of suicide*. New York: Science House, 1970. Pp. 159–164. (Reprinted from *Journal of General Psychology*, 1957, 56, 251–256.)

Shneidman, E. S., & Farberow, N. L. A sociopsychological investigation of suicide. In E. S. Shneidman, N. L. Farberow, & R. E. Litman (Eds.), *The psychology of suicide*.

New York: Science House, 1970. Pp. 227–248. (Reprinted from H. P. David & J. C. Brengelmann (Eds.), *Perspectives in personality research*. New York: Springer, 1960.)

Shneidman, E. S., & Farberow, N. L. Attempted and committed suicides. In E. S. Shneidman, N. L. Farberow, & R. E. Litman (Eds.), *The psychology of suicide*. New York: Science House, 1970. Pp. 199–226. (Reprinted from N. L. Farberow & E. S. Shneidman (Eds.), *The cry for help*. New York: McGraw-Hill, 1961.)

Shukin, A., & Neugarten, B. L. Personality and social interaction. In B. L. Neugarten and Associates, *Personality in middle and late life: Empirical studies*. New York: Atherton, 1964. Pp. 149–157.

Silverman, L., Spruill, N., & Levine, D. *Urban crime and heroin availability*. Arlington, Va.: Public Research Institute, 1975.

Silverstein, A. Acquired pleasantness and conditioned incentives in verbal learning. In D. E. Berlyne & K. B. Madsen (Eds.), *Pleasure, reward, preference*. New York: Academic Press, 1973. Pp. 189–216.

Simmons, J. L. Some intercorrelations among "alienation" measures. *Social Forces*, 1966, 44, 370–372.

Skinner, B. F. Two types of conditioned reflex and pseudo type. *Journal of General Psychology*, 1935, 12, 66–77.

Skinner, B. F. *Science and human behavior*. New York: Macmillan, 1953.

Smith, G. F., & Dorfman, D. D. The effect of stimulus uncertainty on the relationship between frequency of exposure and liking. *Journal of Personality and Social Psychology*, 1975, 31, 150–155.

Sokolov, A. N. *Inner speech and thought*. New York: Plenum, 1972.

Solomon, F., Walker, W. J., O'Connor, G. J., & Fishman, J. R. Civil rights activity and reduction in crime among Negroes. *Archives of General Psychiatry*, 1965, 12, 227–236.

Solomon, R. L. An opponent-process theory of motivation: IV. The affective dynamics of drug addiction. In Maser, J. D. & Seligman, M. E. P. (Eds.), *Psychopathology: Experimental models*. San Francisco: Freeman, (in preparation).

Solomon, R. L., & Corbit, J. D. An opponent-process theory of motivation: I. Temporal dynamics of affect. *Psychological Review*, 1974, 81, 119–145.

Solomon, R. L., & Corbit, J. D. An opponent-process theory of motivation: II. Cigarette addiction. *Journal of Abnormal Psychology*, 1973, 81, 158–171.

Solomon, R. L., Kamin, L. J., & Wynne, L. C. Traumatic avoidance learning: The outcomes of several extinction procedures with dogs. *Journal of Abnormal and Social Psychology*, 1953, 48, 291–302.

Solomon, R. L., & Wynne, L. C. Traumatic avoidance learning: Acquisition in normal dogs. *Psychological Monographs*, 1953, 67 (4, Whole No. 354).

Sommer, B. Mood and the menstrual cycle. Paper presented at the annual meeting of the American Psychological Association, Chicago, 1975.

Spencer-Booth, Y., & Hinde, R. A. Effects of brief separations from mothers during infancy on behavior of rhesus monkeys 6–24 months later. *Journal of Child Psychology and Psychiatry*, 1971, 12, 157–172.

Sperry, R. W. A modified concept of consciousness. *Psychological Review*, 1969, 76, 532–536.

Spielberger, C. D., & DeNike, L. D. Descriptive behaviorism versus cognitive theory in verbal operant conditioning. *Psychological Review*, 1966, 73, 306–326.

Spitz, R. A. The origin of the smiling response. In D. C. McClelland (Ed.), *Studies in Motivation*. New York: Appleton-Century-Crofts, 1955. Pp. 156–167.

Sroufe, L. A., & Waters, E. The ontogenesis of smiling and laughter: A perspective on the organization of development in infancy. *Psychological Review*, 1976, 83, 173–189.

Stachnik, T. J. The case against criminal penalties for illicit drug use. *American Psychologist*, 1972, 27, 637–642.

Staddon, J. E. R. Temporal effects of reinforcement: A negative "frustration" effect. *Learning and Motivation*, 1970, 1, 227–247.

Staddon, J. E. R. Reinforcement omission on temporal Go—No–go schedules. *Journal of the Experimental Analysis of Behavior*, 1972, 18, 223–229.

Stanford, R. G. An experimentally testable model for spontaneous psi events. *Journal of the American Society for Psychical Research*, 1974, 68, 34–57. (a)

Stanford, R. G. Response factors in extrasensory performance. Paper presented at the annual meeting of the American Psychological Association, New Orleans, 1974. (b)

Stang, D. J. Effects of "mere exposure" on learning and affect. *Journal of Personality and Social Psychology*, 1975, 31, 7–12.

Starker, S., & Singer, J. L. Daydreaming and symptom patterns of psychiatric patients: A factor analytic study. *Journal of Abnormal Psychology*, 1975, 84, 567–570.

State Street Center Number Nine Youth Crisis and Growth Center. *Drug use and the youth culture*. New Haven, Connecticut: State Street Center, 1972.

Stein, L. Chemistry of purposive behavior. In J. T. Tapp (Ed.), *Reinforcement and behavior*. New York: Academic Press, 1969. Pp. 328–355.

Steiner, G. A. *The people look at television: A study of audience attitudes*. New York: Knopf, 1963.

Steiner, N. H. *A closer look at Ariel: A memory of Sylvia Plath*. New York: Harper's Magazine Press, 1973.

Stengel, E. *Suicide and attempted suicide*. Baltimore, Maryland: Penguin, 1964.

Stimson, G. V. *Heroin and behaviour: Diversity among addicts attending London clinics*. New York: Wiley, 1973.

Stinchecombe, A. L. *Rebellion in a high school*. Chicago: Quadrangle, 1964.

Stokols, D. Toward a psychological theory of alienation. *Psychological Review*, 1975, 82, 26–44.

Strauss, G. Job satisfaction, motivation, and job redesign. In G. Strauss, R. E. Miles, C. C. Snow, & A. S. Tannenbaum (Eds.), *Organizational behavior: Research and issues*. Madison, Wisconsin: Industrial Relations Research Association, 1974.

Streib, G. F. Changing perspectives on retirement: Role crises or role continuities. In R. D. Wirt, G. Winokur, & M. Roff (Eds.), *Life history research in psychopathology* (Vol. 4). Minneapolis: University of Minnesota Press, 1975. Pp. 301–325.

Strickland, B. R., Hale, W. D., & Anderson, L. K. Effect of induced mood states on activity and self-reported affect. *Journal of Consulting and Clinical Psychology*, 1975, 43, 587.

Szpiler, J. A., & Epstein, S. Availability of an avoidance response as related to autonomic arousal. *Journal of Abnormal Psychology*, 1976, 85, 73–82.

Talbott, J. A. Phenothiazine toxicity in pool shark. *New York State Journal of Medicine*, 1970, 70, 1671–1672.

Tannenbaum, A. S., et al. *Hierarchy in organizations*. San Francisco: Jossey-Bass, 1974.

Tannenbaum, P. H., & Gaer, E. P. Mood change as a function of stress of protagonist and degree of identification in a film-viewing situation. *Journal of Personality and Social Psychology*, 1965, 2, 612–616.

Tart, C. T. Waking from sleep at a preselected time. *Journal of the American Society of Psychosomatic Dentistry and Medicine*, 1970, 17, 3–16.

Tart, C. T. *On being stoned: A psychological study of marijuana intoxication*. Palo Alto: Science and Behavior Books, 1971.

Tecce, J. J. Contingent negative variation (CNV) and psychological processes in man. *Psychological Bulletin*, 1972, 77, 73–108.

Tharp, R. G., Watson, D. L., & Kaya, J. Self-modification of depression. Unpublished paper, University of Hawaii, 1974.

Thompson, L. *Robert Frost: The years of triumph, 1915–1938*. New York: Holt, Rinehart and Winston, 1970.

Thompson, R. F., Groves, P. M., Teyler, T. J., & Roemer, R. A. A dual-process theory of habituation: Theory and behavior. In H. V. S. Peeke & M. J. Herz (Eds.), *Habituation*. Vol. 1. *Behavioral studies*. New York: Academic Press, 1973. Pp. 239–271.

Thompson, R. F., Patterson, M. M., & Teyler, T. J. The neurophysiology of learning. *Annual Review of Psychology*, 1972, 23, 73–104.

Thompson, R. F., & Spencer, W. A. Habituation: A model phenomenon for the study of neuronal substrates of behavior. *Psychological Review*, 1966, 73, 16–43.

Thorndike, E. L. Animal intelligence: An experimental study of the associative processes in animals. *Psychological Review, Monograph Supplements*, 1898, 2 (4, Whole No. 8).

Thornton, J. W., & Jacobs, P. D. Learned helplessness in human subjects. *Journal of Experimental Psychology*, 1971, 87, 369–372.

Tolman, E. C. *Purposive behavior in animals and men*. New York: Appleton-Century-Crofts, 1932.

Tomkins, S. S. *Affect, imagery, consciousness*. Vol. 1. *The positive affects*. New York: Springer, 1962.

Tomkins, S. S. *Affect, imagery, consciousness*. Vol. 2. *The negative affects*. New York: Springer, 1963.

Traynor, T. D. Patterns of daydreaming and their relationships to depressive affect. Unpublished M.A. thesis, Miami University (Ohio), 1974.

Treisman, A. M. Strategies and models of selective attention. *Psychological Review*, 1969, 76, 282–299.

Tryon, W. W., & Radzin, A. B. Purpose-in-life as a function of ego resiliency, dogmatism and biographical variables. *Journal of Clinical Psychology*, 1972, 28, 544–545.

Turnbull, C. M. *The mountain people*. New York: Simon and Schuster, 1972.

Turner, C. W., & Layton, J. F. Verbal imagery and connotation as memory-induced mediators of aggressive behavior. *Journal of Personality and Social Psychology*, 1976, 33, 755–763.

Ullman, M., & Krippner, S. *Dream telepathy*. New York: Macmillan, 1973.

United States Department of Health, Education, and Welfare. *Summary reports: New Jersey graduated work incentive experiment*. Washington, D.C.: Department of Health, Education, and Welfare, 1973.

United States Department of Labor. *Job satisfaction: Is there a trend?* Manpower Research Monograph No. 30.) Washington, D.C.: U.S. Government Printing Office, 1974.

Ursin, H. & Kaada, B. R. Functional localization within the amygdaloid complex of the cat. *Electroencephalography and Clinical Neurophysiology*, 1960, 12, 1–20.

Uyeno, E. T. Effect of frustrative blocking on motivation. *Psychological Reports*, 1965, 16, 203–208.

Valenstein, E. S., Cox, V. C., & Kakolewski, J. W. Reexamination of the role of the hypothalamus in motivation. *Psychological Review*, 1970, 77, 16–31.

Vogler, R. E., Compton, J. V., & Weissbach, T. A. Integrated behavior change techniques for alcoholics. *Journal of Consulting and Clinical Psychology*, 1975, 43, 233–243.

Von Andics, M. *Suicide and the meaning of life*. London: Hodge, 1947.

Walker, P. C., & Johnson, R. F. Q. The influence of presleep suggestions on dream content: Evidence and methodological problems. *Psychological Bulletin*, 1974, 81, 362–370.

Wallerstein, R. S. *Hospital treatment of alcoholism: A comparative, experimental study*. New York: Basic Books, 1957.

Wang, M. B., & Bernard, R. A. Adaptation of neural taste responses in cat. *Brain Research*, 1970, 20, 277–282.

Watson, J. B. *Behaviorism*. (Rev. ed.) Chicago: University of Chicago Press, 1930.

Weiner, B. Role of success and failure in the learning of easy and complex tasks. *Journal of Personality and Social Psychology*, 1966, 3, 339–344.

Weiner, B., Heckhausen, H., Meyer, W.-U., & Cook, R. E. Causal ascriptions and achievement behavior: A conceptual analysis of effort and reanalysis of locus of control. *Journal of Personality and Social Psychology*, 1972, 21, 239–248.

Weingold, H. P., Lachin, J. M., Bell, A. H., & Coxe, R. C. Depression as a symptom of alcoholism: Search for a phenomenon. *Journal of Abnormal Psychology*, 1968, 73, 195–197.

Weiss, J. M., Glazer, H. I., & Pohorecky, L. A. Neurotransmitters and helplessness: A chemical bridge to depression? *Psychology Today*, 1974, 8 (7), 58–62.

Weissman, M. M., Klerman, G. L., & Paykel, E. S. Clinical evaluation of hostility in depression. *American Journal of Psychiatry*, 1971, 128, 261–266.

Wessman, A. E., & Ricks, D. F. *Mood and personality*. New York: Holt, Rinehart & Winston, 1966.

Whitehurst, R. N. Premarital reference-group orientations and marriage adjustment. *Journal of Marriage and the Family*, 1968, 30, 397–401.

Whyte, W. F. *Street corner society*. Chicago: University of Chicago Press, 1943.

Wike, E. L. Secondary reinforcement: Some research and theoretical issues. In W. J. Arnold & D. Levine (Eds.), *Nebraska symposium on motivation, 1969*. Lincoln: University of Nebraska Press, 1970. Pp. 39–82.

Williams, A. F. Social drinking, anxiety, and depression. *Journal of Personality and Social Psychology*, 1966, 3, 689–693.

Wilsnack, S. C. Femininity by the bottle. *Psychology Today*, April 1973, 39–43, 96.

Wilsnack, S. C. The effects of social drinking on women's fantasy. *Journal of Personality*, 1974, 42, 43–61.

Wilson, J. R., Kuehn, R. E., & Beach, F. A. Modification in the sexual behavior of male rats produced by changing the stimulus female. *Journal of Comparative and Physiological Psychology*, 1963, 56, 636–644.

Wilson, P. P. *College women who express futility: A study based on fifty selected life histories of women college graduates*. New York: Teachers College, Columbia University, 1950.

Wilson, W. Correlates of avowed happiness. *Psychological Bulletin*, 1967, 67, 294–306.

Windelband, W. [*A history of philosophy* (Vol. 1)] (J. H. Tufts, Trans.). New York: Harper & Row, 1958. (Originally published, 1901.)

Wine, J. Test anxiety and direction of attention. *Psychological Bulletin*, 1971, 76, 92–104.

Winick, C. Physician narcotic addicts. *Social Problems*, 1961, 9, 174–186.

Winokur, G. Genetic aspects of depression. In J. P. Scott & E. C. Senay (Eds.), *Separation and depression: Clinical and research aspects*. Washington, D.C.: American Association for the Advancement of Science, 1973. Pp. 125–137.

Wise, R. A. Drive and incentive models and the problem of drug abuse. Paper presented at the annual meeting of the American Psychological Association, Montreal, 1973.

Wiseman, J. P. *Stations of the lost*. Englewood Cliffs, N.J.: Prentice-Hall, 1970.

Worchel, S. The effect of three types of arbitrary thwarting on the instigation to aggression. *Journal of Personality*, 1974, 42, 300–318.

Worchel, S., Lee, J., & Adewole, A. Effects of supply and demand on ratings of object value. *Journal of Personality and Social Psychology*, 1975, 32, 906–914.

Work in America: Report of a special task force to the Secretary of Health, Education, and Welfare. Cambridge, Massachusetts: M.I.T. Press, 1973.

Wyers, E. J., Peeke, H. V. S., & Herz, M. J. Behavioral habituation in invertebrates. In H. V. S. Peeke & M. J. Herz (Eds.), *Habituation*. Vol. 1. *Behavioral studies*. New York: Academic Press, 1973. Pp. 1–57.

Young, D. D. B. A three generation study of meaning in life. Unpublished M.A. thesis, University of California, Davis, 1974.

Young, M., Benjamin, B., & Wallis, C. The mortality of widowers. *Lancet*, 1963, 2, 454–456.

Yufit, R. I., & Benzies, B. Assessing suicidal potential by time perspective. *Life-Threatening Behavior*, 1973, 3, 270–282.

Yufit, R. I., Benzies, B., Fonte, M. E., & Fawcett, J. A. Suicide potential and time perspective. *Archives of General Psychiatry*, 1970, 23, 158–163.

Zacher, A. N. Goal rigidity as a variable in mid-life and old age depression. Unpublished Ph.D. dissertation, Washington University, 1971.

Zajonc, R. J. Attitudinal effects of mere exposure. *Journal of Personality and Social Psychology Monograph Supplement*, 1968, 9 (2, Part 2), 1–27.

Zeigarnik, B. Ueber das Behalten von erledigten und unerledigten Handlungen. *Psychologische Forschung*, 1927, 9, 1–85.

Zimbardo, P. G., & Ruch, F. L. *Psychology and life* (9th ed.). Glenview, Illinois: Scott, Foresman, 1975.

INDEXES

Author Index

Subject Index